DIASPORA IN THE COUNTRYSIDE:
TWO MENNONITE COMMUNITIES AND
MID-TWENTIETH-CENTURY RURAL DISJUNCTURE

Statue of Liberty–Ellis Island Centennial Series

Board of Editors

Jon Gjerde, University of California at Berkeley
Vicki L. Ruiz, University of California at Irvine

ROYDEN LOEWEN

Diaspora in the Countryside

Two Mennonite Communities and Mid-Twentieth-Century Rural Disjuncture

UNIVERSITY OF ILLINOIS PRESS
Urbana and Chicago

© University of Toronto Press Incorporated 2006
All rights reserved
Printed in Canada

Published in the United States by the University of Illinois Press
www.press.uillinois.edu

ISBN-13: 978-0-252-03178-6 (cloth)
ISBN-10: 0-252-03178-4 (cloth)
ISBN-13: 978-0-252-07425-7 (paper)
ISBN-10: 0-252-07425-4 (paper)

Printed on acid-free paper

Complete Cataloging-in-Publication data is on file with the United States
Library of Congress.

University of Toronto Press acknowledges the financial assistance to its publishing
program of the Canada Council for the Arts and the Ontario Arts Council.

University of Toronto Press acknowledges the financial support for its publishing
activities of the Government of Canada through the Book Publishing Industry
Development Program (BPIDP).

This book has been published with the help of a grant from the Canadian Federation
for the Humanities and Social Sciences, through the Aid to Scholarly Publications
Programme, using funds provided by the Social Sciences and Humanities Research
Council of Canada.

For Isaac and Maria

Contents

Illustrations follow page 152

Preface

Between the 1930s and 1980s the North American countryside faced a
profound social upheaval of transnational scope. An economic restructuring of rural society occurred, linking intrusive government programs, new farm technologies and science, and increased consumption
and electronic communication. In the process a one-time unified rural
society became fragmented and dispersed. So significant was this
period of change that in the 1970s historian John L. Shover dubbed it
the 'Great Disjuncture.' Families wishing to remain on the farm were
required to accept new levels of automation, specialization, and bio-
chemical agriculture. Millions of farm families unable or unwilling to
make these changes left their old farmsteads and moved to nearby
towns and cities in what became one of the largest migrations in the
history of the continent. Inherited ideas shaped the migrants' responses
to new social realities, but the dispersion also compelled a series of
disparate cultural reformulations. This is a story of a 'diaspora in the
countryside,' a scattering within the heartlands of North America.

This growing cultural and physical separation was especially true for
close-knit, ethnoreligious communities. Scattered accounts of rural Calvinist, Lutheran, Catholic, Mormon, Jewish, and Buddhist communities
attest to this time of cultural change. Mennonites in particular experienced this transformation and dispersion. Throughout North America
these pacifist Protestants of Dutch and Swiss descent, who followed a
centuries-old religious commitment to rural life, faced several options.
Some farm families adapted, commercialized their household enterprises, and accepted new ideas relating to gender, ethnicity, religious
faith, and the environment. Others moved to towns where middle-class
values, evangelical faith, and a symbolic ethnicity beckoned. Regional

cities attracted others and here a kaleidoscopic and dynamic urban culture further fragmented them into numerous social entities. Finally, many Mennonites also found ways of contesting modernity and recreated an old order, agrarian world in isolated farm colonies.

This rural fragmentation is examined by comparing and contrasting two closely related but distinctive Dutch–Russian Mennonite communities located in two corners of the North American grassland. Meade County in southwestern Kansas was a wheat and cattle producing area, while the Rural Municipality (RM) of Hanover in eastern Manitoba specialized in dairy, poultry, and swine production. By systematically comparing these communities, two distinctive responses to the Great Disjuncture become apparent. Significantly, one place was shaped by semi-aridity and distance to major cities, the other by short growing seasons and limited economies of scale. It was also important that one was located in the United States and the other in Canada, for different federal policies and national cultures affected each of the communities. This study also contrasts the cultural changes of these farm families to the cultures their kin constructed after moving to the nearby towns of Meade in Kansas and Steinbach in Manitoba, to the large interior cities (especially Winnipeg and Denver), or to the isolated old order community of Spanish Lookout, British Honduras. This book thus charts not only the fragmentation and dispersion of two rural communities, but follows their emigrants as they reformulated their lives in new settings.

The current craft of history writing rightfully requires authors to engage with their stories in a self-reflexive manner. It requires the author to consider his or her place within the text, to disclose the link of creator with the creation.[1] I am, in fact, closely linked to this story and have met many of the subjects in personal ways. My boyhood was spent on a postwar commercialized and specialized farm near within the community of Blumenort in the RM of Hanover; our farm was a turkey and grain operation, our community was shaped by the Evangelical Mennonite Church, formerly known as the Mennonite Kleine Gemeinde. My dad, Dave, was an outgoing 'poultryman,' a member of the Manitoba Turkey Producers Board, and my mom, Gertie, a fun-loving 'cheerful homemaker,' a member of the Goodwill Mission Sisters sewing circle. Symbols of the Great Disjuncture's agriculture abounded on our farm. They included a variety of innovations: our shiny green, diesel John Deere 3010 tractor purchased in 1961 from Reimer Farm Supplies; our Nicholas Bronze turkeys slaughtered on eviscerating lines at the

Blumenort Co-op Produce; the scientifically balanced feed delivered by large trucks from Steinbach Hatchery and Feed company; the MCP and 2,4-D that neighbor Dietrich Friesen custom sprayed on our lands; the 27-0-0 fertilizer that ag rep Rod Siemens urged us to purchase. And our family was modern: we dropped the speaking of Low German, we hosted non-Mennonite friends, my siblings had 'English' names like Beverly, Judy, Debbie, Bonnie, and Mark.

On Saturdays we visited the wider world of consumption-conscious Steinbach, just five miles down Provincial Highway 12. Here Mom purchased groceries at Penner Tomboy and then crossed the street to shop at the Steinbach Fabric Shop or the Five Cents to One Dollar Store. Dad had his hair cut at Harold Unger's Barbershop. He allowed me to tag along as our car or truck was serviced at the local Chevrolet dealership and here as a boy I feasted on colorful pamphlets promoting cars with such 'worldly' names as Corvair and Corvette, Malibu, and Biscayne. New consumer products thrilled me. I was very proud when in 1964 Mom showed up for Parent-Teachers Day at the Blumenort School wearing high-heeled snow boots, when in 1965 Dad expressed unusual aesthetic sense by ordering a white roof for our new maroon Chevrolet farm truck, and especially in 1968 when he had a transistor radio installed in our new Pontiac, a transgression nicely announced by the firm steel aerial protruding from the car's hood. Evidently my parents had adapted successfully to the new postwar rural economy and in the process unshackled the old ethnoreligious proscriptions against conspicuous consumption and participation in mainstream culture.

The transformation, however, was not without its tensions. At Christmas time in 1961 and again in 1970 I was invited to accompany Mom and Dad on their biannual visits to our Kleine Gemeinde Mennonite aunts, uncles, and cousins in Mexico. Our route to Mexico was simple enough, down the snowy Highway 75 into the United States and then due south on number 81 from North Dakota to central Kansas; here we turned southwest on Highway 54, which took us all the way south to El Paso, Texas, before dipping into Old Mexico. Along the way we spent our first night in Watertown, South Dakota, and our second night in a motel in Meade in western Kansas. I knew that my parents had third cousins in the countryside of Meade County. These distant relatives, like us, were descendants of the 1874 immigration of Kleine Gemeinde Mennonites from Russia, the only difference being that they had chosen the temperate climate of the United States, my ancestors Canada's generous military exemption. My dad's grandfather, Isaac J. Loewen, who had come to Canada in 1874 as an eight-year-old boy, was a first cousin to the Meade County Mennonites' ancestor, Heinrich Loewen, who had come to the Midwest with his widowed mother. And other ties existed in Meade County's Reimer, Klassen, and Friesen clans. Despite these known historic ties, we had no personal acquaintances among the Meade Mennonites and we left town the next morning without making any kinship visits. Judging from the absence of many Mennonite names on the town's main street it was also apparent that these folks did not have the ethnic critical mass we had in Steinbach. From my perspective – the car's backseat – this was wheat land and beef country par excellence, vast sections of ground bearing green winter wheat waiting for the dry, cool months to pass. Clearly, the Mennonite farmers of Meade County pursued a different farm culture than we Manitobans on our specialized poultry farm.

Meade County was the halfway point to our final destination, Los Jagueyes or the Mennonite Quellen Kolonie north of Cuauthémoc in the state of Chihuahua, Mexico. My grandparents had migrated there in 1952 to help create a closely bound, antimodern Mennonite agrarian colony. On our stay in the colony in 1961 when I was seven, I recall visiting Grandpa Isaac's tiny English and German-language bookstore located between the red brick house and the barn. I also recall Grandma Maria, wearing a black kerchief, kneading bread dough, and expressing her wish to be back in Canada. In 1970 at age sixteen I visited again and now I was more aware of the vast cultural differences between my very hospitable first cousins – Edwin, Milton, Arden, and Vernon – and me. We had a gala time taking the three-hour climb up 'Grandparents' Mountain' from where we could look down not only on our kin's village, Springstein, but the entire colony. Despite this fun and my cousins' English-language first names, differences existed: my cousins' language of preference was Low German, their clothing was plainer, their hair much shorter, their exposure to the culture of radio, television, and music even more limited than mine. The cultural difference was again made clear to me when in 1980 as a rookie high school history teacher, I visited tropical Belize in Central America and made my way to Spanish Lookout Colony, founded in 1958 as a Mennonite sub-colony of Mexico's Quellen Kolonie. Now I could marvel at the cultural significance of the migration south. It was anti-consumeristic, wary of evangelicalism, opposed to unchecked farm commercialization, and committed to close-knit communitarianism. I was deeply impressed with my dad's confident cousin Maria (Loewen) Friesen, my affable great-uncle Peter P. Loewen, his thoughtful and knowledgeable son, Menno, and his engaging daughters, Tina, Liesbeth, and Mary, my second cousins.

During the mid-1970s I encountered another community linked to Hanover. I had known as a boy that not all Mennonites had managed to stay on farms. My grandparents on my mom's side, David and Elisabeth Klassen, were subsistence farmers and during the 1950s most of their children, with the exception of the family of my mom and that of my Aunt Annie, left the community and most found work in town as bookkeepers, electricians, hatchery workers, mill hands, or nurse's aides. Other local people, however, went further afield, many to the city of Winnipeg, thirty-five miles to the northwest. Here they found work or pursued university education. As a young university student in Winnipeg in 1973 I discovered numerous former Hanover residents who had lost their rural simplicity. Some appeared quite assimilated. They included my third and fourth cousins: the Ivy League-educated university English professor, Dr Al Reimer, who returned to Steinbach one year to run as a sacrificial lamb for the left-leaning New Democratic Party; Pat Friesen, the brilliant poet known for his book *The Shunning*, a riveting literary assault on Steinbach's religious life; and Marjorie Toews, Annalee Lepp, and Ken Klassen, university history majors from the town of Steinbach who seemed very cosmopolitan to me, a Blumenort farm boy. Innovative in a different way were youth with Hanover ties whom I met at Winnipeg's inner-city Aberdeen Church and at Menno-nite Brethren College of Arts. They included Priscilla Reimer the artist, Ray Friesen the young preacher who refused ordination, Travis Kroeker with sights on grad studies at the University of Chicago, Tim Reimer the gold medalist in philosophy at the University of Winnipeg. These educated second and third cousins had rediscovered their radical sixteenth-century Anabaptist history and found in it a social critique especially relevant in class-ridden, racially divided Winnipeg.

So, Friesens, Reimers, Klassens, Toewes, Loewens, and other members of my clan resided in each of these geographies. They represented an internal North American diaspora created by the forces of the Great Disjuncture. They charted different paths, were informed by divergent cosmologies, found themselves in distinctive social settings, and were defined by antipathies that drew boundaries and formulated 'essential' cultures. I observed that each group, however distinctive, had a complex and seemingly personally satisfying way of making sense and deriving meaning in their new worlds. I wondered what it would be like to have representatives of these various strands talk to one another. Ironically, their only link was a genealogy unknown to most of them and their only commonality occasional nostalgia for a quaint farmstead that no longer existed.

The Great Disjuncture is a story in which I had a personal stake. It is a story, however, that far exceeded my limited world, for it had ties to a social transformation that shook the middle decades of rural North America. That social transformation left a fragmented world, but one in which the fragments had reformulated themselves as diverse, but viable and creative, communities.

Many people have made this book possible. I offer special thanks to professors Maria Bjerg (Universidad Quilmes), Gerald Friesen (University of Manitoba), Jon Gjerde (University of California at Berkeley), Ruth Sandwell (University of Toronto), John Thompson (Duke University), and Marlene Epp (University of Waterloo) for graciously reading the manuscript in its entirety and offering frank and useful criticism. Kathleen Neils Conzen (University of Chicago), Pamela Riney Kehrberg (Iowa State University), Alexander Freund (University of Winnipeg), and Erin Ronsee (University of Victoria) read sections and offered their expertise. Henry Fast (Steinbach, MB), Ralph Friesen (Nelson, BC), Merle Loewen (Ellinwood, KS), Menno M. Friesen (Goshen, IN), Menno Loewen (Belize), and Ruth Bartel (Denver) read sections relating to their respective communities and offered very useful advice. A version of chapter 6, 'The Rise and Fall of the Cheerful Homemaker,' was published earlier in *Strangers at Home: Amish and Mennonite Women in History*, and I thank the editors, Kimberly D. Schmidt, Dianne Zimmerman Umble, and Steven D. Reschly, for helping to improve the piece. Articles that build on the ideas in the book and that contain some paragraphs of this study have been published in the *Mennonite Quarterly Review* and the *Journal of the Canadian Historical Association*.

I am very grateful for the helpful staff at the following institutions and archives: Provincial Archives of Manitoba, Legislative Library and Mennonite Heritage Centre in Winnipeg; Rural Municipality of Hanover, Derksen Printers, and Evangelical Mennonite Conference Archives in Steinbach, Manitoba; the Mennonite Library and Archives in North Newton, Kansas; Meade County Courthouse and Meade County Historical Society Museum in Meade, Kansas; Kansas State History Society in Topeka; the Center for Mennonite Brethren Studies in Fresno, California; Spanish Lookout Bookstore in Spanish Lookout, Belize. Student researchers Tina Fehr Kehler and Myron Dyck provided invaluable assistance with two specific chapters. Several fellowships made this study possible including a Social Sciences Humanities Research Council of Canada fellowship at the University of Manitoba, a Fulbright Fellowship at the University of Chicago and a fellowship at the Centre for Studies in Religion and Society, University of Victoria. Kind and generous people opened their homes and hearts to me and I am deeply grateful that they shared their stories and viewpoints with me: I am mindful of people in Denver, Goshen, Hillsboro, Meade, and Dallas (Oregon) in the United States, Los Jagueyes in Mexico, Spanish Lookout in Belize, and Steinbach, Rosenort, Blumenort, Kleefeld, Landmark, and Winnipeg in Manitoba.

People close to me flattered me by willingly debating the title of this book; Sasha supported my attempt to be ironic with 'Diaspora in the Countryside,' Meg economically suggested 'Scattered,' Rebecca stuck to 'Perfect Strangers,' borrowed from a 1980s TV sitcom. Mary Ann, an avid student of fiction, indulged me in many conversations on the intellectual underpinnings of this book. I dedicate this book to my paternal grandparents, Isaac and Maria Loewen, who took the costly migration path from Manitoba to Chihuahua in 1952, testifying in their action that there is nothing inexorable or inevitable in modernity.

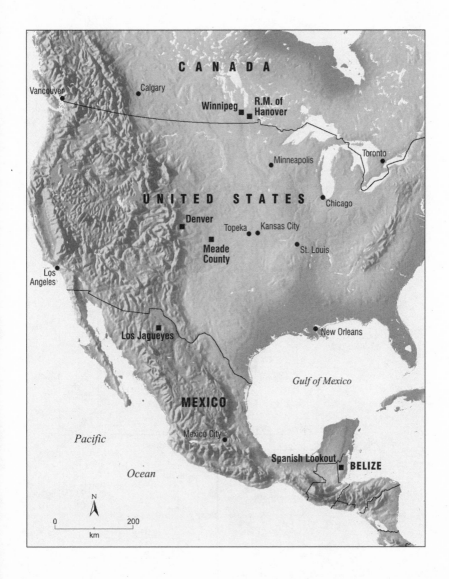

The main Kleine Gemeinde Mennonite-descendant communities in North America.

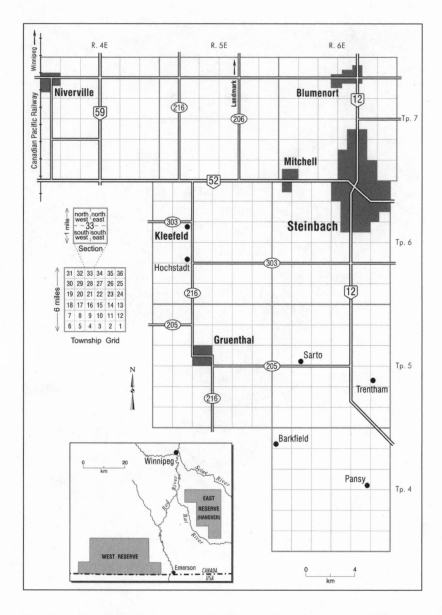

Rural Municipality of Hanover in Manitoba, ca. 1980. As shown in the inset, the RM of Hanover evolved from the Mennonite East Reserve founded in 1874.

Steinbach 1953.

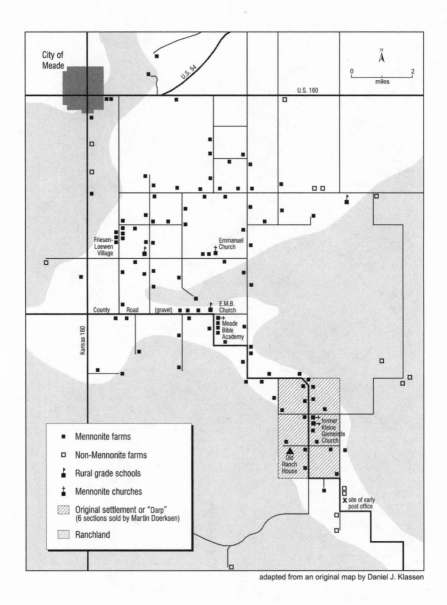

The Mennonite Settlement and scattered Mennonite farms southeast of the town of Meade in Meade County, Kansas, ca. 1950.

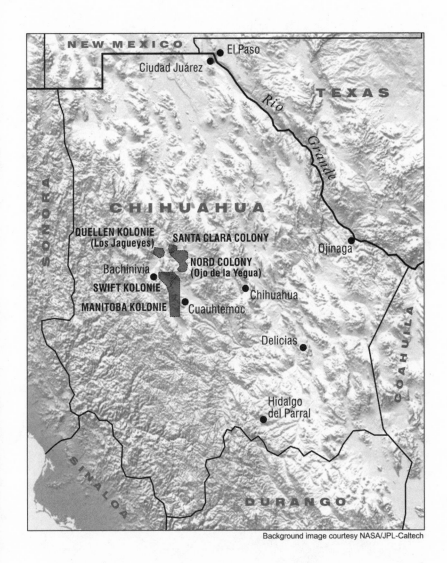

The Mennonite colonies in Chihuahua State, Mexico, ca. 1960.

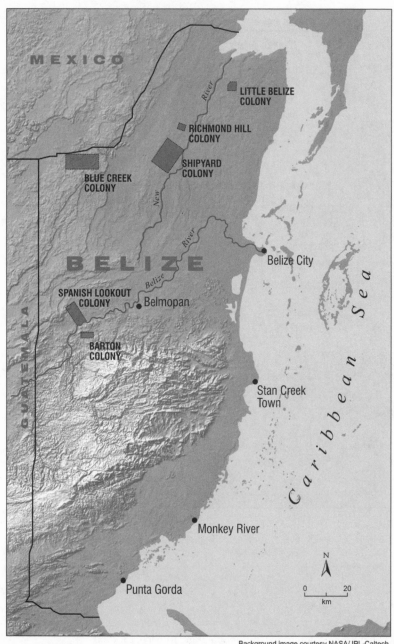

The Mennonite colonies in Belize (former British Honduras), ca. 1980.

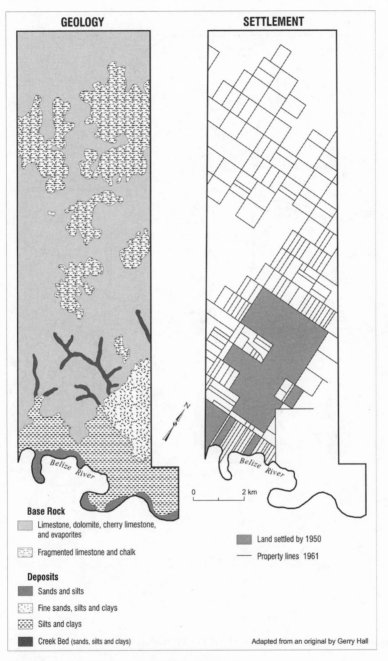

GEOLOGY

SETTLEMENT

Belize River

Belize River

0   2 km

Base Rock

Limestone, dolomite, cherry limestone, and evaporites

Fragmented limestone and chalk

Deposits

Sands and silts

Fine sands, silts and clays

Silts and clays

Creek Bed (sands, silts and clays)

Land settled by 1950

Property lines 1961

Adapted from an original by Gerry Hall

Spanish Lookout Colony, British Honduras.

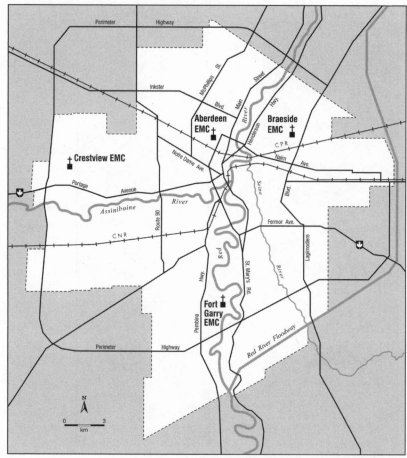

Modified from Welsted, et al, *The Geography of Manitoba* 1996

Evangelical Mennonite Churches (EMC) in Winnipeg, ca. 1980.

DIASPORA IN THE COUNTRYSIDE:
TWO MENNONITE COMMUNITIES AND
MID-TWENTIETH-CENTURY RURAL DISJUNCTURE

Introduction

The middle decades of the twentieth century represented a time of massive, transnational upheaval in the countryside of North America. The midcentury in both Canada and the United States was a time of unprecedented agricultural commercialization, scientific innovation, state intervention, and increased consumption and communication.[1] This book tells the history of that social transformation and associated cultural change by focusing on the rural Mennonite experience. The account begins with a comparison of two communities in separate corners of the great North American interior grassland, in Meade County (Kansas) and in the Rural Municipality (RM) of Hanover (Manitoba). The communities differed in significant ways, but they shared a common fate. A cultural divergence took place within Meade and Hanover as farm people became separated from old ways. Some farm families stayed put but underwent significant economic and cultural transformation as they engaged in a new farm economy. Others faced social dislocation and migrated to nearby towns and interior cities, where they fashioned a diversity of urban lives well removed from the old soil of a communitarian past. A number of Manitoba Mennonite families recommitted themselves to a religiously informed antimodernism by migrating to isolated settings, first to Mexico in the late 1940s and then in a secondary migration to British Honduras in the 1950s. Within a few short decades, from the 1930s to the 1980s, members of the one-time conservative, ethnic farm communities of Hanover and Meade had moved in diverse directions, some farther than others, but all a significant cultural distance. Their composite story reveals a scattered rural people, participants in a rural diaspora. It was a diaspora in the countryside, a literal and virtual uprooting and dispersion of farm families.

In their rural villages, farm-service towns, regional cities, and sectarian colonies they became newcomers within the continent of their own birth.

The dispersion this book traces was not a typical diaspora. In classical literature the word diaspora describes scattered ancient Jewish peoples of the Middle East; it resulted from a dispersion that was often involuntary, frequently violent, and which lead to long-term exile. Biblical texts recount bitter songs of suffering and alienation, a deep nostalgia for a promised land, and a yearning for messianic relief. The spread of Christianity occurred within this context, among the 'aliens of the diaspora ... living out the time of [their] exile.'[2] In more recent historical writings the term describes the scattered migrant communities of particular peoples, usually of European, African, and Asian descent in North America. But the migrant communities also included East Indians in South Africa, Palestinians in the Gulf States, Africans in Latin America, or French Canadians in New England.[3] These were people displaced from homelands, driven by global economic forces that uprooted peasants and craftspeople. They were introduced to new work patterns in disparate countries and compelled to recreate ethnic communities overseas where migrants understood '"home" metaphorically, as well as literally.'[4] Most importantly, they culturally adapted to a new reality of being 'scattered ... widely around the world,' oftentimes as minorities.[5] This culture of displacement and dislocation was recognized and interpreted in this way by post-colonial writers.[6] As comparative studies have demonstrated, this dispersion also brought significant cultural diversity to one-time cohesive and homogeneous groups.[7]

The farm families uprooted at midcentury shared many of these characteristics of diaspora, but their upheaval and dispersion also possessed unique qualities. It occurred within the boundaries of a single continent, over both longer and shorter distances, and over imagined and lived dislocations. But like the ancient and modern diasporas an uprooting was followed by a coalescence, taking neighbors from their farms and bringing them together in new settings, in church congregations, clan gatherings, ballparks, and literary clubs. Mythologies of separation followed, spoken of at family gatherings and in coffee shops and repeated in local histories, that explained the religious or cultural need for the migration, or the economic condition of upward or downward mobility. Rural cultures were profoundly affected, and in this context rose new ethnic identities, gender constructions, class relations, religious understandings, and environmental imaginings. The dispersion of these rural people left strong cultural stirrings; they were nostalgic linkages to an imagined 'homeland,' the historic family farm, where old patterns of kinship, household economy, and communitarian faith had persisted in previous generations. The culture of these intracontinental migrants became fragmented and attached itself to dis-parate and innovative cultural strains, divided by various cultural cross-currents. At the end of a long generation of change, it was clear that an upheaval had taken a closely knit people, rooted in a common history and homogeneous culture, and flung them in numerous directions. All had been asked to reformulate their lives in new settings. They could come back and visit the sites of the old farmsteads – some with nostalgia, others with relief – and recognize that neither those farms nor the self-sufficient rural community of yesteryear's North America still existed. People, closely related and sharing common memories, had charted disparate worlds; they had experienced a cultural, social, and physical scattering. To understand the fragmented North American countryside as diaspora is to understand the profound nature of those changes.

The broad transformation of the mid-twentieth-century North American countryside constitutes the context of this history. Its starting point is the decade of the 1930s, a time in which a common rural culture prevailed in many quarters of North America. The family farm was firmly rooted in a cohesive rural community.[8] Although agriculture had evolved over the course of the nineteenth and early twentieth centuries, most farm households still were independent and self-sufficient, and farms tended to be small and numerous.[9] Most produced a mix of commodities and in doing so the households brought men and women together in a mutual productive enterprise.[10] Relationships within the rural communities were informal and steeped in common understandings. Seasonal roads assured a measure of rural isolation. Local folklore provided each community with a distinctive collective memory, and the cohesion of local society was undergirded religiously by familiar affiliations and sacred doctrine.[11] A collective culture of the rural community existed. A common answer would have addressed Clifford Geertz's question about the 'soft facts' of existence: 'What do people imagine human life to be all about, how do they think one ought to live, what grounds belief, legitimizes punishment, sustains hope or accounts for loss?'[12]

With the lifting of the Depression and the onset of the Second World War significant changes came to North America's rural communities.[13]

Especially during the middle decades of the twentieth century, as American historian John L. Shover argued a generation ago, this rural society and culture was 'overwhelmed' by a broadly based transformation. So profound was the change in economic, social, and cultural terms, that Shover dubbed it a 'Great Disjuncture,' a time of veritable agricultural revolution, in which agriculture became 'transmuted.' Farm production became scientifically driven as expensive new chemicals and medications became broadly used, all in the name of greater productivity. Marketing was often linked to vertically integrated suppliers and processors who used more sophisticated technologies of storage and packaging. They sent products further afield to rising urban populations, and in the process found ways of selling farmers new services, intertwined them in credit schemes, and were first in line to purchase their commodities. Farms began to specialize, and some to consolidate, in specific lines of poultry or in dairy, hog, and beef production, and these joined the wheat farm in becoming fully mechanized with ubiquitous gasoline power and rural electrification. As they did so, they became highly capitalized and financially leveraged. Increasingly too, farm direction was set by rational planning with considerable assistance and intrusion from experts sent out by government departments of agriculture who encouraged farmers to become even more integrated into a global market and national culture.

Thus, argues Shover, life on the farm changed dramatically. As importantly, a massive rural-urban migration set in. New economies of scale and the law of diminishing returns simply meant that many farmers could not make the required transition. The number of farm families who left the old homestead, argued Shover, constituted such a 'mass outpouring,' it might well be designated 'one of the great migrations in history, greater in scope and numbers than the great exodus of European and Asians to the United States in the 140 years from 1820 to 1960.'[14] Striking statistics from census records suggest the phenomenon was a continental one.[15] Between 1950 and 1970 the number of farm residents in both Canada and the United States was cut in half, dropping in the United States from 23.0 to 9.7 million, and in Canada from 2.8 to 1.4 million. Over a longer period the drop was even more profound: the number of U.S. farm residents remained steady during the 1930s at 30.5 million, but declined to 6.1 million by 1980; in Canada the number of farm residents fell sharply in the 1930s from 4.8 to 3.2 million, and then declined further to 1.4 million by 1971. The number of farm residents at the end of the fifty-year period between 1930 and 1980 in the two countries had dropped by 28 million, one-fifth of what it had been.[16] Rural people of all stripes encountered new non-farm and urban worlds with significant social and cultural effects.

Despite implicit agreement among historians that the middle decades consisted of a time of 'profound social consequences' for this new farm economy, the period has been studied less systematically than other eras.[17] In comparison to the years of 'modernization' between the U.S. Civil War or Canadian Confederation in the 1860s and the outbreak of the First World War, the mid-twentieth century has been overlooked. Some noted studies of twentieth-century agriculture end in 1930 or 1940 while others begin in 1970 or 1980. In the United States, Hal S. Barron's influential *Mixed Harvests* suggests that the modernization of agriculture was more or less completed by 1930, while Kathryne Marie Dudley's *Debt and Dispossession* posits that the 1980s spelled the beginning of a late-century farm crisis when farmers dearly paid for brazen optimism and headiness.[18] In Canada several historians take the rural narrative up to 1950, but few historians have built on Gerald Friesen's piece, 'The New West since 1940' or John Herd Thompson's 'Prairie Canada Recast, 1940–1970.'[19] When the mid-twentieth century has drawn the attention of social historians, it has usually not been with reference to rural society, but to suburban culture with its strong consumer impulses, crystalized roles for men and women, electronic communications, welfare state, and geographic boundaries between ethnic and class-based groups.[20] When the mid-century North American farm is the subject of scholarly analysis, farm culture is usually portrayed in broad strokes associated with regional demographic patterns, macroeconomics, and national government policy.[21]

This study of a Kansas and a Manitoba Mennonite community seeks to address the gap in the history of mid-twentieth-century rural North America. No doubt, as religiously conservative, ethnically conscious, socially cohesive farm families, these Meade (Kansas) and Hanover (Manitoba) farm families constituted a minority experience in rural society.[22] As descendants of the sixteenth-century Anabaptist Protestants, noted for their biblical pacifism, adult baptism, and teachings on separation from the wider world, and as inheritors of a centuries-old religious dedication to rural community, the Mennonites may have been a minority even among conservative rural residents. Statistically they were among the last of North America's rural ethnic groups to acquiesce to the forces of urbanization; one 1972 study, for example, argues that fully 65 percent of practicing North American Mennonites still lived in places with fewer than 2500 persons and 34 percent still lived on farms.[23] In this sense the Mennonites provide evidence of a unique experience in the Great Disjuncture; a people left unscathed by earlier continental changes, they finally met the forces of modernization head-on.

This book contends the Mennonites' relevance in other ways than in noting them as exceptions to the rule. In some ways, in fact, the Mennonites merely afford another perspective on changes that affected all farm communities in North America. Certainly they shared sets of experiences with other ethnic or ethnoreligious rural communities – be they of Japanese, Jewish, Ukrainian, Swedish, African American, Dutch, or French Canadian descent – who left familiar, close-knit, conservative rural districts and at mid-century headed for new worlds in towns and cities. These rural people also experienced the call for greater productivity, the rules of global markets, the interwoveness of specialized production, the expense of chemicalized farming, and the bane of vertical integration. In the process they too found themselves more fully integrated in a wider world. They also experienced mid-century cultural changes that nipped away at cohesive farm culture; they faced increasingly specific gender roles, the assimilative force in higher education, the lure of city lights, the sudden appeal of evangelicalism, and the increase in interethnic relations. In the cities, these other groups also found themselves divided from former neighbors by class, religion, politics, and exogamous marriages.[24]

In other ways the Mennonites' very conservatism illuminates the effect of the Great Disjuncture on all farmers. The Mennonites can serve as a barometer of the significance of the mid-twentieth-century forces on the broader farm community. As pacifists and sectarians these farmers were certainly skeptical of the technical advice of government-funded, university-educated agricultural agents, yet their need to survive in the new economy dictated an interaction with these outsiders. As Anabaptists who emphasized a non-conformist, community-centered, and egalitarian world view, the lure of consumer products and capitalist enterprise led them variously to yield to great change or sharply to contest it. As a people committed to close-knit community life within defined social boundaries, it became clear that the forces of the Great Disjuncture played themselves out in everyday life, bringing ethnicity, religion, and inherited social practices in dialectical relationship to create a localized experience of midcentury transformation. Their defined communities offer the luxury of a holistic history, a close examination that reveals no simple, unilinear set of causes. Clearly farm families negotiated a new existence in a new economy. Their ethnicity, religious faith, and inherited sets of social relations affected their response to the new economy, just as the technology and science of the mid-century required of them a cultural response. A study of conservative ethno-religious farmers such as the Mennonites enables an insight into the process that led subjects, equipped with a specific set of historically generated practices within clearly defined social borders, to reinvent and reformulate old teachings and practices in new social situations. The experience of the Mennonites thus can shed light on the significance of the Great Disjuncture for most North American farm families.

Several other assumptions ground this study. The first is that the nature of the Great Disjuncture can be understood not only in terms that are 'centrist and unilinear,' to repeat Hans Medick's warning, but in localistic terms.[25] The significance of government policy, market conditions, and technological advancement become apparent when observed as local experiences. The broad changes created the cultural stuff of the locality, but the interests and behavior of the local community also propelled the broader societal changes. As Henri Lefebvre notes, structures can be understood 'only in so far as they are created at each instance in everyday life.'[26] The second assumption is that social change is not unilinear. Following the counsel of Kathleen Neils Conzen, this study is not about 'the fate of the immigrants,' but rather a study of the 'cultures they created.'[27] In this ambition this book takes seriously Geertz's definition of culture as constituting 'webs of significance,' or as 'structures of meaning in terms of which people do things.' It is a study, then, not of a statically conceived way of life, as if it was only an inheritance, but rather a constantly renewed experience that was recreated every day and every year.[28] The third basis of this study is that the grand modernization thesis cannot in itself explain the rural transformation.[29] A close examination of Meade and Hanover suggests that a social transformation in the countryside was not limited to a predictable evolution from a folk to urban culture, following Robert Redfield's formulation, or from a *Gemeinschaft* to *Gesellschaft* society in the vein of nineteenth-century German sociology.[30] The transformation in the Mennonite communities under scrutiny here spelled not only a change from isolation to integration, closeness to openness, informality to formality. It also included a cultural fragmentation and caused a physical uprooting for the majority of farm families, one that took them in starkly different directions. In their disparate sites of everyday life, the people of this study variously contested, adopted, or moved beyond standardized modern society.

To interpret the localized midcentury experience with a measure of confidence, the two communities – Hanover and Meade – were chosen because they were home to similar branches of the Mennonite people. They were the descendants of the Low German–speaking pacifist, sectarian, farm folk who had migrated to Manitoba in Canada and Kansas, Nebraska, and other midwestern states between 1874 and 1879 from foreign colonies in the southern sections of the Russian Empire, the present-day Ukraine. In the 1930s the majority of Meade and Hanover Mennonites still were conservative farm people. In both places, some had accepted an evangelistic outlook, seeking a more progressive and individualistic religiosity that included a more complete integration in the wider society. Others that included in both places held fast to the old order, bent on continued separation from the broader world. Meade County was home to only two congregations of Mennonites, the somewhat progressive Evangelical Mennonite Brethren and the old order Kleine Gemeinde Mennonites.[31] The RM of Hanover was also home to these two branches of Mennonites, but in addition hosted the more conservative Chortitzer and Holdeman bodies and the more progressive Mennonite Brethren and General Conference Mennonites, the latter two dominated by immigrants from the Soviet Union in the 1920s, the so-called Russländer Mennonites.

While this history touches in general terms on all of these groups, it highlights the experience of the one old order group in both Hanover and Meade, the Kleine Gemeinde Mennonites. As the Great Depression came to an end, the Kleine Gemeinde shared a mindset with other conservative Anabaptist groups: the Old Order Mennonites and Amish of Ohio, Pennsylvania, and Ontario; the Old Colony and Sommerfelder (in some places known as Bergthaler) Mennonites of the Canadian prairies; and the Hutterites of North Dakota, Manitoba, and Alberta. Donald Kraybill and Carl Bowman's definition of these 'old order' groups is apt: they 'question individualism ... talk about obedience, self-denial and authority of church, ... [and] in lieu of civic participation ... emphasize the importance of collective responsibility.' They are members of 'production-based societies that have not joined the world of consumer' culture and they represent an 'audacious challenge to the larger cultural system.'[32] Their own old order commitment to plain living and agrarian culture led many Kleine Gemeinde Mennonites to oppose full commercialization and consumerism of the midcentury decades. For several generations they had selectively adjusted to rural capitalism. Ironically, through judicious market interaction they sought to obtain the financial resources required for their antimodern culture.[33] The midcentury decades, however, presented a new challenge which resulted in the Kleine Gemeinde's fragmentation, in Kansas a church schism in the 1940s produced the Emmanuel Mennonite Church; in Manitoba most members embraced the rise of the newly minted Evangelical Mennonite Conference (EMC) during the 1950s. Perhaps the Kleine Gemeinde Mennonites, along with other conservative, communitarian groups, were among the most resilient of rural North Americans. That they fragmented into urban and rural groups, capital-istic and antimodern, evangelical and old order, serves to signal the significance of the Great Disjuncture.[34]

To understand the full impact of the Great Disjuncture this study not only describes the Mennonites of Hanover and Meade, but also system-atically compares and contrasts their experience in the two places.[35] Indeed, it is another assumption of this study that the process of change can be clarified through comparative history. Among many proponents of this method of historical investigation, Jürgen Kocha has pointed out that comparative study 'allows one to identify questions' of analysis, helps to 'challenge and modify' accepted generalizations, enables the 'testing of hypotheses,' and works to illuminate 'entangled' global or transnational phenomena through localized experience.[36] Certainly a comparative study can suggest some of the broad qualities of mid-century transformation, the composite ways in which the farm commu-nities changed at mid-century. Yet it is unlikely that comparative study will identify the 'culturally innate' as opposed to the 'circumstantial' elements in adaptation as former comparative studies of migrant peoples have claimed.[37] What a comparative analysis of two culturally similar communities in diverse settings can do is to identify the way midcentury transformation was experienced at the local level. As this study will show, it mattered that climate, human geography, ethnic composition, national cultures, and government policies differed in Hanover and Meade. In this instance the two communities represent distinct faces of a composite transformation.

Hanover and Meade were located in specific but different physical environments and political contexts. Their setting in the two corners of the North American grassland – one in Canada, the other in the United States – was significant.[38] Thomas Dunlap has written that in the North

American heartland 'two gradients, temperature and rainfall, shape the country' and the gradients 'run at right angles.' In the first instance, 'temperature falls as we go north. South Texas is subtropical ... At the Canadian border we are in cold temperature conditions [and] a few hundred miles north, European agriculture dwindles out in the oat and canola fields.' In the second instance, the 'Eastern prairies are well-watered but as we climb the great outwash plains [towards] the Rockies, vegetables give way to corn and corn to wheat and only cattle graze in the mountains' rain shadow ... [and in the far] southwest there are deserts.'[39] Hanover and Meade, respectively, were located in the far northeast and the southwest quadrants of these gradients of temperature and precipitation. Meade County of western Kansas lay in the southwestern corner of the arable reaches of the American Midwest where a long growing season and open reaches of land encouraged wheat production, although the semi-aridity of the high plain in the shadows of Rocky Mountains placed a well-defined limit on farming. Eastern Manitoba's RM of Hanover lay in the far northeastern corner of the grassland, bordered to the north and east by the granite rocks, boreal forests, and pristine lakes of the Canadian Shield; its fertile clay lands usually received more than adequate precipitation but it too faced an agricultural limit, that is, the short four-month growing season bordered by the northern winter. The environmental limits of the two corners of the grassland, semi-aridity and frost, demanded different kinds of responses from farmers.

It was also significant that Meade is located in the United States and Hanover in Canada. Increasingly, historians of borderlands regions have compared and contrasted the political environments, and the attending cultures and mythologies, of the two countries that share the North American grassland.[40] Those scholars have usually emphasized national differences. Donald Worster, for example, has written that although the development myth of both the United States and Canada predicted 'the final success of industrial capitalism ... they veer[ed] off into different emphases and implications' that possessed 'continuing power and persistence in the writing of history.'[41] But few historians have compared the ways in which the mid-twentieth-century national cultures or agricultural policies affected local communities in Canada and the United States.

This study suggests that to a certain extent the communities were faced with regional variations of two different, national cultures. On a broad level they were confronted by forces linked to the classic categories of an American 'melting pot' and Canadian 'cultural mosaic'. Certainly in Meade there were hints of what John Higham identified in 1959 as 'the cult of "American Consensus"' with its 'appeal to homogeneity, continuity and national character.' In Hanover, on the other hand, were vestiges of what J.M.S. Careless identified in 1969 as Canada's penchant for 'limited identities,' its concern with region, ethnicity, and linguistic group, 'social qualities that differentiate people,' not those 'that make them the same.'[42] Although their newspapers were equally boosteristic, overt champions of middle-class culture, Meade County's *Meade Globe Press* revealed a culture pointedly nationalistic, patriotic, and militaristic while Hanover's *Carillon News* openly celebrated the ethnicity of its Mennonite majority set in a multicultural region of Canada. As has long been asserted, ethnicity is not innate or primordial, but created in specific historical circumstances, and thus it is not surprising that during this time the Mennonites of Hanover and Meade expressed their Low German–Dutch Mennonite ethnicities in somewhat different fashions.

Different, albeit evolving, national agricultural policies also sent American and Canadian farmers on disparate paths. It would be difficult to overemphasize the significance of the New Deal agricultural policies and the postwar farm support programs of the United States or the Canadian Wheat Board and the 1960s-era marketing boards based on supply management economics in Canada. Those policies, imposed on farms that faced distinct environmental conditions, helped create two fundamentally different farm communities. Certainly, land 'set aside' policies and indirect state support for corporate farm consolidation in part accounted for Meade County's rural depopulation during the 1960s and 1970s. At the same time, the price pooling of the Canadian Wheat Board and supply management economics, specifically designed to guarantee a long-term, sustainable livelihood for small farm families, were factors in the stabilization of the RM of Hanover's population.

Other significant features of the Meade and Hanover Mennonite communities complicate the simple explanations of national and climatic difference in this account. Hanover possessed a critical mass of Mennonites, rooted as it was in an original destination of the Dutch-Russian Mennonite immigrants of the 1870s, the old East Reserve; Meade by contrast was a second-generation settlement, home to secondary migrants who had first settled in Jefferson County, Nebraska. Then too, the two communities related to cities in different ways.

Hanover's largest town lay only 35 miles from the heart of a major regional city, Winnipeg; Meade lay some 300 miles from a similar, albeit much larger city, Denver, and even small cities such as Witchita and Oklahoma City lay 160 and 200 miles in the distance.

These differences were reflected in the histories of the Great Disjuncture in Meade and Hanover. Although a common story can be told of farm folk who did not commercialize and technologize their operations and moved into towns and cities, the Meade and Hanover people experienced rural diaspora in somewhat different ways. Meade farmers faced greater upheaval as a larger percentage of them moved off farms than did farmers in Hanover. Mennonites who re-established lives in the towns of the RM of Hanover and Meade County, that is, in Steinbach (Manitoba) and Meade (Kansas), did so as emerging middleclass entrepreneurs and college-educated professionals, or as members of a working class laboring within the farm service industry or in small factories manufacturing wood or steel products. But the Steinbach Mennonites possessed a critical mass that allowed the speaking of Low German and easy identification with their ethnoreligious identity in town; Meade Mennonites constituted a minority in an Anglo-American frontier town and appeared more reticent about expressing an old ethnicity and more accepting of evangelicalism than their Manitoba counterparts. A third group went further afield by relocating to the regional cities of Winnipeg and Denver; in their new settings they created disparate ethnic and religious identities, including those couched in overtly secular, socially progressive, or evangelistic language. Again, the Mennonites of Winnipeg possessed not only significant critical mass, but were able to secure 'institutional completeness' and maintain closer ties to the countryside; thus whether secularized or evangelicalized, they seemed more ready to count themselves as Mennonites than their counterparts in Denver. Meade Mennonites in Denver made fewer trips 'home' and seemed more ready to align themselves with non-Mennonite churches.

A fourth group, based in Canada alone, came to represent a uniquely Mennonite response to the forces of change in the twentieth century. This was the most conservative of the various groups. It resisted the consumer and nationalistic impulses that invaded the old communities and joined the other ten thousand old order Canadian Mennonites – Old Colony, Sommerfelder, and Chortitzer Mennonites – who in deliberate acts of antimodernism left their country in the 1920s and 1940s. The specific emigrating group on which this study focuses was a remnant of the Kleine Gemeinde. It migrated southward first in 1948 to Mexico and then in 1958 farther south to British Honduras where it established closed, conservative Mennonite colonies in exclusive, rural areas. It would adjust to a rainforest environment, and find solace in greater cultural isolation, bolstered by friendly terms from a colonial government, racialized social boundaries, guarded memories of worldly Canadian society, and an extraordinary desire to forge a close-knit colony.[43]

Thus, the specific groups – farm, town, city – differed internally depending on which side of the forty-ninth parallel they were placed. But if a national divide cut through these social categories, the categories themselves were separated from one another. Farm, town, and city members, and certainly members of the southern colonies, made sense of life with reference to different sets of stories, and competing cosmologies. They each reinvented old identities, both in an ethnic and a religious sense. Each of the groups related to the wider society in different ways, with varying degrees of acceptance and guardedness. Significantly, each constructed a mental picture of an historical trajectory and social space that placed it in opposition to the other. Indeed, each created a strong sense of 'other' in their perception of their counterparts as being inherently different and antithetical. Socially the groups seemed to cherish geographic distance; the space between the original North American rural districts, the regional cities, or the Central American colonies was not always accidental. Culturally the groups engaged in binary constructions, with the progressives labeling the conservatives as blinded, and the conservatives dismissing the progressives as fallen. The city dwellers were capable of denouncing the alleged narrow-minded and myopic culture of their rural cousins. The rural cousins were apprehensive about an alleged groundlessness and rootlessness of their children in Winnipeg and Denver, and at the same time were concerned about the seeming backwardness and primitiveness of their cousins in the southern colonies. Members of the Mexico and British Honduras colonies distanced themselves mentally from their North American rural counterparts who in their minds had yielded to worldly fashion and desire. Usually the cultural distance between the colonists and the city dwellers was too great even for members to conceptualize. They were as sociologist Fred Kniss has written of American Mennonites, the 'disquiet in the land,' following opposing 'moral projects' shaped by divergent 'locuses of authority.'[44] In a sense, too, they were 'perfect strangers,' the title of a TV series in the 1980s. The Mennonites in this book were not unlike the two cousins of the *Perfect*

Strangers sitcom. Balki, the 'Old World' immigrant from the sheep-rearing Isle of Mypos in the Mediterranean Sea, and Larry, an assimilated American middle-class apartment dweller from Chicago, may be cousins and even roommates, but they are separated by many degrees of cultural difference. As the mindsets of these two characters clash, a remarkable cultural dynamic ensues.

To understand the increasingly disparate and complex world of these rural people, this book has selected a specific set of windows – economics, religion, ethnicity, gender, and environmental imagination – through which everyday culture will be examined. Perhaps the windows reveal a degree of arbitrariness, but the vistas reflect both the questions that comparative analysis has generated and those asked by a generation of social theorists and historians concerned with cultural change.[45] They include questions of how people's cultural understandings of gender, ethnicity, class, land, and religion changed in the context of mid-century social transition and the manner in which these categories worked dialectically in creating new and divergent worlds.[46] This book suggests that such categories of analysis not only revealed the complexity of modern society, but also the lived experience of these ordinary agrarian people. The historical actors thought in terms of these specific identities, responded to changes around them in such terms, and worked to create community life built on these understandings.

Moreover, they are categories apparent in the historical record that informs this book. They reside in personal records, the diaries, account books, and letters or memoirs that the historical subjects wrote for their own benefit or for those close to them. They are apparent too in newspaper articles and editorials, in the minutes of church or community organizations, and in local history books, whose writers made their observations public or semi-public. Even the state had an eye for gender, class, and race as it produced statistics, censuses, and tax rolls that were meant to order and even manipulate a complex and evolving society. The same categories appeared in the oral tradition, where subjects in their homes or local restaurants told stories they chose to relate to an enquiring historian. From this body of evidence produced for multiple purposes, a pattern of perceived human experience arises.

These themes unfold in nine chapters. The first examines the economic changes and traces the manner in which technological and governmental pressures shaped the farm and the farmers' mindsets in Manitoba and Kansas. Chapter 2 contrasts the manner in which the concepts of nature and land were imagined by the two communities and explains how that process differed depending on the specific nature of the physical environment and the expressed aims of the farm community. Chapter 3 focuses on life in the small town, the lot of most midcentury farm families, the place in which old ideas of ethnicity and class fundamentally were re-examined. The subject of chapters 4 and 5 is religion, with the attending questions about the nature of shifting belief and practice, changes in ontology and teleology (the ground of being and ideas of destiny), and understandings of salvation and church community. Chapters 6 and 7 raise the question of gender, with one chapter focusing on the evolving but significant change in the concept of femininity among Kansas women and the other on the wholesale social and cultural alteration in masculinity among Manitoba men. The last two chapters explore the reinvention of culture, the disparate reformulations generated by the Great Disjuncture. Chapter 8 is a foray into a miracle of sorts, the deliberate re-establishment of old order communitarianism in the face of a globalizing culture. Chapter 9, no less a subject of wonder, follows uprooted farm families into regional cities where they regrounded their cultures in a more open, secular urban environment.

This book addresses a simple question: how did the rural transformation of the mid-twentieth century affect farm families in general, and conservative, ethnic, and religious communities in particular? By beginning the study with a single Mennonite denomination located at two sites in the North American grassland and in two countries this book attempts to interpret the complex, disparate, and disjunctured transnational worlds of the twentieth century. Perhaps rural society became fragmented, but by following those scattered fragments along their various paths, one also begins to understand the resilience and ingenuity of humans as they recrafted and regrounded their worlds. Each of the evolving groups had elements of cultural shortsightedness and social repression. But none was without a formulation of redemption that encouraged generosity of spirit, rewarded personal creativity, strove for human dignity, and made communitarian concern a central feature of their world view. The descendants of these communities may be surprised to discover that they share a common root with complete strangers in unfamiliar worlds. Outside observers may be surprised at the speed with which two generations travelled culturally from a common farm culture. It is my hope that by tracing this rural diaspora, all readers will participate in a multifaceted story of cultural creativity.

1 The Great Disjuncture and Ethnic Farmers: Life in Two Corners of a Transnational Grassland

The images from the Great Depression of weak markets and drought-stricken plains overshadow a diverse economic and cultural landscape. On one level, no two rural communities of the western grassland were as different as Meade County in Kansas was from the Rural Municipality (RM) of Hanover in Manitoba. Hanover in the far northeast had responded to the Depression from within its physical landscape; its southern sections of rocky bushland enabled subsistence farming and its northern sections of flat, clay prairie held moisture well and allowed grain production through the 1930s. Meade lay far to the southwest, in a region marked by vast, semi-arid, treeless plains; its rolling ground, broken only occasionally by deeply carved ravines, was vulnerable to warm temperatures and high winds. Reflecting these physical traits, Hanover and Meade had practiced distinctive economic strategies during the early years of the twentieth century. A Mennonite community founded in the 1870s, Hanover pursued mixed farming and produced cream, butter, and cheese for the market of nearby Winnipeg, a metropolis of 220,000 by 1921. Meade, lying a significant distance from any significant urban centre and situated on a boundless open plain, showed an almost reckless confidence in monocrop wheat production.

Just as their agricultural histories differed, so too did their responses to the Depression's unstable market and climatic difficulties. Many of Meade's farm families packed up and fled for the well-watered lands of interior California and Oregon, others hunkered down and survived on the subsistence-driven parts of the farm operation, awaiting the refreshing rains and strong markets that came with the Second World War. In contrast, Hanover became a recipient of farm families driven eastward from the open prairie in central and western Manitoba. During the

1930s it found an economic niche in cheese production and through the formation of local cooperatives it survived the Depression handily. Its economic base in livestock and poultry flourished after the Second World War.

Mennonite farmers of Hanover and Meade thus faced the transforming powers of the postwar Great Disjuncture with distinctly different strategies of commercial agriculture. Both carried Depression experiences with them as governments and markets shaped wartime and post-war agricultural strategies. Both localities were cognizant of the limitations and possibilities of their respective physical features, rainfall regimes, and growing seasons. Both were home to conservative Mennonites who had inherited a belief from parents and grandparents that they could nurture their sectarian and agrarian cultures through household-produced commodities and participation in a wider market.[1] Both groups of Mennonites employed technological and scientific innovation, new markets, and even state-sponsored farm programs with a careful pragmatism, in order to secure the old cultural foundations. The rural transformation of the Great Disjuncture was played out on a turf that placed these variables – agricultural experience, inherited religious values, government programs – in dynamic relationship to each other.

The social and cultural result brought a commonality to Meade and Hanover. Both cut themselves loose from the mixed farming that had helped them survive the Depression and both embraced urbanization as an acceptable social option for surplus population. In Manitoba these events steered farmers for the first time into commodity specialization in close cooperation with government programs, exemplified perhaps most publicly by the readily available government-paid agricultural representative, known simply as the 'ag rep.' In Kansas the Depression threatened the very basis of monocrop wheat production and for those farm families who remained in western Kansas, acceptance of the advice of government agricultural agents they knew as county agents and of government support programs also became fully acceptable. In Manitoba, farmers turned to poultry and dairy specialization, in Kansas, farmers returned to wheat, seeking to grow it in a fragile environment and to sell it in an unsteady world wheat market. Meade and Hanover may have been located in distinct corners of the North American grassland, compelled to deal with different physical terrains and national farm policies, but both were members of a global economic and cultural phenomenon that directed farm folk of the middle decades of the twentieth century to make sweeping alterations to old cultures.

The New Agriculture in Manitoba's RM of Hanover

The post–Second World War social change in the RM of Hanover was particularly pronounced. During the Great Depression and the war Hanover's lingua franca was still the West Prussian Low German dialect that Dutch Mennonites had brought with them to Russia in the late eighteenth century. This linguistic retention stemmed in part from the fact that only in 1919 had Hanover's school children been compelled to learn English and that during the first decades of the century Hanover had remained a semi-isolated place without a railway or an all-weather road to the outside world. In the 1930s and 1940s Mennonites in this district still possessed an unchallenged critical mass, a characteristic guaranteed by the new wave of Mennonite immigrants from the Soviet Union during the 1920s, the High German–speaking and pietistically inclined Russländer Mennonites. Hanover's most widely read newspaper was the German-language *Steinbach Post*, which boasted a circulation in the late 1940s of 4000 subscribers and linked conservative Mennonites not only throughout the Canadian prairies, but also in Canadian-descendant Mennonite colonies in Mexico and Paraguay. During these years too, Hanover's economy relied on self-sufficient, mixed-commodity farm households.[2] Two story, white-painted woodframe houses were set adjacent to red-painted, hip-roof dairy barns and surrounded by smaller outbuildings for pigs and chickens, as well as special buildings for milk, machinery, and grain storage. The community was a homogeneous Dutch Mennonite enclave, densely populated by farm families, intersected with relatively small service centers, and linked to Winnipeg, thirty-five miles away, with nothing more than seasonal, dirt roads.

By 1960 Hanover's countryside had a new appearance. Hanover was dotted with modern farms that specialized in poultry, egg, dairy, or hog production. Farms now often sported low-lying, white-colored barns of plywood construction located across the farmyard from the modern bungalow, often graced with decorative limestone brick and painted in hues of green, blue, or brown. Hanover's physical features – its relative lack of fertile land and its proximity to Winnipeg – affected the local response to the new postwar agriculture. Farmers had to become sensitive to new demands for meat, eggs, dairy products, and vegetables from Winnipeg's booming suburbs.[3] As the economic value of these foodstuffs increased, Hanover farms became more intensive operations. Farm sizes dropped, falling from 64.0 acres in 1921 to 54.4 acres in 1941, and then further to 47.0 acres by the end of the war. In the meantime, crop selection shifted to complement the heightened interest in poultry and livestock production. Between 1941 and 1946 wheat production, not Hanover's mainstay in the first instance, declined by 25 percent at the very time that feed grain production increased by almost 30 percent.[4] This trend continued into the 1950s so that by 1956 the oats to wheat ratio on Hanover farms was five times the provincial average.[5] This crop selection in no way represented a hesitation to embrace agricultural science: Hanover farmers applied the herbicides of 2,4-D and MCPA to their barley and oat fields, even if they did so less systematically than the wheat farmers farther west, and they too experimented with at least some synthetic fertilizers.

Leading the shift to full agricultural commercialization in Hanover during these years, however, were not the grain farmers, but the poultry and dairy producers. By 1956, for example, the average Hanover farm kept five times more dairy cattle and poultry than did the average Manitoba farm.[6] Dairy farming, which had saved Hanover during the Great Depression by producing the almost unspoilable cheddar cheese, increased dramatically in the first years after the war.[7] Encouraged by demands for cheese, the number of dairy cows in Hanover had increased by 57 percent between 1931 and 1946, and postwar demand for cheese increased the number even further. By 1949 southeastern Manitoba could boast that it 'made most of Manitoba's cheese and shipped one-half of the milk needed by Winnipeg.'[8] New government-sponsored farm organizations such as the local Dairy Herd Improvement Association (DHIA) introduced registered stock-breeding programs and the notion of record of production (ROP) performance. Technological innovation such as the electrically powered milk machine, refrigerated bulk tank, water pumps, barn cleaning systems, power-takeoff-driven mowers and hay balers, and hydraulic-powered loaders, turned dairy farming in Hanover into a highly technologized and capitalized venture by the mid-1950s.[9]

Even more pronounced was the change that came to poultry production. In fact, by 1951 the size of Hanover's dairy herds began declining just as the size of poultry flocks increased. In his field research in Hanover in 1946, sociologist E.K. Francis concluded that poultry production allowed 'many farmers with small capital and little land [to make] a good living.'[10] Soon, however, the poultry initiatives in Hanover echoed John Shover's description of poultry production in the United States in which factory-like broiler chicken barns and business-oriented farmers 'transformed the wife's source of pin money into the most integrated and mechanized industry of any kind in food production.'[11] Hanover farmers quadrupled the number of their chickens and turkeys from 266,638 birds to over one million in the fifteen years between 1946 and 1961.[12] Farm mechanization and rural electrification provided heat for brooding, thermostatic ventilation allowed for greater bird density, electric lights extended output during the short winter days, and electric motors ran the water pumps and automatic feeding lines.[13] Competing interests from half a dozen local feedmills that produced nutrient-specific, medicated mashed or pelleted feeds, and several eviscerating plants, either private ventures in Winnipeg or a local cooperative in Blumenort, allowed farmers a certain latitude in controlling production costs and securing markets.

A central characteristic of this agricultural transformation was a closer link to the tumultuous postwar world of urban markets and global capitalism. Markets became more accessible even though most of Hanover lay well away from the services of a railroad. During the 1940s and 1950s, scattered across the district about five miles apart and containing 50 to 200 residents, were a dozen small but thriving service centers that had risen with the Depression-era cheese factories. But they were dominated by three larger towns, Niverville in the west with a population in the mid 1950s of 450 persons, Grunthal in the south with a somewhat smaller population, and the kingpin of them all, Steinbach, with a population of about 2500 in the eastern part of the rural municipality.[14] Postwar society entailed increasingly close connections to the world outside Hanover. In the 1940s a paved connection, the Provincial Trunk Highway 59, linked the western reaches of Hanover to Winnipeg and in the late 1950s when the new Trans-Canada Highway passed just seven miles north of the municipality, Provincial Trunk Highway 12 was soon constructed to link the Trans-Canada to Steinbach. Townsfolk could reach Winnipeg, a booming metropolis of 400,000, within an hour. Other linkages to the outside enabled further farm modernization. Rural electrification tied the farm sections of Hanover to the provincial hydroelectric power grid in 1947, the Trans-Canada Pipeline linked Hanover's town residents to Alberta's natural gas in 1957, and in the same year a microwave telephone tower introduced direct dialing to Steinbach, bringing Winnipeg into even closer reach.[15] The economically transformed Hanover countryside had become an 'outpost of urban society,' to employ Shover's phrase, not only in its consumption patterns, but also in its production goals, commodity output, and communication systems.

As elsewhere, farmers in Hanover readily adopted 'business methods,' engaged in such strategies as 'cost-benefit analysis,' and readily accepted 'managerial intervention' by governments. In their limited forays into wheat production they had already learned to accommodate themselves to the Canadian Wheat Board of 1935, and accepted the principle of market manipulation introduced by the intrusive Wheat Acreage Reduction Act of 1941 and the board's enhanced role in 1943 as 'the exclusive marketing agency for Canadian wheat.'[16] In dairy and poultry production they continued to practice cooperative marketing and selective purchasing. In 1968 Hanover's ag rep Rod Siemens could write that 'ten years ago many of the "fortune tellers" ... were predicting doom and failure of the small private farmer because they had discovered the term "vertical integration."'[17] The reason for local success, argued Siemens, was that farmers had fully accepted scientific agriculture and in 1968 the only remaining weakness lay 'in managing the financial and bookkeeping aspects of his business.'[18] Still, farmers were capitalizing their operations in unprecedented ways. A history of the Steinbach Credit Union notes that especially 'the years 1968 and 1969 were marked by the many large loans which were granted to farmers to expand their operations,' loans made despite ever-increasing rates of interest.[19] Financial reporting soon changed too: by 1973, for example, farmers could purchase the mechanical wonder of the 'eight-ounce, eight-digit electronic calculator' for just under $150 from Derksen Printers in Steinbach and in the same year Siemens boasted that at least '100 farmers in Eastern Manitoba' were using the '"Confirm" computer program,' enabling them to master new complex capital gains taxes and confirm their farms financial state at the end of each year.[20] Increasingly too, farmers sought out the services of accountants who with the assistance of tax lawyers began incorporating family farms, all in the name of tax reduction and more efficient financial management.[21]

Mennonites and the Marketing Boards

Most significant of all agricultural innovations in Hanover was the willingness of farmers to look to government for assistance in controlling livestock and poultry markets. In this way they prevented either a return to subsistence farming or the full development of a vertically integrated agriculture. During the 1960s Hanover farmers who had heeded the postwar Department of Agriculture counsel to specialize in different farm commodities organized into producer groups to lobby for their respective industries. Initially they strove to raise tariffs and to remove government-imposed production barriers. In 1957 and 1962, for example, Steinbach's *Carillon News* reported that two local men from the Manitoba Turkey Growers Association, Ben L. Reimer and Dave P. Loewen, had successfully lobbied the department, first with demands for higher tariffs, and then, warning that farmers might 'be forced to quit the turkey business altogether' if the department did not reduce the prescribed amount of fat on a Grade A marketable turkey.[22] Similar efforts to engage government powers were observable in the chicken, egg, hog, and dairy sectors.

More importantly, farmers began to cooperate with government agencies on the basic question of marketing farm commodities during a time in which meat, milk, and egg consumption in Canada was rising quickly.[23] Government's long-term answer became the 'producer marketing board' and its 'supply management' marketing system that entailed a tightly regulated quota system.[24] In 1962 the first reported marketing board in Canada was launched when the 230 chicken broiler producers in British Columbia voted by a 90 percent margin to create one.[25] The implications of marketing boards varied. Dairy producers had one version of them, hog producers another. In December 1962 the *Carillon News* reported that the annual national convention of Canadian dairy farmers in Winnipeg had voted by a majority of 90 percent to support 'united action by dairy farmers ... organized through a single milk marketing board ... [that] would set standards, regulate the market and equalize receipts to producers.'[26] In November 1963 another design was outlined when Herb Anderson, the quiet-spoken president of the Manitoba Farmers Union, told hog farmers that just as the Canadian Wheat Board had proved beneficial because cash-strapped grain farmers no longer caused 'the bottom to drop out' of the wheat market each fall by dumping their commodities, so too the self-interested hog producer should consider the merits of a hog marketing board, especially one that would 'have complete control over the sale of hogs' and allow for the sale 'to the highest bidder in accordance to the true law of supply and demand.'[27] By 1968 farmers were in the process of turning several commodities over to the marketing board system, with beef producers accepting 'promotional and development boards,' hog producers accepting the 'limited joint-marketing desk system,' and poultry and dairy farmers accepting the full 'supply management boards' or quota system.[28]

Advocates of the latter scheme applauded supply management as a farmer-led program, and as one that encouraged equality among farmers, guaranteed production limits, and secured higher prices. As the system came into place a variety of implications for local agriculture became apparent. Mennonite farmers would henceforth see themselves tightly aligned with producers from other regions in the province. Always, the decision to implement the marketing boards was billed as a democratic event headed by the farmers: in February 1968 all turkey farmers with annual production of more than 500 birds were told by the government-appointed Manitoba Marketing Board that they 'could have a vote on organizing a Turkey Marketing Board,' a vote that would eventually pass by 87 percent.[29] Later that year a large majority of Manitoba's 100 chicken broiler producers also asked the provincial board for permission to hold a vote on the issue.[30] Then too, the marketing boards demonstrated that they had real power and even the ability to equalize production among their members: in April of 1968, for example, the dairy marketing board announced that 'producers who had 1967–68 quotas of less than 100,000 pounds and who increased deliveries last year will receive new quotas' while farmers who 'shipped over 100,000 pounds ... may not be able to increase ... quota by the full amount ... shipped.'[31]

The provincial marketing boards now negotiated just how much product each province could export into the national market and then guaranteed farmers a production level. It was announced in January 1973, for example, that Manitoba would enter 'the national egg marketing scheme.' In addition to stabilizing prices and guarding against surplus production, the province would receive an 11.4 percent share of the total Canadian market, based on a five-year average of production.[32] Farmers reported quick results. Local farmers in a 1981 survey all cited significant increases in prices: broiler producers recalled a rise from eighteen cents a pound in 1967 to fifty cents in 1981; egg producers a rise from twenty-eight cents a dozen in the 1960s to ninety cents; and dairy farmers an increase in fluid milk prices from three dollars a hundredweight in 1950 to ten dollars.[33] Farmers had accepted not only the rationality of specialization and scientific advances in production, they had accepted the fullest intervention of a marketing system that took much of the risk of agriculture from the farmers' hands, but guaranteed the survival for the time being of the family farm, at least for a minority of Hanover Mennonites.

Farm Readjustments in Meade County, Kansas

The changes to Meade County paralleled yet differed from those of Hanover. The southeast sections of Meade County represented a close-knit Mennonite community with distinctive ethnic boundaries. Like their Canadian counterparts, the Meade Mennonites were a distinctive people in a community that was disproportionately Caucasian and landowning, recalled by one former resident as possessing 'very few Mexican-American families' and 'no African-Americans ... at all.'[34] In the postwar decades, the original Mennonite settlement at Meade County, having been established on six sections or 3840 acres of rolling range land some eighteen miles southeast of Meade in 1906, was still a visible, distinctly ethnoreligious community. Over time the Mennonite settlement had in fact expanded, filling in much of the gap between the old settlement and Meade with three distinct clusters of farms in the four most southeasterly townships of Meade Center, Logan, Sand Creek, and Odee. Here the majority of the county's Mennonites lived on eighty sections of land, sixty-nine of which were exclusively Mennonite. Thus an elongated community had developed, measuring eighteen by five miles in area and radiating in a southeasterly direction from Meade. By 1948 Mennonites may have comprised only about 20 percent of the county's households or 121 of 631, according to the *Dakota Farm Directory*, but they possessed critical mass in the county's southeast. This distinct settlement was recognized by the wider society of Meade County: news stories such as the June 1947 report in the *Meade Globe Press* that announced simply that 'Settlement Wheat Making 25–30 Bushels' affirmed not only the good fortune of the Mennonite farmers, but the very existence of an identifiable settlement.[35] By 1957 the Mennonite settlement was still described by one local resident as 'a relatively densely populated Mennonite community of 500 people.'[36] This site was a quintessential 'island community,' a place of 'traditional village life,' the social form that John Shover argues predated the Great Disjuncture.

The Meade Mennonite community, however, also differed from the Hanover community in a significant way. Meade County's position in the winter wheat–growing belt of the western Midwest left it with a particular set of farm experiences that affected its strategies for survival in the middle decades of the century. Gilbert C. Fite has described central and western Kansas in the years before the Depression as one of the 'nation's leading wheat' regions and those who stuck it out through the Depression as inhabitants of 'one the world's great bread baskets.'[37] Fite writes that 'the suitability of the soil, the topography of the land, and the early development of machines to handle all aspects of wheat farming contributed to some huge wheat operations involving hundreds and even thousands of acres.'[38] In fact a common strategy in the risky business of wheat production was mechanization and increased economies of scale in a time of shrinking profit margins. Not coincidentally, this corner of the North American grassland was the same region that experienced the Depression-era dust bowl in unparalleled fashion and, in the process, a loss in confidence in agriculture.

The close-knit Mennonite community of Meade County adapted to the conditions of the Depression and the war with various strategies. The family of Ben Classen of Dallas, Oregon, made one kind of adaptation as it left Meade for the west coast in the early 1940s. The relocation came about for two reasons: first, as Classen recalled it, to guard against foreclosure from the 'Federal State Bank as father believed that we would have lost it all if he had not sold;' second, 'mother wanted out because she feared the dust storms' and she knew the family could resettle because she 'had a cousin in Oregon.' Families who remained in the county also adapted, but by readjusting their farm production goals. Meade Mennonites had shifted from mixed farming to wheat production when they left eastern Nebraska for western Kansas in 1906; during the Depression they returned to a diversified agriculture. Between 1915 and 1925 in the face of high wheat prices and field mechanization Meade Mennonite families reduced their cow herds from 3.0 to 1.9 animals per household. During the Depression and the war they increased those herds again, to an average of 4.2 animals per household by 1950.[39] Meade County residents recalled the importance of this return to mixed farming: during the Great Depression 'the cows and the cream cheques were everything, they would even pay for the tractor gas.'[40] Even during the Second World War the mixed-farm strategy was pursued by most farmers. A typical family history notes that after their marriage in 1943 Elmer and Elizabeth Wiens 'took up farming and raised cattle ... They also milked a few cows, had chickens and hogs.'[41] Other sources note that during the war, with the Mennonite boys off at conscientious objector or Civilian Public Service camps, women reasserted an important production role on the farm and that fact alone encouraged the subsistence activities in the farmyard to expand.[42] This strategy did not end quickly. As one Meade County student noted in 1950: 'In the Great Depression and dust bowl years of the thirties the people learned a great lesson that depending only on grain farming was not the best; today this community ... also keeps livestock ... [with] nice large dairies ... such as the Friesens who [have] nice Guernseys, the Isaac Brothers, Peter and John, who each have a large Holstein herd.'[43]

During the 1950s, however, farmers who had survived the Great Depression and the wartime economy once again bolstered wheat production. Wheat was still in western Kansas's blood. A July 1947 story in the *Meade Globe Press* was telling: the newspaper announced that the county was 'more diversified than one might think' and listed not only cattle, but pigs, lambs, honey, and fruit, and not only wheat, but barley, oats, corn, sorghum, and Sudan grass. The figures, however, were more telling than the headline. The record showed that 88.5 percent of the county's planted crop land or 216,500 acres was still in wheat and the only other commodity close in revenue to wheat was cattle, 78,000 head in 1947 on 180,000 acres of range land.[44] Mennonite farm activity adhered to these models during the 1950s. Between 1950 and 1961 total land acreages per Mennonite farm in Meade County rose from 462 to 588 acres, while the number of beef cattle increased from 13 to 34 head.[45] During the same time the number of farms owning milking cows and chickens plummeted.[46] In 1950 82 percent of Mennonite farms in Meade milked at least two or three cows; by 1961 that number had fallen to 20 percent.[47] Chicken production declined too. In 1950 62 percent of the Mennonite farms raised some chickens, in 1961 only 39 percent did. Over the long run it was an even more dramatic fall; 85 percent of farms raised chickens in 1937, but only 7 percent did in 1975. Exceptions existed in this unilinear devolution of the mixed farm as a few households did experiment by specializing in dairy, swine, and turkeys. In 1957, for example, several farmers linked to the Southwest Kansas Turkey Federation accounted for the 25,000 turkeys in the Mennonite community and in 1961 four farmers owned half of the community's dairy cows.[48] By 1980 the turkeys were gone and the dairy herds in decline. For most Meade Mennonite farmers the 1960s and 1970s represented a full return to wheat production. The farmers knew they were on a broad road. As Gilbert Fite notes, 'World War II, the Korean War, worldwide relief efforts ... the requirements of wheat by ... Europe and Japan have placed the Great Plains farmer in a ... favorable market position.'[49] In 1973 the United States exported 1.14

billion bushels of wheat, more than the total production in most years in the 1960s.

Like farmers elsewhere, the Meade families linked promising new technologies to their farm strategies. They continued to embrace greater mechanization, as auction sale records between 1948 and 1960 suggest. One machine listed for sale by seven separate farmers, the combine harvester, was a clear sign of long-term mechanization. The first combine had come to the Mennonite settlement in 1915 and was fully accepted by the 1920s.[50] The auction lists contained a range of combine harvesters – a large, twenty-foot 1930 John Deere number 3, a new but smaller twelve-foot 1949 Minneapolis Moline G4, and others – evidence that combine technology was well-grounded in Meade. Especially innovative was a wide variety of machinery accessories. Farmer John F. Isaac's 1948 auction, preceding his move to California, included equipment with hydraulic cylinder lifts, power-takeoff technology, and electric motor power. His 1936 Chevrolet grain truck had a hydraulic-driven dump, the cultivator was equipped with 'Power Lift,' the tractor had a hydraulic-powered 'front-end loader,' and the grain binder and hay baler were complete with 'power takeoff' shafts that attached to any tractor. The items at these auctions also included a 32-volt, 1800-watt, wind-power charger and a 32-volt Delco power plant, and welders, chicken incubators, and electric fences that used these power sources. Other characteristics of the auctioned equipment reflected the good times of postwar society. Only four of seventeen auctioned combines, tractors, and trucks predated 1945 and in most instances the new equipment was more powerful than the old: Martin Ediger's '½ ton' truck was equipped with a 'V-8' engine and Jacob F. Isaac's 1951 tractor featured an impressive 'six-cylinder' motor.[51]

Allotments, Parity, and Price Support

The single most far-reaching innovation in the Meade settlement, however, was the new array of government programs offered to the farmers and the openness of the Mennonites to them. The Meade farmers had known government intrusiveness during the Great Depression: the Rural Electrification Administration (REA) of 1935 had promoted 'the building of electrical lines to remote locations through a program of low-interest loans';[52] the Works Progress Administration (WPA) of 1935 built grids of graveled roads and placed the unemployed on federally supported roadwork; the Social Security Act provided a new net of

security; the Soil Conservation and Domestic Allotment Act had introduced a new intrusive bureaucracy, including the Soil Conservation
Service (SCS). The once aloof Mennonites readily partook in each of
these programs, and acronyms such as REA, WPA, SCS, and others
became part of their everyday language. One-time Meade residents Ben
Classen and Ben Rempel recalled that during the Depression, after six
straight years of crop loss, the federal government's 'seed loans' program became fully accepted by the Mennonite farmers. They also participated in the 'allotment' programs, receiving government payment
for either storing grain to guard against market flooding or to summerfallow wheat land, actually cutting back on production.[53] The latter
made a special impression on Meade farmers; it was designed 'to idle
the ground,' sometimes for a ten-year period, with remuneration and
an extra fifty dollars an acre if the land remained ungrazed. They also
embraced the WPA that paid for roadwork and ditch-clearing with
horses and scrapers. As Classen and Rempel recalled, accommodation
to these Depression-era programs simply became the 'thing to do.'
Long-time well-driller Corny Z. Friesen agreed: 'Never did the question of taking government funds come up for discussion.' In fact, 'if it
wasn't for the government, I don't know where these guys would be.'[54]

In the postwar years the Mennonite farmers were drawn into relationships with other even more intrusive government-sponsored programs. The choices were many. Indeed in a single issue of the *Meade
Globe Press* in 1948, farmers were offered an extension course in 'Farm
and Home Improvement,' free trees from Fort Hays Experiment Station, labor assistance at the Western Kansas State Employment Service,
a warning that 'tax estimates' were coming due, a two-day wiring
school by the REA, and a report from the Kansas Board of Agriculture
meeting in Topeka.[55] But some programs were more intrusive than
others. The government's International Wheat Control agreement of
1948, for example, promised local farmers 'markets to exporting countries at equitable and stable prices' by guaranteeing wheat export quan-
tities, a five-year ceiling of $2.00 per bushel, and floor of $1.50 per
bushel, decreasing by 10 cents a bushel each year.[56] Under the generous
Commodity Credit Corporation farmers were eligible for government
loans with only wheat stocks serving as collateral. Farmers even had a
choice to pay off the loan, to deliver the grain at a government 'floor
price,' or to wait for the market to rise above the floor and take the
gain.[57] At another stage of this evolving program Meade farmers were
promised wheat and meat support in the form of 'government guaran-

tee of 90 percent of parity,' meaning that upon delivery of a given commodity, the government guaranteed 90 percent of the price registered at the time the farmer enrolled in the program. But the programs came bearing costs to the farmer. In 1952 the county agent reminded farmers that for them to qualify for the 'price support' program they must abide by certain government-set wheat 'acreage allotments' and ensure that 'farm-stored' grain was maintained in good quality.[58] By the late 1960s the *Globe Press* editor could complain of bad times for farmers, 'not only saddled with governmental control, but with weather and each is as unpredictable as the other.'[59] If Mennonite farmers felt hamstrung by government regulations they did not mention those feelings, either in memoir, diary, or interview.

Mennonite farmers became further intertwined in the wider postwar society through their participation in a number of local farm and civic associations. Indeed by the 1950s the once exclusive Mennonites were represented on numerous local boards. Pete E. Loewen was secretary of the 1.5 million-bushel Co-op elevator throughout the 1940s and 1950s, George Rempel served on the Fowler hospital board, Frank Classen was elected vice-president of the Farm Bureau in 1959, and in a single election of delegates for the Agricultural Stabilization and Conservation (ASC) committees in 1959, seventeen of the forty-two candidates were Mennonite farmers and five – D.E. Thiessen, F.N. Ediger, Elias Friesen, Nick Ediger, and P.K. Isaac – were elected.[60] Oftentimes the Mennonites joined these organizations with some ambivalence. The fact was that the Farm Bureau served as a political lobby group for Kansas farmers, promising to 'examine each piece of legislation in Topeka and to evaluate its impact on farmers.' Then too, the bureau sold life insurance, a security system historically rejected by Mennonites. Still, the vast majority of Mennonites, fully seventy-three of the hundred and twenty or so households, signed up for Farm Bureau services in 1947 and among them were the most conservative of the Mennonites, including widows and single-woman farmers.[61] Clearly the Mennonites agreed with the Farm Bureau's support for both the crop loan program and commodity allotment programs, especially its contention that such programs should allow for the 'greatest possible freedom of operation on [the] individual farm.'[62] And clearly too they saw benefits in the bureau's wider range of crop, fire, and automobile insurances.

Mennonite farmers came through the Great Depression and the Second World War with a new willingness to accept the intervention of the state and civic associations in their lives. But many were affected so negatively by ecological disaster and market forces that farming became virtually impossible. Both phenomena – government intervention and market forces – introduced the Meade Mennonites to a wider and more urbanized social milieu. Both took them into a cultural context which pitted a nationalistic imagination against the cultural cohesiveness of everyday life in the Mennonite sections of Meade County.

In both the RM of Hanover in Manitoba and Meade County in Kansas, Mennonite farmers were confronted with the challenge of a global marketplace, of a vertically integrated agricultural industry, and of new technologies. To negotiate their way in this new arena, Mennonites chose one of two options. On the one hand they accepted the active intervention of their governments' departments of agriculture. In Canada poultry and dairy farmers received assistance in organizing into marketing boards that dramatically reordered production and marketing; in the United States wheat farmers accepted government allotment programs that linked aid in marketing with production quotas. In the Canadian marketing board model, consumers of meat, eggs, and dairy products were asked to pay for farmers' security; in the U.S. wheat allotment model the funds came from state coffers. But, more significantly, in Manitoba the marketing boards kept the farm families on the land, whereas in western Kansas wheat allotments more often moved them off.

A comparison of the RM of Hanover and Meade County Mennonite farmers does much more than contrast two national systems. Even though Hanover and Meade were both located on the North American grassland, they represented two distinctive ecological regions measured mostly by differences in length of growing season and proximity to significant urban centers. Meade County's physical and demographic characteristics suited it ideally to wheat production; Hanover's suited it best for specialization in dairy, poultry, and swine. Those very types of agriculture affected the two communities' histories. Economies of scale in the wheat fields pushed men and women off the land whereas the same economic principle in the specialized dairy, poultry, and swine units drew them in. The differences in the two rural communities was apparent not only in their economic strategies, but also in the attitudes the two sets of farmers developed toward their respective environments. In both places government-sponsored agricultural programs shaped commodity production, dictated terms of marketing, and encouraged particular attitudes to environmental management. Ecological differences shaped distinctive responses to the Great Disjuncture, just as markets, state programs, and demographic factors affected distinctive attitudes to the environment. Even during the times of broad change in midcentury agriculture the environmental relationships of two communities of a single ethnoreligious group could be distinctive.

2 Snowdrift and Dust Bowl: The Environment and Cultural Change

The economic transformation in rural Meade and Hanover occurred within a context of cultural change. This latter change, as we will see, revealed itself in shifting ideas of class, ethnicity, religion, and gender, but it could also be seen in the way the environment was imagined and regarded. On the one hand the environment is the soil and ground on which farmers toil, 'a cast of nonhuman characters,'[1] a property sufficiently important to be the premier chapter of any rural history. Certainly, the environment – climate, soil, land, storms, micro-organisms, water – affected human behavior, although less forcefully than during the frontier times of land breaking, road building, bush clearing, and ditch digging, or years of extreme drought or cold. On the other hand there is a history after the environment was fundamentally altered by pioneers, and it included the manner in which the altered environment affected human behavior and culture, including the local economy, cultivation methods, and views of nature.[2] This dialectical relationship was linked closely to the culture of the Great Disjuncture. Both economic imperatives and cultural beliefs linked to the Great Disjuncture determined farmers' relationship with the land, their treatment and their views of it. Their changing cosmologies, religion, ethnicity, and even gender affected their behavior on the land. A rising sense of individualism, increased nationalism, acceptance of new technologies, and new ideas of generational succession changed their perspective on the cultural value of land. Changes in the middle decades of the twentieth century affected not only the farm economy but also human interaction with the environment.

This chapter undertakes a broad approach to the history of human interaction with the environment. It focuses less on the specific manner in which farmers changed their environments than on the complex factors that determined farmers' approach to land management in a post-pioneer era.[3] As such, this chapter accepts Richard White's counsel that histories of human interaction with the environment should be more than the 'Whiggish ... story of environmental sin.'[4] It tries, as White suggests, 'to read environmental history in the way that [we] have to read literature' on any other topic – race, region, and class – 'in order to claim basic historical literacy.'[5] Without a doubt the consumerism and productivity associated with the Great Disjuncture 'came at a tremendous environmental cost' with 'profound social consequences.'[6] But as Simon Schama has noted, environmental history is not only about what humans have done to landscape, but about the way in which human culture has produced the very idea of landscape.[7] The Mennonite farmers' culture and experience compelled them to perceive the land in different ways at different times. Oftentimes land was seen in contradictory ways. It simultaneously could be vulnerable and fragile in the face of human exploitation, hostile to and rejecting of human endeavor, or it could be life-giving, nurturing human body and soul. In this imagining, and in the varied behavior it evoked, the Mennonite farmers themselves were creatures of nature.

The environments of the geographic sites of Manitoba and Kansas can be represented respectively by images of snowdrift and dust bowl. Each represented a stark physical challenge for the farmers. In Kansas the image of the trying Depression-era dust bowl served to order postwar cultivation practices, shape relationships to government soil conservation experts, and create a specific view that land could not and was not meant to sustain an ever-growing population. In Manitoba the challenge was to farm within a 120-day growing season; the imperatives of weather affected farmers' acceptance of postwar technology and agricultural science, and their construction of a postwar farm economy. For a pacifist people, the exigencies of the environment presented a paradox.[8] The craft of farming had always been associated with simplicity, peace, and harmony with a creator God, yet their survival on the land involved overcoming its resistence – dealing with the vagaries of weather, insects, and weeds – and maximizing the soil's potential. The Manitobans outwitted 'Jack Frost' while the Kansans faced down the springtime 'dusters.' Farmers in Kansas spoke of the dark, dust-filled day of 14 April 1935, while the Manitobans remembered the snowstorm of the century, the severe, late-winter blizzard of 4 March 1966. These memories served to inform the range of economic expectation, the order of God's blessing, the belief in communal solidarity, and even the imperative of national duty. Such images were signs of the diverse environmental challenges facing farm communities and foreshadowed the disparate environmental cultures the communities created.

In the Dust Bowl's Aftermath

The reference point for all midcentury Meade County farmers was the Depression-era dust bowl. The combination of drought, heat, dust, and wind could undermine any farmer's best-laid plans. Meade County farmers were constantly reminded of the ecological disaster of the 1930s. Old timers agreed that Black Sunday, 14 April 1935, 'was the darkest day of all ... climax[ing] a three year series of almost unbearable dust storms.'[9] The dust bowl mentality did not end in 1935. A letter by Cornelius and Margaret Siemens of Meade County to friends in Manitoba carried an ominous note: 'the weather is quite windy and dry, seemingly for most it will be a total harvest failure.'[10] And while the 1940s were usually considered years of adequate moisture, several years during the 1950s brought poor or no harvest at all and when crops failed, the culprit was the March or April duster. On 31 March 1955 the *Globe Press* ran a headline that announced the 'Year's Worst Duster Blew Hard.' Then, despite a three-quarter-inch rainfall in the first week in April that promised to 'green up fields,' the weather changed quickly and by mid-April came front page reports of 'High Wind, Dust.'[11] In March 1957 came more warnings that dusters might blow and that precautions must be taken as the soil of any field could 'move bad.'[12] A week later it was announced that farmers were ploughing up their damaged fields of winter wheat and planting maize instead.[13] In early April 1957 when reporters from the Canadian Broadcasting Corporation dropped by the coffee shop of Meade's Lakeway Hotel to 'obtain ... a tape recording of the drought condition in the area,' Meade County's dust had again acquired international status.[14]

If concerns about dusters were more pronounced in some years than others, the concern about adequate moisture was never-ending. The *Meade Globe Press* ran weekly front-page stories on the state of the weather, especially during the October seeding, the March germination, and June and July harvest months. During 1945, even with startling news stories of war, discoveries of oil and gas, and the restructuring of school boundaries, weather conditions and the state of crops captured the front page's lead story in seven of the fifty-four weekly issues. Headlines such as 'Timely Rain "Saves" the Wheat Crop' or 'Over 2 Inches of Moisture Wet-Down Ground in Area' spelled out the main worry.[15] Each story ended with a tally of the total rainfall to date and at the end of each year the annual rainfall was measured against the 19.18 inches annual average precipitation. Farmers knew that May must bring its average of 3.5 inches of rain to fill out the wheat heads, just as they knew they needed the expected 2.6 inches in August to prepare a good seedbed for fall planting. The occasional early November snow-fall, heavy January frost, or significant June rainfall was unwelcomed because it could respectively hamper good fall germination, freeze out the winter wheat, or ruin ripe stands of wheat. Most often concerns returned to issues of drought and wind.[16] The apex of bad weather of course was the tornado that could ruin a wide swath of wheat and turn buildings into 'kindling wood,' as happened to Henry J. Isaac's farm in June 1958.[17]

Rainfall, wind, and inordinate heat marked concerns registered by farmers' diaries. The sparsely written diary of Henry A. Friesen is illustrative.[18] In fact, a comparison of entries penned in 1952 when he was a middle-aged farmer, and during 1968, when he was a retired pensioner, reflect this abiding interest. Of the three allusions to weather in January 1952, one notes a 'windy day' on the eighteenth, one 'very warm weather' on the twenty-eighth, and one 'weather, warm and dry' on the thirty-first. The note for 5 February, 'it was dusty and windy in p.m.,' indicates the close association of the two central concerns. For Friesen, all amounts of rainfall merited notation: typical are statements for 3 February that 'it rained a little during the nite' or for 11 February that 'it rained a little today.' Similarly the arrival of warm, early spring weather was noted: 24 February dawned 'cold and snowy,' and the fact that it coincided with the first day of Rev H.H. Epp's two-week-long revival meeting may have been disconcerting for the ministers, but Friesen seemed as concerned about the fact that just four days later, on 28 February, the 'weather [was] very warm.'

The same range of concerns were registered twenty-six years later in 1968, just a year before Friesen left the farm for his retirement in Meade. On 31 March he recorded that not only was it 'windy this morning,' it 'was very stormy during the night,' and this entry was followed on 3 April with an expression of annoyance that it was 'dusty today' and on the fourth that it was 'windy, dry.' The nature of Friesen's preoccu-pation appears even in his response to rainfall outside of Meade County.

On 22 April while on a two-day trip to Henderson, Nebraska, for a funeral, Friesen laments, 'lots of rain in Nebraska, no rain at home;' a month later on 25 May on a road trip to Des Moines, Iowa, Friesen, without bothering to record the trip's purpose, notes nevertheless that it 'rained' as he made his way through Inman, Kansas, and that it 'rained on the way to Iowa'; a month later, when he took his missionary daughter Elda to Wichita, he notes only that she left 'via plane to Haiti and West Indies' and that it rained in the central Kansas communities of 'Inman-Newton.' It was a big day, worthy of no additional comment, when on 6 May Meade County 'had two inches of rain last nite.' And as more rain came it was carefully measured: .6 inches on 8 May, .8 inches on the thirty-first. The end of the drought-filled summer months, interlaced with 'hot and windy' days with temperatures as high as 104 degrees Fahrenheit, came not only with 'the first good rain this summer' on 17 July, but with precisely .75 inches of rain.

If Meade County farmers measured their sense of well-being in inches of rain and knots of wind, their work patterns were shaped by the seasons of rain, dust, and heat. Weather was a ceaseless preoccupation when raising wheat and running cattle and specific duties attended each season as Helena Reimer's diary for 1948 aptly demonstrates.[19] The winter months required work to ensure that cattle were adequately fed; the usual four-month wheat pasture might be supplemented with high-fibre alfalfa or kaffir bundles or 'hammermilled' feed grain, especially to tide cattle over from the end of the wheat pasture in April to the 'green pasture' on the hay land. But the main task was to coax the arid high plains to produce their maximum yield of grain. Plantings came in spurts throughout the year. Barley and oats were seeded in late March and early April, sorghum and kaffir corn in May and June, and winter wheat in October. In 1948 each period of seeding was preceded by numerous days of 'one-waying,' turning the soil by disker to prepare a seedbed of fine soil for the press drills and to kill as many weeds as possible.[20] June and July brought successive days of combining, welcoming neighbors whose crops were still greenish to lend their combines for joint harvests with the expectation of payment in kind as the harvest proceeded. The beginning of August was less busy – time to cut the sunflowers by the fence, repair equipment, or haul wheat into the barn from the field. At the end of August and beginning of September came the barley and millet harvest using the old threshing machine and presumably allowing the straw to be kept in the farmyard. And even before this task was completed, the traditional fall planting of wheat began with its requirement of another round of one-waying. When this task was completed, the October and November maize harvest began and once again the combines roared in the fields. More chop was required to fatten up the cattle, and thus 'hammermilling' began again and continued through the months of November and December. Those same months marked slacker times, opportunity to 'tighten up the windows,' to pick up heating oil in Meade, fix windmills bent by winter storms, visit Dodge City with eggs and for shopping, and attend neighbors' auctions. For the boys it was a time to help with domestic chores such as washing, but also the season for the methodical 'taking apart' of the tractor for repair. The year's last tasks included the week-long hog kill at the beginning of December and the calculation of the 'income of the year' on December 28.[21]

If the daily work on the Reimer farm of 1948 and the daily concern with weather on the Friesen farm in 1952 and 1968 seem similar, they do mask two decades of change. Donald Worster has observed that the Mennonites of Haskell County in Kansas 'were all residential, diversified farm people – indeed, a most successful model of that declining agricultural order.'[22] This might have been an overly optimistic reading of Mennonite agriculture, but certainly it reflected an agrarian strategy that sustained many Mennonites into the 1950s. Pamela Riney-Kehrberg's *Rooted in Dust* suggests that in southwestern Kansas after the Depression 'farmers moved further and further' from the ideal of a farm that produced both 'sustenance, as well as a cash income.'[23] This judgment fits the Meade County Mennonites. Certainly during the postwar years Mennonites redefined the very notion of environment. But it was a redefinition that came couched in ambiguity and even contradiction. The land simultaneously came to be seen as a vulnerable and abused resource, and as a source of power and wealth. In the first instance it required protection from greed and exploitation; in the second it became the object of heady optimism and overt accumulation, even greed.

Public discussions of the land presented both perspectives. In their newspaper Meade County farmers read at once of a new economic bravado and a new environmental tenderness. Reflecting the first sentiment, industry promised to develop new profitable pathways to exploit and even bypass the environment. In 1948 the *Globe Press* heralded the boast of the nearby Stanolind Synthesis Plant that could produce acids, 'ketones and aldehydes' and in turn 'attract new industries.' In 1954 ads in the *Globe Press* announced General Electric's vision that 'the atom will produce power for homes in five to ten years.'[24] The wheat market also caught the bullish spirit of the time: in June 1947 the *Globe Press* announced that 'local firms ... have done the biggest year's business in history,' and a visit to the Co-op elevator brought the news that '1947 did slightly more than 1946, but they believe the coming year will be a big one for business.'[25] The business optimism was based on the idea that the dust bowl could be beaten. Stories in November 1947 brought promises of 'large scale rain making' in western Kansas with vivid descriptions of how dry ice dropped from airplanes into 'wet clouds' could end the dust bowl threat for good.[26] Other stories promised water not from above, but from beneath, from massive underground rivers said to flow from the Rocky Mountains eastward to the Mississippi River. All farmers needed do was to tap this renewable resource through 'deep irrigation' and purchase an irrigation system for under $2000.[27] Over the course of the decade the *Globe Press* editors readily defended the underground river theory and bristled at the findings of Kansas State University scientists that 'most ground water is rain water.'[28] The exact source of the underground water did not matter to Meade County farmers. They responded to the promise of irrigation and in 1957 alone they purchased seventeen new well systems.

Even as business pursued this seemingly cavalier approach to the environment, it joined government in nurturing a new view of soil and even in making soil conservation an act of patriotic love. Through the Agricultural Adjustment Act of 1933, the government paid farmers to decrease their seeded acreages. Later, the Soil Conservation Act – giving birth to the Soil Conservation Service which in turn created Soil Conservation Districts – made soil a national trust worth saving.[29] In Meade County, soil conservation became a civic duty, complete with a county association, soil conservation week celebrations, and 'special' dinners for county 'ministers and their wives' that emphasized 'man's obligation to God as stewards of soil and water.'[30] Business in Meade County shared in this new enterprise by suggesting that soil had a life of its own. In February 1948, for example, Fletcher Farm Equipment rented the Meade Theatre to screen the color film, *Saga of the Soil*.[31] More importantly, business found symbols of nurture – social or environmental – in American national images. The local Co-op elevator linked social nurture with a national symbol: its ad in 1948 declared that the American 'Constitution came from the hearts of men who believed in the people,' and pointed to 'common people ... investing together.'[32] The local John Deere farm equipment dealership went even further, linking soil conservation to an American symbol: it ran an ad in

June 1947 declaring that 'farming the conservation way is not unlike flying the Old Glory full mast. For the man who generally loves the soil, there is a sense of pride ... in the land defended well against the ravages of erosion and constant harvest.'[33]

If capitalism was sending mixed messages, Meade County Mennonites responded with mixed behavior. They responded enthusiastically to the idea that the land could be nursed back to health. True, the Mennonites testified that what 'carried them through' the dust bowl was nothing less than 'God's help, determination and sacrifice,'[34] but federal government programs on conservation were crucial in this survival. Such government support helped the Mennonites restore the broken land. Through the Soil Conservation Service, Meade County Mennonites helped to restore 'eroded lands with the re-seeding of native grasses ... and the creation of forested shelter belts.'[35] They enrolled in the local Soil Conservation District after its establishment in 1948, voting 127 to 28 in favor of the district's formation.[36] They probably attended the Monday night meetings where slogans were touted such as 'Save the Surface and You' and 'Conservation Means a Come Back for You and Yours.'[37] Mennonites accepted soil conservation incentives to begin or increase contour cultivating, terrace farming, deferred grazing, native grass seeding, legume rotation, and the building of livestock ponds. They planted shelter belts of American and Chinese elm, Russian mulberry and olive trees, Nanking cherry, and honey locust. In addition they accepted the 'soil bank' incentive that paid about $15 an acre to put land into grass.[38] Where land had once been a trust from God, a social mechanism of distance, and a resource base that guaranteed cohesive community, it was now a national trust.

Mennonite farmers also invested in new technologies geared to soil conservation. Unlike other Meade County farmers, the Mennonites did not participate in irrigation schemes, mostly because they could not.[39] In the words of one Meade farmer, 'really, water isn't here in the southeast of Meade.'[40] But Mennonite farmers employed the latest technologies that promised to trap moisture and preserve the soil. Sometimes they purchased the services of custom terrace constructors in an effort to trap rainfall: on 7 February 1952, for example, Henry A. Friesen 'laid out terrace lines on [his] North quarter' and by 6 March the terracing was completed and he 'paid Mr. Harold Shore ... for terracing the 48 acres on the North 1/4, $35.23.'[41] But farmers also invested in a host of new equipment. Inventories of the seven Mennonite farmers who held auction sales in the decade following the Second World War suggest the old ecologically damaging work of one-way diskers was finally challenged.

Farmers had adapted technologically to the horrors of the dust bowl. True, the farmers still listed the soil-pulverizing drag or section harrows and spring tooth harrows and mouldboard plows as part of their equipment inventory. They seemed even to have an abundance of the infamous 'one-way' diskers, be it the Krause K-3, M & M, Angel, or John Deere. But the farmers also listed cultivation equipment clearly meant to counter dust bowl conditions: John F. Isaac had a moisture-trapping 'damming chisel' in 1948; Jacob F. Isaac possessed an environmentally friendly 'rod-weeder' equipped with 'undercutting blades'; Jacob R. Classen owned a twelve-foot 'rotary hoe' in 1956; Martin N. Ediger listed a sixteen-foot Jefferey chisel in 1960. Each of these implements was kinder to the soil than the 'one-way.' The damming chisel or deep chisel was used annually to cut six-foot-wide furrows in pasture or cultivated land along presurveyed 'contour guide lines' to trap rainfall.[42] The regular chisel 'went over the ground' a lot faster than did a plow or deep chisel, and it left soil aggregates and stubble, or as the westerners called it, 'mulch,' to prevent soil erosion.[43] The rod-weeders killed weeds by severing the root system, all the while leaving plant material or mulch on the surface.

If these methods of cultivation suggested a new sensitivity to creation, other innovations meant to protect the soil seemed to contradict the newfound environmentalism of the Mennonites. The herbicide sprayer, for example, promised to kill weeds without disturbing the soil, but of course by employing the latest in chemical science.[44] Among the listed pieces of equipment in the 1950s auctions was a twenty-four-foot-wide herbicide sprayer, owned by the former Mennonite bishop, Jacob Isaac. Isaac in fact had been a leader in the use of herbicides and caught the attention of the *Globe Press*, which announced in mid-May 1948 that 'Jacob F. Isaac ... began spraying bindweed patches on his place Thursday noon with 2,4-D in ester form.'[45] The chemical, introduced in 1948, promised to kill weeds without having either to 'pull or cut' them and to do so leaving 'crops ... undamaged.'[46] Bishop Isaac was not alone. In the summer of 1948 farmer Klaas Reimer attended a 'weed meeting' on 20 July, watched a demonstration on 24 July, had 'the boys spray ... our maize' that same evening, and two days later had them also 'spray the feed grain.' In fact the spraying of 2,4-D had become popular so suddenly, that the local county agent predicted in June that '100 planes' could be expected to arrive in Kansas in 1948 alone to spray the new wonder herbicide. In the same month local dealers reported having sold 'a dozen booms for spraying.'[47] Sprayers came into even greater vogue with the introduction of other herbicides, especially MCP in sodium chlorate form that could be used on milo (sorghum) as well as wheat and barley.[48]

The use of herbicides sent a mixed message. True, it seemed to complement soil conservation concerns, but it also signalled the willingness of the farmer to use radically new methods with uncertain ecological consequences or without regard for the cohesiveness of the community. Certainly, complaints arose after the Second World War that farmers had begun to care less for the survival of the farm community than for the expansion of their personal holdings. The problem, said the dispossessed, lay in postwar bumper crops and the discovery of oil. As one old-timer put it, 'when the crops came, then they got money hungry and then some oil was found and then' it was two clans who 'got all the land they could.' When, after the war, the Mennonite boys 'came back' from the Conscientious Objection or Civilian Public Service camps 'there was no land.'[49]

During the 1950s land became commodified as never before. Even without irrigation and its helpmate, synthetic fertilizers,[50] Mennonite farmers rigorously pursued commercial wheat production. In part because the Mennonites were restricted by dryland farming, they mixed their wheat with other agricultural forms, including dairy, swine, and poultry, although in time cattle alone became the handmaiden to wheat. This strategy led to increased farm size throughout the 1950s and 1960s. Only farmers in high moisture areas could stay on small farms, said common wisdom, but 'here in the high plains region a farmer cannot make a living on 160 acres,' and given the price of wheat at $2 and yielding an average of ten bushels an acre, 'only scarcely on 320.'[51] Kansas Board of Agriculture statistics for the four Mennonite townships – Meade Center, Logan, Sand Creek, and Odee – bear out this sentiment. No sooner had the Depression lifted than the Mennonite farmers seemed pressed to expand their wheat acreages. The total number of acres of summer fallow or land left idle in the four townships, for example, dropped from 32.7 percent of the cropland in 1937, the last of the Depression-era dust bowl years, to under 10 percent in 1950. What had ensued was a decade of above-normal rainfall and heavy crops, sometimes reported at forty bushels an acre, and prices that sometimes neared $3 a bushel.[52] Drought conditions in the late 1950s raised the percentage of idled land again, which reached 38.5

percent of cropland in 1966.[53] But throughout this time, winter wheat remained king and not infrequently the *Globe Press* singled out a Mennonite as master farmer: in June 1959, with 'combines ... whipping through the fields,' the farmer to reach the Meade Co-op elevator with the first load of wheat was Elmer Wiens, reporting a modest yield of eleven and a half bushels an acre of 'Wichita' wheat; in June 1960 the first farmer to finish the wheat harvest was Jake J. Isaac, who, using two combines, boasted a forty-six-bushel-an-acre bumper crop from his summer fallow land and eighteen bushels from his continuously cropped land, the 'best crop he has ever had.'[54] Mennonite farmers stayed the course on wheat, dedicating 69.7 percent of their cropland to wheat in 1937, 62.6 percent in 1950 and 69.9 percent in 1966. Over time, however, the appetite for wheat and the reality of the marketplace led to a steady increase in cultivated acreages per farm family, which rose from 253.5 acres per farm in 1937 to 339.1 in 1950 and 385.5 in 1966. The county with a pre-Depression reputation for large wheat fields was well on its way to restoring that reputation.

A social response followed this economic change. For some time following the war, for example, old methods still governed the sale of land. An outsider's attempt to undercut a land deal in the making by introducing a higher bid was anathema. Thus in 1940 when Henry A. Friesen – age thirty-eight, father of seven children, dependent on a WPA job of hauling gravel and painting, and hungry for land – heard that the farm of Abram Classen was for sale and that negotiations with a prospective buyer were not going well, he refused to move. Even when 'weeks went by [with] ... rumors that the sale did not go through,' he still did not move, for 'the rules of the church were very strict about trying to get ahead of someone else in a sale.' However, one day Classen casually mentioned to Friesen's brother-in-law that he was looking for a new buyer. The brother-in-law 'rushed' to tell Henry's wife, who passed on the information to Henry as he returned home 'tired and speckled with paint.' 'Without eating supper' Friesen drove over to Classen's at once, and 'before the evening was over' he had an agreement. He would buy the 240 acre farm, complete with house, barn, and equipment for $5200, less than $22 an acre, and he sealed it with a $10 down payment.[55] The old honor system had held.

Only a decade later, signs of a new culture arose. Prices reached unprecedented heights in the Mennonite districts, reflecting in part new perspectives on the sale of land. Some former Meade community members insisted that it was 'land accumulating,' well-to-do Mennonite

farmers who drove up prices, making it impossible for younger families to farm. By 1947 'grazing land adjacent to wheat land' on the
southern edge of the Mennonite district was being advertised for $25 an
acre. A 400 acre farm bearing 120 cultivated acres, plus a five-room
house, a two-story barn, four other buildings, a pig pen, and windmill
was advertised for $75 an acre.[56] By the late 1950s land prices were even
higher. The *Globe Press* carried reports of auctions with 'spirited bid-
ding' in the Mennonite territory. In November 1957, for example, at the
auction of the Jacob R. Classen estate, farmer Dick Classen was reported to have paid $130 an acre for a quarter of land of which only 60
percent was cultivated. In July 1959 at the auction of the Lizzie Thiessen
estate, well-to-do farmer and oilman John N. Ediger paid $160 an acre
for a quarter section known as 'dryland without irrigation.'[57] In two
decades land prices had risen sixfold.

Oil and gas discoveries in Meade County certainly affected land
prices. They reflected further a view of soil as principally a commodity.
Land became linked to oil wealth. As the Meade County history notes,
'Meade soil harnesses the energies ... of numerous beneficial minerals,
such as silicone, clay ferrous sand, oil, natural gas and helium.'[58] Oil
and natural gas exploration had an especially powerful effect on the
county's history. Exploration had visited the county sporadically since
1917, with companies drilling and buying up leases, but it was not until
1945 that gas was actually discovered.[59] Gas finds bearing eighty million cubic feet daily and oil discoveries yielding eight barrels per hour
were reported at between 5300 and 7900 feet. Major oil companies
moved into Meade County, 'quietly leasing' huge tracts of land in what
was dubbed the 'hottest spot in the state for oil production.'[60] Local
land prices reflected the new economic condition. Drought could come,
cattle prices might plummet, but Meade County land valuations climbed
through the 1950s for the simple reason that 'local oil and gas equipment was assessed.'[61] In 1957 during a drought year in which farmers
liquidated stocks of cattle because of a shortage of wheat pasture and
hayland, cattle numbers dropped from 19,000 head in 1956 to under
12,000 but county valuations still rose by 2 percent. Farmers were
clearly responding to ads such as the April 1957 pledge from Gas
Royalties Company of Tulsa to 'buy ... gas and oil royalties for immediate cash.'[62] By 1960 Meade County had a mean income that placed it
sixth among Kansas's eighty-five rural counties made it and one of the
seven rich oil counties of the southwest. It was an economic activity
not available to Mennonites in other counties such as Harvey, Marion,

and MacPherson in central Kansas, which were all considerably poorer than was Meade.[63] But neither was it available to the average Meade Mennonite.

As only some Mennonites benefited from gas and oil explorations, old social mores were tested severely. Oil royalties could bolster the financial strength of the traditional mixed farm: 'gas well rent' and 'oil lease' money from a Haskell County inheritance brought Meade resident Helena Reimer over $100 a month, a substantial portion of the household earning in 1940. When drilling came to Meade County, the Reimers' neighbors envisioned a similar boost and embraced the arrival of the oil companies. By 1943 Northern Ordinance Corporation was drilling test wells on lands owned by Henry J. Isaac and Ben Z. Friesen.[64] The effect on the community was negligible, however, until 1957, when reports were filed of extensive drilling 'straight south of Meade' in Mennonite territory, described as 'one of few larger plots in the county that is not under [oil] lease.'[65] Mennonite farmers began to hit the jackpot. In June 1957 came news of a 'light gasser' on A.J. Enns's land amid reports of the high price of $59.13 per acre being paid for 'oil lease.' In October 1959 the Skelley Oil Company announced that 'in the Thiessen gas area' drilling was completed 'for calculated open flow of 6,022,000 a foot per day from ... 5,712 ... feet.'[66]

With the newfound wealth came social disruption. Land prices rose, but so too did tempers.[67] Stories of court action, a traditional taboo for pacifist Mennonites, surfaced. A Canadian minister who visited one of the county's Mennonite congregations in 1959 reported that 'bitter feelings' over an oil lease dispute had driven two respectable Mennonite neighbors, living on the same section of land, to seek resolution through the state court.[68] The informal account had it that one of the church 'brothers' was being barred from sharing in the wealth because the other brother had secured on his own quarter section all the gas wells permitted per section of land. Another account described a dispute between two church members after one, a well-to-do Mennonite land purchaser, refused to share oil wealth found on land he had recently purchased from an uninformed Mennonite farmer. In this instance a settlement was pursued by one of the Mennonite churches. Realizing that the dispute had hurt the 'testimony of our church,' the mediators sought to be 'equally fair to both brethren' and eventually arranged for shared 'royalty payments' of oil production.[69] But other legal suits ensued. In September 1959 the *Globe Press* reported suits that involved Mennonites taking legal action against entities or persons who appeared to be linked to oil interests: in one instance it was announced that 'Jacob R. Friesen is a plaintiff vs Bert Shelly et.al.' and in another that 'Isaac W. Loewen is a plantiff vs Edward P. Boyle, et.al.' The church accounts alone suggest that oil left a heavy imprint on Mennonite culture.

An irony surrounded the history of the Meade Mennonite community's interaction with the postwar environment. Mennonites, the traditional people of the soil, had found in the high plains that their increasingly intensive commercial wheat production led to excessive cultivation. The soil in the fertile belt stretching southeast of the town of Meade was pulverized by of this cultivation method and vulnerable to the drought and wind of the Great Depression. Mixed farming and government soil conservation programs rejuvenated the agricultural lands of the Mennonite settlement during the 1940s. But just as Mennonites responded enthusiastically to new environmentally respected methods of cultivation they also exhibited characteristics of the Great Disjuncture's new farm culture. This approach involved scientific farming with herbicides and synthetic fertilizers, and an acceptance of a new level of farmland commodification. Most telling of the new culture were the conflicts that sprang from the discovery of gas and oil on Mennonite lands. Mennonite farmers had become more environmentally conscious, just as they turned their backs on old communitarian values.

Life between the Snowdrifts

If long periods of dry and warm weather were the curse of western Kansas, short growing seasons spelled the concern of eastern Manitobans. Manitoba's fertile time was bordered by two symbolic windswept snowdrifts, the one that thawed in March and the one that returned in November. Grain farming in the RM of Hanover was confined to the span of its 120-day frost-free growing season from the time in early May when warmth and dryness returned to its clay soils to the time of the first frost and fall rains in September. The history of human–environmental relations in Hanover in the mid-twentieth century is the story of farmers attempting to extract more from the land than it had once given. The period did not mark a fundamental shift in thinking as the dust bowl had in Kansas. The snowdrifts, of course, did not symbolize human misuse of the environment. On the one hand they stood as symbols of the intractable, indomitable Canadian winter: willow and Chinese elm hedges, for instance, were planted less to stop soil erosion than to make the winters bearable, to absorb the icy north-westerlies.

But the snowdrift also signalled a promise in the northern latitudes. Certainly the guarantee of four months of uninterrupted snow cover promised pleasure to the tobogganers, the ice hockey buffs, the snow-drift house builders, the 'fox and goose' trail makers, the snowball warriors, and even to the practioners of the new sports of snowmobiling (or skidooing) and cross-country skiing. Snow's luminescent qualities reflected moonlight and lengthened the short winter days with semi-lit nights, splendid for carolling or carousing, as spirit might dictate. Specifically for the farmers, snow held other promises. Its blanket over a frigid prairie protected the roots of perennial or biannual plants such as alfalfa, hay, and clover from the deep freeze. The brittle cold of winter fragmented the clay aggregates produced by the fall tilling into a fine-particled spring seedbed, and offered a frozen bed for late winter combining or wintertime manure disposal. Winter's retention of precipitation was nothing less than a savings bank, ready at the beckoning of the lengthening April days to turn into instant water for the nurture of spring's first life.

Snow-turned-into-water marked the beginning of each spring. True, the thaw was met with mixed feelings. 'For the seasoned housewife,' declared Steinbach's weekly *Carillon News* in 1967, spring meant 'that the snowdrift at the back entrance has turned into a quagmire' and quagmires could soil clean clothes and fill dry boots with icy water, raising fears of children catching cold.[70] For the farmers, the snowdrift's thaw, when added to spring rains, could easily spell excess moisture and with it, special challenges. As one writer to the *Carillon News* noted, the year of 1967 brought with it an 'early spring' that 'started off rather wet, but once farmers started working there was no looking back.'[71] Spring rains, a hazard to some farmers, marked a benefit to others. The *Carillon News* gave voice to both in its May 1973 comment that 'there should be no complaints about the nearly two inches of precipitation that fell on Monday night' for if they 'interrupted seeding operations slightly ... at the same time [they] much improved the prospects for a good first crop of hay.'[72] Even rains that came after seeding could be detrimental. When three inches of rain fell in the second week of May of 1968, the *Carillon News* reported that not only could the 'heavy rain ... hold up seeding for a week ... it is believed that what was seeded this week may rot' in the cold soil.[73] And if rain didn't hamper spring plans, an early frost could. However, the 'nine-degree frost' of 21 May 1963 was described with reference to damaged fruit trees and early gardens alone, because cereal crops had not yet emerged.[74]

Other features of northern latitude farming brought expectation, but with it, more tasks. The very long, sunny summer days of June caused grain fields to grow quickly, seemingly to full stand within a single month. The hot July sun ripened the stalks, while the dry, sunny August days introduced the conditions for the grain harvest. By mid-August the spring wheat was swathed and windrowed to hasten its ripening. Hanover's position between Lake Winnipeg to the northwest and the Lake of the Woods to the southeast meant that rain could hamper the harvest, especially when south-easterly wind blew. In August 1963 the *Carillon News* reported that 'many wheat stands that looked promising when swathed a week ago, are yielding grain that is badly shrivelled by premature ripening and excess moisture.'[75] The short season, however, meant that no time could be spared between harvest and the preparation of a smooth terrain for next spring's seedbed. Fall tillage also presented an opportunity to kill the inevitable flush of fall weeds. It was imperative, however, that some form of fall cultivation occur in order to bring out the naturally dark color of eastern Manitoba's black Red River and Osborne clay soils, thus ensuring that the spring sun would both warm up and dry out the soils. Some farmers were always lured into the easy route of burning their stubble; most resorted to deep plowing in the 1950s and then during the 1960s switched to deep tilling or chiseling, as the Kansans called it, mostly to speed up the process and save on fuel costs. In either case one of the last tasks of the season was to harrow the tilled land with its lumpy soil aggregates and, if time allowed, to make 'a good permanent drainage system' to counter the 'low pot holes in the area.'[76] Oftentimes the seedbed was ready by the end of September, but sometimes its preparation had to wait until the short, one-week 'Indian summer' of early October and occasionally, as in 1963, until November. As one writer that year noted, 'now that winter is fast approaching most farmers are trying to finish last minute preparations before they settle down to a slower pace,' some even hoping 'to forget about farm worries for a while and go south for three months.'[77]

The same concern to meet the challenges of the March thaw and the November freeze-up appears in personal diaries. According to the diary of Gertie Klassen Loewen, spring seeding on her and husband Dave's farm north of Steinbach in 1963 began on 9 May. Aside from the fact that Dave managed to complete the drilling of forty acres that day, Gertie noted that it 'turned out to be quite cold,' so cold in fact that 'Dave phoned for his [long] underwear.' The cold spring lingered and on 18 May, even as the crop began germinating, Gertie noted that it 'snowed all day.' No other diary notation relating to agriculture was made until 'swathing' time. This cutting of the crop and placing it into a swath or windrow, began in 1963 on 6 August. Given the long summer days of Manitoba, Dave was able to continue at this task until nightfall at 10:00 p.m. And given the dew that came with the northern nightfall, Dave even was able to juggle wheat swathing with clover seed cutting; the former required the drying affect of sunlight during the daytime and the latter, a brittle seed, could be cut with the least amount of shattering or seed loss in the hours just after the 5:00 a.m. sunrise, before the dew evaporated. On 12 August the dew was so sparse that Dave, having gone 'early to swath clover ... started swathing oats instead'; then when it began to drizzle at midday Dave 'went back to clover.' On the thirteenth combining began; the disappointment of the first day's 'very thin' wheat crop was no doubt ameliorated by the fact that brother-in-law Menno Dueck, visiting from Mexico, was available to alleviate the perennial harvest-time labor shortage by hauling the wheat. On the fourteeth when Dave completed the wheat harvest he took the combine four miles northeast to the river lots in the parish of Ste Anne to help his brother John finish his 'mixed grain.' Having helped John finish on the fifteenth, Dave returned to his own land, 'Blumenhof' to swath more grain. On the seventeenth Gertie noted a feat that came with the ownership of a new, fifteen-foot-wide Versatile grain swather. Dave 'finished swathing 80 acres in 8 hours.' The need to keep the combine going on dry days meant that on the twenty-second, even though it was the day that his father Isaac died at age seventy-two, 'Dave combined clover near the highway,' and Gertie 'took him lunch.' By September the combining was more or less complete and on the twelfth Dave and hired hand Jake Klassen 'hauled in bales,' the wheat straw bales to be used as litter for the farm's turkey flocks. During October Dave found time to answer the Canadian Wheat Board's call for the first wheat delivery: in fact on 26 October the urgency to answer the call meant that 'Dave went for a load of grain to Clearsprings after dark[ness]' fell at 6:00 p.m. Snow did not fall that year until late, at least until 7 December it seems, for that was the day 'Ronnie Friesen was here helping Dave chase in the turkeys' from the open range to the barn.

The combination of the imperatives of the climate and the vagaries of a global economy had a dramatic affect on Manitoba farming. In the three decades following the Second World War between 1946 and 1976, the number of farms in Hanover dropped by more than 50 percent, from 1113 to 532.[78] During the 1960s when much of the decrease occurred, Dave and Gertie not only managed to remain on the land, but to expand their holdings. Diary entries for 1963 that marked repeated trips to other parts of Manitoba – Arborg to the north in Manitoba's Interlake district and to Portage la Prairie and Glenboro in central and western Manitoba – to look for farm land, suggest that the couple was not at all assured that survival in Hanover was possible. Nevertheless, by 1973 their own farm had increased in size from 367 acres to 840 acres, and in 1974 an additional 240 acres were purchased. One feature of their bid for survival was the procurement of new technologies to make the most of the short growing season. By 1973 Dave and Gertie had sold their ten-foot-wide John Deere drill that not only made seeding slow and methodical, but that required the land be precultivated to make a workable seedbed and kill the first flush of spring weeds. In 1973 seeding began early, on 1 May, only because the farm had now purchased a sixteen-foot Massey Ferguson disker seeder that required no precultivation and was pulled by a more powerful 120-horsepower 4020 John Deere tractor that came complete with a heated cab and high-mounted night lights. With the new equipment Dave broke an old record in 1973 and in a single day he 'sowed 120 acres.' Given the farm's acceptance of scientific agriculture, seeding in 1973 did require two extra tasks: a preseeding broadcast of granular fertilizer that Dave undertook on 30 April, and the spraying of a postemergent herbicide that Dave began on 29 May. The new technology even lent a bit of leisure and on 30 May, no doubt to celebrate seeding's end and because 'it looked very much like rain,' Dave loaded his fishing boat on the back of his pickup truck and headed one hundred miles northeast to Whiteshell Provincial Park and 'went fishing for the very first time this year.' By 12 June the spraying was completed, although given the specific contingencies of 1973, the sprayer had to be activated again at the end of July to apply an insecticide on 'the field behind the farm for army worms.' The year presented a hot, dry summer and by 30 August the farm had 'finished combining' a good crop at record prices. Thus, gracing the farm alongside the new field tractor was a new 6620 John Deere combine equipped with a dust-free cab and an array of illuminating lights, and a new Chevrolet three-ton grain truck. For the first time, the family could shop much further afield than nearby Steinbach or Ste Anne for the best milling wheat grades or the best feedwheat prices; with winter setting in, the days of 19 and 20 November found 'Dave hauling wheat to Winnipeg,' a distance of thirty-five miles.

Dave and Gertie's experiences illustrated changes in the RM of Hanover generally. During the 1960s and 1970s Hanover farms adopted new technologies, sought economies of scale, and considered the advice of agricultural sciences. A macabre example, perhaps, but farm accidents reported on the front page of a single issue of the *Carillon News* on 4 October 1963 spelled out the range of technologies now considered commonplace: a man 'mangled by a swather PTO [power takeoff shaft],' a toddler breaking a leg after being 'caught in a grain crusher,' and an elderly man happy to be alive after his Oliver diesel tractor 'reared up and overturned.'[79] Other new developments were also noted. In 1963 Hanover's government-appointed agricultural representative or 'ag rep,' Rod Siemens, announced that with five Steinbach-area 'young men ... presently taking courses' at the University of Manitoba, it was obvious that 'more and more youth from southeastern Manitoba are entering university to study agriculture.'[80]

Ag rep Siemens also described increased usage of fertilizers and herbicides.[81] In March 1963 he penned a lengthy column in which he produced a formula for the use of fertilizers 'for this year.' His advice was precise. 'On heavy clay soils use 11-48-0 at 40 to 60 pounds on summerfallow and 16-20-0 at 80–100 pounds on stubble breaking ... for lighter, sandy soils ... mix 10-30-10 and 33-0-0 in equal parts and apply about 70 pounds per acre.' Part of the column was devoted to explaining to farmers that the three sequence numbers referred respectively to nitrogen, phosphorous, and potassium, and the circumstances under which each of the three properties could be depleted. During the same year, Siemens lectured farmers on the use of herbicides. In June he called on farmers to 'apply heavier rates of 2,4-D and MCPA to their crops this year' for 'application of 3–4 ounces will kill only mustard and will allow many harder-to-kill weeds to multiply.' Application of light rates, counseled Siemens, translate into a 'false economy' and have led to a situation in which 'we still have as many weeds on many farms as we had 15 years ago.'[82] Just a month later the point was made again: 'sprayers [should] replace cultivators' as the 'overall operating time on the summerfallow can be cut down by 2/3s to 3/4s in a season by spraying the field with 2,4-D or MCPA in late July or early August.'[83] By 1968 Siemens could write that 'a person who left this area 10 years ago and made a return visit today would see many changes.' 'Using fertilizers' in conjunction with 'soil testing' and 'improving crop rotation' with such speciality crops as 'rapeseed,' which was highly adaptable to Red River clay and Osborne alkaline-prone soils, could lead to the 'complete elimination of summerfallow' and significantly improve the efficiency of agriculture. Farming, said Siemens, had become 'big business' and a scientific approach was imperative.[84]

Still, there were limits to scientific farming. Hidden in enthusiastic descriptions of Hanover's burgeoning agriculture were hints of continued old ways. This is evident even when the *Carillon News* heralded changes in livestock production. In dairying it reported 'drudgery and hard work' had been removed by 'barn cleaners and bulk tanks'; in swine production back-breaking work ended with 'automated feeding and slatted floors'; in egg production 'coolers,' 'cages,' and 'miniature tractors ... with ... scraper blades' had turned farms into 'egg factories.'[85] Significant for an environmental history are the allusions to 'barn cleaners,' 'slatted floors,' and 'scraper blades.' Each spoke of the creation of larger amounts of highly nitrated animal manure. And although no statistics are available, Hanover's 32,000 hogs, 6500 cows, and 1,700,000 chickens and turkeys in 1976 translated into a reality in which perhaps only half of the arable land in Hanover even required synthetic fertilizers to meet new yield targets. The mixed-farming economy also encouraged the cultivation of alfalfa, green clover, and field peas, legumes which replenished the soil with naturally occurring nitrates.

Even old ways of weather forecasting prevailed, despite the introduction of daily weather forecasts on the 'Mennonite' radio station, CFAM, that began broadcasting in 1957. Farmers counselled sons with a rich folklore of environmental tips: begin the spring seeding on the day that the last of the snowdrift thaws in the shelter belts; plant wheat before barley or oats in cool wet springs, the best strategy to avoid seed rot; seed the oil seeds of canola (rapeseed) or sunflowers on the day following the first full moon in May, thus giving these delicate crops the best chance to withstand the frost-inducing full moon of early June; push the combines hard in August to avoid the rains of 'Souptember' and keep October's Indian summer for fall tillage; stop the combine before midnight on evenings with bright red sunsets, for a good night's rest will be required for the next day of hot sunshine; when an all-night southerly blows, combine through the night for by morning the winds will have turned into rain-bearing south-easterlies; if possible, till your most weed-infested land before a stiff frost, for recently exposed quack grass and thistle roots are vulnerable to cold weather; curry favor with the 'farmer in the northwest quarter,' for in Hanover all water drains toward Lake Winnipeg in the northwest and excess water on any given section must drain through the northwest corner.

The same coexistence of old and new ways can also be seen in the farmers' perception of the land. Possession of land itself continued to be laced with cultural value. In the decade following the Second World War Hanover Mennonites went to considerable lengths to find farms for the postwar generation. Local historians have argued that the postwar Kleine Gemeinde Mennonite migration to Mexico was in part a move by younger farm families to find new sources of land. But other Hanover farm families embarked on 'colonization' programs. Two church congregations in particular, the Evangelical Mennonite Conference (EMC) and the Church of God in Christ, Mennonite (Holdeman), established Mennonite farm communities to the east at Whitemouth in Manitoba's Whiteshell region, to the north at Arborg, Riverton, and Fisher Branch in Manitoba's Interlake district, and to the west around Wawanesa, Virden, and Roblin. But other farm families seem to have laid aside any hope of establishing the majority of their children on farmland; farmers increasingly turned farm income into high school and college tuition rather than into new sources of farmland.

Farm wills and church-based inheritance guidelines are particularly suggestive of this new avenue of thought. Old church by-laws that had once specified bilateral, partible inheritance, which put a priority on establishing the next generation of farm families, were rarely printed after the Great Depression.[86] One group that still did so, the Evangelical Mennonite Conference, changed its pitch. A guideline book printed in 1961 by the EMC encouraged 'the making of Wills' with 'the use of good legal counsel.' The primary purpose of the wills was not to protect farm land, but to navigate 'succession laws and inheritance taxes.' Significantly, the authors failed to note that the monies thus saved could used for the purchase of farmland. Their primary concern was that executors be given 'authority to use minors' share of the estate for their own education' and 'to think of the Lord's share.' Educational achievement and the maintenance of church programs had replaced farmland as primary financial goals.[87]

Most wills made by farmers reflected this new view of land. Most apparent was the departure from an old egalitarian practice to a new and more patriarchal idea that the farm belonged to the husband. Increasingly the widow was entitled to only that portion of the farm required for her personal well-being. In the days before his death in June 1954, for example, John P. Penner of Giroux stipulated that he was giving 'my entire estate ... unto my wife Tina ... that she may continue my farming and dairying operations' but added the caveat that when she remarried or when the youngest child turned twenty-one she 'must divide all my net estate ... and all her own net worth ... one third to herself ... two thirds equally among all my children.'[88] Occasionally farmers' wills reflected another innovative approach, more often held by town business people, which specified that the actual enterprises should be passed down to boys, but not to girls. In 1950 car dealer J.R. Friesen provided that his eldest son, Edwin, should have 'the first ... option ... to purchase my interest ... for the sum of $15,000.'[89] In 1952 when printer G.S. Derksen wrote his will, he noted that 'any child, or being a married daughter, her husband' who was an employee of the plant should receive a right to own part of the business.[90] Reflecting a similar culture, gardener Jacob Wiebe of Steinbach bequeathed 'one third interest in my farm in BC' to two sons, but left his daughter Mary $1000 in cash.[91] Other wills suggested that setting up children on farm-land of their own was only one of several goals farmers could pursue. Thus in 1961 when farmer Abram P. Reimer of Blumenort died at age seventy-nine his will noted that it had been 'my practice ... to make loans and advances by portion to my children and children-in-law in various amounts ... and to sell land to them on credit and by oral agreement and to enter such amounts in a book kept by me' and he directed his executors that they should 'take into consideration such accounts.'[92] Increasingly, willed monies went specifically to off-farm ventures. By the 1960s it was common to leave money to the church, although an examination of some five hundred wills suggests that only in 1957 did a Hanover will first made such a bequest and then from an unlikely source; the patron was widow Susanna Peters, the mother of Jacob R. Peters, the executor of the will and owner of Steinbach's Tourist Hotel beer parlor. She left $500 for the old order 'Mennonite Church at Chortitz ... of which Peter S. Wiebe is Bishop.'[93]

Farming in the northern latitudes of Manitoba required farm families to create a specific farm culture that sought to make the most of the short growing season. In the postwar period new field equipment and the use of herbicides effectively lengthened the growing season. Improved lighting and cabs on tractors lengthened the working day, especially in the short days of fall. Herbicides guaranteed earlier seed-ing times, larger yields, and the status-maker of cleaner fields. Still an ambivalence developed toward land. On the one hand scientific farm-ing methods reflected a 'big business' mentality, and yet folklore and especially the widespread use of manure as fertilizer guarded an old farming culture. Then too, farmers venerated the idea of generational succession and through colonization, increased mechanization, and emigration explored ways to perpetuate their agricultural community. But as wills and inheritance practices suggested, the ideal of establishing children on their own farmland was no longer attainable. By 1980 it was clear that the snowdrift presented much less challenge to farmers than did the scarcity of farmland or the high capital costs of establishing a poultry, dairy, or livestock farm.

Despite the differences in their physical settings, Mennonites in Meade and Hanover shared certain fundamental perspectives. As scholars have asserted elsewhere few Mennonite farmers claimed a mystical or romantic union with the land; farmers could 'love the land,' but it was not synonymous with 'love the Lord.'[94] For conservative Mennonites, land historically had provided a geography for the 'Kingdom of God,' the territory for a closely knit congregational life. In the twentieth century, land increasingly came to represent status, a measure of God's blessing, and the financial source for charity. But at no point did land per se have intrinsic redeeming value, even for a people with an inordinate and historic commitment to farming. The Mennonites in Hanover and Meade took pragmatic steps to ensure that the land would produce a bounty. Both communities also shared an openness to the global economy, new technologies, agricultural science, and intrusive governments. As well, all farmers linked agriculture with the creation of order in nature, with the drawing of straight lines on the land, with maintaining fences and even garden rows according to the cardinal directions, and with squaring all farm buildings with the straight line of the road allowance.[95] To an extent they reflected Yi-Fu Tuan's observation that for farmers social 'harmony was ... believed to be a fruit ... of "order on the land"' and 'rectilinearity' a measurable contribution 'to public peace.'[96] Finally, both Meade and Hanover farmers maintained a culture of respect: farmers disavowed Sunday field work, all practised religious rituals of thanksgiving, all gave inordinate heed to weather patterns, and mythologized the bumper crops, the crop failures, and the memorable storms.

Aside from these common perspectives, the communities did have specific ways in which they related to their respective environments and ironies persisted. For example, environmental stewardship was not necessarily commensurate with communitarian commitment. The Kansas farmers, open to ever-increasing farm sizes and rural depopulation, proved to be remarkable in their environmental sensitivity, especially to soil conservation. But importantly, the Kansas farmers did not learn about soil conservation from their religious understanding of creation, but from the government that venerated land as a commodity and national resource. The vulnerable land lay within reach of only a steadily declining number of successful farmers, some rich from oil and others from irrigated land outside the original Mennonite settlement. The Manitoba farmers stood apart from their Kansas counterparts on environmental stewardship. Given the short growing season, they took an almost cavalier approach to cultivation practices. And yet, given their tradition of mixed farming, they engaged the land with relative harmony, not solely dependent on grain for the farm's well-being and more able to use natural methods of fertilizing and weed control. Given the Manitoban Mennonites' critical mass and Canada's state policies supportive of supply-managed agriculture, they built smaller farm units and were less reliant on chemicalized farming.

The dust bowl and snowdrift each demanded specific environmental responses from its farmers that were partly generated by modern ideas of maximizing profit. But in so far as the profits were envisaged for different purposes – varying combinations of individual status and communitarian solidarity – the environment was considered in diverse ways. In their imagination of and behavior on the land these Mennonite farmers developed a sense of social order, they nurtured a cosmology, and they made a living. The specific ways in which the Mennonites of Meade County and Hanover Municipality related to the land also reflected the way they related to each other and to a wider community. It even reflected their subsequent migration patterns. If Mennonites remained on the farms in disproportionate numbers, they were also among the millions of North Americans who made their way into the towns and cities after the Second World War. Because Meade and Hanover represented different rural contexts, the migrations of their farm families to urban centers also differed.

3 'Hold Your Heads High in Your Usual Unassuming Manner': Making a Mennonite Middle Class

During the middle decades of the twentieth century the farm became connected to the town and the wider society as never before. Paved highways, family cars, local radio, national television, and the regional offices of the ag rep and county agent offered consumer products, popular culture, and state support. Farmers who adapted successfully to the new state-nurtured farm economy were richly rewarded, both by the status of landedness within the rural sections and by the procurement of town-based consumer products. Families unable or unwilling to make the adjustment relinquished farm life and instead found a different version of modernity in town, some as entrepreneurs or professionals, many as wage laborers. From the perspective of the city observer – the sociologist, novelist, or newspaper reporter – the small town might well have been 'rural,' perhaps anti-intellectual and stifling, stuck in a localized culture, and inextricably interwoven by kin and church lines.[1] This view, however, was not the perspective of farm folk moving into town or observing from the farmsteads. Newspapers, census records, and local histories testify to the significance of the country town in breaking down old boundaries and networks, and creating new social divisions and new cultural perspectives. The town, as a student of its growth in Hanover noted in 1960, represented the 'Achilles heel' in the destruction of rural isolation.[2] The town-based Mennonites who successfully adjusted to new economic conditions of the middle decades fashioned a middle-class culture, signaled by increased consumption and travel, and by a pursuit of individualized status. The culture that emanated from this discourse affected farmers and town laborers alike by providing a cultural standard, a common aim. In the process most Hanover and Meade Mennonites revisited their inherited cultural identities, reinventing old ethnicities, and reimagining their national affinities.[3] In the classic words of Maurice Halbwachs, their 'collective traditions or recollections' were in fact new 'conventions that result[ed] from a knowledge of the present,' their 'traditions and present-day ideas ... exist[ed] side by side,' in dialectical relationship.[4] Their memories sprang from a new social imperative, for it was 'in society that they recall[ed] ... and localize[d] their memories.'[5] The past was about to be changed to fit the Mennonites' social present.

The residents of Steinbach, Manitoba, faced these cultural choices from within a town in which Mennonites dominated and a country that was beginning to celebrate its multiculturalism, a movement that culminated in Canada's 1971 official policy of multiculturalism. The Mennonites in Meade County's town of Meade found themselves in a very different circumstance. They were a minority in an Anglo-American town that itself was located in a region especially in tune to a strongly conformist American nationalism and quite aware that it had a 'primary appeal nationally ... as the setting for a romantic historical myth,' the great American frontier.[6] Despite these differences the Mennonites of both places sought a respectable entry into the wider society as full members of the middle class and endeavored to turn their old ethnicities into new articles of broad cultural value.

Hanover's Town-Based Middle-Class Society

From the 1930s to the 1980s the towns within the Rural Municipality (RM) of Hanover continued to grow in size. Places such as Steinbach, Niverville, and Grunthal held economic opportunities for farm folk who were moving in search of wage labor or business opportunity. As an ethnic block settlement called the East Reserve during the late 1800s, Hanover had once boasted numerous European *Strassendörfer*, but few of these farm villages had contained more than 150 residents. By the First World War the town of Steinbach had distinguished itself from other villages by refocusing its attention on merchandising and growing to a population of 500. This number increased slowly over the next thirty years and changed only to reflect a similar growth in the overall municipal population base. Between 1946 and 1961, however, the town's population grew significantly. During those fifteen years, as the population of the rural sections of Hanover decreased slightly from 6843 residents to 6771, the population of Steinbach almost doubled, rising from 1900 citizens to 3739.[7] By 1958 Steinbach was touted as 'among the fastest growing centers in Manitoba' by the province's Bureau of Industrial Development, and was seen as one that would 'continue to grow and flourish.'[8] In town, farm men and women found work as laborers in the growing service sector and, increasingly, elderly farm men and women retired to the town's suburbs or to its new 'Rest Haven Invalid Home.'[9]

The standard narrative of Steinbach's growth appears in more than one history book. One history that was commissioned in 1971 by Derksen Printers, the owner of Steinbach's weekly newspaper, the *Carillon News*, and written by its engaging editor, Abe Warkentin, proudly enumerated the accomplishments of Steinbach's entrepreneurs. The list included the smithies and lumberyards of yesteryear, but grew much longer as its focus turned to the mid-twentieth century. It described the modern car dealers who had turned the town into Manitoba's 'automobile capital,' the vertically integrated poultry and dairy industries, the small manufacturing interests of clothing and cabinets, and the nationally focused truck transport companies. The kingpin of Steinbach businesses, though, was Loewen Windows, a company that turned to manufacturing wood products during the 1920s, capitalized on the postwar building boom, and heightened religious interest by producing church pews, doors, and then windows. By 1975 it employed hundreds of workers, many of them displaced local farm families or Mennonite migrants who had returned to Manitoba from a two-generation sojourn in Paraguay or Mexico.[10]

The booster history book ignored class divisions. True, common church membership, a culture that rewarded deference and humility, and close blood ties between owner and worker ameliorated some competing class interests. When in October 1973 Cornie Loewen, president of Loewen Windows, announced that 'there is no unemployment in this region, for everyone even remotely interested in a job there's lots of work' and requested twelve new workers at once, he spoke with the confidence of a town father. Business persons who created work for town folk were accorded civic honors. Workers who failed to respond, who complained, or who contemplated unionization, were belittled. When the *Carillon News* reported in 1973 that Loewen Windows was finding it difficult to hire workers, it also noted that the Lund Boat factory 'could use about 8 more' workers, A.K. Penner Lumberyard had a 'shortage of good drivers,' and even the A&W Drive-In restaurant had a 'problem in hiring enough ... car hostesses.' The story lamented that the labor shortages were driving wages through the roof, and cited the example of 'farm labourers [who are] demanding $500 a month when $250 was once enough.'[11] Workers who felt denigrated kept their murmurs low, but they existed nevertheless. A week after the labor story in Steinbach, Grunthal's John D. Klassen, dubbing himself 'an unlearned man ... labourer (lowest class) by trade' wrote to say that the 'answer in one word' to the labor shortage was 'wages.' The 'starting salary' in Steinbach, he argued was no more than $2.50 an hour, compared with Winnipeg's union 'starting rate ... for the lowest form of labour' of $4.60 an hour. He concluded that although 'I myself really don't advocate unions ... for Steinbach, I personally think that would be the pill to cure their [employee shortage].'[12] Special derision was reserved for workers who actually unionized. When the very first union came to Steinbach in 1973 it organized the four-man police department and met with outright contempt from the town council.[13]

Another mark of changing culture in Steinbach was the openness of town entrepreneurs to government programs. True, at the foundation of Steinbach's heady growth was a strong sense of independence. In fact the local member of Parliament, Jake Epp, a Mennonite, had made laissez-faire economics center stage when he entered federal politics under the Progressive Conservative banner in 1972. Only days after taking his seat in Ottawa the rookie parliamentarian decried 'the technocrats in government [who] are saying that most rural areas are not going to survive.' Instead he called on government to 'give direct tax incentives to ... small rural business in order to encourage growth' thus ensuring that 'less money ... be taken out of the private sector' because the 'free enterprise system is the only long-term employment creator.'[14] The reality was that Steinbach made full use of government programs designed to underwrite industries in rural districts. Indeed, six months before Cornie Loewen spoke of employee shortages at his millwork firm, the company made a $750,000 expansion with a $141,000 federal government grant through the Department of Regional Economic Expansion program, popularly known as DREE.[15] In April of 1973 when the provincial government under left-wing New Democratic Party (NDP) leadership announced 'complete elimination of health insurance premiums effective June 1' no one objected. Even the brash, newly elected Conservative, Bob Banman of Steinbach, who had run on the party theme of 'Freedom of Choice and Opportunity Now' and beat out the seasoned Liberal incumbent Leonard Barkman's 'In Touch with the People,' was silent.[16] Provincial and federal government intrusiveness was now woven into the very fabric of Steinbach. The *Carillon News* looked back in 1973 and philosophized that 'until about 1963 ... whenever there was a project for the care of the aged in the southeast there was a church behind it,' but now 'governments are taking more and more of the initiatives.'[17]

If an increasingly open community allowed government programs in, it also cheered citizens who left and tasted of the wider world. Consider, for example, the travels of Steinbach's middle class.[18] Like other postwar places the town was abuzz with the promise of the airplane, and in 1960 it was announced that the town was to receive an airport 'big enough and wide enough to receive a big DC 3.'[19] With regularity the *Carillon News* announced the growing trend of holiday-related air travel, noting in a single issue in February 1960 that 'Mr. and Mrs. J.H. Brandt will leave Friday by plane ... for Hawaii' while 'Mr. and Mrs. George F. Loewen left by plane on Sunday ... for Florida.'[20] The advent of the family car, though, affected many more people directly. As geographer John Warkentin's 1960 study of Hanover noted, postwar society was marked by a 'new found prosperity [that] provided the means to buy cars, and new roads [that] opened the way to larger centers where the new buying power could be utilized.'[21] Indeed, local car dealers made it their special goal to turn Steinbach into a regional automobile sales center; through relentless advertising, car auctions, and the construction of 'ultra-modern' dealerships, the Steinbach dealers were able to sell 1000 used and new cars in 1955 alone and saw this number rise to 5000 units in 1960.[22] By December 1957 the local newspaper reported that given the eight head-on collisions of the year, Hanover could even join the rest of Canada in declaring the car accident as the leading cause of death among its youth.[23] The macabre allusion pointed to a new lifestyle in which the traversing of both physical distances and social boundaries had become the norm. The same allusions would provide Steinbach with the grist for its successful argument for a four-lane highway to connect it to the four-lane Trans-Canada twelve miles to the north; reconstruction of Highway 12 began in the spring of 1973.

Burgeoning Steinbach brought the residents of the RM of Hanover the culture of consumerism.[24] This development was more than a 'leisure ethic'; it was, to use T.J. Jackson Lears's terms, 'an ethic, a standard of living, and a power structure.'[25] Social scientists who had visited Hanover in the 1940s were struck by Steinbach's 'appearance as a boom town' and described the town's 'Main Street ... lined with substantial business buildings equipped with large show windows and neon signs' and argued that there 'was nothing provincial about the garages and stores, the beer parlor and at least one of the cafes.'[26] Newspaper stories celebrated the commercialization of the once treed and quaint main street. The December 1954 story of the end of a 'familiar landmark' was not entirely a lament; it reported that the 'former J.R. Friesen residence,' a grand, two-story house built from the profits of Ford car retailing and once 'situated under the big maples at the north end of town has been moved to ... Hanover Street where it will be used to [house] the Invalid Home.'[27] Many other stories and numerous aggressive advertisements in the *Carillon News* documented not only the rise of a new postwar consumer culture, but an incipient fascination with any and all new consumer items. In February 1949, for example, it reported that the new wonder bread spread, margarine, had been purchased by 'about every household' by 4:00 p.m. on the day it first appeared in Steinbach. In 1957 the newspaper described 'hundreds of women' and even 'more men' who came to see the 'wonder' of the $1900 microwave oven featured at Penner Electric. In the same year 'hundreds' again filed 'through the J.R. Friesen [Ford dealership] showroom ... viewing the new Edsel cars.'[28] Steinbachers and their neighbors, however, did more than observe, they spent. By 1951 the whole of southeastern Manitoba spent over 13 million dollars in the retail sector, six times the amount of 1941.[29] Significantly for Hanover's overall prosperity, half of its consumption money for 1951 was spent in its own town, Steinbach. And while much of this money purchased appliances, cars, and new bungalows, it also bought new services – utilities, license fees, and permits. From 1950 to 1953, for example, hydroelectricity payments rose by 58.4 percent, automobile insurance payments by 171.6 percent, and telephone costs by 177.6 percent.[30]

Steady economic growth through the 1960s and 1970s signaled that both the RM of Hanover and the town of Steinbach were full participants in midcentury urban and industrial growth. But their participation in it had been accomplished on terms that brought together not only technological achievement, agricultural science, and transportation links. A critical mass of ethnically conscious residents seemed to translate into a strong commitment to the community and into finding economic opportunities at home. This ethnic characteristic also drew hundreds of Mennonite return migrants from Latin America, especially from Paraguay's Menno Colony, thus providing the town with a strong and deferential labor force.[31] The sense of belonging and the conditions for business expansion led dozens of pragmatic Mennonite entrepreneurs to capitalize on both the easy access to Winnipeg's consumer market and on government programs meant to bolster economically challenged regions. The community remained cohesive in 1980, but not without significant alterations in the borders that had formerly isolated it from its neighbors.

Hanover's New Middle-Class Ethnicity

The middle-class culture of Steinbach and hence, too, of Hanover, can be seen in a reinvented and even a reified Mennonite ethnicity. Mennonites were beginning to think of themselves not so much as a peculiar, Low German–speaking religious group – a separate people – as an ethnic group, the descendants of migrants with a particular history. Ironically, as an ethnic group Mennonites saw themselves as just another component of Canada's multicultural landscape. Aiding this shift in the RM of Hanover was its location in polyethnic southeastern Manitoba. According to the 1961 Canadian census, southeastern Manitoba was a quintessential multicultural region, the only district in Manitoba in which Anglo-Canadians constituted less than 10 percent of the population. In the southeast five distinct groups – French, Mennonite, German Lutheran, British-Canadian, and Ukrainian – shared the cultural landscape, and each still inhabited distinguishable ethnic enclaves.[32] Over time voices for assimilation could be heard: in 1973 the editorial pages of the *Carillon News* celebrated the fact that 'Steinbach is not as isolated, withdrawn and Mennonite' as it once was, for 'it's a bigger world' today and 'the ethnic groups are beginning to mix.'[33] But the declaration was as much an assertion of the existence of ethnic consciousness as an announcement of its demise.

Indeed, the very mixing that accompanied the new postwar economy also brought the urge and the resources to define a Mennonite ethnicity. Residents now engaged more fully in 'symbolic ethnicity' by seeking to objectify and celebrate the past while knowing that it could be pursued in English as well as in Low German.[34] The postwar era was a time of the writing of family histories, of genealogies and massive clan gatherings that drew former residents 'back home' from places across western Canada and the western United States. They came to old farmsteads and to churchyards to hear speaker after speaker embellish the stories of the olden days. They stopped for photos of the clan, they found their places in huge genealogical charts, and they elected the history book committees that would compile all the information for posterity. This concern was the story behind *Plettentag*, the gathering of four hundred descendants of pioneers Cornelius and Sarah Plett in July 1945; it too was the story of 'Reimer Day,' the meeting in 1954 of seven hundred descendants of Klaas and Helena Reimer, the early-nineteenth-century founding family of the Kleine Gemeinde Mennonite church in Russia.[35] It was the surge behind Mennonite Genealogy Inc., begun in 1968 by the local grocer, A.A. Vogt. He boasted information on 180,000 persons and when the company was expanded by his daughter, Margaret Vogt Kroeker, it declared its aim to be service to an immigrant people in a 'stable' world 'trying to find their identity.'[36] Nostalgia even drove a discovery of 'Mennonite foods' and by far the best-seller in the Mennonite world in Canada was the 1000-recipe *Mennonite Treasury of Recipes* printed by Derksen Printers in Steinbach in 1961. Twelve years later, after selling 42,000 copies, the printing company ran off another 4000.[37]

In 1949 Steinbach's Mennonites heard their member of Parliament, Franco-Manitoban René Jutras, declare to them, 'hold your heads high in your usual unassuming manner [for] you have cut yourselves an honourable place among the Canadian communities.'[38] The occasion was a day of history commemorating the seventy-fifth anniversary of the coming of the Mennonites to Manitoba in 1874. Local history buffs had invited old-timers to reminisce, youth to thank their elders, elders to give short sermons and MP Jutras to bring greetings. Jutras's utterance came at the conclusion of a recitation of the Mennonites' historical achievements in agriculture and industry. Those comments assured the Mennonites that their history now warranted that they be seen as respectable, middle-class Canadians. It also required that they redefine the very notion of Mennonite history. Mennonite heritage no longer found its grounding in sixteenth-century stories of a 'golden age' of Anabaptist martyrs, forebears whose ultimate religious sacrifice had been recorded in the 1000-page *Martyrs' Mirror* of 1660 and had nurtured a compelling Mennonite identity.[39] In the postwar culture, one no longer strove to emulate the values of the past; one strove to move beyond its limitations. After 1947 the *Carillon News* ran regular 'progress editions,' in which each business was encouraged to juxtapose its humble beginnings with booming, recent achievements. Typical was the ad for Steinbach Flour Mills, which displayed a photo of its old mill built in 1892 alongside one of its newer, 1920s-era five-story building, which through 'modernizing and enlarging' could provide a service 'second to none.' But an ad for the Steinbach Credit Union in 1957 expressed the new view of history most clearly: after announcing that its assets had risen tenfold in ten years, it asserted that 'the past is ... only ... a gauge for things that are and the present ... a measuring stick for things to come.'[40] Mennonite history in Western Canada was now increasingly the story of primitive, but hard-working late-nineteenth-century pioneers, people quite like other prairie Canadians, facing the obstacles of the frontier and overcoming them.

By 1960 Mennonite ethnicity in Hanover had come to be defined as a contemporary cultural expression. One example of this was that the Low German language had become the medium of comedy and self-deprecation. Local author Arnold Dyck's Low German *Koop en Bua* novelettes became Hanover bestsellers in the late 1950s with reports of sold-out editions in 1960. If the parental language of the heart had become encased in comedy, the old social ways of the Mennonites were about to be showcased for the wider world.

The Mennonite Heritage Village museum north of Steinbach became a central symbol of the new ethnic identity when it was constructed in 1967 on forty acres of land. Anchored by a high, multiple-peaked exhibition hall, the museum featured a replicated pioneer Dutch-style windmill, a conjoined house-barn, a grass sod 'semlin,' a 'plain people's' church, and other 'Mennonite' buildings. One of its main proponents, schoolteacher John C. Reimer, declared in 1960 that the new museum would be a 'show window on the past' and would measure 'the progress that had been made'; clearly it was not intended to separate Steinbach from the rest of society by reminding residents of its sectarian faith. Significantly the museum's construction was heralded as the Steinbach Chamber of Commerce's 'contribution to Canada's Centennial celebration in 1967.'[41] These developments echoed Maurice Halbwachs's observation that the 'memories' encased in such institutions as museums resulted not from actual memories but 'in order to answer questions which others have asked ... or that [are] suppose[d] they could have asked.'[42] In the 1967 centenary Canada was seen to be asking questions about the worthiness of the Mennonites and at the museum in Steinbach, Mennonites were preparing their answer.

What the museum foreshadowed, the centennial celebrations in 1974 of the first coming of Mennonites to Manitoba realized: ethnicity was linked to a set of 'collective memories' that could change; ethnicity could be donned or discarded as events dictated. True, the venerated Manitoba Mennonite history teacher, Gerhard Ens, was invited to Steinbach in 1974 to offer lectures on sixteenth-century Anabaptists.[43] But in the pages of the *Carillon News* much more attention was given to propelling and capitalizing on symbolic ethnic identity than to religious introspection. Member of Parliament Jake Epp sought national attention for the Mennonites by asking the postmaster general to issue a commemorative stamp of the anniversary. The Town of Steinbach promised its residents more than $30,000 in fireworks and related celebrations. Entrepreneurs cashed in, the most eager no doubt a local clothing retailer who featured male models in front of the museum's replicated Dutch windmill wearing the latest seersucker jackets and gabardine pants, the very antithesis of traditional Mennonite garb. The only limit to the commercialization of ethnicity was when entrepreneur Alvin Franz sought to have the town pass a 'mixed drinking by-law' to enable him to build a new hotel 'in time for the expected influx of visitors' during the centennial.[44] Led by committed Mennonite preachers, townsfolk defeated a referendum on the by-law and in the process turned Steinbach dry. Ironically, the voters had managed to equip the town with a new symbol of its evolving middle-class ethnicity; temperance was coming to be equated with Mennonitism.

Further exemplifying the mixing of middle-class values and ethnic self-perception were the response to radio, movies, and television that emanated from Hanover's towns. Open hostility greeted the Playhouse Theatre when it opened in Steinbach in 1946 and began screening movies such as *Frenchman's Creek*, which featured a young, dashing couple spending '24 reckless hours' together.[45] By 1957 the theater had become the focus of such community opposition that it pulled up roots and relocated ten miles north to the French-Catholic parish of Ste Anne. Less hostility greeted the arrival of television in June 1954. But townsfolk would have seen the significance of the *Carillon News* story of television's debut; the first set it discovered was located in the lobby of the local men's-only pub, the Tourist Hotel, where two elderly patrons were celebrating TV as the greatest wonder since the cream separator had arrived sixty years earlier.[46] Radio was another matter. Although Hanover lagged behind the rest of Canada in acquiring the radio, it had become a widely accepted medium in the municipality by the end of the Second World War.[47] In March 1947, for example, Steinbach miller Peter F. Barkman was featured on CBC Radio boosting January-placed 'early chickens,' and in the same month the Steinbach Bible Institute was visited by the singing 'radio group,' the Gospel Light Messengers.[48] In the mid-1950s CBC Radio even advertised its nightly Arthur Godfrey show and the homemakers' *Trans-Canada Matinee* in the German-language *Steinbach Post*.[49]

Hanover residents, however, would not fully embrace radio until they controlled the medium. Local Mennonites voiced grave concerns about the listening habits of the youth. By the late 1940s Hanover youth were in fact tuning in to the *Western Hour* on Winnipeg's CJOB and a few years later listening to the 'blaring disharmony' of Elvis Presley on the city's more youthful station, CKY.[50] In this context local residents began to read of plans in Steinbach's *Carillon News* for a radio station located in Altona, Manitoba, to be owned 'exclusively by Mennonite sharehold-ers.'[51] The moment came on 1 March 1957 when the 'Mennonite' CFAM first aired. Ironically, what promoters dubbed as Mennonite had an uncanny resemblance to Canadian middle-class culture. The main thrust of CFAM programming, declared the promoters, would be 'farm news and market prices,' and the 'good music' of the 'favourite classics played by the best orchestras in Europe and America.'[52] To be a Menno-nite now was to be a respectable member of middle-class Canada.

The language of the new ethnicity spoke to a new confidence that Hanover Mennonites displayed in their relations to the state. Thus, school consolidation came to Hanover in 1968 with relative ease. Only 53 percent of eligible voters in Hanover even bothered to vote on the issue in the December 1967 poll. Conservative elements, of course, raised concern. According to the *Carillon News* some folks 'fear that education is taking their children too far afield' and 'point to university where ... professors smoke pot and advocate free love.' Others argued that the Department of Education and other 'pro-unity supporters were trying to bribe' the most conservative of Hanover communities with promises of new school buildings, hoping that at best they would vote for the proposition or at worst would simply abstain.[53] In fact by early January 1968 'an official complaint' had been 'lodged with the County Court Judge of St. Boniface' with regard to 'irregularities occurring during the event.'[54] Most residents, however, seemed resigned to the new school system. Arnold Reimer of the rural district of Landmark in the Hanover school district, argued during the ensuing trustee elections that he hoped better farm district-town relations could be fostered and that he for one could not criticize Steinbach's support for school central-ization; its residents were only 'working for their town as ... was only proper.'[55] In the end only the conservative Holdeman Mennonite con-gregations undercut consolidation by establishing their own private elementary schools, although even they seemed less concerned with consolidation per se than with 'the radios and TV ... [that] were being used' by their neighbors.[56]

Ironically, this refashioned sense of Mennonite ethnicity allowed Hanover to anchor itself in a wider world. Certainly the Imperial Oil Company was acting ahead of itself when in June 1947 upon its invitation, Steinbach farmers 'packed to capacity' a hall to watch films and hear a program about farm innovation. The petroleum company even bade the sectarian farmers to begin the evening with the singing of 'O Canada' and ended it with 'God Save the King.' Other national images entered the lexicon of everyday Mennonite life.[57] The front pages of the *Carillon News* fully shared the concerns of the typical Canadian. Images of the Cold War, for example, seemed foremost among Hanover concerns in 1957. In a startling March issue, readers of the *Carillon News* were warned that should 'the Red Air Force ... attack [Winnipeg] with their five megaton Hydrogen bombs on the Ilyushin jet' the residents of rural Hanover would face 'certain death' as the prevailing northwesterly winds would carry radiation into the heart of the municipality.[58] As a precaution, Hanover joined the rest of the country in appointing a blue-ribbon 'civil defense advisor,' Steinbach mayor K.R. Barkman. Like other towns Steinbach was on the watch for Communists. Mennonite cooperatives may have dealt with Peoples' Co-op in Winnipeg but when the left-leaning Ukrainian Canadian-based co-op announced plans in 1963 for a dairy processing plant in Steinbach the *Carillon News* went on the offensive. It disclosed that the co-op's assistant manager, Andrew Bileski, was a card-carrying 'Communist' and cited the co-op as a major revenue source for the Canadian Communist Party. It then stuck to the story despite countercharges of 'McCarthyism' from the co-op.[59] When during the same year the provincial NDP spoke of 'production for use and not for profit' at its annual convention the *Carillon* editor smelled 'the molasses' of 'Khrushchev's Socialist Utopia.'[60]

In 1973 the Steinbach town council even smelled socialist rot in the unionization of its local four-man police force. Council members spoke nostalgically about policing in a simpler yesteryear. In the 1950s Constable Ben Sobering could publicly chide 'now-a-day ... kids' who 'get too much money to spend' and in the 1960s he could still assure the community that 'the amount of marijuana brought into Steinbach' from Winnipeg 'was nearly negligible.'[61] More importantly, the unionization of the tiny police force introduced another symbol of Steinbach's inclusion in a wider Canadian community. Riding in to rescue law and order in Steinbach in the summer of 1973 was the Royal Canadian Mounted Police, which took over local policing. In October of that year the *Carillon News* devoted an entire section to a 'salute to the RCMP' and heralded it for being a force that 'quietly and incorruptibly [took] the law into the far places of the country' and did so with 'tact, courage, understanding and diplomacy.'[62] The specter of the Cold War and the steady arm of the RCMP were now appropriated and mixed with a restated Mennonite ethnicity. Both served as part of the cultural repertoire of the middle class that developed in this Mennonite town during the Great Disjuncture.

Town Life in Meade

Just as the marketing boards and new technologies allowed only some of the Canadian farm families to survive the postwar decades, so too the government-driven wheat support system and new science of grain production saved only some of the American farmers. The Great Depression was especially hard on this section of the United States, and Meade County's population fell during the 1930s and early 1940s. But while popular images trace a westward migration of dejected and displaced dust bowl folks to the West Coast, many remained and found economic opportunities by moving to nearby small towns. This movement gained momentum as economic forces associated with the Great Disjuncture commenced. Reflecting the exodus of families from farms during and after the Second World War, the town of Meade's population grew by 26 percent during the 1940s, rising from 1400 to 1763 persons, and then during the 1950s by another 14 percent to 2019 persons in 1960.[63] Eventually the global economy of the second half of the century caught up with both county and town. During the 1960s both stagnated, following the trend in Kansas that saw rural population decline from 850,000 to 760,000, or from 39 percent to 34 percent of the state's total population.[64] During the 1960s Meade County's population fell from 5502 to 4912 and the population of the town of Meade from 2019 to 1899.[65]

No matter its demographic patterns during the middle decades, more and more Mennonites considered the town of Meade home. True, many Mennonites, like their American neighbors, were simply leaving the county; statistics tell this story, showing that the number of Mennonites in Meade County declined by 20 percent in the 1930s, from 1409 persons in 1930 to 1153 persons in 1940, and then further declined to 1019 persons by 1950.[66] True too, the Mennonites who stayed in the county also stubbornly struggled to stay in their rural homes. In fact their numbers declined less dramatically than those of their neighbors.

In the three southeastern townships in which Mennonites had the highest numbers – Meade Center, Logan, and Sand Creek – the rural population fell from 980 in 1946 to 956 in 1954, a drop of just 2 percent. In the meantime in the four most northwesterly townships – Fowler, Crooked Creek, Mertilla, and West Plains – home to only six Mennonite families, the population dropped from 1425 persons in 1947 to 1059 in 1954, a drop of 26 percent.[67] Reports even pointed to rural residential clustering among Mennonites. In 1957 high school principal Walter Friesen noted that in the original Mennonite settlement southeast of Meade 'some houses and the church have been vacated and moved' while another village, a 'quaint settlement of houses' in the 'northwest edge of the community is ... disintegrating'; but he noted that a third village not part of 'our kinship unity' and described as 'by the academy' or close to the private Mennonite high school, was still growing.[68] The most pronounced demographic trend among the Meade Mennonites during the middle decades, however, was migration to the nearby town of Meade.[69] Phone directories, for example, record a drop in the number of rural Mennonite households, from 107 in 1951 to 96 in 1970, at the very time that they show an increase of Mennonite households in town, a rise from only 12 households in 1951 to 59 households in 1970.[70]

The move to the town of Meade entailed a dramatically new social milieu for the Mennonites, still described in 1957 as a people 'close to the soil, loving the independence, freedom and quietness offered on the farm.'[71] Postwar Meade was the antithesis of a quiet social milieu. It was in an expansive mood and cherished close links to a wider America. Its newspaper, the *Meade Globe Press*, reported regularly, for instance, on the activities of the National US Highway 54 Association that heralded its turnpike as the fastest route from Chicago to the 'Sunny Southwest' and the 'Land of Enchantment,' and certainly the shortest route from Kansas City to Los Angeles.[72] Highway 54's traffic was regularly counted with numbers up by 188 percent in 1948 alone and in 1956 averaging four thousand cars per day.[73] In fact when talk of 'Super Military Highways' began after the war, the Highway Association made a strong pitch for such a freeway. When it learned in the late 1950s that the interstate system would not include the 54 but pass to the north in the form of the I-70, the association predicted that the state would 'soon' be forced by the very volume of traffic – 'more east-west cross Kansas than any other highway, bar none' – to expand the highway into four lanes.[74] And as elsewhere in the 1950s, what could not be linked by pavement

could be made closer by air. Meade fathers purchased land for a land-
ing strip as early as 1941, rebuilt it in 1947, and eventually developed it
into a full-fledged regional airport that boasted hangers for nineteen
aircraft and an asphalt runway measuring 3400 feet.[75]

Boosterism and consumerism characterized postwar Meade. Amid
talk of prosperity, a sense of urgency dictated a full embrace of capitalism. 'In the coming years,' said one merchant in August 1945, 'it will be
survival of the fittest in the business picture – dog eat dog' and he, for
one, was battle-ready.[76] When a former Meade resident returned after a
thirty-four-year absence and expressed 'amazement' at Meade's growth,
the editor of the *Meade Globe Press* told him to return in ten years and he
would witness even greater changes – more 'black top,' an airport, three
thousand residents, and tourist cabins: 'A pipe dream, you say. Man
alive, all of that is on the drawing boards with money to pay for it.' With
the promise of 'diversified' agriculture, the region's 'huge oil and gas
pool,' the 'sterling character of the people,' and an average net worth of
$7000 per person, 'the county can weather storms and droughts and
depression.'[77] Citizens even anticipated paying for rising urban services. The *Globe Press* noted in October 1947 that 'taxes like Topsy have
just growed,' but added the explanation that given a 'new school set up
and the natural development of this section,' higher taxes could be
expected.[78] Radio was employed to boost the town even further. In
April 1948 station KXXX of nearby Colby was brought in to do a live
broadcast, complete with a 'round table,' 'man on the street' interviews,
and 'local music' on the occasion of Meade's first County Exposition
where most business establishments hosted trade booths.[79] And as
elsewhere in North America, the town's car dealers were especially
aggressive in their advertising, running Detroit-derived ads that promised cars 'graced' with 'lower lines' and 'wrap around windshields,' but
cars of power; the Ford was the 'most powerful ever built,' Chevrolet
possessed a 'sensational V8,' Dodge a 'Hy-Fire V8.'[80] And judging from
annual 'tag' sales for cars, this town was excited about automobiles.
Meade was far from ending with a whimper.

Understandably Mennonites entered the urban fray tentatively. Those
who were compelled to consider off-farm activities first tried to set up
businesses in the countryside. A 1947 Meade town business roster may
not have listed a single business with a Mennonite family name, but
Mennonites engaged in business nevertheless.[81] Their niche lay in rural
Meade County. One observer noted in the 1950s that because Menno-

nites 'use many machine[s] ... here, we find some of the best equipped machine and repair shops [including] Rempel Machinery and Repair, H.L. Friesen Machine Shop specializing in motor overhauls ... Dick's Repair and many farmers have their own repair shop.'[82] Other rural-based services arising from rural electrification and soil irrigation included Classen Electrical Wiring, Rempel Electric, and Friesen Windmill and Well Drilling. In 1949 David and Martha Classen opened their Country Store to serve the farmers' postwar consumer needs, but it closed just seven years later on account of 'farmers moving into town.'[83] Even when Mennonites began locating their businesses in town they usually pursued enterprises with strong rural roots.[84] In fact several businesses were actual transplants from the rural Mennonite settlement: Rempel's Auto Repair was a three-generation farm-based repair shop when it moved to town in 1960,[85] and Henry L. Friesen's machine shop and Corny Z. and Henry Z. Friesen's Windmill and Supply store were similar rural transplants. Even as they expanded their businesses the focus remained rural: John K. Friesen's business may have been a state-of-the-art enterprise that won a state award in 1959 and linked up to St. Louis's Ralston Purina Company, but his business still featured a feedmill that served local Mennonites. This rural concern was also the focus of the expanding businesses of Henry L. Friesen's Case dealership and Corny Z. Friesen's irrigation and well-drilling enterprise.[86]

Even the most flamboyant of the postwar town-based Mennonite businesses, Meade Manufacturing, had strong rural ties, although its business focus signalled that farmers increasingly were interested in comfort and even leisure. Begun in 1946 in the countryside southeast of Meade, the machine works was owned by Clarence and George Isaac, sons of the conservative Mennonite Kleine Gemeinde leader John F. Isaac.[87] In 1950 it relocated to Meade, and although it was said to exhibit a 'streak of inventiveness' when it introduced a 'riding lawn mower,' it directed most of that ingenuity to the improvement of farm machinery, producing 'sur-seeders,' fertilizer applicators, and combine cabs.[88] The company grew quickly and in 1958 the Isaac brothers constructed a massive new brick building to house the factory.[89] By 1966 when it celebrated its twentieth anniversary it boasted a plant of 67,000 square feet that employed almost one hundred workers and sold products throughout the American Midwest and Canadian Prairies. During the late 1950s and 1960s Meade Manufacturing introduced new products, most notably the motorized 'Travel Inn' campers in 1959, but also air-conditioned cabs for tractors and combines when the rights to the Logue Evaporative Cab Cooler were purchased in 1968 and redubbed '"Artic" Breeze.'[90]

As some rural Mennonites came to the town of Meade to seek economic power, others came as wage laborers. Again, they came tentatively. At first Mennonites ventured from their rural settlement into town only for temporary or casual work. Youth who once had found casual labor on neighboring farms now more often found it in town. In March 1948, for example, the sons of Klaas and Helena Reimer took work 'assembling equipment' at the Hartshorn dealership in Meade. Young married men used town employment to bridge the time gap between initial household formation and generational succession of the family farm. Exemplifying this pattern was Pete Loewen who worked in town between 1953 and the late 1960s when his father retired. Then with his savings and a family loan, Pete rented the old farmstead until an opportunity arose in 1973 to purchase it outright.

Middle-aged farm men, too, incorporated wage labor into their household economic strategy. The biography of Herman and Esther Harms notes that when the young couple returned to Meade County after the Second World War they 'moved back to a farm nine miles south of Meade [and then in] April of 1954 Herman was employed at Meade Manufacturing until ... 1978.'[91] Increasingly, farm families left the farm, moved into town, and found permanent work as wage laborers. The biography of Aaron Warkentin notes that while at first his family 'lived on a farm four and a half miles south of Meade ... later they moved to the town of Meade [where] Aaron worked in [the] Co-op elevator for many years.'[92] Similarly the biography of Menno Wiens describes a man who 'was born and raised on a farm southeast of Meade,' but then moved his family into 'a home he had built in 1962' in Meade where he was 'employed at Friesen Windmill.'[93] And as the boast of Meade Manufacturing revealed, the workers increasingly saw wage labor as a life calling: in 1968 the company announced that 'the Employees Profit Share' stood at $50,000 and that in the preceding year it had paid out $10,000 in 'production bonuses' to employees.[94]

In time Meade became home even to the Mennonite elderly. Typical was the story of Peter F. and Katherina Isaac, described by the *Meade Globe Press* in June 1957 as having 'made their home in the City of Meade' after having 'spent 49 years on their farm southeast of Meade.'[95] Time and again in local newspapers and in family histories the move to Meade to retire was described as one of the last major events in the history of the family. In 1962 the county's two Mennonite churches jointly erected a large senior citizen's home, the Lone Tree Lodge, in Meade. This venture introduced yet another event in the life cycle of the Meade Mennonites. The family history of Elisabeth (Classen) Reimer, for example, notes that although Elisabeth 'remained on the farm for a number of years' after her husband David died in 1943, in 'December 1963 she moved into Meade' and then spent 'her latter years' at Lone Tree Lodge.[96] By the 1970s Mennonites in Meade had all the appearance of a people who had found a new permanent home in town.

Patriotic Imaginings and Mennonite Ethnicity

Mennonite businessmen made cultural integration into the town of Meade seem natural and effortless. Their worlds simply seemed to expand. As Meade Manufacturing grew in the early 1950s so too did the world of its owners, the Isaac brothers. They took to the road and traveled widely, from the National Garden Supply Association trade show in Oakland to the National Hardwares Association show in Chicago in 1954 alone. They associated with regional organizations such as the Western Kansas Manufacturing Association Board, for which Clarence Isaac was chosen Meade's representative in 1954.[97] Unfortunately for the county, these ties could turn on Meade as they did in August 1969 when George Isaac announced that he was relocating to California 'to devote ... time ... to other business interests they hold there.'[98] Even though the company reported in October 1969 that it planned 'to increase production' and fill 'up the empty buildings in Meade' with capital it hoped to raise in Meade County, by December of that year it announced that it would begin producing 'five or six of its most popular models in Dinuba, California,' and a year later it closed its plant in Meade.[99]

Moving in smaller worlds, perhaps, Mennonite businessmen who remained in Meade nevertheless traveled outwards, becoming full-fledged members of the Meade establishment. Their associations ranged from business links such as the one that named Henry K. Friesen chairman of the Meade County Trucking Industry Committee in 1954, to civic societies such as the link that crowned Corny Z. Friesen president of the town's Kiwanis Club in 1975.[100] Other Mennonite businessmen now boldly set out to meet the entire Meade citizenry with the best of postwar consumer products: in 1954 Nick and George Reimer called Meade residents to the town's Palace Hotel to witness their very own lawn and garden methods that had been reproduced at the 'lovely home of the Joe Ross family ... on South Cedar Street'; in 1960, when Isaac Electric had its grand opening in Meade, it advertised not electrical farm supplies but the latest array of household gadgetry including air conditioners, dishwashers, and TVs.[101] By the 1970s other Mennonites in Meade owned a florist shop, a motel, a restaurant, and a car dealership.[102]

Yet the image of the easily integrated Mennonite businessman is problematic. A cultural settlement remained to be worked out. The fact was that Mennonites in Meade represented a cultural minority in a dizzying world of consumeristic, civic, and nationalistic symbols suggestive of an assimilative vortex. The front page of a single issue of the *Globe Press* in 1948 featured stories of nine different social and civic groups – the Chamber of Commerce, 4-H Clubs, Home Demonstration Units, Young GOPs, the basketball teams, the Farm Bureau, a Gas and Oil Royalty Group, and the Red Cross.[103] Although they would relate to some of these organizations, the Mennonites in Meade County still seemed to be the quiet in the land. Mennonites appeared infrequently in the newspaper's social columns. Even though the paper recreated weekly social interactions with immense detail – it published parking tickets, high school football results, visitors from other cities, all discharges and admissions to the Meade hospital – few Mennonites were listed in the post-war years. The gossip section 'Local and Personal' of 1947 bears not a single reference to a resident bearing a Mennonite name: it lists Mr and Mrs Earl Fisher as visiting Liberal, J. Bob Wilson home from KSU, Lydia Rogers visiting Dodge City, Jess McKinney arriving from Los Angeles, but no Mennonites.[104]

The images of Meade's cultural life in the *Globe Press* also often contradicted the Mennonites' traditional quiescent and nonresistant values. In Meade's public imagination the year 1874 signified not the coming of pacifist Mennonites from an increasingly militaristic Russia as in Manitoba's Hanover but the year of the county's 'Lone Tree Massacre,' in which Cheyenne warriors killed six white surveyors. In 1954 the local Chamber of Commerce considered reenacting the killing's eightieth anniversary but declined when time constraints undercut hopes to 'make a really big thing of the re-enactment.'[105] The historical imagery in Meade County recorded a culture of the 'wild west.' In 1952, for example, the Chamber of Commerce helped raise the profile of the local tourist attraction, the Dalton Gang Hideout, which commemorated local heroine Eva Dalton's assistance to her out-law brothers; it was timely assistance, for the Hideout went on to attracted more than 30,000 tourists in most years of the 1950s and 50,000 annually in the 1960s.[106] For the Mennonites the law of the frontier and indeed law itself was always an outside force. Sheriff Arlie Johnson, elected to his post for most years between 1953 to 1981, was stationed in Meade. He was applauded for never shying from pursuing justice even if it meant 'shooting at tires,' arresting vagrants, chasing 'juvenile delinquents' at 'over 100 miles per hour,' 'pulling up ... rowdies or tending to accidents on Highway 54' – seventy-five in total and five fatal crashes in any given year – and he was often rewarded with a front-page *Globe Press* photo of taking charge of the handcuffed culprit.[107] Only occasionally did Johnson's work involve the Mennonites. True, in December 1947 the sheriff swooped into the Mennonite settlement to impound the Bishop Jacob F. Isaac's recently purchased car on information from the FBI that it was a stolen item; on another occasion Johnson attended a report that 'Mrs. Abe Z. Friesen' upon returning from church opened her house door to a 'man standing inside holding a gun.'[108] But generally the local law lay outside the Mennonite settlement and so did Meade's fixation on the wild west.

Mennonites were at odds too with the cultural forces of wartime, post-war, and Cold War America. The Second World War was especially difficult for the Mennonites and Meade breathed patriotism. During 1945, for example, eleven of the fifty-four lead headlines in the *Globe Press* bore reference to Meade's war effort – a local boy killed in Germany, three involved at Iwo Jima, many soldiers 'battle weary' and 'hungry for home life' (all to be listed in an honor roll inscripted at the Court House), many citizens responding to the 'Mighty Seventh' War Loan Drive or the 'E-Bond' sales.[109] As late as 1948 the bodies of fallen Second World War Meade boys returning to the county were met with a town-wide ceremony: businesses closed during the funerals, the fire whistle blew, and a military escort of ex-servicemen paraded.[110] As the Cold War loomed the militaristic language in the county soared. In a highly reported talk to the Meade County Kiwanis, a U.S. military captain warned that the 'communist propaganda is snowballing in the press of the country' and the time has come 'to give out propaganda to our own people reselling them on the merits of democracy.'[111] Meade was also regularly visited by U.S. military recruiting personnel who brought stories of faithful 'local boys,' the one who enlisted for a three-year tour of duty, another who had made it piloting the 'new 5-star DC 6.'[112] Local residents were reminded often of the terror of nuclear war, especially once Meade County was designated a 'reception area' for evacuees for Wichita and Hutchinson, which were declared 'critical target areas' because of their defense plants.[113] Overall, the citizens of Meade County knew they were rooted in the nation: 'Kansas may be in the "Bible Belt" and her rolling prairies in the "dust bowl,"' declared one editorial, but it was ahead of most states in the purchase of U.S. savings bonds. When patriotism languished, Meade's American Legion was quick to notice. In 1954, for example, the Legion criticized the 'many firms in Meade [which] do not own ... flags to fly' and announced in ominous language that it was 'making up a list to order flags.'[114]

The Mennonite place in this world of militaristic nationalism was not easily negotiated. Farmers recalled how during the Second World War they came to town quietly; as German-speaking pacifists they sought out as little attention as possible. They told stories of how they used only English on the telephone lines, even though Low German was still the lingua franca of the Mennonite settlement. In the years after the war, old-timers were said to have voiced 'sadness ... that things are not as they were in the "Friejahr"[,] ... a single word amplif[ying] the glorious past with a sentimental and emotional past, of years gone by, never to return.'[115] Commentators from the 1950s predicted that 'community customs and cultural traits will quite likely have less influence in the future ... [as] group life characteristic of the community will be somewhat broken.'[116] Over the years the Low German language came into disuse and Mennonites rarely spoke of their pacifist ideals or historical symbols in public. True, some events gave the label 'Mennonite' an increased respectable public meaning by legitimizing it through acts of charity. It was worthy of a public account in the *Globe Press* when in August 1947 'the two Mennonite churches in the Settlement ... again started a drive for flour for the relief of hungry people in Europe.' It was an especially impressive move as the *Globe Press* called for a county-wide response; 'under the plan,' announced the Mennonite leaders, the 'wheat may be donated at elevators or money may be left at the bank.' To add credibility to the drive, the organizers reported that 'in 1945 the Settlement ... donate[d] ... 2440 sacks of flour.' Just three months later, in October 1947, the *Globe Press* ran the headline story announcing that 'Mennonite Friends Lead Kansas Wheat for Relief.' It was noted that while 4000 non-Mennonite Kansas churches had collected $17,000 for the Kansas Wheat Relief Committee, Mennonites had collected $50,000. Rev Milton R. Vogel of the Kansas Wheat Relief Committee was quoted

as saying that 'surely if other great churches of Kansas were contribut-
ing in comparison to the small Mennonite groups ... wheat would be
flowing ... by the carload to the starving peoples of the world.'[117] In 1965
another set of favorable reports appeared on Mennonite aid, specifically on the local work of the Mennonite Disaster Service (MDS). In
June came a report that when a local dairy barn burned to the ground
'two units of MDS cleaned up the ashes, rebuilt fences and made the
farm premise presentable.' Just a month later came a report of the MDS
at work after local flooding with the claim that 'every person who came
into contact with [230-person] MDS [unit] at work in Dodge City and
Garden City has high praise for the group.'[118]

Meade Mennonites were boldest when they found ways of linking
their story to that of the nation. Mennonites who recalled the founding
of their 1906 settlement did so by appropriating the status of pioneers
and as such nothing less than full-blooded American frontiersmen. In
this sense Mennonites could wear their ethnic badges with some degree
of pride. Their participation in county historical celebrations during the
1960s and 1970s were occasions in which members did not deny their
Mennonite heritage but held that heritage up to represent the best of
America. In 1961 when Meade County celebrated its seventy-fifth anniversary, Kleine Gemeinde descendant Mennonites who had avoided
participation in the county's fiftieth anniversary in 1936 came out in
full force, offering among other items a male vocal quartet from the
Emmanuel Mennonite Church to sing in full harmony 'Church in the
Wildwood' and 'Faith of Our Fathers.'[119] With similar confidence Mennonites represented theirs as a frontier story in local history books
during the 1970s. In one of their own publications that celebrated the
thirtieth anniversary of the founding in 1943 of the Emmanuel Mennonite Church, a single sentence related to an upheaval that gave birth to
the church[120] while a longer section described the early Mennonite
settlement on open prairie 'some 20 miles south of Meade.' At a place
'where seldom anything else had been heard than the howl of ... a
coyote ... voices of children and parents broke the silence' and here in
'an area ... previously ... numb to human schedule' business and industry had become 'a vital part of life.'[121] Mennonites similarly represented
themselves in the 1975 *Pioneer Stories of Meade County*.[122] While acknowledging that Mennonites had once been known by their dresses of
'dark color' and their shirts with 'no ties,' writer Peter J. Rempel emphasized the Mennonite contribution in subduing the frontier. No sooner
had they left the train in 1906 than they 'angled across the country' to

the site of their settlement. Here, according to Rempel, the pioneers spent their first night on 'buffalo grass.' Then even though there 'was not much wheat grown' this far west, the Mennonite settlers activated the 'sod breaker ... probably bought in Meade' and planted wheat in the same spirit that their forebears had planted the finest of 'Turkey Red' when they first arrived in the United States in the 1870s.[123]

Mennonites had negotiated a niche for themselves in the public arena of Meade County. Perhaps Meade County Mennonites lacked the critical mass to publicly remember their history and make it an integral part of southwestern Kansas's tradition. But even given the social composition and cultural tenor of postwar Meade County and Meade, the Mennonites had found the narrow window in which to assert a symbol ethnicity.

Many farm families did not have the capital to acquire either the finite sections of wheatland or the technology to specialize in a given meat commodity. These rural folks were compelled to move or lured into town. But the town milieu in the North American grassland could differ significantly, depending on which side of the forty-ninth parallel the town was located or whether a particular immigrant group possessed the critical mass to shape the town's culture. Meade in Kansas and Steinbach in Manitoba differed in their midcentury cultural offerings. Steinbach was set in the heart of a community in which Mennonites constituted a majority and here they struggled to make the very word 'Mennonite' represent the best of middle-class behavior and culture. The Mennonites of Meade County represented a minority, only about 20 percent of the county's population, and the public face of the town of Meade often seemed to be the very antithesis – Yankee, militaristic, patriotic, and Republican – of the Mennonite world. As such there was much less room for a type of Mennonite ethnicity to take hold. A further difference was that Steinbach would grow during these years, from 2000 in 1946 to 3700 in 1961 and then to 5200 in 1971 and 6700 in 1981; Meade grew too, from 1400 in 1940 to 2000 persons by 1960, but then it dropped to 1900 persons by 1970.[124] Its location on the wheat lands of the highly technologized western Midwest could not sustain the town over the long haul; Steinbach's location near Winnipeg and its strong homogeneous demography factored into its continued growth. The Great Disjuncture left in its wake two communities with distinctive economic, social, and cultural histories.

Both the American and Canadian families who relocated to their respective towns found themselves in distinctively new economic and social environments. In Steinbach the newcomers founded farm service businesses or entered into wage labor in one of the car dealerships, grocery stores, or especially the millwork factory. In Meade farm families similarly founded enterprises linked to farm service or products, while others became the labor force that sustained those enterprises. It mattered not whether the town was American or Canadian, ethnically homogeneous or pluralistic, cultural recreation was in store for both. Meade and Hanover Mennonites who began the century with a strong sense of peoplehood in Europe found it necessary to redefine that ethnicity at midcentury. Mennonite ethnicity in the 1950s can be described as 'symbolic,' to use Herbert Gans description of 'third generation' ethnicity; it can also be seen to have been 'class-oriented,' taking a particular rung in what John Porter has described as the 'vertical mosaic'; it may be seen as a cultural 'invention' as portrayed by Kathleen Neils Conzen and others; or as a piece of 'national identity' in the way described by Orm Overland.[125] Ethnic flowering was stronger in Hanover, perhaps because Canada had never exerted a national standard on its citizenry, perhaps because of the culturally homogeneous nature of the municipality's founding. Ethnic decline was in the works in Meade, the tenor of American patriotism and power of the imagined nation could not be escaped and in any case the pluralistic nature of Meade provided little ethnic cover for the farm families who moved in from the county's southeast. But in both cases the Mennonites' ethnic traits were asserted in anniversaries, celebrations, the media, and even in the marketplace in such a way that the communities entered and were not barred from their respective national communities. In Kansas the Mennonites described themselves as proud pioneers of the frontier; in Manitoba Mennonites were welcomed as equally proud contributors to a multicultural mosaic. Ironically, the traits each was required to possess were not particularly unique; both prescribed ways in which the once sectarian and humble Mennonites could 'hold up their heads' in a midcentury society.

4 Joy and Evangelicalism: Rediscovering Faith in Kansas

North American rural historians often describe the conflict between conservative, ethnoreligious communities and the wider individualistic, English, liberal society.[1] Studies of specific conservative rural communities – Dutch Reformed, German Catholic, Swedish Lutheran, Jewish, and Mormon – have focused on the perennial search by devout people for ways to 'stand apart in the world.'[2] This search produced a battle between persistence and accommodation that seemed constant. During times of social transformation the religious commitment and intense debates about faith among these distinctive groups, immigrants, or ethnic minorities seemed stimulated in new ways. The great European migrations to the North American grassland in the decades before the First World War certainly had tested the immigrants' faith, their cosmologies, and their moral codes. The mid-twentieth-century social transformations saw an even greater testing among some conservative, rural, ethnoreligious communities. Old ideas sometimes were used to interpret and accommodate those changes. More often, in the rural districts during the midcentury decades, such groups embraced new symbols of religious faith, tried new institutions, drew new lines of authority, and even emphasized new emotions.

For rural Mennonites two distinctive religious responses were especially important. Some Mennonites, as will be discussed in chapter 8, took the path of religious retrenchment: tradition was reinvented in an intentional attempt to 'stand apart in the world' with refurbished old order social codes, cultural symbols, and religious teaching. For many other Mennonites a religious reorientation that celebrated evangelicalism became the chosen path. It too was a conservative way in that it guarded biblical authority. Yet it was progressive in that it emphasized a personal assurance of future bliss in heaven, an orderly engagement with the broader society, and scripture that spoke of 'joy,' the 'joy of salvation' and the 'joy of the redeemed,' or 'pure joy' and 'glorious joy.'[3] Faith was personal, it emphasized social integration, and it was oriented to the future.

For the Mennonite communities of Meade and Hanover, facing the social changes that accompanied the Depression, the Second World War, and the Great Disjuncture – dislocation, individualism, assimilation – this evangelicalism held special appeal. Certainly it did not contradict the rise of a respectable, middle-class identity. Then, too, it promised to refashion old communitarian practices and symbols, inherited social boundaries, and ways of seeing order in the world that seemed staid and out of step with a new, more integrated, and interwoven world. In their religious practices, these evangelical Mennonites reconsidered spiritual disciplines, reimagined their worlds, and regrounded their beliefs.[4] They reordered moral codes, redrew new mental maps of community networks, and recast foundations of social order. Ironically in the very call to engage the wider society, new forms of social separation became ritualized.[5] This new religious way of thinking often made the migration of post-Depression and postwar Mennonites into towns and cities more orderly and certain. Indeed, middle-class life in urban centers now attained a new religious sanction, and even an imperative; as it seemed that only in towns and cities could one truly affect the broader world. The very idea of an identifiable Mennonite community was altered as the social dispersion and economic realities of the Great Disjuncture set in.[6] Given their lack of critical mass in southwestern Kansas, that is, within a Midwestern milieu of evangelical Protestantism, the Meade County Mennonites broke more radically with their past than did their counterparts in Manitoba. The starting point, however, was similar.

In the 1930s the Meade County Mennonites were members of two different Mennonite congregations. The larger, more conservative and communitarian Kleine Gemeinde and the smaller, but more progressive and revivalistic Bruderthaler shared some common characteristics. In the early decades of the twentieth century both churches had benefited from their relative isolation. Control over local public schools, an emphasis on pacifism, a reliance on the Low German language for household and High German for church communication, endogamy or intermarriage, and a commitment to farming were characteristics of both congregations. Between 1906 and 1930 the two congregations had nurtured a closely knit, exclusively Mennonite community in the south-east corner of the county.[6] Both churches were affected by the changes to their society during the Depression, war, and postwar economic transformations. But the most notable shift occurred within the ranks of the larger and more conservative of the two congregations, the antimodern, old order Mennonite Kleine Gemeinde. At the center of the Kleine Gemeinde's[7] transformation was the evangelicalism that pervaded the midcentury American, and especially Midwestern American, religious scene. Indeed, evangelicalism was at the root of the old church's demise in 1943.[8]

Scholars of midcentury American society have long argued that religion in the United States provides a fundamental mechanism of social integration. Sociologist of religion Will Herberg argued in his now-classic work of 1955 that second- and third-generation immigrants found a pathway into American society by assimilation into one of three wide religious representations, Protestant, Catholic, or Jew. Such associations, suggested Herberg, were 'both genuinely American and ... familiar'[9] at the local level. Other scholars have suggested a particular role for evangelicalism in the America of the midcentury, a time of pronounced religious fervor in the United States. Church historian George Marsden, for example, has demonstrated that during the post-war decades two-thirds of Americans attended church with some regularity and more than four-fifths of Americans saw the 'Bible as the divinely inspired word of God.'[10] More importantly, this was a time of the awakening of Protestant evangelicalism, a personal yet disciplined and outgoing religiosity.[11] It presented a religious understanding that drew rigid social boundaries between the true Christian community and the modernistic world of the city.[12] Other church historians have posited that together, the personal joy and the social discipline of evangelicalism proved effective in the new society.[13] W.G. McLoughlin notes that evangelicalism represented a 'fundamental ideological transformation necessary ... in adapting to basic social, ecological, psychological and economic changes.'[14] Martin Marty has gone even further, suggesting that mid-twentieth-century evangelicalism occurred 'concurrent[ly] with the development of a new stage of modernity.'[15] That stage was a time of 'electronic communication, rapid transportation, mobile and kinetic styles of living, affluence and a sense of entitlement in large publics.'[16] Unlike the fundamentalism of the 1920s, here was no 'voice of dissent' against the cultural establishment. Rather, evangelicalism was a 'means of providing ritual process for applicants to the approved world.'[17] These evangelicals, argued Marty, were Protestants who 'still held to the traditional fundamentals of the faith, but were trying to reenter ... in the mainstream.'[18]

Among those seeking to enter the mainstream were the farm families who had been uprooted from their close-knit and familiar worlds by postwar economic forces. The traditional countercultural teachings and practices of the sectarian Mennonite farmers were especially tested in this more town-oriented milieu. For the Meade County Mennonites evangelicalism was literally a 'godsend.' It offered them both a continued measure of community cohesion and a legitimacy in the wider world.

The Schism of the Winter of 1943

In 1937 when the Meade Mennonite community emerged from the Great Depression, it was clear that this 'dark moment' had shaken the community to the core.[19] Still the Kleine Gemeinde, the largest of the county's Mennonite churches, was determined to hold its ground. It would seek to repel modernist culture, and bolster its antimodernist symbols, set in a sincere understanding of biblical teaching and Christocentric discipleship. Old-fashioned dress codes were to be respected: no neckties for the men, uniform black kerchiefs for women. Personal amenities were dismissed as frivolous and cars were kept plain: the once banned window-fitted 'glass car' was now accepted, but chrome bumpers were not and members were expected to paint them black.[20] Christ-like simplicity was to rule all events. Weddings, for example, were to take place only during the regular Sunday morning worship service and flowers, candles, and bridal attendants were discouraged.[21] Prayer was kept silent and in humble uniformity; 'at the beginning and at the end of each sermon' all members would 'kneel for silent prayer.'[22] Elaborate church programs, mission projects, and church budgets were unknown: the bishop and preachers were unpaid farmers and 'when relief money was needed ... special meetings were held for these collections.'[23] The youth were baptized by pouring, not by the more common Protestant method of immersion, and they were inducted into church membership without much fanfare, usually near the time of marriage, almost as an automatic, albeit sacred, rite of passage into adulthood.[24]

The emphasis from the pulpit was on ethics, humility, and loving obedience, not on doctrine, belief, and joyful certainty. Bishop Jacob F.

Isaac's October 1937 exposé on the biblical injunction, 'the greatest commandment,' to 'love your neighbor as yourself,' was a representative teaching, an expression of idealism coupled with a lament for under-achievement. He first dismissed his own abilities: 'I must confess that I achieve this duty so poorly even though my desire to do so is great.' Then, putting fundamentalist doctrine to question, he noted that 'Love is the only thing that one can take with one to heaven; creed, hopefulness and all other things stay. The person who does not have [love] cannot partake of the Kingdom of God. And yet it seems that love so easily grows cold ... If we spend time alone with God, and pray for our neighbor, or for our enemies, how can we then speak or think ill of our neighbor?'[25]

For the Kleine Gemeinde the social networks of the wider rural Mennonite settlement southeast of the town of Meade held special meaning. A key compoment in this understanding was the geographic context of the Kleine Gemeinde – it had two churches, the north and the south church – because the tradition of alternating services at the two rural sites brought community members into an especially close communion. As one Kleine Gemeinde member noted, 'everyone in the [village] where the services were held would prepare for company ... it was perfectly acceptable to stop without an invitation for [the noontime] Sunday dinner ... and stay for the afternoon.'[26] A further network tied the congregation to the Canadian branch of the Kleine Gemeinde, centered in the Rural Municipality (RM) of Hanover in Manitoba. The monthly binational church organ, the *Christlicher Familienfreund*, was published in Canada, and it kept the two small national communities informed of one another's activities, including illnesses, births, travels, and calamities.[27]

In 1937 the binational Kleine Gemeinde community took a last stand in defense of the conservative and nonconformist way of life. That year a corps of eleven Kleine Gemeinde preachers and their wives from Manitoba traveled in a convoy to Meade County to participate in a six-day conference that stretched from Saturday 23 October to Thursday 28 October. The Americans seemed pleased to have the Canadians visit: 'With ardent anticipation,' wrote one Meade congregant in 1937, 'we await the time when we may have in our midst the anticipated guests from Manitoba; we bid all of you welcome.'[28] The Canadians were especially welcomed because together they would reaffirm the church's conservative reformist idealism dating to its origins in the Mennonite commonwealth in New Russia in 1812.[29] The Canadian minister, David P. Reimer, youthful editor of the *Familienfreund*, noted the meeting as a 'serious undertaking.' Church leaders would do nothing less than ear-nestly ask, 'Lord, what is the path that we are to take?' The conference itself identified twenty-three different issues that were threatening the old church body and each issue was met by an expressed recommit-ment to old teachings.[30] On only one of the issues did the minister compromise: young members could attend college, but only because it is 'required that public school teachers have high school education.' Only those who were seen morally fit by the preachers would beallowed to do so. Most of the conference resolutions were simple reassertions of the simple, communitarian values of an old order Mennonite society. Members must resist mixed bathing and 'useless pleasure' such as sports, photography, jesting, and 'vain conversation.' Radios and musi-cal instruments could not be allowed. Expressions of common humility were reaffirmed, including unison singing from the centuries-old, Ger-man-language *Gesangbuch*, uniform black-colored head coverings for women, and exclusive dependence on the church for aid in time of death and illness. Religious cooperation with evangelistic churches and their songfests and foreign missions was discouraged.[31]

In southwestern Kansas this 1937 reaffirmation of an old order prac-tice was difficult to maintain. Meade, of course, was the very bastion of patriotic fervor and a broadly accepted evangelistic code colored both the town's small sectarian groups like the United Brethren and Pentecostals, and a range of more broadly based churches such as the Nazarenes, Baptists, Methodists, and Lutherans. Several of these churches hosted revival meetings that the Mennonite youth attended surreptitiously.[32] Only the Episcopalians and Catholics were completely outside the purview of discontented Mennonites.[33] The presence of the other Mennonite congregation, the Bruderthaler, made matters even more tenuous for the old order Kleine Gemeinde. By 1937 the Bru-derthaler had renamed itself the Evangelical Mennonite Brethren or the EMB as it was popularly known.[34] From its fledgling start in Meade County in 1910[35] the EMB had grown, constructing a church building in 1921, opening a Bible school in 1927, overtaking the local Mennonite Brethren church in 1930, and enlarging its church building in 1936. By 1937 its church roster of 170 adult members put it among the largest congregations in the broader EMB conference in the American and Canadian West and further postwar growth (membership in-creased from 182 in 1947 to 251 in 1952)[36] brought one Mennonite revivalist to declare that the Meade EMB 'has grown into a real power-ful church.'[37]

The attraction of the EMB was obvious. It spoke the language of doctrinal certainty, it promised personal joy and peace, it called for confident interaction in the wider world, and it offered Bible school education. It was also certain of the dispensationalist teaching common in American evangelicalism, assuring the faithful of their place in the divinely ordered, precise unfolding of world history. In June 1943 the Meade EMB hosted the annual conference of its fellow churches in Canada and the United States. Here the EMB give moral support to the newly established 'Mennonite' Grace Bible Institute of Omaha,[38] a school that promised 'a strictly "Bible-based" learning environment.'[39] At the wartime Meade conference too, the EMB celebrated a foreign mission budget of over $40,000, much larger than the $1100 devoted to the older concerns for relief and refugee programs.[40] And at Meade, members heard EMB leaders explain the dispensationalist view of the end times: history would end soon, a time of 'tribulation' and the final 'judgement' would follow; but most important was the hope for the 'rapture,' the moment when Christ's church would be joyously transported to heaven.[41] Meade farmers were also impressed that, although these ideas emanated from faraway places where their leaders had studied, from Moody Bible Institute in Chicago and Northwestern Bible Institute in Minneapolis, the preachers were still Mennonites. They were simple men, insistent on biblical pacifism. They did not wish to turn fundamentalism into a public spectacle, but to share the gospel within church revival meetings and person-to-person in everyday life. As one historian has noted, the EMB avoided 'the militancy of [fundamentalist movements that] failed to correspond with the EMB's more "quiet" ways.'[42]

The EMB's evangelicalism began attracting numerous Kleine Gemeinde members by the early 1940s. The fledgling Meade Bible School expanded its program in 1941 by hiring three part-time instructors and in 1942 by naming a new principal, Orlando Wiebe, a graduate of Tabor College, a Mennonite institute in Hillsboro in central Kansas. The Meade school promised to provide 'young Christians an opportunity to grow through prayer and the studying of scripture.'[43] As one observer recalled: 'the evangelistic spirit of the Bible School soon captivated many of the Kleine Gemeinde youth.'[44] These youths began campaigning for the Kleine Gemeinde to adopt evangelicalism. Sometimes their crusade mixed elements of charivari and simple impatience with the old ways: on one occasion they broke into the church on a Saturday night and rearranged the church pews and the pulpit, nailing them in new positions to resemble a mainstream Protestant church spatial layout with the pulpit at the end of the sanctuary rather than at its side. On another occasion they took 'away the lead from the song leader' during the Sunday service, and sang the old German hymns 'loud and fast,' racing ahead of both leader and the older folks.[45] Sometimes the campaign for change was a simple request to the bishop for evangelistic youth services and prayer meetings and when permission was denied, the youth moved ahead anyway with its own ad hoc meetings.[46]

In time the youthful members called for a full revamping of church programs and leadership. The criticism began to focus particularly on Bishop Isaac, who had been elected to his lifetime position in 1913. But Isaac would display the same strength of character for which the congregation had chosen him thirty years earlier. He chose to go on the offensive. He promised 'a more spiritual basis' at the same time that he publicly chastised church 'gossipers.'[47] He chided them for being overly critical. In their eyes, scolded the bishop, 'the church members are all bad, they can no longer be met honestly ... Everything is construed as bad, the preachers are no good anymore, instead of praying for them, they are being gossiped about, and so they stand alone and no longer have any friends.'[48] The mistrust was mutual. As one of the reformers indicated, 'feelings of distrust ... against the elder had developed ... to such an extent that the congregation did not want him as a leader even though he would consent to some of the desired reforms.'[49]

The crisis came to a head in late 1942 and early 1943. An informal group of concerned members contravened a centuries-long tradition of lifetime leadership and asked Bishop Isaac to resign. One of the reformers recalled that the bishop's 'reply was that he [had been] ordained by God and [was] there for life ... and demanded that he be honored as an elder.'[50] In early January word spread quietly that a complete break was the only way to assure meaningful reform. The old system of alternating church services between two church buildings, set four miles apart, now served as the very mechanism by which the reformers took over the church. On 31 January 1943 the Sunday morning worship was scheduled to be held in the south church, located near the bishop's farm. But only the bishop, his family, and four conservative families showed up.[51] The rest of the congregation made plans to begin a separate service. Three weeks later on 21 February 1943 the majority of Kleine Gemeinde members met in the north church and were led in worship by Henry R. Harms, the retired pastor of the EMB church, who had been invited by the dissenters.[52] The event was filled with emotion, even though the official history of the newly founded church records simply states that 'a committee of five was appointed to work together with two other [Kleine Gemeinde] ministers and a committee from the EMB Church in organizing a [new] church.'[53] Serving notice of their ultimate intent, the dissenting majority now invited Rev Harms to lead the new group.[54]

Having broken their ties with the past, it took the new body a year to recast the very structure of church and ideology. In March and April 1944 the new congregation met several times, and each time took dramatic action. During one of these meetings the break of 1943 was made unequivocal as members accepted a written document that outlined the steps of the break and declared a wish to 'carry on regular church services.' The refashioned body chose the new, English-language and evangelistically inclined name, the Emmanuel Mennonite Church. It planned a revival meeting, aimed now at 'definite conversion,' and sought from each church adherent an 'individual ... confession of faith in the Lord Jesus Christ as his own personal saviour from sin.'[55] It demanded that members make a commitment to a new, fresh start. Each member had to assure the leadership that 'the past, as concerning God and men, had been set in order' and each was asked to present 'a public testimony that they have a genuine, living, heart-acceptance of Jesus Christ.'[56] The new congregation put leadership on a new basis: instead of the old ministerial of life-term preachers and deacons, a church council of five respectable community laymen was elected for a set term.[57] The chairman of this council now led church membership meetings and his committee led the church in hiring, not electing, a spiritual leader. The leader was now known as pastor, not bishop or elder, and he would more often be a man of education than one of relative wealth.[58]

Nothing short of a reformulation of ecclesiology underlay these changes. Where once the concept of church had been synonymous with the community itself, it had become an institution that would compete for individuals, leaving itself open to the very idea that some individuals might choose not to join. It was, like evangelicalism elsewhere, a religion that 'surrender[ed] its suzerainty.'[59] In order for this more personalized concept to work the church program itself had to expand dramatically. This it did over the next five years. By December 1944 an annual meeting was held in which leaders were elected to a plethora of new offices: Sunday school superintendents, members of a trustee committee, a church secretary and a treasurer, ushers, a song director, members of a prayer meeting, a young people's committee, and a monthly Sunday-night worship service committee. Old social networks in which people visited without invitation seemed to be declining and could no longer be relied upon to unite the members: in April 1945 the church saw the need to officially set aside 'the last Sunday in the month ... to visit in the Settlement' and in December 1946 it approved of a plan 'to send out get well and sympathy greeting cards in the name of the Sewing Circle.'[60] It was evident that the new concept of a proactive church built on personal salvation was working. By August 1944 even the five most conservative families who had sided with Bishop Isaac asked to be admitted to the new church and in September, twenty youth were baptized upon expressed 'personal faith.'[61] Evident too of the new view of the church was an unprecedented move in November 1947 to debate the merits of the ban, the historic practice of ostracizing errant members; the question was, 'when shall it be done and why, and what it means.' The discussion was followed by an unprecedented decision: 'to grant ... [the] request' of a young woman who seriously had fallen from the grace of the church to simply resign and thus avoid the stigma of excommunication and the ostracization that accompanied the ban.[62]

By the 1950s a degree of cultural homogeneity had re-entered the Mennonite settlement. The ideological language of the Emmanuel and EMB churches was similar. The two churches frequently shared in evening services, Sunday school festivals, and missionary meetings. One observer noted in 1957 that the services were indistinguishable: both churches sang '[English] hymns and gospel songs in full harmony,' used 'piano music ... special vocal music by a choir or ensemble,' practised 'audible' prayer, and heard English-language 'sermons, about 30 minutes long' that were either 'evangelistic, bringing people to an acceptance of Jesus Christ' or 'instrumental, teaching the Bible and helping Christians to translate Christianity into daily practice.'[63]

Crossing into the Wider World

Part of the ideological consensus that descended on the Mennonite settlement southeast of Meade in the 1950s made the crossing of the old boundary between country and town, ethnic settlement and wider county, a particular virtue. During the 1940s and 1950s Meade Mennonites redrew boundaries. They now fully identified with grand dichotomies informed by the struggle of the United States to contain the Soviet Union, of saved Americans to convert unsaved Americans, and even of upstanding Protestant Republicans to counter suspect Catholic or Jewish-oriented Democrats.

Mennonites now sought to identify themselves not as the remnant of an ethnic group, but as another denomination willing to contribute to the social and spiritual well-being of the wider county. Both the Emmanuel and EMB churches began to cooperate with other county churches. They listed their services in the church section of the *Meade Globe Press* and gave the impression that among the various offerings – Lutheran, Catholic, Baptist, Methodist, Nazarene, Presbyterian, Episcopal, Apostolic – the Mennonites were just another denomination. Like the other more evangelistic churches – Apostolic Faith and Nazarene – the Emmanuel and EMB churches in publishing their weekly church calendars added the postscript, 'you are welcome to come and worship with us.'[64] In February 1948 both the Emmanuel and EMB churches joined the Meade Ministerial Association, and significantly, Orlando Wiebe, pastor of the EMB, was elected president.[65] In May of the same year when Dr Don Gilbert, a widely known religious author and journalist came to Meade County to 'interpret current events in light of scripture,' both Mennonite churches joined with the Baptists, Nazarenes, Apostolics, and Methodists in sponsoring the event.[66] But most significantly the Mennonite churches began cloaking their special programs in a language that would draw the approval and participation of the wider county society. When Peter Dyck, the popular European coordinator of the Pennsylvania-based Mennonite Central Committee's postwar refugee program came to report at the EMB church in September 1947, the event was advertised in the *Globe Press* as 'free to the public' and the Dyck story described as one 'more thrilling than fiction' itself. A similar fanfare attended the May 1948 visit of the Mennonite choir of Tabor College, Hillsboro, to the Emmanuel Church. The choir was billed on the front page of the *Globe Press* as 'one of the state's finest voice aggregations' to which the 'public is cordially invited.'[67] Of course, relief work and choral singing might be construed as Mennonite markers.[68] But overall, the public language of the Mennonites had become similar to that of other evangelistic churches in the county.

The Mennonite churches, however, also felt the evangelical imperative to proselytize. The support of foreign missions was, of course, the concern of all evangelical churches. In fact, only six months after its official start, the Emmanuel church decided to 'invite the Ecks [Mr. and Mrs. Marvin M. Eck] here for examination ... to see if we want to support them in the mission field [in Africa].'[69] A commitment to re-forming fellow Americans themselves followed. Few were as outgoing as Jacob R. Friesen, a one-time stalwart Kleine Gemeinde member. In the 1940s he sold his windmill sales and repair business to his sons and set out criss-crossing the United States by car bearing the sign 'Jesus Saves' and distributing up to 200,000 pieces of evangelistic literature a year. His aim was simple, to 'win as many souls as he had sold windmills,' 5000 in total.[70] But Friesen was unique only in that he took to heart what Meade Mennonites were now saying and appointed himself as God's ambassador.

Most Mennonites were more reticent, although most agreed that it was imperative to try to convince friends and associates to embrace evangelical Christianity.[71] A sentiment with which Meade Mennonites now identified was expressed by young John L. Friesen, who died after a lengthy fight with cancer in 1945. During his last days, it was said, he had grieved not only at the thought of leaving his wife and three small children, but also that 'during his life he had done so little for the Lord' and had not 'witness[ed] more for the Lord and [won] souls for him.'[72] A feeling pervaded the congregation that the old boundaries should be crossed more aggressively. Yet a lingering ambivalence to opening the cultural borders remained. In July 1956 when a non-ethnic Mennonite, Bob Gillett, applied to the Emmanuel Church for membership, members seemed to be caught offguard. Members asked whether in fact the church could 'consider baptizing a person who doesn't have a Mennonite background.' The answer came hesitantly: 'if a person has a desire to become a Mennonite and is willing to ... abide by our constitution, we [may] go ahead with baptizing and exception [sic] into our church ...'[73] A similar struggle between teaching and behavior was manifested in November 1958 when the church grappled with the problem that it had not, since its inception in 1944, sent out its own missionary. In a lengthy discussion, members agreed that 'the commission of the church' was to engage in overseas evangelistic missions and confessed that 'we feel that more could be done in spreading the gospel.'[74]

Meade Mennonites found the border-crossing exercise easier when it meant identifying with county neighbors, not transforming them. A common dread of communism provided such an opportunity. It was simply easier to denounce totalitarian Russia than consumer-driven America. EMB historian Kevin Rempel argues that during the 1950s 'the EMB directed its fire at anything which even vaguely resembled communism,' attacking labor unions, a social safety net, and the 'social gospel' of more 'liberal' churches.[75] Henry L. Friesen's 1947 article in the Globe Press may have contravened the style of most Mennonites and aroused some skepticism, but the general thrust was not strange. Friesen wrote of the following experience: 'On the evening of September 23, 1947 about 11:30 at night I was awake. All at once I heard a loud rap in another room. And I listened and ... asked the Lord what He wanted me to do ... At that moment seemingly a loud voice came to me and said, "Cry out. Wake-up America, Communism is going to overtake you ..." I was extremely frightened ... [and] I started praying what should I do. He revealed ... "[Tell] the people [to] repent of their sins, turn to God and pray for the protection of our country – this anti-Christian nation." Dear reader, won't you join in repentance and pray?'[76] Few people responded publicly to Friesen's plea, but without question they shared his fear of communism and his identification with the 'imagined community' of America. Ending the three-generation-long practice of rejecting participation in state or national politics, Meade Mennonites now became overt political supporters of President Eisenhower, Senator Andrew Shoeppel, Congressman Cliff Hope, and other Republicans.[77] By 1956, 49 percent of the 262 eligible Mennonite voters in Meade County voted and in the townships in which they dominated demographically a greater percentage of votes went Republican than elsewhere.[78]

Erecting Evangelical Boundaries

Evangelicalism may have been the very conduit to the outside world the Mennonites sought, albeit on their own terms. But it was also the very guarantee of continued boundary maintenance. Ironically, the religious fervor that told Mennonites they must engage the outside world was now a new justification for their separateness. The Low German language, anti-consumeristic preaching, and biblical pacifism were no longer the hallmarks of a separate identity; instead, evangelical purity was.

This aim was especially apparent in the language employed by Meade Mennonites to keep the education of their children in their own hands. In both the 1940s and the mid-1960s Meade Mennonites opposed rural elementary school consolidation that threatened to close public schools with names such as 'Sunrise,' 'Lilydale,' and 'Pleasant Hill,' schools that they had run virtually as private institutions. In both instances the Mennonites lost, but not without making strong arguments in public. In late 1945 and early 1946, for example, Mennonite parents hired a lawyer and 'went to court to try to ... stop consolidation.'[79] At the 'legal hearing' in the Meade County District Court they insisted that consolidation would undermine their 'Christian' values. Some parents like Isaac Classen agreed with the school officials who scolded the Mennonites for opposing consolidation in order that 'you folks could remain to yourselves down there' in the southeast corner of the county.[80] But others appealed to patriotism: 'we are all Americans living in this great country of ours,' argued Jacob Wiens; providing children with a 'good religious training ... will only make good honest citizens out of them.'[81] More often Mennonite parents simply insisted through their attorney that 'control of the schools would slip out of their hands and ... their children would not be educated by Christian instructors.'[82] What parents wanted, argued Henry Harms, the pastor of the Emmanuel church, was to 'have the influence of good Christian teachers' who daily would ensure the 'reading of the Bible and prayer.'[83] Mennonites now identified themselves with a language and a set of concerns with which Meade County residents sympathized, but the language was used to separate themselves from those residents.

A similar formulation that employed evangelical language to build a social border for the Mennonites was expressed in the founding of Meade Bible Academy, the MBA, a private Mennonite-run high school located in the heart of the Mennonite settlement. This was the old EMB Bible School that changed direction in 1944 by adding high school courses such as English, history, algebra, and music and then in 1948 turned exclusively to providing a full four-year, state-accredited high school education.[84] Mennonites immediately and enthusiastically accepted the new school. Few Mennonite students ventured the eighteen-mile distance to Meade for their education.[85] By 1954 high student enrollments compelled the erection of a large, new, brick building, complete with an 'auditorium-gymnasium' and administration wing. The school remained open until 1966 when financial difficulties due to falling enrollments and rural depopulation forced it to close.[86]

During its heyday the school's cultural language was a buoyant evangelicalism, even though ethnically it was almost entirely Mennonite. The trustees of its board were all Mennonites, more than 80 percent of its fifty-seven teachers that taught there over time had ethnic Mennonite names, and its student roster consisted almost entirely of similar traditional Mennonite names.[87] But the academy was member in the Midwest Association of Evangelical Schools, and the members of the school assembly were assimilated to an evangelical culture and language. Neither the academy's six-point list of purposes nor its doctrinal

statement bore reference to the term 'Mennonite' or to distinctive Mennonite tenets. Among the school's stated aims were to 'strengthen young
Christians,' 'develop ... talents for the Lord's service,' and 'build Christian character.' The doctrinal statement was generic fundamentalism:
the inspiration of the scripture, the trinity, the virgin birth, the deity of
Christ, personal salvation through Christ, a belief in the final resurrec-
tion and in heaven and hell, an affirmation of the reality of Satan, and a
stated hope in the second coming of Christ.[88] Walter Friesen, who
carried out a major survey of the school in 1957, noted that the basic
difference between the public high school in Meade and the rural academy was that the latter sought to persuade 'young minds to ... accept ...
Jesus Christ as a personal savior and ... prepared ... Christian workers.'[89] In a 1957 poll, 90 percent of the students (fifty-five of sixty-one)
agreed that 'a Christian's primary task' was to be a 'witness ... to
others,' to bring them to 'a saving knowledge of Jesus Christ.'[90]

A cursory look suggests that the school wanted nothing more than to
tear down old boundaries. In fact a special imperative seemed to be to
equip students with the tools for entering the wider world: the 1957
school curriculum prescribed three units of English and two in American history and government, but only one each in mathematics, science,
and health.[91] No course in German was offered and only 7 percent
of students thought it should be.[92] Students represented themselves as
the best of middle-class American citizens. In Friesen's 1957 poll,
91 percent of the students believed that attending the academy made
them 'better citizens.'[93] Indeed the only reference to Mennonite tradition in a March 1959 issue of the student magazine, the MBA Progress,
was to a fund-raising event that promised in the language of symbolic
ethnicity, 'an old-fashioned Dutch supper ... featur[ing] traditional Mennonite dishes,' including 'baked ham, "prune mosse," fried potatoes
and homemade breads and rolls.'[94] The students even looked 'American:' the official photograph of the graduating class of 1954 depicted
eight young men and women, each of the men in suits and wearing ties,
each of the women with kerchiefless permed hair and wearing a tight-
fitted suit.[95] And the students sounded 'American': their sports teams,
for example, were the Eagles and Eaglettes.

Still, the main thrust of the school was not to eliminate old boundaries but to reformulate them, to regulate them, and to provide judi-
ciously executed crossing points. The school might have spoken the
evangelical and nationalistic language of its American neighbors, yet it
guarded against interaction with those neighbors. It was not surprising
that the school explicitly forbade 'attendance at movie theaters, danc-

ing and card-playing,' but it also forbade competitive sports with 'any public high schools.'[96] The headline of the *MBA Progress* on 13 February 1959 read 'Friends Tromps MBA,' a week later it stated, 'Corn Bible Academy Trounced MBA', and a week after that the sports columnist noted that 'the ball stealin', pass thievin'' MBA Eagles won against 'Berean.' The tromping, trouncing, and thievin', however, was entirely within a network of private evangelistic institutions. Students in Friesen's 1957 poll registered few complaints about the school, but they recorded 'considerable agitation' against the policy of no games with public schools and complained about the 'geographical and cultural isolation' of the school.[97] Parents and community elders, however, were pleased: the school met their wishes 'to keep young people near home under the cultural and religious beliefs and practices deemed important by the community.' As Alvin Kleinsasser, pastor of the EMB church, noted candidly in the mid-1950s, the school served to protect the teenaged students during 'years when the student is yet formative.'[98]

The school met its purpose. Meade County sheriff Arlie Johnson, who participated in Friesen's survey, might have meant his comments as criticism, but the community elders no doubt read them with satisfaction. The school, according to Sheriff Johnson, was succeeding in preparing the youth for the 'complex civilization in which we live,' but as Johnson saw it, the students could do more to accept the 'down to earth endeavor to understand other segments of our population, their beliefs, fears and prejudice to other groups.'[99] It was a cultural understanding that came slowly. Even after graduation the path from the MBA high school led not to the heart of county life, but to other Mennonite-dominated institutions. According to the 1957 study, more than 80 percent of the graduates of MBA reported regular attendance in Mennonite churches; only 12 percent attended other churches and the majority of these consisted of a '"fundamental" Protestant church.'[100] The same study indicated that of the 59 percent of high school students who went on to post-secondary education between 1948 and 1956, 88 percent had spent some time at either Tabor College in Eastern Kansas or Grace College in Omaha, both predominantly evangelical Mennonite schools; only 22 percent had attended public universities and colleges in Kansas.[101]

Still Mennonite in the 1970s

During the 1960s and 1970s the Meade Mennonites became more comfortable with foreign missions and mainstream American evangelicalism. Indeed in early the 1960s the Emmanuel church went on the offensive, literally outdistancing its sister church the EMB by relocating to the very heart of the county, downtown Meade. Although the May 1963 decision was made in part because more and more Mennonites lived in Meade, a church document of 1974 noted emphatically that the decision had been taken after 'realizing the greater [evangelical] outreach possibility in the town of Meade.'[102] It was clear that any reservations church members had about encountering the wider world had dissipated. Architecturally, the new Emmanuel church in Meade was distinguishable not for its inherited plain lines, but as a trendsetter. Between 1964 and 1975 Meade's Baptist, Catholic, and Lutheran churches each constructed similar steep-roof, open-ceiling, dark-brick buildings, with educational side wings set back from the street front.[103] The Emmanuel church had overcome an earlier reticence and now donated twice as much money to foreign missions as it did to the local private high school and four times as much as it did to foreign relief.[104] It now readily participated in community-wide evangelistic programs by supporting such events as the 'Ford Philpot Crusade in the Dodge City auditorium,' encouraging attendance at Billy Graham films shown in other town churches, and hosting non-Mennonite speakers such as Mr Steven Peterson of the Evangelical Enterprises.[105] The church now supported eighteen missionaries, many from its own congregation. And its rhetoric was unequivocal: the pastor of 1974 called upon members to remember that 'darkened hearts everywhere need to hear the Gospel,' and that 'the church must now, as never before, reveal to the world next door and beyond that Jesus Christ is the only answer.' Here was rhetoric laced with Americana: he spoke about 'a new and challenging frontier ... [that] is, the frontier of unclaimed [unsaved] lives' and promised committed members a church that is 'strong' and 'free.'[106]

The Emmanuel church's birth in 1943 was considered a halfway measure by the 1970s. The original departure, it seemed, had not fully evolved into evangelicalism. Even the church of the 1950s, though it might have called itself evangelical, still bore signs of a communitarian approach in its statement of faith that declared as its first principle to 'believe and teach the scriptures.' The first aim of the constitution of the 1970s was to present 'Jesus Christ ... so that individual sinners may come to a saving knowledge.'[107] The 1950s constitution made its primary social responsibility the advancement of 'the doctrine of nonresistance in word and in deed' and called for members to continue separating themselves from the 'ungodly world'; the 1970s constitution replaced this aim with that of becoming 'responsible and useful citizens within our society' and explicitly declared that 'the church ... must not isolate itself from the community' and that 'activities ... that further community betterment should be considered opportunities to manifest the love and compassion of Christ.' Where the old constitution had prescribed some of the inherited symbols of communitarian uniformity such as ceremonial foot washing and the 'devotional head-covering,' the 1970s document emphasized belief. Unlike the document of 1950, the one of 1970 included subjects such as the 'depravity of man,' the 'return of Christ,' heaven and hell, angels and Satan.

In a decision with far-reaching consequences both the Emmanuel and EMB churches altered their positions on biblical pacifism. This historic Mennonite teaching was a difficult stance to defend in Meade County in the 1960s. The county could well boast of its patriotism and its preparedness to support military ventures overseas. By 1970 almost 25 percent of adult males in Meade County were veterans, 105 men of the Vietnam conflict itself.[108] The more assimilated EMB moved on this issue first. Its local record reflected that of the wider EMB conference, which saw 15 percent of drafted men engage in active combat duty during the Second World War and 41 percent during the Vietnam War.[109] In 1954 when Dick Isaac, a young Second World War veteran, died suddenly in Wichita, the local EMB permitted a military honor guard to assist at the funeral.[110] By the late 1950s the church had dropped the requirement of pacifism for prospective members. The Emmanuel Mennonite church took a similar, albeit belated, path. In 1957 when it considered amalgamating with the local EMB church it objected to the latter's obfuscation on biblical pacifism. By 1975, however, the Emmanuel church had also dropped the requirement, noting candidly that although it would continue to 'recommend [alternative] civilian service' over combat duty, it recognized that 'some Christians believe that according to scripture they should participate fully in ... military service' and that the church 'should accept for membership' persons holding such positions.[111]

Despite the more overt evangelical theology and the weakening stance on biblical pacifism, both the Emmanuel and EMB churches in Meade clearly presented themselves as Mennonite denominations. In fact the EMB church opposed a growing sentiment among its sister congregations in Nebraska and Oregon to exchange the name Evangelical Mennonite Brethren for Evangelical Bible Church. The Emmanuel church, although one of few independent Mennonite churches in the United States, also resolved to maintain the sectarian designation. Both churches were leery of the proactive social critique of the Pennsylvania-based Mennonite Central Committee, but both readily supported its material aid and disaster service agencies.[112] The Emmanuel church, for example, noted in the early 1970s that although 'man's basic problem is sin' and that sin can be corrected 'with the blood of the Lord Jesus Christ ... we must not neglect ... social issues, disasters and human needs that can properly be handled.'[113]

The strongest sense of Mennonite continuity in the 1970s came from existing church rosters. By 1968, twenty-five years after the initial break and five years after moving into town, the Emmanuel church's membership roster listed only two families with non-ethnic-Mennonite names. The EMB, which was even more overtly evangelical but remained geographically within the original Mennonite settlement, had an active membership list of 131 with not a single non-ethnic-Mennonite name. Evangelicalism had proven itself not by redrawing the church boundaries, but by providing a pathway out of the county in which the traditional farming economy was faltering. Between 1966 and 1968, when eleven members of the Emmanuel church left the community, six joined Mennonite churches of other conferences in Kansas, Colorado, and California, but five joined evangelistic churches.[114] In 1976 the EMB church roster contained forty-three 'non-resident' members; it was here that non-ethnic Mennonite names appeared. Each of the eleven persons bearing a non-Mennonite family name seems to have been a former Meade Mennonite woman who had married a non-Mennonite man and now lived in Manhattan or Wichita in Kansas, in cities in Illinois or Nebraska, or in foreign mission fields.[115] At home in Meade, old ethnic boundaries persisted, albeit cloaked in evangelistic language.

Between 1930 and 1980 the majority of Meade County Mennonites reformulated the foundation of their culture. The social basis of a communitarian and nonconformist ethnoreligious identity had weakened. Technology, government programs, and farm markets demanded increased farm sizes, more concerted interaction with a wider world, and migration into town. Religious faith and ethnic identity were marshalled anew to make sense of this new world, to chart a path through the hazards of social change.

Evangelicalism promised the Mennonites a more certain cosmology and teleology and a new legitimacy in a new society. It was a faith with an element of individualism that allowed for an easier interaction with the rapidly changing American culture. It provided for a stable pathway out of the agrarian community for it now associated the concept of 'world' not so much with a wider geography, but with a licentious lifestyle. Now the one-time sectarians were armed with a religious language and cosmology that not only had currency in the wider world, but made a sustained interaction with that world a social imperative. Ironically, these evangelical principles justified social distance from the wider world for those who chose or were able to remain in the county. And by avoiding the world the devotee seemed in fact to gain greater credence in the wider society. For those who wished or were compelled to leave, evangelicalism provided an articulated moral code and an important new definition of an imagined national community. Evangelicalism thus allowed the Meade Mennonites at once to maintain old boundaries by emphasizing the moral difference between local community and worldly society, but also the rationale to cross those boundaries.

Clearly what sociologists of the 1950s claimed to be seeing, an assimilation into mainstream America, was occurring. Mennonites were dressing, speaking, and thinking like their American neighbors, but they were using these symbols and structures to ensure continuity and group identity in a new, more urbanized, and commercialized society. The Depression-era and postwar social upheaval recast old boundaries. During this time of economic growth and social dislocation the joyfulness, the assurance, and the hopefulness associated with evangelicalism was both a grounding for communal continuity and a bridge to the wider world. Within the community the 'joy' was a measure of religious sincerity; on the paths that led to the broader world the 'joy' legitimized a new set of cultural interactions.

5 Beyond Shunning: Reconfiguring the Old Manitoba Bruderschaft

Site of Religious Conflict

Just as the midcentury social changes in Kansas demanded a religious response, so too did those in Manitoba. As in Meade County, religious understandings in the Rural Municipality (RM) of Hanover and the town of Steinbach were put to the test. In Manitoba, however, change came more slowly and gradually. It was as if the critical mass of Mennonites, and particularly conservative Mennonites, in places such as Hanover filtered the evangelical enterprise to some extent. Nevertheless, opposing communitarian and evangelistic concerns became locked in an intense and dynamic relationship within the local community, pitting rural churches against town churches, but also setting members against each other within individual churches, rural or town. Conservative churches in Manitoba, however, did not disintegrate, they fragmented. These schisms were exacerbated by emigration of the most conservative members to exclusive Mennonite old order sites in Latin America, a shock to the Manitoba community.

In Kansas a sure measure of change was the rise of evangelical fervor; in Manitoba it was the ongoing debate in the inner sanctum of the church between conservatives and evangelicals over the emotionally charged and highly symbolic practice of shunning, that is, the ostracization of errant members. For conservative communitarian Mennonites this controversial practice was a sign of continued willingness to combat the ways of the world – its modernism and its consumerism – and defend the old Anabaptist 'two kingdom' cosmology. For the progressive, evangelistic forces, the shunning was clearly out of step with modernity, individualized religiosity, and easy association with an

English-speaking, consumeristic, and capitalistic world. As the most obvious elements of old order religiousness declined, its proponents nevertheless found ways of reasserting its philosophical foundation. The shunning of errant members was clearly not the only way of guarding old ways.

The site in which to observe this debate most precisely was the *Bruderschaft*, or the 'brotherhood meeting' as it came to be known in English. The Bruderschaft was a meeting of male adult baptized members called by the bishop to discuss congregational and community life.[1] In the more conservative churches, Bruderschaft was the place where communal norms were identified, doctrines and ordinances were debated, and a religious practice expressed in everyday life was reformulated.[2] Unlike the evangelical agenda, the communitarian concern of the Bruderschaft was not discussed in the public media; its witness was public only in its everyday behavior, its own shunning of modernity. The language of communitarianism was kept within the church in sermons, but even more intensely within the record of the Bruderschaft itself, records that were shielded by their trustees from the potentially unsympathetic eyes of outsiders.[3] The Bruderschaft rested on the assumption that religious meaning could be found neither in a public witness for the evangelization of individuals nor in public calls for social justice in the wider society or the state. Its ideology was based on an old-order perspective, the old Anabaptist 'two kingdom' ideal. This teaching suggested that the congregation was an exclusive body of committed Christian disciples and a traditional agrarian idea that the church held moral authority over geographically defined community. From a modern perspective the Bruderschaft was antithetical to the liberal ideal of the inviolability of individual freedom. Not surprising, poets and novelists found in this antimodern site a demon in need of exorcism. In Steinbach descendent Pat Friesen's poetic work, *The Shunning* (1980), the bishop excommunicates the innocent, 'quiet, serious' Peter Neufeld, with 'all the weight of the brotherhood behind him[,] a brotherhood of brothers.'[4]

For the conservative Mennonites of Hanover the Bruderschaft was a site where members recommitted themselves to the old order. It did not matter which of the existing old order church denominations in Hanover one visited – the most populous Chortitzer church, the Sommerfelder transplant from south central Manitoba, the pietistic Holdeman Mennonites, or the Kleine Gemeinde – the Bruderschaft was the very expression of communitarian ideals. Each of the conservative churches used the Bruderschaft to articulate and enforce a discipline of the every-day. The recorded minutes of its proceedings reveal a process by which a church body brought old ideals of communitarian solidarity into a dialectic with new ideals of individualized religious meaning. The Bruderschaft helped distinguish among competing ways of thinking about faith and everyday life. Here lay the crux of culture, reflected not as the record of a 'coherent whole' but, as Fredrik Barth writes, as a process by which people 'interpret ... the here and now so as to be able to respond to it.'[5]

The Manitoba Kleine Gemeinde Bruderschaft

The Bruderschaft of the Kleine Gemeinde Mennonites in the vicinity of the RM of Hanover included the congregations located in the town of Steinbach and the nearby farm districts of Blumenort, Kleefeld, and Prairie Rose (Landmark). It usually met about once a month or when a pressing issue arose. As in Kansas, the Manitoba Kleine Gemeinde found its task exceptionally difficult during the 1930s and 1940s. The church had not joined the migration of some 8000 conservative Menno-nites to isolated colonies in Mexico and Paraguay during the 1920s. Nor had it rejected new technologies as had the Swiss-American Old Order Mennonite and Amish churches. And it had turned down a third option of adopting beliefs and behaviors selectively from the revivalist tradi-tion as its Holdeman Mennonite counterpart had. If the Manitoba Kleine Gemeinde had not adapted earlier, now at midcentury it was finally compelled to devise new ways of dealing with the ever-encroaching world. Exacerbating this tension was the fact that the Kleine Gemeinde represented the largest church in rapidly growing Steinbach, and that this congregation, along with two rural congregations with which it had close ties, Kleefeld and Prairie Rose, seemed especially open to the individualized and personal message of evangelicalism. They seemed to stand at loggerheads with the most conservative of the four congre-gations, the large and well-to-do Blumenort congregation, located just five miles north of Steinbach.

On the surface, however, the church was united. It was a rural-oriented, communitarian body intent on confronting the technology, fashions, and culture of the wider world. Like its counterpart in Kansas, the Manitoba Kleine Gemeinde of Hanover and area during the 1930s was still led by a farmer-bishop, untrained in formal theology and elected to the post for life. In southeastern Manitoba this bishop had a mandate to provide leadership over each of the four church districts and chaired the joint Bruderschaft meetings. In 1930 the bishop was Peter P. Reimer, the successful Blumenort farmer elected at a Bruderschaft in 1926. His mandate was not only to lead the four church districts as a single church body, but to do so with the assistance of a corps of lay ministers, also theologically untrained men – farmers, businessmen, and schoolteachers – hailing from each of the four districts.

At the Bruderschaft the bishop, ministers, or even lay members frequently issued general admonitions. Many of these pronouncements reflected an underlying dualistic view of society, which recognized a division between the faithful community and the wider world. Typical was the statement offered at a July 1934 meeting that 'being a light to the world' required that 'we keep ourselves aloof from the world.'[6] Often the misdemeanors that violated this calling were specifically identified: in February 1934 it was members who played musical instruments, a worldly 'act denounced by Menno Simons' himself; in August 1938 reprimands were directed to specific members in the congregation for 'the consumption of strong drink'; in June 1936 it was members who engaged in the 'social gathering of the sexes in co-ed bathing, completely unsuitable for Christians'; in October 1941 the 'tobacco afflicted members' were censured.[7] Each instance was a sign of 'conformity to the world' which contradicted the following of Christ in true simplicity and humility.

The Bruderschaft was especially concerned to ensure that each member was in agreement with these admonitions. And thus it also took upon itself the role of encouraging attendance at the biannual communion service. For these Mennonites the *Abendmahl* or communion service was an essential communitarian rite that celebrated God's grace through the sacrament of the consumption of bread and wine, the symbols of Christ's crucified body. A crucial component of this sacrament was that the elements be consumed in a social setting, thus indicating social harmony. Adding to this sense of unity was the practice that took literally Christ's injunction in the gospel of John to 'wash one another's feet, even as I have washed yours.' The serving of the bread and wine and foot washing were the two pillars of the communion service. The very participation in it was a pledge of loyalty to the entire community and to its teaching of nonconformity to the world. Attendance was absolutely imperative. Thus in the 1930s the Bruderschaft's leaders still made it their business to note each person who was absent from the communion table and in the week following the service 'approach' all absentee members.[8] Such members either were asked to attend the next communion to show their unity with the congregation or to attend the next Bruderschaft to state publicly the reason for their show of disunity.

The Bruderschaft also strove to ensure unity at the borders of the community. Members who were tempted to participate in government or government programs, for example, were encouraged to remain aloof from the lure of power and seek only the resources of the community. Thus in March 1936 the Kleine Gemeinde ministers sent a message to the brethren that 'it would be a better testimonial if we as a church would aim to live without [government old age] pensions.'[9] Later that year when Steinbach farmer Peter Penner considered running for the RM of Hanover municipal council, the church offered its opinion that this 'was not advisable' for 'as Christ notes, "my Kingdom is not of this world."'[10] Stronger measures including excommunication were almost automatically levelled against members who took political or civic positions that violated the church's traditional stance on pacifism. In October 1933, for example, when Steinbach resident Jacob Fast agreed to accept a local judgeship the Bruderschaft quickly agreed to 'ask by [official] letter, for his resignation.' Eight years later during the Second World War, when a certain John Barkman became the first Kleine Gemeinde member voluntarily to enlist in the armed forces, the ministers 'unanimously declared that we feel that according to the Word, the church must separate itself from him,' and postponed the actual excommunication just long enough that they might 'speak with his wife and if possible with him.' The Bruderschaft took a similarly dim view of members who married non-Mennonites and this act too almost automatically spelled excommunication. Thus in October 1935 when Heinrich Warkentin married a non-Mennonite the Brudershaft agreed that Warkentin should be sent a letter declaring that 'we no longer consider him a brother.'[11] And in May 1938 when Mary Siemens 'married an "unconverted person," a Frenchman,' the church secretary recorded unequivocally that 'it was decided that [her] sinful fall constituted a reason for excommunication.'

If the basic church structure appeared unshaken in the 1930s, serious division had nevertheless developed in the congregation of the Manitoba Kleine Gemeinde. Bishop Peter P. Reimer was a rural conservative from Blumenort, while several of his junior ministers were public school-teachers and entrepreneurs from Steinbach and Prairie Rose. Much of the history of the Kleine Gemeinde between 1930 and 1960 was a contest between town and country, especially between the town of Steinbach and the largest of the rural districts, Blumenort. That contest was played out within the Bruderschaft. Here town and country debated ideas of right and wrong, the nature of the church and of social boundaries, and the best methods of attracting the next generation of youth into the church. The Bruderschaft minutes speak of constant debate. The Steinbach ministers were the advocates of Protestant church methods that included Sunday schools, protracted revival meetings, English-language services, musical instruments, youth societies, and foreign missions. The Blumenort ministers held out for older agrarian approaches that pursued a strong church community through social separation, German-language services, plain dress, a cappella singing, and farm or rural vocations. But these were not merely divergent practices, they reflected divergent world views.

This debate lay at the heart of the historic Meade, Kansas, conference of 1937. The Manitoba ministers who attended that six-day conference may have driven together in convoy, but they held disparate ideas. The town progressives disagreed with the rural communitarians. The conference's central issue, to arrest the trend of 'leaving the way of the Lord,' pitted town schoolteacher-preachers against country farmer-preachers. The ministers at Meade noted that 1937 was the 100th anniversary of the death of Kleine Gemeinde founder, Bishop Klaas Reimer, back in Russia and that just as the Kleine Gemeinde's founding in 1812 had been set amidst 'dark clouds of disunity,' so too was their own conflict in the 1930s. How could the Gemeinde 'stand up for the truth' in a mid-twentieth-century world and maintain the 'little herd,' the small, culled flock of true believers?[12] At the conference the progressives may have received a significant concession on high school education and teachers' college, but on the central question of church discipline the conservatives would not give way. They were adamant that members who gave in to worldly ways must not only be excommunicated, but shunned, banned, and ostracized by other church members.

The entire ministerial still agreed on the need for strict church discipline. In fact the very first resolution read that 'no member has the right to leave the church for the purpose of avoiding church discipline.' In the past the church had recognized the resignation of members, an act serving the interest of both the church and the errant member, avoiding undue disruptiveness in the former and the circumvention of the dreadful shunning in the latter. But in 1937 the concern was that some members would 'resign from the church only in order to live more freely in the world.' In other words errant members were resigning from church membership before the Bruderschaft could excommunicate them and in this manner avoiding the ban and social ostracization. The Meade meeting seemed to acquiesce to the conservatives by ensuring that sin would have no escape hatch.[13] And strengthening their hand was the decision to excommunicate members who routinely avoided the church communion services.[14] The ministers, however, could agree on these harsh measures only because they would agree to disagree on the nature of shunning. Progressive ministers balked at the strict application of shunning, especially the idea that the excommunicated should be barred from attending Sunday worship services. Thus, 'on the question of whether excommunicated members should be allowed to attend church service, the resolution states that there are differences of opinion about this, and that [we] want no schism because of these differences.'

The fact that disagreements arose with regard to excommunication should not be surprising. The act of banning a member was a socially searing event and the Bruderschaft itself never took such banishment lightly. Indeed, excommunication was always a moment of great solemnity. In May 1935 the Manitoba Kleine Gemeinde excommunicated a Blumenort man, married, father to several young children, and in his early thirties. But it banned him only after citing him for a host of misdemeanors including a serious fist fight with 'a brother,' attendance at 'Lady Barber Shops' and other 'obscure houses,' and 'continued use of tobacco even after being approached by three ministers.' The young father's defiance of ministerial counsel set off the process that ended with the rite of excommunication. The Bruderschaft secretary recorded the associated series of events. The offending member's 'confession has not been found sufficient, so we decided that we would all jointly bow and kneel in prayer before God so that each member might examine himself and discern how one should vote, how to help this fallen brother, and then to vote, and if a majority votes for excommunication, then to place the [brother] into an excommunicated state. So we trust in our hearts that the Lord will be gracious to him.' It concluded with the hope that these actions will result 'in a confession to leave his former walk.' Shunning followed and its harshness was effective. After two months of ostracization, on 21 July 1935, the man from Blumenort was reinstated into full fellowship after having made the required 'heartfelt confession.'[15]

The very practice of shunning, however, was being undermined in the increasingly pluralistic midcentury society. Church discipline was usually not as neatly executed as in the case of the Blumenort man. In January 1941, for example, when it was reported that a young woman had 'confessed to having fallen deeply,' the Bruderschaft debated her situation vigorously. In the end it decided against disciplinary action because many brothers felt that her 'fall was that of a sinner before God' and hence 'no further ... action is required by the church.' At another occasion in April the Bruderschaft carried out an excommunication, but made it clear that no shunning should occur. The case involved a 'brother ... [who] married a sister of another church denomination.' According to church tradition the Bruderschaft felt compelled to ban him from membership, but it was a half-hearted dismissal for the brethren added the codicil that should the brother and his bride wish to 'join our church ... it shall be possible.' Another case pointed to the difficulty of enforcing the ban. In June when an elderly excommunicated businessman from Steinbach died, the Bruderschaft noted with some consternation that church members had interacted with other 'excommunicated brethren' at the funeral and cited some members for having eaten at the same table as the 'excommunicated.'[16]

The tensions surrounding these three events point to two opposing world views. One espoused more individual choice, the other an idealized communitarian solidarity. The severity of disagreement on shunning was evident in a question Bishop Peter P. Reimer asked his fellow ministers in October 1941: 'Do we hold and practice the shunning of excommunicated members rightly' or were past practices in fact not rooted in scripture? This became an agenda item at a Bruderschaft five months later. At that meeting it was obvious that many brethren felt that shunning no longer worked, especially in the increasingly pluralistic towns. Still the bishop seemed especially anxious to attain unity on this central question and he asked the Bruderschaft to meet again in 'five or six weeks' and 'in prayer, under the examination of God's word, and through a vote come to unity' on the issue.[17]

The meeting on the ban did not occur as scheduled for the worries of the war intervened and the special Bruderschaft was held three years later, in September 1945. When it finally came, the meeting had a single agenda item: 'This consultation was so to say finally organized to advise with regard to the shunning of excommunicated people because the understanding on shunning for a long time has been diversely viewed within the church.' Bishop Reimer, as always, was in charge of the meeting, but this time he also outlined the very manner in which the question was to be debated. As he put it, three imperatives required consideration: the authority of scripture, the teachings of Mennonite forebears, and present circumstances. Reimer led the assembled men through a study of scripture, noting that various members aligned themselves with different texts. Some took a New Testament injunction by St Paul as recorded in the book of 2 Thessalonians 3:14 literally: 'if anyone refuses to obey what I have written ... have nothing to do with him, so that he will feel that he is in the wrong.' Others were in favor of an even stricter application found in the Old Testament book of Ezekiel 44:6: it called the faithful to 'be careful about which men are admitted to the temple' and to avoid going 'beyond all bounds ... by admitting ... the uncircumcised in heart ... to frequent my sanctuary and profane my temple.' But then this teaching was contradicted in the New Testament book of Romans 10:17, which stated that 'faith comes from what is preached.' Clearly the church could not hold to all three biblical texts. How could the sinner come to faith if barred from the temple, that is, from hearing the Word of God?

Bishop Reimer's answer to the conundrum was to suggest that church members follow 'the simple spirit of God' and 'loosen up on worship service attendance' but 'tighten up on personal encounters in order to win more.' The resolution that came from the meeting reflected Reimer's vision: 'Within the context of our time we believe that ... as shunning cannot be totally understood ... that we no longer consider it a disorder when excommunicated [members] attend a worship service ... However, to separate [from the errant member] in general eating, as in business and social encounters we shall become stricter.' The resolution attempted to bridge two worlds; in the urbanizing world preaching, not social ostracization, would change an errant member. But the resolution added a caveat rooted in communitarianism – shunning was still the way in which 'the excommunicated members can be won through love.' An attempt had been made to keep an old teaching through compromise. That the compromise would not squelch the cacophony of discordant voices was apparent from the recorded verbal dissension of 'two brethren' who argued after Bishop Reimer had spoken that 'shunning was not even scriptural or necessary.'[18]

Establishing an Old Order in Quellen Kolonie, Mexico

The September 1945 resolution with regard to shunning was a hollow declaration. During the very years that conservative members were clamoring for a clarification of the church's stance on excommunication, they were also recognizing that the four Kleine Gemeinde congregations – Steinbach, Kleefeld, Blumenort, and Prairie Rose – were too diverse to continue operating as a single church unit. As early as September 1936 the joint Bruderschaft considered whether or not 'as the church grows larger, that each church site be allowed to run more of its own affairs.' It borrowed the English word 'district' from the public school system to clarify its meaning. Through the early 1940s this question of church districts was raised annually. At one Bruderschaft in February 1942 Bishop Reimer seemed to be pleading for the end to the idea of a unified, central church: 'everything has become too large and complex, and at this point ... it is time to consider specific districts each under its own leader or bishop.'[19] The official separation of the church into districts finally occurred after the war, in October 1945.

It soon became clear, however, that even the separation into districts would do little to restore peace to the beleaguered Gemeinde. In the very year that Bishop Reimer reasserted shunning as a form of church discipline and divided the troubled Gemeinde into districts to accommodate the progressive town preachers, he faced a rebellion from the far right, from the followers of his ultraconservative cousin, farmer-preacher Cornelius R. Reimer. So worried was the dissenting Cornelius Reimer about the Gemeinde's drift to modernity that he led a small group of like-minded members to meet separately in a schoolhouse in the district of Heuboden, near Kleefeld.[20] In December 1945 Bishop Peter Reimer summoned cousin Cornelius to a special Bruderschaft to explain his rebellion.[21]

Two opposing views were expressed at the meeting. Cornelius Reimer argued that his separatist Heubodener group was right to oppose substantive shifts in the lifestyle and teaching of the wider Kleine Gemeinde church: there was too much pride, too much association with the world, too much smoking and drinking, too weak a position on shunning, too much verbal prayer, too easy an association with non–Kleine Gemeinde preachers, too much harmony singing and use of musical instruments, too much voting in government elections, and too great a support for the Zeitgeist infused at the evangelically oriented Steinbach Bible School.[22]

The younger evangelistic preachers from Steinbach responded, countering the rebel Cornelius Reimer and putting forward an alternative interpretation of the state of the Kleine Gemeinde Church. Steinbach farmer and lay preacher Peter Kroeker asked how 'pride' could be identified when 'we live in a different age'; businessman and lay preacher Peter Friesen wondered whether the word 'Gemeinde' really entailed unified practice in all things; Steinbach Bible School teacher Ben Reimer wanted a debate based on scripture; and the most recently elected Steinbach preacher, schoolteacher Peter J.B. Reimer, a first cousin to his namesake the bishop, suggested that the brethren leave this 'sorrowful' exercise of lamenting and get on with the 'spiritual' work, presumably the work of evangelization. The making of two sections of the Kleine Gemeinde was underway. What the younger progressives were asking for with their privileging of scripture, spiritual work, and the autonomy of the local church was for a church that would still be Mennonite, but able to negotiate its way in a wider English-speaking world through the language of evangelicalism.[23]

The December 1945 meeting did not establish the desired unity. It did ferret out the voices that became even more pointed in subsequent meetings. On 31 December, three days later, a second round of debate ended with the conservative Cornelius R. Reimer declaring that he 'could not see that we can get together today ... [for] we are simply not one in the spirit.' Just two months later in February 1946 Bishop Peter P. Reimer made his move. He openly sided with the conservatives by releasing a document entitled, '*Eine Aufrafung der Kleine Gemeinde*,' literally, 'a wake-up call to the Kleine Gemeinde.' It was an ironic title for it implied that revivalism and evangelicalism were lulling the congregations to sleep. Kleine Gemeinde members, he wrote, needed to be alerted to their traditional calling to 'enter by the narrow gate' and to refuse to 'mind high things'; true church work could not be pursued so long as 'pride and worldliness force their way among us.' Bishop Reimer repeated in detail the points of the December 1945 meeting, but he interwove them with biblical authority. The language was stronger, the gulf between current practice and past principle were sharply defined. Weddings with elaborate dress desecrated a 'holy and orderly' moment. Choral music countered the 'simple and graceful' songs. Alcohol consumption linked one to an 'unrighteous' world. The use of provincial courts to collect debts was an idealization of individual rights. Attending the 'newly classified and graduated Bible schools' led to the veneration of 'learned scribes,' the very practice condemned by Christ. The open communion service undermined its stated purpose, that is, to bring together only the faithful and thus to bolster unity amongst God's people. Women's failure to wear the prescribed and uniform headdress, the black kerchief, violated 'unity and simplicity.' Sports resulted in 'joking, amusement, greed, and lust.' Bishop Reimer noted that these were not rules that led to salvation, but teachings based on 'our perception of the gospel and on our forebears.'

Although the Manitoba Bruderschaft endorsed it, this conservative position became the ideological basis for a migration that began in 1948 and eventually involved eighty-five families, 15 percent of the Manitoba Kleine Gemeinde. The move took them to Chihuahua State, Mexico. There, in a mountain valley of the eastern Sierra Madre, they joined about twelve thousand other mostly Old Colony Mennonites whose parents had emigrated from Canada in the 1920s to avoid Manitoba and Saskatchewan's assimilative school laws.[24] In Mexico they created a separate Kleine Gemeinde colony guided by its own Bruderschaft. Translating the name of the Los Jagueyes ranch purchased from Alberto Estrada into the German equivalent, *Quellen Kolonie* (Springs Colony), they created an idealized conservative, old order community.

An early barrage of letters to the *Christlicher Familienfreund* documented the year-long migration effort. In July of 1948 an advance guard of families loaded trucks with farm machinery and cars with personal effects and headed south to Mexico. There they established an outpost and, importantly, planted the first oat fields and gardens. During autumn came a steady stream of families, each taking their tearful farewells in Manitoba and heading out for the long road trip down US 81 to Kansas then southwest on US 54 through Meade County where ties with distant relatives were strengthened, past the 'wondrous' Carlsbad Caverns, southwest to El Paso to face the red tape at the border. Heading into Mexico the migrants adjusted to the sight of 'dark' people, before moving onto the high, semi-arid plain of Los Jagueyes to break the land, construct red clay brick houses, and begin the long process of institution building.[25] In all of this, letter writers thanked their Canadian brothers and sisters for their prayerful support. As Heinrich and Elisabeth Plett noted in a December 1948 letter, 'When we think back to Canada, to all the beloved members and friends, we feel very indebted to be thankful for all the love and prayers that have been directed to us.'[26]

The migration itself, however, was much more than a physical move, it was an embrace of an old communitarian religious faith that emphasized Christian discipleship. Even before a new Bruderschaft had been established, letters from the migrants justified the relocation as redemptive, worth the pain the church members endured. 'It would probably be perfect in this world if we could all stay and work together,' wrote Johann and Tina Reimer in February 1949. 'How and what the Lord has in mind that He scatters his children so [far] in the world, that is not to be understood,' they wrote, 'but, no doubt, it will serve to the best; on that we can trust completely.'[27] A strong feeling of religious submission and trust also developed; it was articulated with the words, 'here we sow with tears, there we harvest with joy.'[28] And, clearly alluding to a fear that several of the early migrants voiced, migrant Albert Plett counseled his fellows in May 1949 with the following semi-apocalyptic biblical teaching: 'prepare ... for when the Lord will appear [for] the day that he will come as a thief in the night will be much more serious ... than when a thief comes and wants a little money in this world.'[29]

Bishop Peter P. Reimer's own depiction of the reestablishment of the Kleine Gemeinde and its Bruderschaft in Mexico in the spring of 1949 was more temperate, but firm nevertheless. His address that reestablished the Bruderschaft was replete with words such as 'unity,' 'unison,' 'reaffirmation,' and 'historic authority.'[30] The new Bruderschaft possessed moral authority that was rooted in the very act of migration. Members' agreement was recorded in their letters. Be as those who 'ground themselves in the true faith,' wrote farmer Jake K. Friesen in October 1949. He then added a special message to 'Canadian ministers' to 'render that for which you have been called.'[31] Widower Heinrich E. Plett had a message for Canadian youth: do not be like 'the one who places his hands on the plough and looks back, he is not ready for the Kingdom of God. Do not look back on Sodom as Lot's wife, nor [as] the children of Israel to Egypt. Run patiently through the struggles.'[32] Still others pointed out the logical outcome of remaining in Canada and enjoying its more sophisticated economy. As farmer Isaac P. Loewen noted, 'Yes, there are great advances being made [in Canada], as in highways, hydro electricity, hospitals, etc. These are very useful to have; but do we too eagerly partake of this, to try it out? My thinking is not that we should suppress these things, but if we take part so completely, will we not be too easily [tempted to] fight for the government of this world?'[33]

The increasingly progressive Canadian churches created a countertext that challenged the legitimacy of the conservatives' migration. The text became especially important because parts of it were crafted by missionary relatives of the very migrants who had fled the evangelistic tendency in Canada. Ironically, these missionaries travelled to Mexico and used their kinship links at Quellen Kolonie to commence evangelistic work. In fact, one of the most progressive Canadian ministers, the Steinbach schoolteacher Peter J.B. Reimer, took a Mennonite Central Committee assignment in the town of Cuauhtémoc to help establish hospitals and schools in the region just as the migration of the conservative Kleine Gemeinde began in 1948. Oral tradition suggests that the controversial, conservative preacher Cornelius R. Reimer, who had been elevated to bishop after Peter P. Reimer's death, looked skeptically on the Steinbach minister's presence and deflected his offer to give a sermon at Quellen Kolonie.[34] But even more troubling was the move by the evangelistically minded Manitoba Kleine Gemeinde to send missionaries to Quellen Kolonie itself, to use it as an initial base from which to conduct missionary activities among the colony's Mexican neighbors. One Manitoba missionary recalled the ambivalent situation: 'We knew where we were heading since our relatives waited for us in Quellen [Kolonie], probably with some trepidation. Would we be accepted by the rest of the Kleine Gemeinde out there? ... Later we found out that in Mexico some spiritual leaders had fears of the "black cloud" coming from Canada.'[35] A history of that mission effort notes: 'It appears that God used the immigration [to Mexico] as a springboard for the new [missionary] work, even though the group wanted to simply start life away from the progressive changes going on in the Kleine Gemeinde Church in Canada.'[36] By 1954 when the Manitoba missionaries in Mexico converted and baptized a Mexican citizen, Ernesto Palominos, a new point of conflict arose. Palominos was not accepted by the Kleine Gemeinde at Quellen Kolonie and the Manitoba missionaries cited the church for racism saying it was no better than the Jews who in Acts 10:28 uttered 'you know that it is forbidden for Jews to mix with people of another race and visit them.'[37]

At about this time the Quellen Kolonie Bruderschaft acted to make the migration to Mexico an act of total separation from the Manitoba churches. Continued membership in the Canadian church initially had survived the migration. After Bishop Reimer died in 1949, senior Manitoba ministers regularly traveled to Mexico to assist the congregation with baptism, communion, and the election of ministers until 1952, when Cornelius Reimer was chosen as bishop.[38] Ironically, this was the very year that the Manitoba Bruderschaft voted to replace the old name of Kleine Gemeinde with the new designation Evangelical Mennonite Church or EMC as it quickly came to be known. This too was the year in which the Steinbach church purchased a piano and began plans to sponsor the opening of a church in Winnipeg for its increasing number of city members. Cornelius Reimer made these changes in Canada the occasion to see his vision of the church in Mexico fulfilled. Citing the Manitoba EMC for 'worldliness' he led his Bruderschaft to agree to secession from the Manitoba church in 1955.[39] A secession letter was sent to the Manitoba Bruderschaft, which in turn reported to its members that the Mexico church had written to say that it 'will not be able to remain with us any longer as differences between us and them are too great.'[40] Others members expressed a deeper remorse: a more evangelistic member in Mexico caught in the middle noted that this was a 'sorrowful road ... which in such a situation created sadness and heart ache.'[41] The response from the Manitoba churches was to assist the more evangelistic members at Quellen Kolonie to establish a tiny separate congregation, known locally as the *Westgruppe*. A growing sense developed among the Mexico Mennonites that the Canadians had compromised and were on the fast road to assimilation. After the 1955 schism fewer Quellen Kolonie members wrote to the *Familienfreund*. Those who did delivered news of health and death, aiming more to strengthen kinship networks than church ties. In 1958 a further division occurred when the more conservative half of Quellen Kolonie moved even farther south to British Honduras. In this Central American country they established the ultraconservative Spanish Lookout Colony, making the social fragmentation from the Manitoba church community irrevocable.

A Cosmology Fit for Town

The imposition of the district concept and the migration and separation of the Kleine Gemeinde's most conservative sector allowed the Steinbach church in Manitoba to become even more progressive in the increasingly pluralistic environment of the 1950s. This progressivism was accompanied by an intense and ongoing debate with sister churches in the countryside and its own Bruderschaft or 'Brotherhood Meeting,' as it became known in the 1950s. The town church did not have the same social control over its district as did the rural churches and church growth could not be assured through natural increase and application of church discipline. The children of town members did not necessarily join the church upon marriage, nor did youth who wished to be baptized necessarily join the church of their parents. Even in the 1940s half a dozen of the churches in rapidly growing Steinbach offered more glamorous programming and were more evangelistic than the Kleine Gemeinde. Shunning was not a useful form of church discipline in town and the Bruderschaft no longer had control over the community. But even as the shunning was put aside, old communitarian concerns found ways of leaving their imprint on the new evangelicalism.

On the surface the history of the Steinbach Kleine Gemeinde or the Steinbach EMC as it came to be known, paralleled that of its sister church, the Emmanuel Mennonite Church in Meade County, Kansas. The Steinbach EMC became a strong proponent of proactive evangelistic services. It endorsed an interchurch program to construct a massive, thousand-seat, woodframe auditorium dubbed the Tabernacle, to host community-wide religious crusades, emotional revival meetings.[42] It participated in the establishment of an evangelistic children's summer camp on Red Rock Lake in eastern Manitoba's picturesque Whiteshell Provincial Park. It was instrumental in expanding the local Steinbach Bible School to include high school education and broader Bible training for youth and aspiring ministers. Its members helped establish the locally based Western Gospel Mission that sent preachers throughout the Canadian prairies and especially to communities dominated by conservative, old-order Mennonites, inviting people to consider personal, evangelistic revival. Steinbach ministers such as Peter Friesen spoke of faith in personal and emotional language; his diary of 1943 notes in overtly evangelistic language that a Tabernacle revival meeting had led 'Brother Barney and his wife ... [to] give ... themselves up to the Lord; praise him; prayers are answered.' Two years later his diary records attendance at a 'short-course evangelistic school' in Indiana where listening to two non-Mennonite American revivalists left him 'just melted in yielding to the spirit.'[43]

It was not long before the Steinbach church's agenda of ridding itself of old-order ways confronted the practice of shunning. After 1945 each of the Hanover Kleine Gemeinde church districts convened its own Bruderschaft and in contrast to the Bruderschafts of the rural districts the Steinbach meetings reflected an increasing leniency toward church discipline. True, a September 1947 resolution from Steinbach ministers states that 'we want to keep the shunning on the excommunicated brethren.' Other signs, however, indicated another spirit.[44] In 1946, for example, younger minister Ben D. Reimer noted defiantly in his private papers that he was against shunning, or as he put it, withholding 'hand and kiss' from an excommunicated person.[45] And Steinbach's Bruderschaft itself moved cautiously on matters of church discipline. In September 1946, for example, it discussed the 'fall' of a woman's marriage; the problem was that the young woman, without adequately repenting, had joined the new, non-Mennonite, evangelistic Emmanuel Church in town. Even if the Bruderschaft had wanted to exert discipline, excommunication and shunning had little effect in a pluralistic community, and the church's only recourse was 'to deal somewhat patiently with the sister.'[46] The clearest sign that the Steinbach church was waffling on the ban was that it was cited for that very transgression by rural leaders. In April 1948 Peter P. Reimer, by then bishop of only his home church, Blumenort, wrote the Steinbach congregation to admonish it for allowing the use of musical instruments, for supporting the local Bible school with its fundamentalistic and dispensationalist teachings, and for weakening its resolve to maintain the practice of shunning, or as he put it, 'keeping the ban.' The Steinbach members responded defiantly from within their own Bruderschaft: '[We] agreed that we could not change our ways,' read their minutes, although they added their intention to 'work along' with the wider church wherever possible.[47]

What 'along' meant was clear at a joint Bruderschaft that was held to reorganize the Kleine Gemeinde after the Mexico-bound exodus in December 1948. The town church agreed to support selected Kleine Gemeinde programs, including the German-language *Familienfreund*, Mennonite Central Committee relief projects, and joint youth meetings called the *Jugendverein*. They even agreed to a common church worship calendar in which local preachers occasionally visited neighboring churches, even if it meant the uneasy mixing of town and rural preachers. The Steinbach Bruderschaft even agreed that the radio was 'very harmful, dangerous, yes, and even poisonous,' and noted that radio as signalled by 'those aerials on cars' also seemed a sign of pride and ostentation. Finally, the Steinbach assembly concurred that its venerated Western Gospel Mission's practice of accepting women missionaries who wore 'bobbed hair' and men who used 'jewelry' needed 'regulating.' How could messengers of Christ dress in worldly fashion?

But Steinbach refused to maintain the old practice of shunning errant members. Increasingly even their simple excommunication without shunning was abandoned as a form of church discipline. With reference to the question 'How are we to deal with those members who marry outside a Mennonite church?' the church secretary noted a deep division: 'Several were for excommunication, others merely for registering [our views] via letter.' Those who supported the former approach expressed a concern that 'we do not diminish [the use] of excommunication'; the latter responded that 'we do not want to be too strict.'[48] When the matter of shunning was raised again at 'a special Bruderschaft' of all four Kleine Gemeinde church districts in February 1949, it was clear that the old practice would have to change. The elderly Bishop Peter P. Reimer and the most conservative members of the Kleine Gemeinde had relocated to Mexico. In answer to the question of how 'shunning [is] ... to be administered,' the Bruderschaft was content to register the feeling 'that it is difficult to administer,' and express a 'need to examine it fully in the future.'[49]

This note signalled the Steinbach church's final intention to leave shunning in favor of evangelicalism. During the 1950s it openly pursued church growth. It became the strongest advocate of the ideologically significant name change from Kleine Gemeinde to Evangelical Mennonite Church and the short, crisp acronym EMC. It also dropped its insistence on plain dress for its members. By June 1947 the Steinbach ministers had already gained such a reputation for open-mindedness that they were asked by a young businessman, Cornie P. Loewen, to accommodate his fiancee who at their upcoming wedding 'would like to dress as is the present fashion' – that is, in a long, white wedding dress instead of the traditional dark and inconspicuous dress.[50] By the 1950s Steinbach's progressive lay minister and travelling evangelist, Ben D. Reimer, openly derided concepts of plain dress.[51] Instead of warning members to remain aloof from urban life, the Steinbach church now became a leading force in establishing an EMC church in Winnipeg's north-end working-class district, on Aberdeen Avenue.[52] During the 1950s Steinbach also shed the old, simple, German-language services adopted instead English-language worship services that included the singing of upbeat gospel songs that by 1952 were accompanied by a piano.[53] Throughout the late 1940s and the 1950s it flaunted another long-standing practice and opened its doors to evangelistic missionaries and revivalists without regard to religious denomination.[54] Members recall different details about revivalist messages pitched in the late 1940s – Hyman Appleman from Chicago giving hope to parents that wayward children would 'be saved,' Hyman Goldstein from California 'exhorting sinners to come forward,' – but the idea was the same, an outsider coming to turn Mennonite youth to God.[55] The church business minutes record these events through the 1950s: 'Rev. Balaster' impressed the church by showing a 'film' in 1955; 'Missionary Norm Taylor from the Northern Canada Evangelical Mission' visited in 1957; 'Mr. Flumbaum, the Jewish missionary in Winnipeg' came in another year.[56] As a result, the Steinbach EMC became the happening place in the town's religious landscape. It grew by 62 percent in the 1950s alone and had attained 520 members by 1960. This growth made it the largest EMC church in Manitoba and enabled it to justify the construction of a handsome new steep-roofed, open-ceiling, 850-seat sanctuary in 1959.[57]

The transformation of the Steinbach EMC, however, was not a whole-sale adoption of evangelicalism. It is true that the church now employed excommunication only for the most egregious of wrongdoings, including adultery, apostasy, and outright crime. In 1957, for example, Steinbach's Brotherhood banned a middle-aged father who declared to the ministers that he could not 'any longer believe that there is a God.' In that year, too, it banned a member whose 'wayward life' landed him in provincial jail.[58] But throughout the 1950s the church battled to keep some semblance of the old conservative, anticonsumeristic, and simple lifestyle. Time and again, the Steinbach ministerial dealt with the 'wedding' and 'jewelery' question. It was concerned with the 'worldly dress' of both the grooms and the brides, and especially they balked at the 'double ring' ceremony that sanctioned and indeed exhibited the wearing of ostentatious jewelery. Only in 1958, after years of opposing this practice on moral grounds, the church ministerial finally accepted 'wedding rings and wedding dresses, as "quite all right" if ... conservatively done'; but again it warned against 'excess.'[59] But even then the ministerial asked itself whether there was 'anything that can be done about it, as it seems always to be used more.' The new pastor, college-educated Archie Penner, promised to 'present something based on scripture' to the membership but acknowledged that 'it will require much grace.'[60] The opposition to the public display of jewelery, however, lingered on and as late as 1964 the ministerial voiced concern that its members were practising 'double ring weddings ... directly in opposition from what had been counseled.'[61]

Even if the town church no longer employed excommunication, it continued to criticize members who openly engaged in the 'ways of the world.' Sometimes concerns were raised euphemistically: prayer was invoked for a 'sister's ... great sorrow about her daughter ... who is presently in Ontario.' Oftentimes frivolity was noted: 'our young members ... [who] are attending ... hockey games in Winnipeg and other places,' 'the spiritual condition of the construction camps where some of our members work'; the brother who 'lives so worldly' and will be 'taken into the work.'[62] Overt confrontation was even employed when the church observed questionable business practices among its members. In 1964 a popular farm equipment dealer in the church was confronted on a questionable – and according to some an even illegal – business financing scheme. When the man allowed his name to stand as a minister the other ministers asserted that they had 'annoying misgivings' with the businessman. When he was actually elected, the Brotherhood took up the entire painful issue. Eventually so much pressure was put on the minister that he resigned his post.[63]

The Steinbach EMC also maintained a semblance of communitarian concern in the wider town society, driven as it was by evangelical schools, consumer impulses, and the messages of mass media. In 1959 pastor Archie Penner earned a Master of Divinity degree from Wheaton College in Chicago and published his thesis as a book under the title *The Christian, the State and the New Testament*. The book issued such a powerful argument for the continued separation of Anabaptist people from government that the Wheaton College examiners considered Penner 'un-American.' Mennonites, argued Penner, could accomplish little by engaging in the self-serving electoral process; only as a corporate body could it act 'as the preservative of society.'[64] During Penner's tenure as pastor, the Steinbach church reasserted its traditional convictions, including the principles that military service contradicted its Anabaptist faith, that Calvinist ideas of predestination undermined concepts of free will and moral responsibility, and that religious calling demanded social responsibility. In 1963 when the Baptist Church–dominated Winnipeg Bible Institute, the very school Pastor Penner had once attended, asked to be invited to the Steinbach EMC to 'bring a program' the ministerial was unequivocal: 'we are not very happy to have them come because 1) they are aggressively against non-resistance, 2) stress eternal security too much, 3) are on socially shallow ground.'[65] Only a small step separated this position from the one that led the church to share its moral values with the entire town of Steinbach. Thus in 1964 the ministers of the Steinbach EMC urged all members to sign a petition 'against liquor advertising' in the local German-language *Steinbach Post*. In 1965 the church wrote the English-language *Carillon News* that it was deeply concerned about the billing of movies in the newspaper. And in the same year it voiced a concern about the 'presentation of Mormon music' on the local radio station, CFAM.[66] If the town church could not escape the modern world, perhaps it could influence its moral posture.

Even as it asserted itself in public, the EMC moved to end forever the practice of shunning. In 1960 a joint meeting of all members of the wider EMC ministerial, which had grown from five to twenty-one churches in a mere twelve years, reaffirmed the need to 'practice the scriptural teaching of avoidance.' But the motion had little effect. By this time neither of the EMC's two largest churches were actually practising it. In the large rural district of Blumenort the ministerial had already concluded that it was ineffective and in a pluralistic society even repressive. In the Steinbach church, opposition to it had become overt. In 1961 minister Peter J.B. Reimer tabled a historic report on the practice of shunning and concluded that rarely had it been practised in complete strictness 'during the 2000 years since Christ' and that in Russia only the EMC's forebears, the Kleine Gemeinde Mennonites, had practised it strictly. Both Steinbach and Blumenort were seeking an equilibrium that combined evangelicalism and communitarianism. By setting aside the shunning they signalled their intention to engage the dynamic midcentury world as individuals. By objecting to military service and the concepts of predestination they insisted that the ethical dimension of an old Anabaptism still had currency.

The Bruderschaft in Manitoba's old order Mennonite churches was a social site in which old and new ideologies interacted with the everyday lives of church members. This patriarchal meeting of male members did more than approve annual budgets and elect church officers. It was also much more than a meeting of the members. It was a centuries-old social gathering in which religious meaning was enforced, contested, and reformulated. In worship services preachers could exhort, entreat, and encourage. At annual church conferences elected delegates could debate general policy. But at the monthly Bruderschaft members rose to debate old and new ideas; ministers censured specific behaviors with reference to biblical teaching; the bishop exerted his moral authority by marshalling the ultimate church mechanism of social control, the excommunication and the shunning. The Bruderschaft was more than the most dynamic of church gatherings among conservative Mennonites. It was the site of contesting cosmologies.

An examination of one conservative Bruderschaft, that of the Mennonite Kleine Gemeinde of the RM of Hanover and the town of Steinbach, shows a congregation at a crossroads. At this particular juncture in history, it faced new technologies, popular cultures, and integrative state activities that fundamentally changed rural life. It was a time of religious volatility. The deliberations of the Bruderschaft express vividly the painful adjustments that a rural-dominated church group underwent as rurality itself was transformed. But it also provides insight into how ideology and cosmology evolved. For Mennonites, inherited ideas of community pointed to an exclusive, communitarian body literally applying the principles of a simple lifestyle, non-violence, and humility to the everyday. This relationship was made more complex by the social changes that occurred in the middle decades of the twentieth century. The large Steinbach Evangelical Mennonite Church in Manitoba may have given up on the shunning and may have openly accepted evangelicalism, but it also maintained inherited principles concerning pacifism, an old amillennialistic view of the end times, and its traditional support for the relief and refugee work of the Mennonite Central Committee. If it had ended the literal shunning of the sinful, it nonetheless continued to shun in symbolic terms the social forces of mid-twentieth-century Canada.

6 The Rise and Fall of the Cheerful Homemaker: Womanhood in Kansas

Mennonites Redefining Gender

'I made butter, sewed and set 10 hens'; 'I worked hard at "keeping Saturday"'; 'I worked hard at cleaning the chicken barn'; 'I and Helena sewed and did the chores.'[1] These were some of Helena Doerksen Reimer's entries in a March 1949 German-language diary, descriptions of the everyday life of women on a Meade County, Kansas, farm.[2] In 1952 another Mennonite woman in the *Meade Globe Press*'s 'Coffee Chatter' column created a text that represented a different female world. This unnamed newspaper correspondent described the local 'Cheerful Homemakers' Home Demonstration Unit (HDU) that met regularly for all-day meetings to discuss an array of issues: topics such as 'smart shopping,' 'dressing attractively,' and 'global awareness' were followed by 'coffee and dainties' or 'coffee and chiffon cake.' By the 1970s a third female experience was depicted by Mennonite women in the local Meade history book. They wrote that they spent most of their time, once their children were grown, at their professions in the town of Meade. They were teachers and nurses, but also bookkeepers, hairdressers, motel managers, cooks, gift-shop owners, dental assistants, and business secretaries.[3] The three texts – the farm household diary, the Coffee Chatter columns, and the history book notes describing women's professions – illustrate three distinct patterns of work and leisure in Meade County between 1930 and 1980. They also demonstrate the sequence of change in the cultural worlds of rural women. The symbols and systems of meaning that expressed their principles and the values and views of life they espoused changed dramatically in the mid-twentieth-century decades.[4]

The changing roles of farm women over time has been the focus of much enquiry. Some historians argue that the very social context of the pioneer or frontier family farm provided women with important degrees of power and status. The argument continues that this autonomy was lost as agriculture became more commercialized and technologized and as urbanization began undermining the old basis of the farm community. In the 1980s Martine Segalen posited that although women in the nineteenth-century French countryside were in a subordinate position legally, the household economy produced a particular 'man-wife relationship ... [that was] based not on the absolute authority of one over the other, but on the complementarity of the two.'[5] Numerous works in North America have reflected this reasoning.[6] Other works, however, have questioned this dichotomy. Veronica Strong-Boag in Canada, for example, argues that the farm household's productive side did not guarantee that men and women 'pulled in double harness'; rather it often meant that women 'pulled a double load.' Deborah Fink in the United States adds the caveat that although 'the economic autonomy arising from women's participation in production has been a necessary ingredient in their gaining control of their lives ... the organization of labor within the nuclear family undermined [the farm household's] liberating potential.'[7]

This ongoing discussion raises the possibility that the women of Meade County may have experienced the world in a particular way. It highlights the importance of the county's semi-arid wheat culture and its long distances from larger urban centers. It also suggests that religious and ethnic context shaped distinctive gendered identities. It opens the path to determining the significance of social and economic changes associated with the Great Disjuncture, especially the effect on women of the farm household's embrace of mechanization, economies of scale, government programs, and consumer culture.[8] It even argues that the importance of the changing nature of the media in which women expressed social change – the personal diary, the newspaper column, and the hagiographical history book – shaped the degree of gender self-consciousness, the very nature of femininity, and the expressions of female autonomy in women's lives.

In Meade County the women's environment was shaped partly by environmental and partly by economic forces. Gender relations were affected by 'the disheartening, endless, numbing succession of dirt storms and drought conditions' of the Great Depression.[9] They were also affected by the unstable wheat economy that followed the Second

World War. The shift from wheat production to mixed farming during
the Depression and then to a highly mechanized commodity specialization in wheat and cattle during the 1950s affected household social
relations, increasing the economic significance of women during the
Depression and diminishing their influence in household production in
the post-war period. But demography and ethnicity also affected Mennonite women's lives, especially the Meade County Mennonites' traditional emphasis on social boundary maintenance and household
self-sufficiency. The evangelicalization of the Meade Mennonite churches
and with it the development of 'symbolic ethnicity' and acceptance of
North American Protestantism made for easier interactions with the
wider world and emulation of female models in that world. The evolving economy in the 1970s that caused the end of many farm households
both compelled and enabled the Mennonite women to break from the
Cheerful Homemaker mold, consider smaller families, and return to
remunerative work. In each instance – before, during, and after the era
of the homemaker – womanhood was defined in distinctive ways. Each
era may have provided men with specific privileges; each era too required that women adapt their own responses to the world in order that
they might establish their own roles and meanings within it.

The history of Mennonite women in Meade County is more than a
history of one of the sexes. It is a history of gender through the perspective of the women. Though this chapter focuses on the worlds of women,
the voices of their men are never far in the background. The three
phases of Mennonite women's history in Meade also reflected the evolving experience of Meade Mennonite men. The women of the farm
household in the 1940s joined with their men in maintaining an agrarian culture based on commercial wheat production and self-sufficiency
in foodstuffs. Their men found their measure of worth in an organic
community and they realized that the household's economic well-being
relied on the farm labor of their wives. The Cheerful Homemakers of
the 1950s lived on increasingly large and technologized farms where
their husbands were machine operators, marketers of farm produce,
and participants in government programs. These men often measured
success by land ownership and farm equipment acquisition, but also by
access to consumer products and leisure. The women who in the 1970s
found employment in town had husbands who were compelled to
accept the wage labor or the professional salaries of their wives in order
to strengthen household finances. These men had left the restricted
economy of wheat production to make their homes as members of an

ethnic minority in an American town. They also constructed their own gendered world in broadly based trade associations, church men's clubs, and civic organizations. As economic and social changes linked to the Great Disjuncture swept Meade County, the relationship of women and men were transformed. So were the very notions of what constituted the culture of a particular gender.

The Female Farm Householder

Helena Doerksen Reimer's 1949 *Tagebuch* (diary) describes a life centered around the Mennonite household.[10] The numerous suffixes of *sehr* (very much) that followed descriptions of work signify the amount of hard work she directed to the economic strength of the Mennonite farm. Helena's diary clearly intends to outline the contours of the farm household. It is the economic record of the entire family and even of a wider kinship network. Her diary documents the work of fifty-seven-year-old husband Klaas, a carpenter and farmer who spent days each month building in nearby Meade, Fowler, and Dodge City. The diary also lists the work activities of her teenaged sons, Bernard, Gerhard, and Johann, including the seasonally varied farm work: fencing in winter, planting rye and sorghum in spring, harvesting the wheat in June, endless days of 'one-waying' (disking) in July, planting winter wheat in September, and repairing equipment in November. And the diary describes the many times that Helena's married daughter, twenty-five-year-old Helena Jr and husband Martin Bartel, came to help out.

More important, the diary places Helena's own work within the context of the household economic unit. Her descriptions, for example, of the Monday wash, Tuesday ironing, Saturday dusting and baking are placed on the same line in the diary as the activities of Klaas and the boys. Moreover, much of the work Helena describes is also overtly productive, generating direct income for the family. Her view of the house is both domestic and economic. Here, as she describes it, eggs are cleaned and prepared so that Klaas, or Klaas and Helena together, can take them to the market in Dodge City. Here too, Helena uses the DaLaval cream separator to generate another commodity to take to the creamery in Meade and old methods are used to prepare butter, yet another commodity. The raw materials of these commodities are secured by Helena in the barnyard. Each morning she begins the milking of the ten cows until the boys finish their chores and continue the task, then she feeds the pigs and tends the two barns of chickens. This latter activity includes gathering eggs from the layers, feeding the fryers, and, as time allows, cleaning the barns and setting the brood hens on hatching eggs.[11]

A second document, the financial account of the Reimer household kept by Klaas, undergirds Helena's implicit perception of mutuality. The farm was typical of western Kansas Mennonite farms. It consisted of 420 acres, 230 of which were planted to winter wheat and 50 to feedgrains – maize, kaffir, oats, and barley. Moreover, the Reimers kept 10 dairy cows, 150 chickens, 14 pigs, and maintained an orchard of 10 peach and 10 cherry trees for home consumption and local markets. By the end of the year, the sector of the farm involving Helena that produced the chickens, eggs, cream, and hogs earned $1549.26. This total was less than 20 percent of the $9534 income derived from grain and cattle sales, but it was twice as much as the $766 Klaas brought home from carpentry. Arguably the net profits of the barnyard were proportionately larger than the gross figures indicated. They required few technologies and had tapped little of the $1191 spent on tractor, truck, and car fuel and oil. Finally, another of Helena's contributions to the family income appeared in the $559 in oil and gas royalties from land that she had inherited from her parents in Haskell County. Both Helena's diary and Klaas's account book suggest that the couple saw their roles in the operation of the farm economy as being interdependent.[12]

Helena's diary also documents her role in community formation, especially in nurturing relationships among other women in the ethnic community. One means of doing so that her diary suggests is the operation of a small business selling vinegar. The German nomenclature, 'Henry A. Friesensche' – in which the feminine suffix 'sche' denotes that the person is Mrs. Henry A. Friesen – suggests a formality for the sake of the diary; Mrs Friesen's visit on 7 January to purchase vinegar doubtless entailed no such formality. The same familiar female culture would have attended visits from 'Menno Wiensche' (Mrs Menno Wiens) and 'Sam Friesensche' (Mrs Sam Friesen) who dropped by on 5 July for vinegar purchases. The diary describes visits to relatives and neighbors, sometimes with her husband, but also, as on 24 January, while Klaas was at 'H.H. Reimers,' 'I [and] Heinrich, and Helena and Martin, were at Helena and Susie's.' Occasionally it notes that she helped out at the neighbors, as on the 19 March hog-butchering bee, when 'we both and [daughter] Helen and Martin and [sister] Helen [H. Reimer] helped butcher hogs at the parents, while Bernard and Gerhard helped butcher an ox at "Gerhard H. Doerksche."' The diary describes her participation in the Emmanuel Mennonite Church not only during worship services but at special evening services and the women's sewing circles that produced clothing and blankets for international distribution by the Mennonite Central Committee. Clearly Helena's world was set in household and ethnic group for her diary describes relatively few visits outside the immediate community. Only occasionally does she accompany Klaas on trips to market the eggs and butter or to purchase a new batch of chicks in Dodge City. Only occasionally does she travel to Fowler 'with Gerhard and Helen to the doctor' or visit auction sales in Meade or Fowler.[13]

If the old-order Mennonite concern for self-sufficiency undergirded women's productive roles in farm households, traditional Mennonite inheritance practices – the partible bilateral inheritance of both Dutch and Swiss Mennonites – bolstered the prestige of those roles within the community.[14] 'Father was very insistent that the inheritance be kept equal,' recalled one Meade man who left the community in the 1950s.[15] 'Each one of us, the boys and the girl, got 80 acres upon marriage and each of the children got a small house, John a $3000 trailer home, and I, a small house,' recalled a woman in another family.[16] The tradition of providing early gifts of land to each of the children in lieu of inheritance was also well established. Thus, in August 1959 when Jacob E. Loewen at age seventy-one divested himself of some 380 acres of land each of his children, sons Henry and John as well as daughters Elizabeth and Bertha, all married with children, received about 80 acres of land.[17] Despite the fact that tax rolls did not necessarily reflect the female lineage of land (often listing, for example, only the husband's name), 28 of 170 Mennonite landowners in Meade County in 1950 were listed as women.[18] And evidence suggests that women's ownership of land translated into at least a degree of female autonomy. Women were not dependent on marriage to secure a livelihood; in addition to four operating Mennonite farm households headed by widows in Meade County there were two headed by unmarried spinster women. What is important for female self-perception was that the 'Bartel sisters' were seen as farmers: they were listed in the farm census in 1950, a diary entry notes that they purchased the services of a custom hammermill owner in 1949, and a newspaper listed them alongside male names on the Farm Bureau roster in 1948.[19]

It is also apparent that the culture of female land ownership sanctioned a degree of matrilocality, female-directed residential patterns. Official church histories mention the deeply valued religious service of

Rev Henry Harms, a 1912 Meade settler. A family history offers an explanation of why he had come to Meade County in the first place: 'Maggie and Rev Henry Harms' were the 'children of Anna and Peter B. Thiessen' who stayed in Meade after they 'bought Grandma Thiessen's farm.'[20] It was even a recognized fact among men that the key to wheat farming often lay in the inheritance of their wives: 'I couldn't farm,' related one Meade man, 'the quarter section I bought from my Dad for $500 down, $500 due each year, borrowed with interest, was not enough ground. My brothers all went into farming; they had enough through their wives to buy land.'[21] These experiences support the findings of scholars who have linked land ownership and status among women.[22]

The description of Helena Reimer's life, ordered by mutually interdependent work roles in the farm household, reflected a broad social reality in the Mennonite district of Meade County in the 1940s. Family histories of farms in this decade allude frequently to husband and wife working together and sharing an identity with the farm: 'following their marriage [in 1943] ... they took up farming and raised cattle ... milk[ing] a few cows, [and raising] chickens and hogs.'[23] Farm census records suggest that the sector of the farm associated with women continued to be economically important until the 1950s. The percentage of families who owned a few milk cows dropped only slightly between the Depression and the early 1950s, from 94 percent in 1937 to 82 percent in 1950, which suggests that despite a decade of good crops and high prices the female sector of the farm continued to have economic relevance. It was similarly significant that the percentage of farms tending 200-bird chicken flocks dropped only slightly, from 78 percent in the Depression year of 1937 to 62 percent in 1950.[24]

The world of Helena Reimer in the 1940s was grounded in that farm household. Women saw their work as economically productive and interdependent with that of the men. Both Helena's diary and Klaas's financial record reflected female production of commodities and women as land inheritors. The religious values Mennonites associated with the agrarian existence and simple lifestyle led the conservative Mennonite farm women to react to the Depression and the war with a commitment to farming a mix of commodities. The culture of bilateral inheritance similarly encouraged mixed farming by providing women with land and by ensuring that each of the children of most families received a small acreage. Womanhood was intrinsically tied to the idea of gender mutuality within the farm household. As memories of the Great Depression and the Second World War began to fade, as a burgeoning wheat market provided new financial openings, and as a new round of mechanization and the lure of consumerism entered the picture, Mennonite ethnicity and ideas of gender began to change.

The Cheerful Homemaker

One night in October 1963 on Highway 23 just outside the town of Meade, a 'family vehicle' driven by thirty-year-old Mrs Bea (Bessie Mae) Morrow Cornelsen struck a cow. It was a serious accident. Bessie Mae, who it seems had left the high school football game of the Meade Buffaloes early with her six children, ages three months to eleven years, had to have them 'checked out' at the Meade hospital. And the injured cow had to be killed. For the local *Meade Globe Press* the accident was shocking, but for the purposes of social history the event illuminates the new world in which women lived. Bea Cornelsen was not an economically productive farm-based woman; her life was centered around children and included significant degrees of mobility and new forms of leisure. This tragic meeting of car and cow on K23 reflected this set of new social realities. Since women no longer milked cows in daily life, this may in fact have been the only cow Bessie Mae encountered in 1963. According to 1961 records she lived in Meade with her husband Anthony and the children.[25]

The social basis of Bea Cornelsen's world, however, reflected a new economic reality not only for town women but for farm women. At midcentury they saw their productive roles on the farm decline in importance. Larger and more mechanized farms made the dairy and chicken sectors seem insignificant, altered the culture of labor, and generated a cash flow that was more easily directed to store-bought products.[26] In this context a new description of women arose. Meade Mennonite women who began their households in the 1950s and 1960s usually referred to themselves as 'homemaker' and 'housewife,' a step removed from the designation of 'farmer' or 'farmwife.' A family vignette written by Katherine Friesen for the Meade County history book notes that she and her husband Pete 'purchased their first home on 160 acres in 1954 ... and called it Horseshoe Farm.' It further describes Pete as 'active in farming' and Katherine as 'a homemaker, enjoy[ing] added talents of painting and various crafts.'[27] Similarly, the family history of John and Katie Bartel written by daughter Arlene notes simply that after moving from Manitoba in 1960 John became 'a carpenter' and did 'some farming' while Katie was 'a housewife.'[28]

Specialized wheat farms of the 1950s continued to require help from women. They drove tractors to plow the land, hauled grain, baled, and brought food out to the field. Representations of this kind of work, however, suggest a new perspective. Elda Friesen writes of her work in the field in decidedly more negative terms than her work in the farm-yard: 'I would have to plow with the old 22-36 International ... a beast to handle,' and although instructions were to keep 'the guide along [a neat straight] line,' Dad, coming 'back to the field ... could never recognize anything straight.'[29] She writes of her work in the dairy in a different tone: 'I was always so pleased ... if I could have the milking done before Dad or any of my brothers would come home to help.' Food prepara-tion differed depending on the type of harvest technology. During the harvest Elda recalled 'dislik[ing] helping pack the meals into the trunk ... and driv[ing] out across the straggly stubble while squinting to keep the dust out of my eyes ... never [being able to make out if] the combine operator was motioning me to come to the opposite end of the field with ... dinner or wait in place.'[30] Coincidentally, male descriptions of women bringing food to the fields supports the female perspective. Menno Friesen, who spent his teenaged years in the 1950s on a wheat farm, reports that 'men were almost kings at lunch during the harvest' when 'fine farm meals were bought to the field' by women who 'served well' and helped ensure that meal 'time was a celebration.'[31] If the men felt like kings on the fields, women waited their turn for feelings of worthiness in the house or farmyard. Elda Friesen's description of barnyard threshing employed words such as 'very exciting' and 'fun to watch' and described a different pattern of meal consumption: 'at noon they would stop the machinery and come to the house' for 'delicious dinners,' drinking 'eagerly' and piling 'their plates high.'[32] The house and barnyard held a tradition of female autonomy; the field seemed to undermine it.

The new economy also introduced a new level of consumerism that affected the social patterns and culture of women. The 1947 switch from wind-driven Delco power plants to continuous power supplied by the Rural Electrification Agency and the construction of natural gas pipe-lines through the county in the 1950s brought significant changes to the inventory of household appliances. The local manager of CMS Electric Co-operative, Carl Zink, promised that subscription to the co-op's ser-vice would make 'farm life more pleasant.'[33] Evidently he was right. The April 1948 auction sale of the Isaac household included a clothes mangle, an oil stove, a wood stove, an 'Oak Heater,' a gasoline-powered washing machine, and cream, butter, cheese, and meat production equipment. By comparison the May 1960 auction sale of the Ediger household listed not only wares reflecting a more affluent life – a living room suite, 'steel kitchen cabinets' with '"formica" ... tops,' and a riding lawn mower – but appliances requiring heavy electrical usage such as an Admiral air conditioner and a Maytag oven range fuelled by natural gas.[34] Mennonites also began to patronize other stores such as Ideal Grocer and Marrs clothing store, and judging from the new vogue of 'permanents' cited by church elders, the hairdressers in Meade too.[35]

Falling fertility revealed a third change in the lives of Meade Mennonite women during the 1950s. The birth rate had already dropped during the Great Depression and the Second World War. Now, in contrast to the rest of the country that witnessed the baby boom, the fertility decline among Meade Mennonites continued uninterrupted. In the eight years between 1953 and 1961 the number of children per Mennonite household fell by 22 percent, from 2.7 to 2.1 children.[36] At the same time, the average age of a woman bearing her first child rose from 23.1 years to 25.6 years.[37] Reasons for this decline certainly include economic and hence educational factors, but a religious explanation can be offered. At least one historian has linked fertility decline with the rise of pietistic evangelicalism, a change that encouraged women to think of having 'fewer children of "greater spiritual quality."'[38] This reality was reflected among Meade County Mennonite women as evangelicalism strengthened in the 1930s and 1940s. In 1944 after the evangelistic Emmanuel Mennonite Church was founded on the remnants of the old Kleine Gemeinde, the view that children should be converted or at the very least that the church's duty was to mould their Christian life at an early age became standard among Mennonite families. Within months of the church's inception a Youth Meetings organization was begun and over the next decade the issue of youth involvement in church programs was repeatedly raised.[39] In 1955 the Emmanuel Mennonite congregation even considered 'dedicating children,' a practice described as a 'public dedication of children to the Lord by parents.'[40] Mennonite women also began employing the language of 'child psychologists' to explore 'correct ways' of child rearing.[41] In one meeting in June 1954 Meade Mennonite women concluded that while 'love [was] the most important' in child rearing, it was also important to 'recognize him, make him feel wanted and needed, and not forgetting the spiritual element.'[42] As housewives Mennonite women had recast the duties of motherhood.

The decline of household self-sufficiency, the rise of consumerism, and the plummeting of fertility occurred in the context of a significant change in the very notion of American womanhood. Feminist scholars have long designated the 1950s as a decade of domesticity when the 'feminine mystique' placed women in economically unproductive roles in homes, turned them from producers to consumers, and separated them more completely from the world of men. On one level this is true for Mennonite women in Meade County. A comparison of the obituaries of mothers in the 1930s and those of the 1960s suggests that the staid concept of women's 'duty' was replaced by such virtues as goodness, gentleness, dedication, and spiritual nurture to children.[43] At wedding parties in Meade County one sees the creation of men and women as 'incommensurable opposites,' in the language of Thomas Laqueur, different not only biologically but ontologically with the bride distinguished from the groom by color and elaborateness of dress.[44] A June 1957 wedding report of a Meade Mennonite couple, Levi Isaac, son of the former Kleine Gemeinde bishop, and Wynelle Hamm, a graduate of Meade Bible Academy, is illustrative. The report described Wynelle not only as 'lovely,' but as wearing a gown of 'frost white silk organza and venice lace over taffeta, fashioned with moulded basque bodice, shirred short sleeves and scoop neckline edged with lace ... [and] a chapel-length train.' It further reported that the bride had been given in marriage by her father and that Levi, wearing a 'dark tuxedo,' waited to receive her.[45] These were not the wedding garments of the 1930s.

As Mennonite women visited town for consumer goods and made child rearing more public, they also began joining and actively participating in publicly funded, state-spawned Home Demonstration Units, commonly dubbed HDUs. The HDUs in Meade County, as elsewhere, were supervised by special 'home demonstration agents' who worked closely with the school superintendent, county agricultural agent, and county health nurse to advance the cause of 'homemaking, health and safety.' Scholars suggest that the HDUs arose in part because government and business believed that farms would become more productive if women simultaneously turned their attention from the wider farm to the narrower world of the house, and from the closed neighborhood to the wider nation.[46] Significantly, however, Meade Mennonite women resisted joining HDUs between 1918, when the first unit was established in the county, and 1952, at the very time that female farm production in Mennonite households dropped. Significantly too, when Mennonite women did join the HDU movement they avoided joining established units and organized their own, distinctly Mennonite chapters. The Cheerful Homemakers and Live 'n Learn clubs founded in 1952 consisted almost entirely of Mennonite women.[47]

These Mennonite units reflected the new social reality of increased mobility and leisure. They also provide the student of Mennonite gender with a new text of womanhood. In one sense, the language of the units differed little from that of the Mennonite sewing circle that Helena Reimer would have attended in the 1940s; women met monthly, they opened meetings with prayer, they often adopted community service projects. But overriding these older features were a new agenda and a new language.

The language was, first, that of a new middle-class, consumer-oriented, and domestic femininity. In fact, the core of ideas expressed through the HDU reports suggest that Mennonite women had exchanged a view of themselves as household producers for a self-perception of themselves as middle-class, consumer-oriented home managers. The women, for example, used many of their meetings to discuss table settings, interior decorating, the creation of home spaces, and the organization of domestic chores; no discussion of farm work, even in the poultry or dairy sectors, was recorded. The Cheerful Homemakers also openly expressed a concern with the physical appearance of fashionable dress and the female body. Representative of their lessons was the one from February 1957 in which 'Mrs Corny Classen and Mrs Herman Harder' spoke on 'How to Dress More Attractively.' The women were introduced to the concept of 'counterdressing' to alter the appearance of those who were 'too tall or too short' and then they discussed more informally the 'problems ... that different members had.'[48] A set of new symbols was acquired from the wider commercial world to script their more domestic, genteel lives that farm women of the past would have rejected. These symbols sometimes reflected their views of marriage. At one of their meetings each woman brought a wedding photo to show during roll-call, at another meeting they all wore their wedding dresses, and during yet another meeting, a 'Valentine's Day Special,' they made 'heart-shaped jello' desserts.

Ironically, the Cheerful Homemakers used a public forum to legitimize their new lives of domesticity.[49] But like women elsewhere who engaged in what historians have dubbed 'maternal feminism,' these women extended their domestically based virtues to the public arena. Their own newspaper reports point to a new preoccupation with a wider world beyond their immediate neighborhoods. The women heard lessons on 'global awareness,' they discussed 'my favorite radio program,' they attended regional meetings of HDUs, they opened meetings by 'singing "America,"' and they met to discuss 'our voting privileges and responsibilities as citizens of our country.' Women also extended their services to the world outside their homes. The official histories of the Cheerful Homemakers and Live 'n Learn clubs suggest that the unit members thought of themselves as servants, not of the poor as in the older sewing circles, but of public institutions, including the senior citizen's home, the hospital, and the 4-H clubs.[50] In some instances women spread the word of the new virtues of happiness and discretion. Indeed, they prescribed a standard of behavior and of female virtue that the women of the more difficult, physically strenuous, and communitarian world of the 1930s and 1940s would have found odd. In February 1957 when the Cheerful Homemakers presented a program to the Meade Bible Academy they began with two songs, 'Always Cheerful,' and 'Kind Words Never Die,' and followed it with 'a comical skit ... by six ladies [suggesting] ... not to say things we don't want repeated.'[51]

The women of the 1950s used their images as nurturers and custodians of moral virtue to gain entry into the public world in and around the Meade Mennonite community. This strategy is most apparent in the overtly public, although subservient, roles that women assumed in the increasingly evangelistic Mennonite churches, especially in the new Emmanuel Mennonite Church. In the old Kleine Gemeinde church tradition lines of patriarchal authority from the male bishop to the all-male council of ministers and deacons and further to the general male brotherhood, were clear and simple, and women held no official position of public authority. The birth of Emmanuel Church's more individualized theology and more complex church structure presented women with new, more public roles. The church's new agenda of actively winning souls, both those of its own youth and those of non-evangelical communities, required committed service from all members, women as well as men. Between 1944 and 1964 Emmanuel Mennonite women became Sunday school teachers, participated in church elections, served on the Mission Extension Department and, most important, entered foreign mission service. By the 1950s the all-male council of the Emmanuel church noted that 'if a sister feels the call to enter into the Master's service ... the minister or church board [shall] ... give her their attention.'[52] Indeed, it was considered a special vocation that could well steer a woman from the calling to have her own children. Thus, when Morocco missionary Elsie Regier was courted by Peter Z. Friesen of Meade in 1949 he was faced with the objection from Elsie's colleagues that her 'Arabic was too good to waste ... time raising children.'[53] Clearly women 'felt the call' and when they volunteered for missionary work, the church hailed them in special public forums, such as the August 1964 'farewell for Lena Isaac who is leaving for service in Morocco.'[54]

Even the acceptance of the idea that young women might train for traditionally female professions of nursing and teaching was gradual. Women who had pursued professional degrees in the 1930s and 1940s recall having to resist older, agrarian notions of women's work and marriage. When Minnie Classen announced her intention in the late 1930s to become a registered nurse, she is said to have 'tested the system' and to have faced 'great opposition ... great reluctance and admonishment from ministers and Grandma Friesen.' Ironically, the opposition was so strong that she, as a pacifist Mennonite, was forced to covertly join 'the U.S. Cadet Nurses Corps' to obtain 'help with expenses and tuition' until she 'graduated in 1946.'[55] Other women resisted old ideas that only farm households guaranteed security and fulfilment. 'I had to ask for permission to attend high school,' recalled one 1948 graduate of Meade Bible Academy, and then 'when I wanted to go to Tabor College for teacher's training, Dad suggested that this would be unnecessary if I wanted to get married.'[56] Even when secondary school education became acceptable for young women in the 1950s, elders sought to steer women to homemaking. During the mid-1950s, for example, it was said that the 'most pleasant and best equipped room' at the Meade Bible Academy was 'the home economics room' with the latest in electric and gas cookstoves, refrigerators, and electric sewing machines.[57]

By the 1950s it was becoming acceptable for young women to consider teaching and nursing careers, but only if they were confined to a time before marriage or the birth of children. There were young Mennonite female schoolteachers in the Mennonite-dominated rural districts of Goodwill, Lilydale, Sunrise, and McNulty.[58] Moreover, a 1956 poll at the private Mennonite high school indicated that of the approximately thirty female students, nineteen intended to become nurses and several others schoolteachers, secretaries, or missionaries.[59] And even though only five girls indicated that they wished to be become 'housewives,' it was agreed that professionally trained young women should return to 'homemaking' after marriage. Moreover it was inconceivable that women could both pursue professions and raise families.[60]

The Meade women of the 1950s had made consumption and nurture the public hallmarks of true womanhood. They had exchanged a productive role on the farm for a creative life of domesticity. Ironically, they also turned this new conception of domestic womanly duty into a highly publicized role, first as homemakers and then as Mennonite church workers and service professionals. Here are signals that in limited ways these public roles could be turned to economically productive work.

The Professional Woman

By the 1970s another group of women was beginning to challenge the image of the farm-based homemaker.[61] An increasing number of married Mennonite women in Meade County were finding paid work in town. It could be seen as the third part of a pattern, severely telescoped perhaps, but not unlike the one described by Louise Tilly and Joan Scott, 'a U-shaped pattern of female productive activity – from relatively high in the pre-industrial household economy, to a lower level in the industrial economies, to a higher level with the development of the modern tertiary sector.'[62] The western Kansas farm economy that had made wheat and cattle production profitable in the 1940s and 1950s had also resulted in a restricted farm economy, reflected the inflation of land prices, higher input costs, and increasingly expensive equipment, all in what John Shover describes as an economy of 'diminishing returns.'[63] In this economy women's productive work once again became necessary. At the same time an increasingly complex society with a more complete social safety net for the elderly and for farmers, and a consumer society that produced more medical services and offered more stores of food, clothes, and home furnishings, provided more opportunities for women to seek paid work outside the home.

The growth of the service industry and of government offices significantly altered patterns of female employment in Meade County. These patterns are apparent in county and state records that reveal, for example, that women in their twenties more often than men left the county to acquire postsecondary education and that these same women returned to work in the county. In 1970, for example, 22 percent more women than men in Meade County had received a college education (355 to 290). In this context the number of women working in public places increased slowly and steadily from 13.2 percent of the total waged workforce in 1940, to 28.3 percent in 1960, and to 33.8 percent in

1970.[64] More significant was the rapid entry into the workforce of married women, whose numbers rose by almost 50 percent during the 1960s, from 27.0 percent to 39.8 percent of all married women.[65] Although quantitative data are not available to document the married Mennonite women returning to work, family biographies note this as an increasing tendency. They suggest too that Mennonite farm families, once committed to agriculture as a religiously sanctioned way of life and to an ethnically homogeneous rural community as a safeguard against 'worldliness,' were now turning to town life for economic security.

Several different subpatterns are evident in Meade County Mennonite women's work in the 1970s. Some farm women found productive roles on farms that were similar to those of their mothers during the 1930s and 1940s. A few Meade County farms had pursued an avenue of commercialization, not through winter wheat production and cattle ranging, but through a similar route to their distant kin in Hanover, Manitoba, specialization in hog, dairy, and poultry production. Although men assumed primary roles in these barnyard-based farm economies, women seem to have played more crucial roles here than on wheat farms. Ike and Anna Reimer who married in 1958 established a farm that illustrates this pattern: their acreage was one of two Meade Mennonite farms specializing in hogs and included a herd of 250 sows in 1975. A family history of the Reimers notes that Anna was a 'housewife ... help[ing] with the hog chores and quilting ... in her spare time.'[66] More women, however, seem to have found work as a direct result of an increasingly narrow and specialized farm economy. Sometimes they worked the small farms, which averaged less than 250 acres, while husbands found work in nearby Meade.[67] In 1961 Martin and Helen Reimer Bartel, for example, owned a small farm that had 100 hogs, 20 beef cattle, 120 acres of wheat and sorghum, and 5 milking cows: Martin recalled later that while 'I worked for Meade [City] Manufacturing [Company], Helen ran the mixed farm, teaching all the boys to drive the tractor.'[68] More often women contributed to the household economy by working in town, reactivating professions they had acquired as young women in the 1950s. The story of John and Anna Siemens who married in 1941 and had five children between 1943 and 1951 was typical. Their farm was relatively small; in 1975 they harvested 160 acres of wheat, marketed 26 cattle, but had no hogs or dairy cows, and John worked for the local Friesen Windmill company. When the two youngest children – twins Lois and Loel – turned sixteen in

1967, Anna went to work as a 'medication aid' at Lone Tree Lodge, the senior citizen's home in Meade.[69]

Most often, however, the couple left farming altogether and both husband and wife drove into town to work or moved into town to be close to their jobs. The story of Herman Harms and Esther Wiens is illustrative of this pattern. After they married in 1945 they moved to a small farm where in 1951 they cultivated 158 acres of wheat, marketed four head of beef, milked three cows, and raised fifty chickens. A family history notes, however, that after '1954, Herman was employed at Meade Manufacturing [where he worked] until September 1978 [when] the plant closed.' It adds that 'in 1970 [after raising three children] Esther started to work at Lone Tree Lodge as cook on a part time basis.'[70] Married women, especially those with school-age children, also found roles in family-based town businesses. Thus, Betty Isaac Friesen of Friesen's Machine Shop worked as a 'secretary' and Phyllis Grunau Rempel of Rempel's Auto Repair as a 'part time book keeper.'[71] During the 1970s as married women began to work at positions throughout the growing tertiary service sector – as business managers, hairdressers, novelty-shop clerks, dental assistants, secretaries – their numbers in the workforce rose even higher.[72] A few married Mennonite women like Mary Klaassen played even more active roles, 'manag[ing] the Meade Motel ... and later own[ing] Mary's Variety and Fabrics, all in Meade.'[73]

The increasing number of working women came with several new developments. Fertility rates continued falling among Mennonite women. The number of children per family in the countryside that had fallen from 2.7 to 2.1 children during the 1950s decreased to just 1.6 children per household in 1975. Similarly the age of a woman bearing her first child, which had risen by two years in the 1950s from 23.1 to 25.5 years, rose another full year in the 1960s and early 1970s to 26.7 years. The number of women who lived in town rose sharply, from ten married women to fifty-nine married women in the years from 1961 to 1970.[74] The everyday language of even the older Mennonite women began to be English; Helena Doerksen Reimer, for example, moved into town in about 1963 and on the very day of the move changed the language of her diary from German to English.[75] The number of elderly Mennonite women who lived with their children after their husbands died decreased too as homes became even more private and the social safety net spread to include a Mennonite-run senior citizen's home in Meade. Finally, Mennonites began moving beyond old ethnic boundaries. The mostly Mennonite Cheerful Homemakers and Live 'n Learn clubs still met, but Mennonite women of the 1970s joined other women's organizations, the interethnic Sunnydale Homemakers, the Sorosis Club (an affiliate of the General Federation of Women's Clubs), and even the Meade Business and Professional Women's Clubs.[76]

The evidence for these new social realities also points to a new culture of Mennonite womanhood. The hundred or so biographies of Mennonite families in the local Meade history books reflects a new female representation. Significantly, the data rarely mention the family's ethnicity, its church affiliation, the name of the Mennonite minister who married or baptized the couple, or the woman's rate of childbearing. These would have been the signposts of community membership in an earlier time. What is noted in these texts is the work and profession of family members, and importantly, the work and profession of married women. Sometimes women's work, and more important their inexorable pilgrimage through trying times of child rearing towards a life of gainful employment, receives more space than the story of their men's careers. Thus the biography of Roy and Alma Regier, who were married in 1956, notes in two lines Roy's employment at Meade Manufacturing and CMS Electric; it devotes four lines to how 'Alma taught two years ... and after their marriage taught one year ... [and] while the children were growing up Alma did substitute teaching, custom sewing and taught piano.' Finally, it adds that 'Alma is now in her fifth year of teaching first grade.' Similarly the historical section of John and Anne Reimer's biography noted in three lines that before their marriage 'Anne graduated from the Gretna Mennonite Collegiate and from the Tuxedo Teacher's College [and] after that she taught for three years in her home school' and added in a single line that 'John attended the McNulty School near Meade.'[77] The Mennonite woman's legitimization now lay not in her lineage, her effort in the farm household, or her domestic life, but increasingly in her publicly recognized profession.[78]

A 'U-Shaped' Trajectory

Women's lives changed during the course of the post–Second World War rural transformation. Farm mechanization, commodity specialization, and state-sponsored HDUs changed the social configurations in which Meade women lived. In this context women lost their economically productive roles, but acquired the cultural resources to engage in a new middle-class society. With the continued evolution of the farm economy, especially an agriculture of 'diminishing returns,' women returned to 'paid' work, usually in the town of Meade, as laborers or as college-trained professionals. With these changing work patterns came alterations in social networks, falling fertility rates, and increased levels of education. Scott and Tilly's idea of a 'u-shaped' trajectory in which economically productive farm women of an earlier time set a pattern for later professional and town-based women seems to reflect the social reality in Meade County.[79]

Mennonite women in Meade County did more than change patterns of work. They redefined womanhood. The central texts that revealed the lives of women in the 1940s were the diary and account book, which suggested a mutual relationship between husband and wife in the farm household. The central texts of the women from the 1950s were the newspaper columns that recorded the activities of the local HDUs, a confident public record of middle-class home management coupled with public-service roles and the new virtue of cheerful nurture. The third text, the local history book and within it family biographies, reveals a new set of values, encased in trajectories of professional and economic achievement.

Rural women in the twentieth century were affected by dramatic social transformation. Their lives were radically altered by shifts in technology, education, state intrusiveness, and popular culture. The specific ways in which they changed, however, were affected by local variations in environment and economy and by interweaving community practice and ethnic identity. The rapid rate of rural depopulation in the Meade County wheat land, the intrusive postwar government institutions, and the quickly evolving sense of Mennonite ethnicity in a Midwestern milieu telescoped the u-shaped trajectory of which Scott and Tilly have written. Certainly the Tagebuch, the newspaper column, and the history book biographies tell only part of the story. Significant overlaps existed – farm women could work part time in towns, the Mennonite HDUs were still functioning in the 1980s – but the three texts point to an evolving set of gender identities that was carried along by the Great Disjuncture. They point to three groups of women who fashioned elements of domesticity and autonomy from their circumstances that were economic, cultural, and religious in nature. Each group of women found new ways to develop autonomous and meaningful lives within societies that continued to produce new expressions of male dominance.

The same narrative also signalled a change in their view of themselves in relation to the men and with this u-turn came a shifting account of the men themselves. Helena Reimer's diary reveals a mutuality of production in the household economy, albeit encased in an authoritative, church-based patriarchy. The HDU reports suggest a new gap between the worlds of men and women, encouraged by increased mechanization, more intrusive government programs, and closer associations with the civic life in the town of Meade. The successful man was a winner, but now as even the occasional HDU indicated he had also learned to channel his aggressiveness, assuming the mannerisms of charm and chivalry. These were the men in the Cheerful Homemakers' 1960 headline announcing that 'Husbands Host Homemakers at Valentine Party,' followed by a story of them 'donning chefs hats [and] serv[ing] waffle and eggs and home-made ice-cream,' thus ensuring that 'all unit members were proud of their husbands and felt it was a Valentine's party in the truest sense.'[80] The party chef was a man who made overtures to women from an outside world and visited the domestic space for only a moment.

As women returned to the workplace and joined the men in mutual endeavor, a new manhood arose. Meade high school notes describe young men who seem vulnerable, alienated from strange workplaces, in need of male companionship: as one young female high school student put it in 1959, for true happiness in marriage to exist the 'man must have friends besides his wife to help and encourage him.'[81] The same source describes men in need of an outlet outside of work for a measured male aggressiveness: consider the featured 'scholar' of Meade Bible Academy in 1948 – Frank, a 'left guard in basketball, always in a cheerful mood, kind and gentle in his ways.'[82] But the new man also knew how to appropriate an observed farm-based manliness to a white-collar world: 'Dad's fierce determination,' noted Menno M. Friesen who left the farm to pursue a dream that eventually led to a doctorate in English, 'gave me a model for securing an education ... [and] beneficial survival techniques during my years on university campuses.'[83] Manhood now seemed more intentionally constructed, based on channeled emotions and borrowed models.

As the Meade women began charting new lives in town during the 1970s they proudly linked economic productivity with true womanhood; as men took up positions off the farm and alongside professional women, they found ways of reasserting masculinities linked to imagined roles of yesteryear. The image of the rise and fall of the Cheerful Homemaker ironically contradicts the very pattern of Scott and Tilly's metaphor of the 'u-shaped pattern of female productive activity.' The fact is that each of these groups of women, in dialectic relation with the enabling and limiting features of their social environments, created a narrative that granted them meaning, dignity, and agency.[84] But the u-shape metaphor has another limitation. Gender for both women and men may have taken a u-turn of some kind, but it in no way meant that either gender ended anywhere near the same place they had started. The Great Disjuncture on the wheat plains of western Kansas expressed itself in significantly new ideas of gender, for both women and men.

7 Poultrymen, Car Dealers, and Football Stars: Masculinities in Manitoba

Social Change and Masculinity

Just as the effect of the Great Disjuncture on gender in the Mennonite community of western Kansas can be observed in a case study of women, so the changing views of gender in the Mennonite community of eastern Manitoba can be seen through a study of manhood. The forces associated with the Great Disjuncture affected the meaning of femininity and the structure of women's roles in both Kansas and Manitoba. The same social forces reshaped the very idea of masculinity in both places. Men rethought the meaning of respectable maleness as they accommodated the rising consumerism in society, commercialism in agriculture, and rural depopulation.[1] In the postwar era both Manitoba and Kansas men found themselves on highly technologized farms shaped by intrusive government programs and scientific discovery. Both sets of men also lived in farm households that de-emphasized food self-sufficiency and encouraged women to partake of a suburban-based consumer culture. Just as the 'cheerful homemaker' in Kansas was accompanied by the commercialized wheat producing man or town businessman, so too the Manitoba male farmers, entrepreneurs, and sportsmen were accompanied by women separated from the productive side of the households. If the cheerful homemaker and office worker reflected not only a new femininity but a broader gender transition in Kansas, so too the poultrymen and car dealers pointed not only to a new masculinity but to new set of gender relations in Manitoba. Given the more diversified and stable farm economy of eastern Manitoba and its critical mass of Mennonites, gender in Manitoba played itself out in somewhat different ways than it did in Kansas. Both the differences and the similarities can be illuminated in the study of gender through the perspective of Manitoba men, their sense of masculinity, and view of women. Gender relations in both Hanover and Meade may not have changed in precisely similar ways, but both turned Mennonite men and women in a similar direction.

It is a truism by now that as society underwent change so too did masculinity.[2] Some characteristics of masculinity changed little: most historians agree that men over time have usually equated masculinity with superordination over women, over boys, and over men they considered to be of lesser quality. But historians also agree that different cultures created this arrangement differently. Anthony Rotundo argues that aggressiveness – sometimes checked through self-denial, sometimes voiced in passion – was an overarching American male characteristic; Robert Nye posits that in France masculinity was tied to 'honor' and 'courage' in such a way as to enhance personal prestige; Michael Roper and John Tosh suggest that in Britain masculinity entailed 'sexual domination' and 'discourag[ed] emotional expression,' a combination that led to a 'fragility ... at the psychic level.'[3] Despite the appearance of some degree of national stereotyping, clearly gender constructions are not universal and reflect a dialectic with local or national cultures. Those constructions also change over time. Joy Parr has noted in her prize-winning book *The Gender of Breadwinners* that German-Canadian men in nineteenth-century Hanover, Ontario, lived in a highly stratified society where 'maleness' for the factory-owning man lay in hard work, austerity, self-control, and oneness 'with the men he employed.' But in the twentieth century 'the new ethics of masculine identity ... required that virility be separated from physicality ... money could trump muscle in the ranking of manly prowess.'[4]

In Manitoba's Rural Municipality (RM) of Hanover and the town of Steinbach, homogeneous agrarian worlds declined as global markets, communication technologies, and integrative governments worked in concert to change the social foundations of society. Before 1945 the Mennonite groups here had venerated the true man as one who was 'quiet in the land,' submissive to state authority, humble among neighbors. and committed to the advancement not of self, but of the household and community. The measure of a man lay in the maintenance of social status not in the earning of it, and the greatest achievement for any man was to create the same situation for his children. A sign that this sense of masculinity could not last was apparent in the changing nature of Mennonite religious leadership; here farmer-bishops gave way to educated, often schoolteacher-pastors. The authority of the former was more deeply rooted, based on an organic identification with the cosmology and virtues of the community. The authority of the latter was based on personal skill, energy, and performance. The difference in the maleness of leaders was evident in the contrast between Bishop Peter P. Reimer who led the old order Kleine Gemeinde Mennonites from the RM of Hanover to Mexico in 1948 and Revivalist George Brunk from Pennsylvania who visited Hanover in 1957. The humble, quiescent, demurring presence of Reimer stood in contrast to the American visitor. Brunk not only promised the *Carillon News* the 'largest gospel effort ever put up here,' he did so with flare and confidence. The newspaper reported that Brunk look 'like a ship's commander ... at 6 feet 4' and reminded 'one of Billy Graham, who incidentally is one of his close friends.'[5] Many Mennonite church histories have a chapter devoted to this change in leadership type and many other Mennonite biographies highlight the traits of individual energy and personal skill of noteworthy twentieth-century leaders.[6] Parallel changes affected the lives of Mennonite men in their everyday society and the meaning ascribed to being male clearly underwent a transition. A major shift in the Mennonite understanding of masculinity occurred when Mennonites left the farm and took new roles in town, but also as the farms were transformed into commercialized, technologized, and highly capitalized ventures.

Arguably the gender reconstruction experienced by Mennonite men was especially pronounced. Pacifist, quiescent, sectarian Mennonites did not have at their disposal images of the aggressive male who might provide them with models of how to survive in a more market-driven, open, and urban economy. The Americans had their cowboy, the English their gentlemen, and both, like many Canadians, had the war veteran. Marlene Epp has written that as conscientious objectors (COs), the Mennonites were 'heroes of the faith' within their community, but in the wider 'world the CO frequently had the opposite image, and countering the public image of nonresistance cowardice has been a major effort for the church.'[7] Mennonite men found their sense of maleness in belonging to the Bruderschaft, undertaking religious duty and service, and taking the church-sanctioned role as household patriarch. But they also found it in the everyday. Here a veneration for hard work and an incipient materialism, that is, a fetish for things seen in the myriad photographs of massive traction steamers, large, two-story houses, and towering poplar windbreaks, were the marks of success.

Thus when the nature of agriculture and indeed the social basis of rurality changed at midcentury, so too did the basis for masculinity. In the process, one may argue, a new Mennonite man was created. The man of the 1950s and 1960s was an individual achiever, an ambitious and aggressive person, and possessed of a sense of manhood that sanctioned passion so long as it was channeled rightly. In the old agrarian world patriarchalism was assumed even as men and women shared lives of economic mutuality; in the new more individuated world of the later twentieth century, male worthiness seemed more tenuous, a status that had to be won daily. Status in the old world came from being a restrained, sober, quiet, conservative member of household and community. In the new world it came by moving ahead of the community, stripping away worn authority, proving individual merit, being forceful, expressive, and openly competitive. In the old world, the true man bridged generations, passing on teaching and patrimony to ensure lineage; in the new world the man of status was the self-made man.

The New Mennonite Man in Steinbach

Evidence of a transformed masculinity is not difficult to find. Old sermons are replete with descriptions of an agrarian and communitarian masculinity and family histories describe the makings of the ideal old-order man. Both texts describe agrarian male virtue. Official teaching from church pulpits berated men who sought to distance themselves socially from others. The biography of Steinbach's Peter Dueck, Kleine Gemeinde bishop from 1901 to 1919, is revealing in its unrelenting criticism of 'evil businesses' that are 'continually enlarging,' of men who take on public office and vote, and of men who purchase cars or dress in 'worldly fashion' in displays of ostentation. Conversely, few preachers criticized a man for purchasing too much land, owning too much livestock, possessing too large a barn. Indeed, a measure of a successful man was one whose household acquired enough property to place each son and daughter on a piece of land.

Nostalgia-filled biographies written during the mid-twentieth century underscore these agrarian values. The 1958 depiction of pioneer brothers Klaas, Abram, Peter, and Johann Reimer of the districts of Steinbach and Blumenort is revealing. During the late nineteenth century the four brothers had not only been Hanover pioneers, but had served as community leaders. One was a successful merchant, another a deacon, a third a preacher, and a fourth a village mayor. Yet the description of each in the Reimer family history was phrased in terms not of publicly recognized achievement but of craft- and farm-based masculinity. The dominant story within the biography of Abram Reimer, the deacon from Blumenort, has him putting a haughty apprentice in his place by moving an anvil with a single arm, after the apprentice tried but failed to move it with all his strength. The biography of Peter, the Blumenort farmer-preacher, portrays his courage as a boy when he skated home on the Busuluk River in Russia after dark, as wolves howled nearby. The biography of Johann, the Steinbach village mayor, has no information on his public office, but includes a story of a terrible injury he incurred by refusing to let go of a runaway team of horses. As if to underscore these private, household-based acts of bravery, the biographer of Klaas Reimer, the well-to-do Steinbach merchant, ends his account not by citing the well-known particulars of the man's wealth, but with a meaningful quotation: 'I always find it difficult to leave my family for I love them dearly and leave taking is always a painful experience for me.'[8] Masculinity in the world of Mennonite agraria held little room for public accolades and records of individual achievement; it was rootedness in a venerated and organic community.

By the mid-twentieth century these images were changing. In the RM of Hanover and the town of Steinbach three groups of men in particular illustrated the extent of the change. They were farmers who commercialized the dairy and poultry production sides of mixed farms, car dealers and lumber barons who benefited from the technological and consumeristic impulses of the postwar boom, and young men who found in football and hockey new outlets and new expressions of manhood. The changes did not constitute wholesale cultural transformations. A culturally rooted ambivalence visited each of these groups of Mennonite men. The successful poultry producer was buffeted by uncertain North American markets, the successful businessman built his success on surging consumerism and materialism, the football and hockey players displayed stealth, deception, exhibitionism, and certainly violence. All these traits were at odds with old ideas of pacifism, simplicity, and self-sufficiency. But what made them part of a redefinition of Mennonite manhood was that these men still thought of themselves as Mennonites. The sportsmen spoke Low German and the football players even dubbed themselves with a name resounding with Mennonite ethnic symbolism, the Dutchmen. The car dealers were the financial backbone of the more progressive of the Mennonite churches and certainly sold many of their cars in Low German. The poultrymen and dairymen had direct links to farms that had once been the mainstay of the agrarian community.

The new Mennonite men recognized strict boundaries of acceptable behavior. The true man must distinguish himself from lesser men. However, although the new Mennonite man was more success-oriented, cosmopolitan, and aggressive, these characteristics had limits. One senses from the way they are described that some images of masculinity were more venerable than others. Images of a suspect masculinity in pacifist and puritan Steinbach would have included the following men described in various *Carillon News* articles. Jim Toews of Toronto, the 'tall, young airman' with a 'glint of the west in his eye' who no longer remembered 'a great deal about Steinbach' may have impressed one observer in 1949 as a fitting 'example of [Steinbach's] fine stock,' but he would have drawn the suspicion of the majority of townsmen. 'Us lucky fellows' – sixty-nine-year-old George Goossen and seventy-eight-year-old William Friesen watching the town's first television in June 1954 while sitting in the Steinbach pub – may have made local news, but their link to the pub disparaged the very invention they were heralding. When farmer Jake Kehler rejected the idea of a livestock marketing board in 1954 because 'I don't want to be told when or what to sell' and 'I feel like minding my own business' he was too individualistic even for the most successful town entrepreneur. Certainly when Rev Boyner, the 'peppery leader' of Steinbach's Pentecostal Church threatened to 'sue' the town in 1957 for stalling on issuing a building permit on his Bethel Tabernacle he was being less than humble and deferential. When Gilbert Friesen, the town's own Rhodes Scholar, was sent off to Oxford in September 1960, he was honored with a private 'enjoyable' dinner with 'several Winnipeg students ... present,' but his gentle personality, untimely death in England, and intellectual and artistic bent, seemed to have conspired to shut him out of any of the town's history books.[9] Each of these men had in their own way crossed the boundary of acceptable masculine behavior. Perhaps the true man must be able to negotiate his way in the new postwar society, but he must not break the values of sobriety, pacifism, simple-mindedness, and quiet deference to authority.

A final requirement for the new man was that he establish himself as separate from women. In the new postwar Hanover, life was more gendered than ever. In 1946 a writer to the *Carillon News* criticized the Bethesda Hospital for using only 'the man's name' in its birth announcements and satirically wondered whether Steinbachers no longer believed that 'women would have to bear children.' The *Carillon*'s response was to apologize to women readers and, in what would have been considered to be a half measure by progressives, change its policy by adding the prefix 'Mr and Mrs' to the 'man's name.' Neither the writer nor the newspaper were advocates for women's rights; they were the harbingers of a new view of the gendered family in which women primarily were associated with children and men predominately with the public world.[10] Although many women were working outside homes in Steinbach during the 1950s, most men and women occupied different worksites. In 1960, for example, when Steinbach boasted '1000 gainfully employed' persons and recorded 408 of these workers as women, it also portrayed a highly gendered worksite: 137 men but only 10 women worked in Steinbach's four largest car dealerships; 150 women but only 11 men worked at Steinbach Apparel, the clothing factory.[11] Where women did work side by side with and gained positions equal to those of men, they received special recognition. In 1954 when Mintie Reimer retired as the RM of Hanover's executive secretary she was accorded recognition for having been the 'only Mennonite woman ever to have attained such a position.' But Mintie herself noted that she was no ordinary female. In her first 4-H club competition, she said, 'I placed ninth in the baking competition, but won first prize for my steer.'[12]

Ironically, as men found themselves in more gendered social spaces they also seemed to find it more necessary to assert an aggressive and outgoing manliness. In the 1950s poultrymen, car dealers, and football stars gained the greatest public recognition. The very categories would not have been considered 'manly' in an earlier generation. Tending to poultry was a woman's job that required nurture and a direct tie to the kitchen; selling consumer goods in Sunday clothes as was the lot of the car dealers would simply have been beyond the pale; sports was the world of boys that grown men left upon baptism and marriage. By the mid-twentieth century each of these activities became an indicator of the very essence of successful manhood.

It was the small self-sufficient farmer who became the object of burlesque and even spoof. The countryside was not a place for men, but for the foolish. In 1960 the editor of the *Carillon News* argued that the town of Steinbach should establish a park and save the urban dweller from ending 'up in some mosquito-infested, poison-ivied corner, made more dangerous by the presence of an angry bull or a biting dog.' As the editor noted, a park would secure 'the beauties of nature right here within walking distance.'[13] Farmers who were too closely tied to nature were parodied. No writer rose to a higher level of affection and admiration than did Arnold Dyck, the Steinbach author of the highly popular, Low German-language *Koop en Bua* series of novelettes published in the 1950s. Dyck's was an account of '*Struckforma ... gaunss dijchtbie de Natua*' – that is, 'bush farmers ... completely close to nature,' residents of Hanover's southern parkland who raise 'bush and stones,' shoot at dogs, think of Saskatchewan as an exotic land, and are held in disdain by commercialized wheat farmers.[14] The countryside had lost its redemptive value in the century's middle decades.

The Poultrymen

The most obvious gendered change among male farmers occurred in the poultry-raising sector.[15] A new breed of farmers adapted to the physical and economic realities of the RM of Hanover, engaged aggressively in a market economy, and in the process recast old gender roles by identifying themselves as 'poultrymen.' Their farm vocation was refashioned by the Manitoba Agricultural College and Extension Service. These institutions, according to Jeffrey Taylor, worked to create a new 'composite image' of the 'farm man' as an 'efficient producer,' a 'market participant,' and a 'family head.'[16] The poultrymen also were directed by local hatcheries, eviscerating cooperatives, and feed mills, often vertically integrated enterprises seeking to join the North America–wide movement to commercialize poultry production. Local feed companies that marketed 'Pep Feeds' and 'Surgain Feeds' indirectly appealed for a more aggressive stance in the production of poultry, but Steinbach's leading feedmill's offering of 'Poultry Man's Laying Mash' and other 'Poultry Man's Feeds' was a direct declaration that men were setting aside old taboos.[17] So too were regular appeals from Steinbach Hatchery and Brookside Hatchery for poultrymen to purchase their chickens and from Blumenort Co-op Produce, a slaughterhouse, for poultrymen to sell them their commodities.

Poultry became a man's world. Men who turned to poultry were legitimized with visits from 'government men' bearing imposing titles. In January 1946 Steinbach Hatchery and Brookside Hatchery published an invitation to farmers, with a special 'Attention Poultrymen' salutation, to come and meet none other than Mr W.A. Bronson, 'Chief of Special Products Board of Poultry Marketing Services, Ottawa, Canada.'[18]

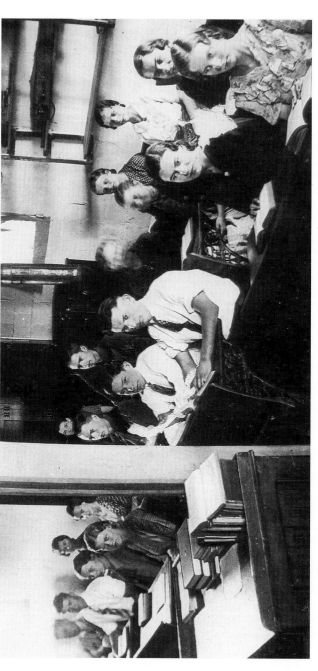

Students at the Meade Bible School during the 1936–7 academic year. The Bible school was one of dozens located in rural Mennonite communities in North America and served to introduce a more personalized and evangelistic faith into the communities. This Bible school eventually evolved into the Meade Bible Academy, a bustling private highschool during the 1950s. A similar school, Steinbach Bible Academy (later Steinbach Bible College) was begun in Manitoba in the 1940s. (Merle Loewen)

Seventy-six year old Aganetha Friesen Reimer in 1950, still dressed in old order Kleine Gemeinde garb, featuring a dark dress and head covering, holding a planting. Aganetha was one of the last Meade County residents born in Russia (January 1874), just months before her clan's migration to Jefferson County, Nebraska. Her husband, Klaas B. Reimer, predeceased her in 1931. (unknown)

A family photograph of Jacob F. and Maria (Dueck) Isaac, of Meade, Kansas, and their small sons Lee and Al in 1940. Jacob was the last bishop of the Kleine Gemeinde Mennonite Church in the United States. Maria, a Canadian and one-time student of the large Prairie Bible Institute of Three Hills, Alberta, was Jacob's second wife. While Jacob's tie-less shirt and Maria's dark dress indicate their commitment to old-order ways, the fact that this is a studio photograph indicates that the Kleine Gemeinde Church was in transition. Four years later the vast majority of the members of the Kleine Gemeinde revolted against Isaac's leadership, left that church, and formed the independent Emmanuel Mennonite Church. (Merle Loewen)

The John H. Reimer farmstead in Meade County, Kansas in about 1950. (Mennonite Library and Archives)

Here a 22-36 McCormick Deering tractor pulls a one-way disker on the Henry A. Friesen farm in Meade County. These diskers were replaced in the 1940s and 1950s by soil-conserving tillage equipment. This particular tractor, manufactured in the 1920s, was upgraded in the late 1940s with an electric starter and rubber tires; the small wheel located on the boom in front of the tractor was a locally invented steering aid. (Menno Friesen)

Dave Classen's country store in the Mennonite Settlement southeast of Meade, Kansas, 1951. The small store's popularity was marked by its $24,000 in annual sales of frozen food, gasoline, and books. The car would eventually undermine the 'Settlement' as Mennonites began traveling to shop in the town of Meade. (Mennonite Library and Archives)

The family of Henry A. and Margaret L. Friesen, about 1945. Henry and Margaret farmed in Meade County, but with the exception of one son, all their children left the county. From left to right: (back row) Margaret Jr, who became a teacher in Inman, Kansas; Daniel, who became a businessman in Denver, Colorado; Menno, who earned a PhD and taught for a time at Drake University, Iowa; Pete and his wife Katherine (Reimer), farmers in Meade; Marvin, who left to farm in Van Horn, Texas; (front row) Elda, a nurse who settled in Lancaster, Pennsylvania; Margaret Sr; Esther, who met her Swiss Mennonite husband doing voluntary service in California; Henry. (Menno Friesen)

The initial buildings of the Kleine Gemeinde Mennonite village of Springstein at Quellen Colony (Los Jagueyes Colony) in the Bustillos Basin of the eastern Sierra Madre Mountains, north of Cuauthemoc, Chihuahua, Mexico, 1950. These primitive earthen brick buildings housed the young families of Bernard and Helen Loewen, and Cornelius and Helen Friesen, the vanguard of the Isaac and Maria Loewen clan that relocated from Manitoba to Mexico in 1952. This clan was a small part of an 8000-person Mennonite migration from Canada to Mexico in the 1920s and 1940s. (Dietrich Loewen)

Leaving Sunset Court motel in Meade, Kansas, en route to Mexico. Before the coming of the interstate system Meade lay on the busy New York–Los Angeles route that included Highway 54. It also lay along the route used when Manitoba Mennonites moved to Mexico in the 1920s and 1940s. Here Manitoba resident Gertie Loewen and her daughters Judy, one year old, and Beverly, three years old, are seen to embark on the last leg of the four-day road trip to visit the relatives of her husband Dave (the photographer) at Quellen Colony, Mexico, in the spring of 1954. Although Meade County was the home of Dave and Gertie's third cousins, they were unacquainted with them. (Gertie Loewen)

Three five-year-old cousins in Quellen Colony, Mexico, in 1968. Lesley Plett and Peter Dueck, on the left, are sons of members of the Kleine Gemeinde Mennonite church; Mark Loewen on the right, is a guest from Canada whose parents were members of the Evangelical Mennonite Church. Note the traditional shirt styles of the Mexico boys and the more fashionable pullover of the Canadian boy. (Gertie Loewen)

Spanish Lookout Colony, British Honduras, February 1963. Resident Venus Kornelsen and his brother-in-law Dietrich Loewen visiting from Mexico examine a palm branch. At the time the colony was still preoccupied with turning a rain forest into an orderly farm settlement consisting of straight roads and farm fields. (Dietrich Loewen)

The Kleine Gemeinde Mennonite Church building in the village of Schoenthal at Spanish Lookout Mennonite Colony, British Honduras, February 1963. The plain church structure was an adaptation of Canadian design, but note the veranda and the absence of glass windows, early adaptations to blazing heat in British Honduras. (Dietrich Loewen)

A typical farmstead at Spanish Lookout, British Honduras. The house is an adaptation of the popular one-and-a-half-story frame farmhouse of the Canadian prairies, with the exception of being constructed on wooden piers, half a meter above the ground, and the open windows. (Dietrich Loewen)

These two African-Belizeans worked for the Mennonites when they first settled in British Honduras. Names like Gordon Elias and Dario Martinez were household names to the Mennonites, but it cannot be ascertained that they are the men depicted here. Living among non-Caucasians marked new cultural and social challenges for the conservative Mennonites. (Dietrich Loewen)

The six children of Clarence and Vera Dueck of Spanish Lookout, British Honduras, in early 1969 (from left to right), Margaret, Wilma, baby Edward on the lap of Betty, George, and Lawrence. Note the palm tree in the back and the tin-roofed building on the left. (Dietrich Loewen)

Beverly and Judy Loewen sitting on a snow drift that appeared each winter between their family's farm house and barn. Manitoba's northern continental climate usually brought snow that remained on the ground for four to five months of each year. Children played in it, while farmers relied on it to protect perennials and to provide moisture for spring plantings. (Gertie Loewen)

Manitoba farmer Herbert Peters and his sons Art, Willie, and Siegfried, and dog Spotty, in their modern dairy barn in the Rural Municipality of Hanover, Manitoba, January 1958. The barn features Manitoba's very first mechanized 'Badger' manure disposal system consisting of an electric motor-driven chain-lined drag that pulled the cow dung outdoors. Herbert Peters, unlike most of his neighbors, was born in the Soviet Union and was part of the 1920s immigration of the so-called Russlaender, progressive Mennonite refugees. (*Carillon*)

Elizabeth Reimer, age fourteen, and friend Bella Barkman, combining with a Model 55 John Deere combine harvester in the Rural Municipality of Hanover, Manitoba, September 1968. Elizabeth's father, Irwin Reimer, the owner of the combine and seen disembarking, is custom combining for his neighbor Henry Barkman, the owner of the Dodge truck. Unlike in Kansas where combine harvesters cut standing wheat, Manitoba's short growing season required wheat to be pre-cut and then dried in a swath before it was harvested. The self-propelled combine harvester became popular on both Manitoba and Kansas farms in the 1950s. The Manitoba farms were located on the very eastern edge of the Canadian prairie, note the tree line on the horizon. (*Carillon*)

These fashionably-dressed young telephone operators in Steinbach, Manitoba, in August 1957, represented a vanguard of young women who found job opportunities in Manitoba's consumer-based postwar economy. A modern dial system took over this manually-operated switchboard in 1959. (*Carillon*)

The formidable Dutchmen football team of Landmark, Manitoba, in 1957, helped make rough and tumble sports among grown Mennonite men respectable. However, as most of the players were of Kleine Gemeinde Mennonite background (note the surnames of Penner and Plett below), they were also severely criticized by the elders. From left to right: (back row) Corny Penner, Henry Penner, Paul Plett, Wilmer Penner (quarterback), Les Penner, Stan Plett, Vic Hildebrand; (front row) West Plett, Dan Loewen, Elmer Plett, Johnny Reimer, Willy Plett, Albert Plett, Wes Penner. (*Carillon*)

A crowd of almost two thousand wait to hear Pennsylvania Mennonite revivalist, George Brunk, in Steinbach, Manitoba, June 1957. Brunk's charismatic preaching style drew thousands while his simple evangelical message of repentance and joyous certainty of salvation helped weaken the old-order Mennonite religious message of humility and pacifism. (*Carillon*)

In May 1960 the last of the traditional Mennonite house-barns was demolished in Steinbach, Manitoba. The owner of the property, the flamboyant car-dealer A.D. Penner, front and bent over, was criticized for allowing progress to erase all signs of the olden days. When he ordered the old building bulldozed he had his eighty-four year-old mother, Susanna Penner, offer a symbolic spanking. The event precipitated serious discussion on the building of a museum in town; in 1967 the Mennonite Heritage Village Museum opened its doors. (*Carillon*)

Women in Steinbach, Manitoba, swarming the town's new Stylerite Department Store's '9 a.m. door crasher' when it opened in June 1960. The local *Carillon News* was a booster paper that highlighted all grand openings in town, while the women of Steinbach made history by becoming savvy participants of a consumer society. (*Carillon*)

The major car dealers and salesmen of Steinbach, Manitoba, in the 1950s. The cowboy hats marked just one of many promotional tactics used by these Mennonite men to lure customers from Winnipeg and Manitoba's southeast region to purchase family sedans in their town. Only their names still suggest their simple agrarian backgrounds: from left to right they are Henry Peters, John (JD) Penner, Abe (A.D.) Penner, Charlie Penner, Harry Fast, Bill Giesbrecht, unknown, Art Berg, Clarence Fast, unknown, "Yappin" John Klassen, Harvey Klassen, Dave Epp, Jake Peters, Frank Klassen. (*Carillon* and Frank Klassen)

Main Street, Steinbach, Manitoba, looking northwest, May 1975. (*Carillon*)

Archie Penner lectures at a meeting of the Mennonite Student Fellowship at the University of Manitoba in Winnipeg in 1968. Penner was the former pastor of the Evangelical Mennonite Church (EMC) of Steinbach, Manitoba, and in 1968 was working on his doctorate in history and religion at the University of Iowa. He had been brought back to speak to students on the theme of religious faith and science. Leaning against the blackboard is Glen Klassen, a graduate student in microbiology at the University of Manitoba. Penner and Klassen would eventually become the first EMC members to earn doctorates, Penner in 1971 and Klassen in 1979. (Evangelical Mennonite Conference and Glen Klassen)

Jake and Lydia Epp at breakfast with their seven-year-old daughter Lisa in 1972. Jake Epp, at the age of 33, was elected as a federal Progressive Conservative Member of Parliament in that year. He became the first Mennonite from Manitoba's southeast to be elected to a federal post and later became a prominent cabinet minister. Epp, a champion of laissez-faire government and lower taxes, considered himself more an evangelical than a Mennonite and is credited for the inclusion of 'God' in Canada's 1982 constitution. (*Carillon*)

And men began to organize special poultry associations. By September 1946 a local 'Hanover Turkey Breeders' Association' had been established. By 1949 meetings of 'turkey breeders,' 'capon raisers,' or 'Barred Rock ROP stockmen' were becoming highly publicized and regular affairs. In January 1949 after a meeting of 'turkey and poultry breeders' the *Carillon News* conjectured that 'gauged by the enthusiasm of local poultrymen,' this could well become an annual event. Later that year it was announced that a 'Poultry Show,' the 'biggest in Manitoba,' had just been held in Steinbach.[19]

Individual farmers were now singled out and cheered on in their endeavor to commercialize the production of poultry. In 1947 farmer Arnold Barkman's flock of 'several thousand' turkeys and farmers Ben L. Reimer and Jake U. Klassen's breeding stock of '70 broad-breasted turkey hens' received recognition in the local weekly. Farmers who demonstrated innovation in poultry production were accorded special status. Significant honor, for example, was accorded the 'poultrymen from the Ste. Anne and Blumenort areas' who won top prize for their eggs at the April 1960 Canadian National Exhibition in Toronto. Sometimes the men were recognized for the both the innovation and size of their enterprises. In March 1947 when Steinbach Hatchery's owner, Peter F. Barkman, announced that his company had defeated nature and placed '20,000 January chicks' he did it on CBC radio's 'Monday Farm Broadcast' under the designation of 'local chick magnate.' In October 1955 the *Carillon News* ran an article on a 19,000-bird turkey farm, in which owner J.P. Tanchak was described as a 'rancher,' his farm as the 'Ridgeville Turkey Ranch,' and his workers as the 'four men on his ranch.' And in newspaper stories, efficiency and technology became associated with poultry. Steinbach Flour Mills advertised its new bulk-feed truck delivery service in 1959, a service that it declared in print and picture allowed farmer D.G. Klassen and his twelve- and fourteen-year-old sons to 'raise ... 70,000 broilers a year.' A sure sign of the new prestige of poultry production and the erosion of old gendered and labor assumptions surrounding it was the fact that in 1960 the longest and most modern of the Hanover broiler-chicken barns was being erected by Steinbach's foremost merchant, Frank Reimer, and its largest egg-layer operation by one of the town's leading car dealership owners, John D. Penner.[20]

Hanover farmers were aware of a certain agricultural dichotomy that stemmed from the frontier years of the 1870s. The confident wheat producer had settled on the open prairie west of the Red River on the

Mennonite West Reserve, whereas the subsistence-oriented households had chosen the bush and lowlands of the East Reserve, the district that evolved into the RM of Hanover. As sociologist E.K. Francis noted in his field research in Hanover only in the northwest sections of the municipality were there 'larger ... grain growing' operations: the 'most widespread type' of farm in Hanover was 'the medium-sized mixed farm ... emphasizing dairy products and to a lesser degree poultry and eggs.'[21] By the 1950s assumptions about farm productivity and wealth had changed. Dairy and poultry now were the growing farm sectors, following the lead of American vertically integrated enterprises and incorporating the latest technology. As one observer noted in 1954, 'there may have been a time when farmers in the Southeast would have cast an envious glance in the direction of the straight grain farmer, who ... seed[ed] his grain in spring, harvest[ed] it three months later, then t[ook] off for California.' Now, declared the writer, the advantages of dairy and poultry farming have been demonstrated.[22] No one could conclude any longer that the wheat producer was more in tune with market forces and technology than the poultry or dairy farmer.

With the commercialization of the mixed farm, women were excused from the farmyard. Now only vestiges of women's association with poultry production remained. At Hanover's Agricultural Fair in 1955, for example, each of the twenty-nine prizes for cattle production was awarded to a boy or man; twenty-two of the fifty-one prizes for the raising of Leghorns, Barred Rocks, Sussex, and other poultry, however, went to girls and women. But it was a sign of a passing arrangement. Significantly, the *Carillon News* coverage of the December 1949 Steinbach Poultry Show mentioned numerous men but only one woman: 'Mrs. Jim Steele,' an Anglo-Canadian from the nearby Clearspring settlement, was present to observe 'the new way of marketing poultry.' A similar rearrangement appeared in dairy farming. In February 1949 the *Carillon News* could report that 600 'dairymen' had gathered at the annual meeting of the Manitoba Dairy Association; the former guardians of the dairy cows and their milkers, that is, the 'over 100 women' who were in attendance, 'took part in the special program arranged for them.' Judging from the ads for the 'McCormick Deering' milking machines, Ford's 'hydraulic touch' front-end loader, and the 'Badger' barn cleaner, dairying had become a mechanical world and hence, as agricultural historians have argued, a man's world. Most telling that mechanization had ushered women from the dairy barn was a 1959 ad for the 'Badger Barn Cleaner.' It noted that the 'Krentz Farm' of thirty-six milking cows south of Steinbach could now be 'look[ed] after' solely by sixteen-year-old Reggie Krentz and still ensure that he had sufficient 'time to complete his education.'[23]

The underlying reason for this gender shift was that poultry and dairying had become associated with the wider world. Men who participated in the raising of chickens and turkeys were no longer isolated Mennonite farmers. Steinbach's Brookside Hatchery made a December 1946 appeal for local farmers to join the Canadian initiative to provide Britain with a million cases of fresh eggs. Brookside declared with an air of importance that 'if we wish to hold the British market for Canadians we must ship fresh eggs in October, November and December.' When local farmers spoke of the problems of poultry raising, the subject rarely had to do with the logistics of manual chores. Rather their problems and their challenges lay in the elusive market. In 1955 the *Carillon News* announced that according to local turkey raisers, 'turkeys are birds that are hatched and grown in the west to keep the producer broke and the buyer crazy ... Turkeys are hatched in the spring, mortgaged in the summer and lost in the fall.'[24] Moreover, these problems were associated with international events. In 1957 when the new Conservative government of Prime Minister John Diefenbaker raised tariffs on incoming American farm produce a local representative on the Manitoba Turkey Association noted that he was 'jubilant,' for 'our turkeys were getting old in storage' and 'we got action the next day after the tariff went on' as 'prices went up 2½ cents right away.'[25]

The poultryman and the dairyman had introduced a new concept of manhood to Hanover. Manliness may have been associated with a market-driven economy, profit motivation, and separate spheres on the wheat farms of Western Canada. It was now associated with the farm sectors traditionally the sphere of women. The debut of the poultrymen and dairymen signalled not only that men had taken over a sector of farming once associated with women, but also that men who had grown up on small mixed farms geared to self-sufficiency and generational succession now saw their roles in new ways. Success merited attention and attention brought the new designation of 'rancher' 'magnate,' and 'breeder.' These designations separated true men from undaring men, men from boys, and most importantly, men from women.

Car Dealers and Fellow Businessmen

More visible and self-assured than any poultryman was the Steinbach district businessman. His reputation became the very explanation of town life. As geographer John Warkentin noted in his 1960 study of southern Manitoba, the main reason that Steinbach alone of all RM of Hanover villages had risen 'well above the level of a rural trading centre' was that its business leaders 'are extremely aggressive and dedicated to hard work to the exclusion of every other activity but church work.'[26] Town businessmen signalled in these postwar years that they had moved well beyond the task of providing services to farmers. In 1957 Steinbach Chamber of Commerce president, car dealer, and wholesaler, John D. Penner, hinted that Steinbach businessmen were reconsidering their support for the local Agriculture Fair: although '15 years ago business people in Steinbach [depended] largely on agriculture,' he argued, now in 1957 they were playing in a larger league, with 'neighbouring cities, including Winnipeg.'[27]

The men who were looking to Winnipeg most publicly were Steinbach's five largest car dealerships: J.R. Friesen and Son was the town's oldest car lot and reputedly even the oldest Ford dealership on the Canadian prairies; Penner Motors and Penner Garage were owned by two brothers, farm boys from Blumenort; Loewen Garage, selling Chevrolets, was run by P.T. Loewen, brother of Steinbach's prominent lumberman C.T. Loewen; and the company of L.A. Barkman, the son of a conservative Holdeman Mennonite family, sold Pontiacs.[28] During the 1950s the five car dealerships built their business through extensive advertising and unrelenting hyperbole. In addition they sponsored sales promotions, car giveaways, 'Automobile Extravaganzas,' car discounts to local ministers, and sales pitches using the direct-dial long-distance service to Winnipeg. When the Penner brothers, A.D. and John D., introduced the first car auction in 1955, they achieved the sale of '48 cars in three and a half hours' as well as the admiration of 'officials from the Ford Motor Company from Winnipeg.' They had achieved it all with the 'usual Penner flare for show and precision.' Always the salesmen were depicted as forceful and energetic persons. A.D. Penner lauded his five salesmen in an October 1955 ad as being the 'driving force in helping 300 families choose 1955 Dodge cars and trucks.' All the while the salesmen insisted boldly and shamelessly that the hoopla was merely in the interest of the consumer: 'There's a flyer in the mail,' announced one Penner Garage ad in 1955, but 'don't drop dead – just come in and share the wealth.'[29]

This flashy, energetic, colorful presence was far removed from the owners' Kleine Gemeinde Mennonite roots. Most flamboyant among the dealers was A.D. Penner. A local history juxtaposes his town-based success to the time in 'the early Depression years [when] a gangling farm boy from Blumenort ... wanted to try something a little different from milking cows and feeding pigs.'[30] That Blumenort farm boy now enjoyed the lifestyle of conspicuous consumption: he drove large Chrysler cars, flew a private airplane, attended the Emmanuel Free Church, and helped establish the town's Fly-In Golf Course. Penner was at the helm of creating a new place for businessmen. In the late 1940s and 1950s the large, two-story houses of Steinbach's first genera- tion businessmen – J.R. Friesen, H.W. Reimer, C.T. Loewen – were moved and the large maples uprooted to make room for growing businesses and car lots.[31] In March 1960 the *Carillon News* reported that 'things aren't as simple as they used to be in the peaceful Mennonite "darp."' Penner and several other businessmen had purchased a set of lots and gardens on the south side of town 'to plan a rather exclusive building subdivision' with '100 to 120 foot frontage[s]' and bearing a 'boulevard of flowers.'[32] They were doing so, said the newspaper, with 'some justifiable pride.'

Most deliberate of Penner's departures from an agrarian past was the destruction of Steinbach's last house-barn in 1960. When Steinbach had been founded as a farm village in 1874, the wooden framed house-barn built especially for easy access of women to livestock signalled pioneer success. By 1960 the town's only house-barn was an abandoned, sag- ging, unpainted, shingle-sided building located at the corner of Main Street and Victoria Avenue, the gateway to Steinbach's commercial center. Significantly, the rotting building sat just across the road from A.D. Penner's ultramodern Chrysler car dealership – bright red, flat- roofed, and graced with grand show windows. In May 1960 Penner, who also owned a road construction company, announced that one of his huge D9 Caterpillar bulldozers was in town and he intended to demolish the old house-barn. Immediately Penner was petitioned by retired schoolteacher John C. Reimer of the local Mennonite Historical Society to stop the destruction in the name of history. To strengthen his case Reimer asked Mr. Hart Bowsfield, Manitoba's provincial archivist, to drive from Winnipeg and help confront Penner. As the *Carillon News* put it: 'right up until a few minutes before the bulldozer blade crunched into the rotting timbers ... Bowsfield and local members of the society were in [Penner's] office ... attempting to obtain a stay of execution.'[33] Penner was unrepentant: he had offered to sell the commercial property to the historical society 'at cost' and since it had not been able to raise the funds his crew would proceed. With typical flare Penner excused himself from his office and crossed the road with his elderly mother to offer a photo opportunity. As cameras clicked, the huge D9 crushed the building and a grinning A.D. bent over to allow his mother to mock spank him. The message was clear: while the historical society might think him a reckless 'boy,' the massive, masculine D9 would do its work in the name of progress.

The new masculinity, however, came with confusing behavior. How could a man dressed in Sunday best, selling consumer goods that had little economic merit, be a man at all? How could men sell cars that during the 1950s were often advertised with photos in which fashion-ably dressed women competed for attention? How could they sell products that boasted graceful lines, sparkling chrome, and soft rides? No doubt the salesman's occupation was made more acceptable by advertising encapsulated in profoundly male language. In 1957 each of the new cars used the word 'bold' to describe its advantage: the Pontiac at L.A. Barkman Inc. declared its 'boldest advance,' the Meteor at Penner Motors a 'bold new way,' the Dodge at Penner Garage a 'bold and revolutionary' design. The ad for Meteor went the furthest, con-trasting the 'bold clean cut' machine to the older 'plump, static' car. And each car ad also emphasized ever-increasing power and size. The 1958 Lincoln was said to the 'most powerful Lincoln ever built,' a car with '300 HP, hushed and ready to fly' and inside 'everything you touch turns to pampering power: electric door locks, 6-way power front seats, power lubrication.' For those finding themselves out of range of the Lincoln, the Meteor promised all that a family could desire in language that emphasized size above all else. The ad for the 1957 Meteor at Penner Motors declared 'the Big M for '57 is dream-car styled, but family-car big – by far the biggest Mercury you've ever seen. New length, width and wheelbase.'[34]

The car dealers were only the most flamboyant of Steinbach business-men. In 1955 C.T. Loewen and Sons' lumberyard and wood products factory employed 101 persons, Barkman Hardware 56 persons, and dozens more worked at M.M. Penner's lumberyard, the half dozen grocers, the hatcheries, feedmills, farm equipment dealerships, the sew-ing factory, service stations, and cafes. Many of the larger businesses had deeper roots in Steinbach than the car dealers, most were less dependent on advertising, many were based on old crafts – skill with steel, wood, and cloth – and most were less eager than the car men to exhibit their good fortune. What newly established car dealers and second-generation lumbermen and retailers had in common, though, was the amalgamation of two images; the old agrarian ideal of hard work and the new urban fixation on power were combined to construct a new notion of true manhood.

Often the businessmen spoke of self-reliance, family unity, and 'puritan' values. But their references entailed a look to the future, not to the past. In one 1960 ad Steinbach businessmen celebrated the fact that the railway had bypassed the district in the '1880s,' a fact that led pioneers to discover that 'there was only one thing you could rely on and that was yourself.'[35] But this was hardly a pitch for a return to a self-reliant, isolated Mennonite community. A triumphant cry by Steinbach car dealers, in bold red letters, announced an upcoming, 'Automobile Extravaganza,' explaining that there was 'Lots of Steam in Steinbach Even Without a Railroad.' In 1954 at the occasion of his fiftieth wedding anniversary lumberyard owner Martin M. Penner was lauded by his wife, Elizabeth, for his part in holding 'the family together.' It was an old virtue, but had been achieved in a new way: Martin had done it using his 'powerful, aggressive personality.' This personality, said Elizabeth, 'caused him on several occasions to go ahead and ... complete a scheme which friends deemed impossible ... This very forcefulness' had 'held the family together and caused them to enter every enterprise as one unit.'[36] Other of Steinbach's businessmen were described in similar language. Frank Reimer, Steinbach founder of the nationally focussed Reimer Express Lines noted that his training had included the idea that when the Bible declared 'six days shalt thou labor ... it meant six days not five ... it didn't mean "thou shalt fool around" [or] ... thou shalt quit when the job is only half done.'[37]

Hard physical work apparently had preceded his stunning business success. The businessmen may have relied on mental power to negotiate the new postwar society, but they all insisted that it was a love for physical work that had launched their upward mobility. Many of the businessmen had stories of how they had toiled as youth: A.D. Penner had milked cows; C.T. Loewen had been a gun-toting frontier cowboy; Frank Reimer had driven a truck, earning $35 a month, single-handedly loading hundred-pound bags of flour, working till midnight and then rising at 5:00 a.m. 'whistling.'[38] Most of the men sent the message that by providing others with the opportunity for physical work, they, the businessmen, were not so much reaping rewards as serving their communities. A 1947 company history of C.T. Loewen's lumber firm notes that 'Canada's most modern' recently completed bee-supply factory had its roots in the Great Depression after 'Mr. Loewen planned on how he could employ at least a few of the [community's unemployed] men who were so eager to work.'[39] The town fathers' confidence may have been rooted in 'forceful' and 'determined' personalities, but they felt a manly tie to any male willing to exert himself physically. They even boasted a solidarity with failed West Reserve wheat farmers who during the Depression came east to Hanover's southern parkland and established subsistence farms. These men were worthy because they were hardened by a municipal council that 'refrained from dealing out "unearned money."' The Hanover council had seen to it that 'all who were able to work were given an axe or a pick and told: "now earn your warm meal a day."' And because they were 'thrown without much mercy upon their own resourcefulness, they discovered many opportunities for rehabilitation.' Above all, these men turned 'mechanical hobbies into gainful employment,' serving in the creation of 'prospering workshops and factories.'[40] This culture of earnest hard work Steinbach happily passed on to the next generation. In 1960 when six twelve-year-old children in town were asked the question, 'what is a gentleman?' only young Tony Sawatsky answered that a gentleman 'treated ladies in a knightly fashion'; five of the six respondents described a gentleman as 'hard working' and 'kind.'[41]

If the businessman had a nemesis it was not the honest wage laborer but the male schoolteacher. No doubt the teacher was respected and possessed self-respect. Elementary schoolteacher Mel Toews's outlook is described by novelist Miriam Toews in her book *Swing Low*: 'I would prepare my students for the world outside, beyond our little town and I would teach them to express themselves.'[42] But a different perspective was emerging in the local weekly. Town businessmen sometimes let it be known that the male schoolteacher lacked a full measure of respectable masculinity. Reportedly a common saying among local businessman was that 'schoolteachers are boys that are not men, and men that are not boys.'[43] Schoolteaching was after all a profession that men shared with women. Indeed, even after a massive 30 percent hike in teachers' salaries in 1957, a married man was still promised only $300 more than an unmarried woman who received 'a basic salary of $3500.'[44] The male schoolteacher would have smarted at the words of a young Steinbach woman who said that if her future husband, the 'breadwinner,' made less than $3000, life certainly 'wouldn't be much fun.' Local barber John Unger's analysis did little to add to male status: 'these salaries' are a good thing, interpreted Unger, because they could lead 'many girls to finish high-school and go to Normal School.'[45] If Arnold Dyck had parodied the bush farmer, the *Carillon News* now did not shy from an occasional ribbing of the schoolteacher, the man who had outgrown his britches. In January 1960 the *Carillon News* noted a town rumor that a 'local schoolteacher ... got himself ... into hot water' for having denounced Catholics, but also for having suggested that 'Steinbach businessmen are, by and large, a bunch of crooks.'[46] At Steinbach Collegiate, the graduating class let it be known that if higher education was the route to success, teacher's college was less manly than another university-based career: in 1960 as ten boys and ten girls prepared for 'teacher's college,' twenty-one boys and one girl indicated they were headed for 'university.'

But the very highest status was always accorded the businessman. In one 1970 *Carillon News* fictional portrayal of social mobility a man named Joe, 'being a bit above average,' earns a Master of Arts and becomes a 'high school teacher,' but then 'always wanting a bit more, he jumped from teaching to an executive position in a business firm.' He ultimately failed because he refused to consult his business colleagues or even his wife; thinking he was 'smart enough' he relied only on his 'degrees' and 'his own original ideas.'[47] Male teachers, of course, could be redeemed as history teacher Jake Epp demonstrated in 1972; that year he was elected member of Parliament and his charismatic cries that 'government governs best that governs least' quickly made him the darling of Main Street entrepreneurs and a model for other schoolteachers.

The forceful, aggressive, self-made men in Steinbach venerated a combination of hard physical work measured in product and mental determination measured in profit. A mix of old and new ways also tempered their view of Christianity. A local history tells the story of the travelling salesman who checked in at Steinbach's Tourist Hotel and asked 'what do people do for fun around here?' He was told they 'work and go to church.' That story may be apocryphal, but it stood at the heart of Mennonite masculinity.[48]

These men believed in a clean, sober, godly town and went out of their way to build it. But often as businessmen bent on moralistic duty, they worked not through their own churches, but through their own associations or parachurch organizations. It was the members of the Chamber of Commerce in 1954 who recorded their support for prohibition; thirty-two to two were opposed to licensed beverage rooms, twenty-two to twelve against any kind of alcohol sales, including those at the men's-only beverage room on Steinbach's Main Street.[49] It was businessmen who served on the board of the Red Rock Bible Camp and the

Steinbach Bible Institute and who spearheaded the construction of the thousand-seat Tabernacle revival meeting hall. They were the Gideons who, dressed in sharp suits and wearing friendly faces, visited each grade five class in Steinbach every year to hand out New Testaments. And they were the benefactors of projects they deemed important. They gave, but on their own terms. An often-repeated story of C.T. Loewen, the lumberman, was that when he traveled the countryside to collect unpaid bills he carried bags of flour as gifts to debtors who were too poor to pay up. Individual businessmen also supported foreign missionaries, but often in ways they chose. The giving could be spectacular, unexpected, and anonymous. In September 1957 a local businessman was said to have 'shocked' a missionary conference at Steinbach's Emmanuel Mission church 'into momentary dead silence' by his anonymous donation of $24,000.[50] Local businessmen, no doubt, were pleased that Manitoba's *Trade and Industry* magazine named Steinbach's John D. Penner 'Man of the Month,' but especially because it declared that Penner was 'living proof that it is possible to reach a high pinnacle of success in business without letting the economic venture become the most powerful factor in ... life.'[51]

The new man in the Steinbach business community was forceful, determined, and aggressive. Traits that in an earlier farm-based generation were suspect now became venerated. They promised personal success. Providing work for the unemployed, making a profit for the family, and offering support to evangelical missions were manly successes. Each was achieved through individual initiative and personal merit, and it was important that they were achieved and not inherited.

Football Stars and Sports Enthusiasts

If the car dealers had developed a sense of manhood that was separated from physical exertion and from an organic sense of togetherness, another form of nonagrarian manliness tried to recapture the physical and communitarian forms, albeit with the same competitive spirit and division of labor seen in town businesses. This was the athletic Mennonite.[52] He was the product of town life, and he represented boys who worked for bosses and not for their fathers, boys headed for the self-made professions or business, not the inherited farm. Clearly they were the products of a new society that was directed by radio, and increasingly by television, to the culture beyond Mennonite boundaries. As athletes they increasingly were seen as a positive cultural response to and preparation for the new postwar society. Sports activities were even seen as manly, not trivial boyish pursuits to be put aside when manhood arrived. Indeed, sports activities marked the very passage to manhood.

Sport itself was not new in the Steinbach district. As early as 1923 a Steinbach Sports Club expressed an aim to 'to provide funds for the promotion of skating, hockey, snow shoeing, baseball, tennis and other sports.' The club seems to have had some impact in associating sports with manhood: its first president was twenty-four-year-old J.J. Reimer, who was not only the son of a respected Kleine Gemeinde merchant, but a married man.[53] In 1937 the local Kleine Gemeinde Mennonite churches asserted the old value that with regard 'to entertainment ... it is all right for children to play ball ... but that believers [adults] should not take part in such games.'[54] The debate over adult participation in sports intensified as Steinbach grew in size and as more families left the farms.

In January 1947 Steinbach was enmeshed in heated verbal exchanges over construction of an indoor ice arena. Non-Mennonite banker T.G. Smith chided local businessmen for being so 'busy with their private affairs' and churches for being so 'engrossed with problems of their own congregations' that they ignored the need for a 'modern ... recreational centre.'[55] Smith had opened a debate on the foundations of Steinbach culture. Those who opposed Smith had other matters in mind than the cost of a new facility. Writing in the *Carillon News*, Abram Friesen argued against an arena: Steinbach, he said, had prospered because of 'hard work and faith in God,' not sports and railroads. Abram Toews from Saskatchewan wrote to counter Friesen, saying that he knew 'a dozen towns' – Ukrainian, English, Norwegian – and each had prospered by embracing all four components, 'faith in God, hard work, railroads and sports facilities.'[56] Sport in his mind was neither infantile nor heathen. Peter Toews replied, blaming the very debate on town life: if we had kept to 'the faith of our fathers ... we would not have this town problem' because we would 'be an agricultural people [whose] ... young people ... have plenty of exercise.'[57]

He was right. Historians suggest a link between competitive sports and a time in history when fewer and fewer men expressed their manliness in outdoor physical work and within cohesive family units. Michael Oriard's *Reading Football* argues that this link centered on an anxiety about manliness: 'without football, masculine anxiety might have been more acute; without the anxiety, football might not have survived its injury-plagued probation.'[58] Anthony Rotundo argues that competitive sport was the answer to American urban society for 'team contests demanded a strength, vigor and physical assertiveness that undermined the ease and debility of modern affluence.'[59] Increasingly this too was the view of Steinbach residents. Sports turned boys into men, not men into boys. A February 1947 poll indicated that 90 percent of Steinbach townsfolk believed that 'a closed-in arena would be beneficial to the youth,' although only 69 percent thought that the town could afford such a complex.[60] Community leaders even described a new path from boyhood to manhood, using language rooted in postwar terminology. Schoolteacher P.S. Guenther wrote that sports organizations were needed not only because 'young people have atomic energy to use,' but in order to 'channel sound, healthy individuals and build a sound community.'[61]

The presence of adult men on Hanover district sports teams after the Second World War was an even more powerful indicator of a new linkage between sports and masculinity. Hockey had a special appeal. In 1959 when Chuck Toews, who had once tried out for the Detroit Red Wings, quit the Steinbach Huskies Hockey Team, he was thirty-seven years old and was honored for his leadership, 'always ... a live wire in the dressing room no matter what the score.'[62] A week later when another Husky star, Dennis Guenther, quit after having scored two hundred goals in eight years, he did so not because he had outgrown hockey, but for specific health reasons.[63] Hockey fever even infected the most conservative of Mennonite districts. In the Blumenort district, for example, hockey came to be seen by elders as a routine, if troubling, passion for young Mennonite men. In 1958 the rural district's Blumenhof Black Hawks hockey team trounced town teams to win the first championship of the Hanover Tache Hockey League. The series was said to have had 'lots of thrills,' as Blumenhof 'marksmen' 'out for revenge' won the championship and during the final game produced a hero, John Penner, who although suffering from a dislocated shoulder, scored a 'hat trick.' Grown men were speaking a foreign language.

Of all the sports teams in the southeastern Manitoba Mennonite communities, the Landmark Dutchmen were the most remarkable. Located in the Mennonite community of Landmark a few miles north of the RM of Hanover (but within the borders of the Hanover School District), they developed a sports dynasty that began in 1954 as a touch football team playing against teams from other local districts. By 1957 the Dutchmen played tackle football and regularly engaged Winnipeg teams. Three years later they joined the Manitoba Intermediate Football League as the only rural team, and within a few years raised enough interest in Steinbach to form a joint Landmark-Steinbach Dutchmen football team. Enthusiasm for the team was infectious. As the *Carillon News* reported in 1957, football, 'a little virus [usually] cultivated in the action-mad ... cities and larger towns has infected the inhabitants of ... Landmark, a village which ... is not much more than its name suggests.'[64] The reason for the interest was readily apparent for the Dutchmen's wins were stunning: Dutchmen vs Winnipeg's United College, 40–7; vs Winnipeg's Daniel McIntyre Collegiate 48–0; vs Steinbach 36–12, 18–8, and 36–0. The Dutchmen were invincible.

The Dutchmen were especially significant in that they presented themselves as possessing the best characteristics of the Mennonite community. 'We were the Dutchmen,' noted its quarterback, 'because we were Mennonite; Franco-Manitoban teams could be Saints and Habs and Flying Frenchmen, we were the Dutchmen.'[65] But the football stars were Mennonite in another sense: an increasing number of community supporters saw the players as exemplary men of moral character. In 1957 the Dutchmen's quarterback, twenty-two-year-old United College student Wilmer Penner, who returned home from Winnipeg on weekends, was singled out for special praise as a skillful and modest athlete. Farmer J.J. Hildebrand, who had set aside a piece of his farmland as a field for the football players, did raise a concern about the game's roughness. But he supported the boys because 'boys need an outlet for their excess energy,' and in part because '[I] can think of no better example for them than coach Wilmer Penner.'[66]

If the community accepted an athletic version of masculinity, the Evangelical Mennonite Church (EMC), the descendant body of the old-order Mennonite Kleine Gemeinde, had not yet come to this conclusion. Indeed, the football field and hockey rink were contested sites. That both the Dutchmen and the Black Hawks teams consisted not only of pre-baptized teenaged boys but of baptized church members in their twenties made matters especially worrying. After the Black Hawks hockey team was formed in 1958, the Blumenort EMC church issued an official warning: 'we definitely want to distance ourselves from hockey.' And after the Black Hawks won the 1958 championship the church demanded and received 'a confession that ... they had participated in hockey' and counselled players to seek 'new lives and to be witnesses for Christ.'[67] The Dutchmen drew even greater opposition from the church. The *Carillon News* could pay homage to the Dutchmen's 'snappy ... jerseys,' and 'shiny blue helmets [that] gleamed in the sunlight.'[68] But the preachers from Landmark's Prairie Rose EMC church were apprehensive at seeing 'grown men wearing helmets, with all the appearance of men from space.'[69] By 1960 the church became more assertive in its opposition: its pastor, Frank D. Reimer, reported that 'on the sports question [s]everal brothers have been excommunicated and ... [we] want to place on probation [other] brothers who have taken part.'[70]

The ministers who opposed the football team worried that it would open the way to further worldly associations. They repeated the idea that for baptized church members to play football was akin to being 'unequally yoked together' with unbelievers. The team spirit, the rough codes, the exhibitionism, and the frivolity contradicted the tenets of the humble Mennonite man. The problem, of course, was that few of these young men were committed to much less able to make farm life their vocation in the postwar economy. The Landmark football players were almost to a man heavy equipment operators, truck drivers, and schoolteachers. They found in football the physical outlet and base of comradery an earlier generation had found in the farm household. Here, too, they found the avenue to competitiveness and exhibitionism that were the hallmarks of postwar society. The controversy over football arose because it now claimed to be a legitimate expression of masculinity. In the old Mennonite scheme of things only boys could play ball; now sports could occupy a place within the very heart of Mennonite manhood.

Women and the New Masculinity

The poultrymen, car dealers, and football stars expressed a new Mennonite masculinity. They defined manhood in a society in which the currency of humility, communitarianism, and pacifism was faltering. Assertion, and notably individualistic assertiveness, was a requirement if a man was to survive in the postwar marketplace and consumer society. Ironically, the worlds of the poultrymen, car dealers, and football stars would have been deeply suspect in an earlier generation. Poultry raising had been a woman's concern, sales of consumer products a religious taboo, and all sports child's play. Now the very marks of success were constructed in terms of the commodification of suburban-directed food production, the exhibition and sale of consumer goods, and the ability to engage in physically demanding games of leisure. As men left earnest hard work and humble communitarian endeavor for white-collar, town-based vocations, the need for personal exertion and a mythologization of physical work seemed to increase. Mennonite men as pacifists had not inherited a cultural repertoire that would guide them from the farm or village into town or city. But they adapted quickly enough, accepting the very behavior and ideals that identified urban and capitalist men in the wider North American society.

Just as the gender constructions of both the Meade women and men evolved during these years, the respective gender roles of both Hanover men and women changed. The wives of the late-nineteenth-century Reimer brothers – Margaretha Klassen, Maria Reimer, Maria Plett, Aganetha Barkman – charted their lives in large families, self-sufficient households, matrilocal residence patterns, and patriarchal church congregations. Their daughters and granddaughters of the 1920s and 1930s lived in similar settings in a Hanover still described as a rural place steeped in 'pioneer conditions,' lagging behind other Manitoba regions in 'commercial success' and the acquisition of technology.[71] With the coming of rural electrification and access to suburban food markets and hence too of farm specialization, the roles of women on farms changed dramatically. Unlike the women of the HDUs in Meade County, few Hanover women joined civic organizations, but they did acquire a more urbanized culture. Alongside their sisters in town they frequented Steinbach's Marvel Ladies Apparel, coveted the appliances at Penner Electric, shopped for sleek cars at J.R. Friesen and Son Ford.[72] They found new sources of fulfilment in church-centered sewing circles that focused on producing clothing and blankets for war-torn Europe.[73] And they too skipped the baby boom, participating as Mennonites elsewhere in an unusual fertility decline during the 1950s. In disproportionate numbers they came to embrace town life (11 percent more often than men) where they found wage labor or attended high school with declared plans to become nurses, secretaries, and elementary schoolteachers.[74] And in town a new breed of women assumed public profiles: missionary Susanna Plett home from Bolivia spoke to large audiences of both men and women in Steinbach in 1949; the trailblazing municipal executive secretary Mintie Reimer retired amid great public fanfare in town in 1954; native daughter Anna Regier was honored as the first woman from Steinbach to earn a doctorate when she visited from her Minnesota college in 1960.[75]

If the female names of Susanna, Mintie, and Anna acquired public currency and this in turn encouraged women to move beyond the newly rooted 'feminine mystique,' other women questioned the mystique by asking questions about the seemingly new norms of masculinity. The local newspaper may have accepted assertiveness, individual achievement, and exhibitionism as the marks of the real man, but discerning women were less impressed. Perhaps they were driven by nostalgia, but they seemed to idealize the very image of the humble, self-sufficient farmer that popular literature and newspaper discourse now ridiculed. The bête noire in their estimation was the urban father who revealed undue aggressiveness, self-centered preoccupations, and excessive independence. In Steinbach that opposition came from both women and men and was expressed in the magazines of the Mennonite churches. The Evangelical Mennonite Conference *Messenger*, first published in 1963, carried numerous articles that chastised the new urban father for ignoring and being unable to identify with his children. In 1964 Margaret Reimer, the wife of the former Steinbach Bible Institute principal and evangelist Ben D. Reimer, submitted an article that implicitly criticized a father for having 'visualized [his small son] as a man,' telling him 'to hold your shoulders back,' and snapping when he 'softly, timidly, with a sort of hurt, hunted look in [his] eyes' disturbed father in the library.[76] In 1970 Helena Dueck, the wife of local schoolteacher Ben B. Dueck, offered a Father's Day tribute to her father who had never earned a 'university degree,' taken a 'world tour,' or accumulated 'great riches.' Instead, he had enjoyed 'long hours and hard work.' Above all through 'his high-souled, simple-hearted honesty' he had been able 'to relate to his family ... in a way that psychologists today are trying to bring.'[77]

Just as a new image of the Mennonite man had woven its way into the fabric of society in the RM of Hanover and town of Steinbach, it was already being questioned by those left outside this class-based masculinity. The middle class of the Great Disjuncture sustained the new masculinity. Its sharpest critics would be found among the strangest of bedfellows, in the conservative Mennonite colonies of Mexico and British Honduras and in the university classrooms that drew Steinbach's surplus population to nearby cities such as Winnipeg.

8 Reinventing Mennonite Tradition: Old Ways in the Jungles of British Honduras

The most conservative of the Mennonite farmers of Meade and Hanover were profoundly concerned that the mid-twentieth-century world was undermining their faith and weakening their ability to guard their inherited culture. In postwar Manitoba they were among many old-order Mennonites who stood up to modernity and migrated to isolated agrarian colonies in Latin America. In 1948 about 1200 of these Mennonites headed to Paraguay and about 800 to Mexico. The two countries held special appeal because during the 1920s after the passage of assimilative school attendance acts in Manitoba and Saskatchewan, almost 9000 conservative Canadian prairie Mennonites had moved south, 7000 to Mexico and 1800 to Paraguay. The large migrant group of the 1920s and the smaller group of the 1940s consisted of various Mennonite denominations including the Old Colonist, Sommerfelder, Chortitzer, Saskatchewan Bergthaler, and Kleine Gemeinde Mennonites. Each group shared a common Anabaptist faith commitment to a plain, communitarian, nonconformist, Christian lifestyle that challenged the forces of assimilation in modern Canada. They all shared a willingness to undertake drastic measures to confront those forces. In migrating south they answered an old challenge preached from Mennonite pulpits, they were *Nachfolger Christi*, literally 'followers of Christ.'

Among the post–Second World War migrants were 150 Kleine Gemeinde Mennonite families (595 persons) from Hanover and a smaller Mennonite settlement, Rosenort, fifty miles to the west on the 'other side' of the Red River. The initial migration had taken them to Chihuahua State, Mexico, where they established Quellen Kolonie at Los Jagueyes, about fifty miles north of the town of Cuauhtémoc. There they had established a Low German–speaking Mennonite colony complete with private schools and church-based governance over a small land territory. They had committed themselves to separation from worldly society and culture including military service, the language of the host society, and state social security programs. In 1958 a secondary migration ensued after the Mexican government introduced an intrusive social welfare scheme, the Seguro Social. This time about half of the Kleine Gemeinde Mennonites in Mexico migrated farther south to British Honduras, later renamed Belize. This social fragment found its place at Spanish Lookout Colony in the western jungles of Cayo district near the Guatemala border. There a second conservative Kleine Gemeinde Mennonite colony was established.

The aim of the migrants was to seek the maintenance of old ways, the traditions of their parents. From one perspective these newcomers to British Honduras suceeded in the transplantation of old-order society. They were similar to the conservative ethnoreligious immigrants described by leading immigration historians: in their 'isolated rural areas [they] ... had less need for the invention of ethnicity since the more particularistic collective consciousness ... serve[d] their needs for community.'[1] Rural villages, it was implied, could best be explained as changeless societies of rote and habit; to employ Benedict Anderson's concept, they were 'primordial villages of face-to-face contact' without need to be 'imagined.'[2] On the one hand this consideration is true for the Kleine Gemeinde Mennonite migrants to British Honduras. Old loyalties and social networks survived the migration, and the old dialect of the everyday, Low German, remained the lingua franca. The Kleine Gemeinde Bruderschaft continued to be the most powerful governing body. Agriculture was the vocation of the vast majority of members, roads were rough, and colonists were separated from the wider world. Spanish Lookout Colony was in this respect a changeless, traditional society.

Still, it can be argued that the aim of antimodernity required a significant cultural reformulation in the jungles of British Honduras. In this respect these migrants were similar to other conservative Anabaptist groups.[3] An anthropology of Mexican Old Colony Mennonites, for example, appeals to works by Ernest Gellner and Eric Hobsbawm to argue that life on the colonies 'is a continual process of reconstructing identity, which includes the ongoing reinvention of the notions of "tradition," the "Welt," history, change, place and social structure.'[4] A study of an Amish community in Iowa sets aside the 'static terms' of 'boundary maintenance,' and employs the thinking of Pierre Bourdieu, Carlos Ginzburg, and others to argue that the Amish were driven by internal 'dispositions [that] are acquired by [unexpected] historical experience and are engaged in historical situations.'[5] The conservative order of Spanish Lookout Colony in British Honduras also relied on a series of dynamic adaptations that remade or even 'reinvented' the old traditions. They did not simply persist in transplanted communities. Rather these antimodernists adapted, creating new symbols of separation, reinterpreting recent history, and creating new associations.[6] Even the most conservative and separated rural immigrants adapted to new environments and to changes in the wider society. In this process came new ways of organizing community, new immigration-rooted stories, and new cultural maps that gave the immigrant farm community a particular place within the host society. Like immigrants elsewhere they found ways, in Werner Sollors's words, to have their 'ethnicity ... present (invent) itself as a "natural" and timeless category.'[7]

Spanish Lookout reflected this dynamic and ongoing task of cultural reformulation. Despite its remote location across the Belize River near the Guatemala border some sixty miles inland from Belize City, it became a well-known community. By the 1970s it had attracted attention from geographers, sociologists, journalists, and government agents who were surprised at the successful adaptation of this thousand-person, Euro-Canadian community to a tropical, Third World environment.[8] Here in British Honduras tradition and adaptation existed simultaneously. Geographer Jerry Hall's in-depth 1970 study of the colony's agriculture emphasized this paradox: these farmers were 'ultraconservative' Mennonites whose agricultural system reflected a complex and shifting combination of 'tradition, trial-and-error experimentation, and local Mayan technology.'[9] Material adaptations had ensured that old ways would persist. An examination of Spanish Lookout Colony records – the colony mayor meeting records, the church brotherhood minutes, and the colony history book – suggests that the dichotomy pitting traditionalism against capitalism constitutes an inadequate understanding of the society. Ironically the purportedly traditional social mechanisms and self-identities may be new, economic and environmental innovations old.[10] But certainly their traditions were not sterile; they were made and remade at every turn as the colonists confronted new situations and tried to be true to their religious calling.

The Kleine Gemeinde Mennonites' first decade at Quellen Kolonie north of Cuauhtémoc in Mexico from 1948 to 1958, marked a period of cultural experimentation.[11] During that decade they elevated communitarian authority to a new level. The governing body of the congregation, the all-male Bruderschaft (Brotherhood) guided by the *Diener*, the ordained ministers and deacons, initially became the sole legal owner of colony land. Furthermore, the Bruderschaft sanctioned the power of a newly created secular governing arm, the *Vorsteher Komitee*, literally the committee of village mayors, but more generally the colony administration. This body in turn ensured the colony's isolation and self-sufficiency by creating a centrally planned economy, a colony transportation network, and a system of land distribution. This colony governance that had been developed in Mexico was re-established in British Honduras in 1958. During their first twenty years in British Honduras, however, Mennonites continued to evolve as inherited perceptions blended with the unique features of life in the new land to create a new subcategory of Mennonitism.

First, the colonists turned the very act of settling in the difficult rainforest of Central America into an occasion for increased group cohesion and then into a symbol of renewed religious commitment. They reviewed the very idea of 'being Mennonite.' They de-emphasized the High German language and made the Low German dialect a language of the church; they re-examined links with familiar Dutch-Canadian Mennonites and sought new associations with conservative Swiss-American Mennonites, and they seriously reconsidered their ties to their Kleine Gemeinde kin in Mexico. They also debated the use of technologies, including cars and trucks, and introduced new ideas of spirituality, especially stressing inner peace and joy. Unlike their college-educated kin in Canada they did not emphasize the stories of their sixteenth-century Swiss and Dutch Anabaptist ancestors, the focus of a midcentury 'recovery of the Anabaptist Vision';[12] instead they venerated a golden age of simple, pioneer life in western Canada. They also reconsidered their relationship to the outside world. They capitalized on their status as English-speaking agricultural innovators within a Third World economy to embark on a relationship to the British Honduras government and society in which the Mennonite colonists worked from a position of status and influence. This ethnoreligious community spoke of persistence, but in the very act of maintaining the old, it reinvented itself, renewing its religious commitment, refashioning its identity, and creating new methods of social organization.

Imagining a Jungle Community

The very act of migration was culturally dynamic. In migrating, the Mennonites had of course resorted to an old social mechanism.[13] Having been faced by the threatening Mexican government Seguro Social initiative and the aggressive presence of Canadian-based Evangelical Mennonite Church (EMC) missionaries they sought a place more amenable to their old order ways. They migrated to a new land where they could trust the state and secure social isolation.[14] As their history book explains, they found British Honduras 'attractive' because it was 'a colonial possession under the government of Great Britain.'[15] In December 1957 the Kleine Gemeinde delegates and representatives of the even more conservative Old Colony Mennonites of Mexico received a special charter of guarantees from the British Honduras government that included military exemption and German-language parochial schools.[16] The Mennonite migrants knew this document as their *Privilegium*, their official charter of privileges. In their minds, this document was similar to the ones their ancestors obtained when they migrated from West Prussia to Russia in 1804 and from Russia to Canada in 1874.

If an old pattern was relived it did not, however, signal a static society. A Spanish Lookout history tells a story of increased group cohesion and even a flourishing of group identity during the time of the migration. The move, for example, was based on a corporate decision: when the first two Mennonite delegates to British Honduras returned to Quellen Kolonie in early 1957 they 'arranged a large public meeting' and shortly thereafter an 'official' four-man delegation, including a church minister, traveled to British Honduras with authorization to purchase a suitable tract of land and negotiate a charter of privileges.[17] When these delegates came upon the 18,000-acre parcel of high-jungle land that came to be known as Spanish Lookout Colony they considered its benefit for the entire envisioned colony. The land had potential links to outside markets, it was possessed of 'heavy loam soil,' and featured an established sawmill, and so they chose it at once. But, importantly, they did so on behalf of the prospective colonists. As Delegate John D. Friesen recalled: at sunset after a day of scouting, sitting on the bank of the Belize River, 'I made the comment to the three [men] ... that if this land actually was for sale, it should become ours' and 'this comment was heartily endorsed.'[18] The four delegates then sought out the owner's daughter, 'Miss Olga Burns,' and after only a short delay they negotiated the deal on behalf of Quellen Kolonie in Mexico.

The move itself invigorated corporate identity. Colonists traveled in groups. The very first contingent that left on 5 March 1958 from Quellen Kolonie consisted of five single young men, four young married couples, and three large unrelated families, totalling forty-five persons. Importantly, it was headed by the Quellen Kolonie colony mayor, Peter F. Friesen. After a grueling train and truck trip through Mexico's steaming Campeche and Quintana Roo states they arrived at the British Honduras border. Here, their published accounts note, they were welcomed by friendly officials because 'they realized that we were the Mennonite colonists that they had been expecting.'[19] The first weeks at Spanish Lookout similarly drew the members together in an unusually close association. No sooner had the first contingent crossed the shallow Belize River and taken over the sawmill and its 'old two storey house' than the foundations of an intricately organized community were laid. Five small, colony-owned common houses, the largest measuring eighteen by twenty-six feet, were first constructed. Then came the corporately organized task of cutting more lumber for permanent houses. This process coincided with the clearing of the jungle to survey a base meridian line and establish road allowances. Next, muddy roads were built and graveled and more building sites laid out.[20]

Even early difficulties became the grist for illustrations of increased cohesion. The tragic drowning of sixteen-year-old Margaret Friesen in the Belize River just four days after the first group's arrival brought heart-wrenching shock and grief, but also heightened emotional ties within the community.[21] When forty-nine-year-old Maria Friesen, the wife of the colony mayor, sprained her ankle, the community recognized her as a heroine, a 'selfless servant,' because, when discovered 'at the bottom of the stairs' leading to the makeshift communal kitchen, it was said that she had been in a 'partial lying ... position kneading her dough.'[22] Even the act of traversing muddy roads by foot became an event of communal unity. Farmer Klaas C. Penner made the following entry in his October 1960 diary:

It was very wet today. Daughter Lena, son Cornelius and myself carried our eggs to the store at Peter D. Reimers' ... As we went farther north we met John J. Reimer ... [on his way] to the store on foot. We also met our Bishop H.J. Dueck who was carrying ... egg fillers ... on his back. Of course, all of us went barefoot. We had enough time to rest and visit for a while. I am reminded of verse # 6 of song 450 in our German song book ... of the fellowship that we may have with each other as we walk with each other on the road of life, visiting and sharing with each other our experiences, whether ... on the mountain or in the valley of life.[23]

Within this dynamic enterprise, colonists took time to re-establish an array of institutions that further strengthened the close sense of community. Significantly, the renewed institutions were not especially traditional. The Bruderschaft, the *Dienersitzung* or Ministerial Council, the parochial school system, and the colony mutual aid system were re-established not 'as in past centuries' but in the words of the Bruderschaft secretary, 'as in Mexico.'[24] When in June 1958 at its very first meeting the Bruderschaft selected Rev Abram J. Thiessen as its 'church leader' it hastened to add that it was 'for the present time' only and within two months invited the popular Bishop Cornelius R. Reimer from Mexico to conduct Spanish Lookout's first baptism service and its first communion service.[25] By August the Bruderschaft had set up the parochial school again. The school houses with their coverings of 'four-foot wide palm leaves' were definitely new, but relatively new too was the church Bruderschaft's decision that three fathers and one preacher make up the school committee and that 'as in Mexico' the Bruderschaft should democratically 'elect' all schoolteachers. By September the Bruderschaft had also re-established the colony mutual aid society, the *Hilfsverein*, 'as in Mexico,' with a mandatory investment of one quarter of one per cent of each household's total value. Then in October the Bruderschaft decided to meet monthly 'as in Mexico,' signalling that the church body would be much more than the overseer of moral issues as in Canada. Instead, it would be the ultimate community authority, overseeing all colony institutions dealing with education, mutual aid, physical infrastructure, and farm economy.[26]

A final reinstated organization was the Vorsteher Komitee, the committee of the colony administration. Once again, here was an organization that was first established in Mexico in 1948 to take care of all temporal needs at Quellen Kolonie. The first Spanish Lookout Vorsteher or colony mayor was Peter F. Friesen who had held that office in Mexico; in British Honduras, according to the colony history, Friesen 'just continued his term.'[27] Significantly, despite the colony administration's importance during the early months of settlement, the Bruderschaft remained the preeminent body of colony governance. It elected the temporal colony mayor and made it clear that this elected official was ultimately responsible to the Bruderschaft.[28] Within months of undertaking the arduous settlement of Spanish Lookout when Friesen fell ill, suffering from the mental strain of the relocation, it was the Bruderschaft that intervened. It attempted to 'encourage' the colony mayor, defining more clearly his duties, and then lightening Friesen's load by electing two assistants, one immediately and the other 'once the others have come from Mexico.' Then on 28 November, the colony administration's activity once again came under the scrutiny of church leaders when it was criticized for using 'so much money on colony roads' that it was unable to repay its loans to individual colony farmers. It was the church Bruderschaft that bailed out the temporal colony administration by soliciting greater contributions for the colony's mutual aid fund.[29]

Organizations had been created to meet the communitarian, old-order needs of the exclusive Mexico colony during the 1950s, and now during the 1960s and 1970s in British Honduras they continued to evolve in the even more exclusive Spanish Lookout colony.

Building a Religious Community

The innovations that the British Honduras church took from its short sojourn in Mexico were only the beginning of a generation of change. A sign of adaptation to new circumstances was the June 1958 decision to forego the construction of a woodframe church and construct instead a temporary 'palm roof under which the church should have its services.'[30] Another sign of the new circumstances of British Honduras was the moral issue raised at the first June 1958 Bruderschaft and one that dominated the moral agenda during the first year. The issue was the mode of dress in the tropical environment, more hot and humid than any climate these Dutch–North German Mennonites had ever encountered. One problem concerned 'privacy in the river and the danger that both sexes are bathing with too few clothing and in too close a proximity to each other.' This issue provoked debate until April 1959 when river bathing as a sport was again criticized and a stipulation laid down that women and men should bathe on alternate days.[31] A second problem arose in the spring of 1959 as ministers planned for the spring baptismal service. The question of dress was raised again: 'whereas baptismal candidates have traditionally been dressed in dark clothes, but now in the hot weather do not wear jackets, should the boys be encouraged to wear shirts that are not too lightly colored?' By June the Bruderschaft had adopted a new policy: 'young men are to wear dark shirts' at baptism.[32]

If the jungle experience forced the church to consider new paths of conservatism, so too did two unexpected events in 1958 and 1959. Both effectively pushed the community to a greater self-awareness and to a more exclusive position than its founders had envisioned. The first event came to light during Bishop Cornelius Reimer's September 1958 visit to British Honduras. Reimer reported to a seemingly surprised Bruderschaft that although a majority of Mexico colonists had voted for the relocation to British Honduras not everybody intended to move. Indeed, it seemed that the Mexicans wanted to strengthen, not dismantle, Quellen Kolonie. The Bruderschaft was told that 'those who don't want to move to British Honduras ... want to have a ministerial election in Mexico.'[33] Within months the matter became even more serious when individual members, including Colony Mayor Friesen, spoke of leaving the difficult jungle and returning to Mexico. Other sources recall that Bishop Reimer himself now cast the doubters as 'murmuring Israelites' who rather wished to return to their Egyptian taskmasters than find freedom in the Promised Land.[34] Records indicate that the Bruderschaft and the preachers strongly reacted to the movement to return to Mexico. In October the Bruderschaft sent a warning to the Mexico church; do 'not vote too quickly' for a slate of new ministers, a clear step, if it were taken, to refurbishing the Mexico colony.[35] By late 1958 and early 1959 Spanish Lookout ministers worked to head off any return migration, a sentiment that increased as the difficulties of farming in the jungle became fully realized. The ministers could not forbid, but they could convince: in November the ministers advised a 'poor man ... against it'; in January they 'convinced' a brother who 'wanted to go back to Mexico' to stay; in February they warned a woman not 'to return so soon ... if she had come here in faith,' even if it was for the purpose of marriage; in July they answered a more general murmuring of 'people [who] are asking why did we move' with the short rebuttal, 'they have the social security there.'[36] The decision to migrate to British Honduras had acquired moral language.

This sentiment became more rooted following the shocking news from Mexico in the spring of 1959 that Bishop Cornelius Reimer had died of a stroke at age fifty-seven. Spanish Lookout people had clearly expected Reimer to move to British Honduras and his death marked a painful disruption in leadership. On 3 April colony ministers asked bluntly, 'how will we carry out the work in the absence of Bishop Reimer?' Then they pledged themselves to 'guard against the church work falling behind.' As a priority, the youth 'would be spoken to so that they will be converted ... and then someone will be appointed to baptize them.' Then in August 1959 after reasserting the biblical basis for a lifelong term for bishop, the Bruderschaft elected the newly arrived and 'orderly' Heinrich J. Dueck as their very own Spanish Lookout bishop.[37] Some colonists saw Dueck as more conservative than Reimer had been. He was said to 'favor having things more simple' and preached his first sermon on the published points of an 1899 conference in Manitoba where progressive Mennonite church practices as well as photography, musical instruments, funeral eulogies, and government jobs had been condemned. Increasingly the leadership and influential lay members venerated the first and second generations of sojourn in Canada, especially the years between 1899 and 1919 when a popular conservative bishop from Steinbach, Manitoba, Peter R. Dueck, had rigorously opposed the telephone, fashionable dress, English-language schools, town businesses, and the car.[38]

During the 1960s the Spanish Lookout church became markedly more conservative not only than its counterpart in Canada, but than the Quellen Kolonie church in Mexico. Some people now even developed the idea that the 'chaff' had remained in Mexico and the 'kernel' had been salvaged by the move to British Honduras. Indeed, the clock was turned back. Car ownership, accepted by the Kleine Gemeinde since 1919, became a mark of ostentation in British Honduras. Even ownership of half-ton trucks was criticized and some elders lauded Old Colony Mennonites from British Honduras's Blue Creek Colony for excommunicating farmers who equipped their tractors with rubber tires rather than the traditional steel wheels. By the mid-1960s the swing to the right climaxed in a church schism. An ultraconservative group inspired by an American Amish subsect denounced all engine-based technology and vestiges of the market economy. These conservatives cited the leadership of the deceased Bishop Cornelius Reimer as having been too 'soft' and charged Spanish Lookout preachers with 'preaching against things, but not legislating against them' with excommunication and shunning.[39] In 1964 some members boycotted a communion service because it was led by Mexico ministers and in 1968 amid 'much heartache and tears' the protesting group moved out of Spanish Lookout.[40] It then created an even more exclusive and isolated colony at nearby Barton Creek and distinguished itself by practising subsistence agriculture, relying only on draft power, and asking all members to dress in dark clothes.[41] Within the first decade of their sojourn in British Honduras, the settlers had accepted an increased asceticism and geographic exclusion as standard Mennonite behavior. The very presence of Barton Creek placed a check on any modernistic trends at Spanish Lookout.

Within the close-knit conservative community at Spanish Lookout all members were closely link together as an ethnoreligious community. They willingly seemed to accept the moral scrutiny of other members and they, in turn, accepted as sacred the duty to scrutinize others. The church services leading up to the annual baptism during the 1970s illustrate this commitment to community. Baptism itself came not only after the youths had been instructed in church doctrine, but after five different sessions of moralistic examination. At one public Bruderschaft meeting, the moral state of each of the nine candidates was announced: the first candidate, it was stated, had a 'good testimony,' the second 'is willing,' the third 'needs more assurance,' the fourth had 'nothing to impede her' in her spiritual quest, the fifth was 'free,' the sixth possessed 'more joy' than previously, the seventh was clearly 'born again,' the eight was 'mindful of the Saviour,' the ninth was 'obedient.'[42] But the life of older church members was also constantly probed. Conflict among members received special attention. In a single year during the mid-1970s ministers responded to a variety of relational problems among members. For example, they reviewed the failed relationship between an employee and an employer and noted that during discussions with these members 'numerous issues were opened up.' At another time they dealt with a parent's grievance with respect to a schoolteacher, a situation the ministers helped solve, but with a resulting 'lack of neighborly relationship.' On a third issue ministers intervened to examine the 'agreement between [two] brothers ... who want mutual forgiveness' but sadly, one of the brothers still left the meeting 'troubled' by the other brother's 'expressions.' At another juncture a decision was made to 'open old wounds' in the relationship of two other men because 'what serves mostly to heal, we should do.'[43] This was the language of remarkable community cohesion.

By the 1970s, however, this communitarian definition of 'being Mennonite' began to be questioned. The laity at Spanish Lookout had tasted the prosperity of the colony's impressive agricultural achievements. Increasingly ministers believed they saw signs of ostentation or vanity. In March of one year the Bruderschaft heard a strict warning from Bishop Abram Reimer that the colony's youth must be drawn to 'a purer faith' and encouraged in this endeavor through the 'rules of the parents.' In July of the same year Reimer outlined a series of attitudes that he believed undermined the purity of the congregation, including vanity, greed, envy, animosity, and ambition. He also raised the concern that church members were 'mocking brotherly admonitions' and 'talking about them in public.' Just a week later when the bishop outlined the case of a truck driver who had confessed to 'carousing' the Bruderschaft was left with the rhetorical question: 'is it necessary for the maintenance of our life here [on the colony] to have such an intense truck-based trade?' At a later meeting in September the bishop noted that not only were the youth and banned members wavering in the faith, but so too were the members who owned 'multicolored trucks, watches, cameras, and radios.' Ministers reinvigorated their house visits and as they did so they discovered other problems – personal disenchantments, marriage tensions, sibling rivalries, and deeply felt concerns from some members that the church was too worldly and from others that it was too conservative.[44]

The church did not stand still. At the very time that Bishop Reimer outlined the moral problems in public at the Bruderschaft, he and the cohort of ordained ministers were troubled by a deep-seated self-doubt and were confronted by the progressive ideas of a young minister, Jacob Barkman. Within the ministerial meetings he began emphasizing the 'working of the Holy Spirit' and publicly suggested that 'self righteousness' resulted from an emphasis on a conservative lifestyle. In their private meetings ministers seemed attracted to this idea, that an emphasis on inner spiritual life would rejuvenate the church. At a February 1975 meeting the ministers discussed 'the spiritual state of the church, prayer life, etc.' In April the ministers heard Bishop Reimer ponder the questions 'How do we sustain the church's condition? How free are we of legalism? Or, how free are we in the spirit?' Two months later in June the ministers discussed the concept of inner 'peace,' asked 'how does one acquire this?' and reaffirmed that 'the Christian is entitled to a peace that is higher than all understanding.' A 1976 meeting with the ministerial of the Mexico Kleine Gemeinde church was held to discuss 'those things we once considered dangerous ... [an emphasis on] spiritual life, harmony singing, Sunday School.' Then, too, in 1976, the election of Jacob Barkman as one of three colony bishops furthered this idea.[45] Other signs of an increasingly personal faith was the change from preaching by reading formal sermons in High German to preaching extemporaneously in the familiar, everyday dialect of Low German. Clearly, a more personal approach to faith was now considered possible.[46]

Events, however, soon raised suspicions and dampened the new interest in personal spirituality in the main church. Of special concern were reports that some leaders had been drawn to the spirituality of the Chinese American evangelist Watchman Nee; not only had they studied Nee's book, *Release by the Spirit*, but they had made an unsanctioned trip to California to visit Nee.[47] Especially difficult was a schism that developed as a result. Members wishing for a stronger emphasis on inner spirituality become impatient with the slow moving Kleine Gemeinde and seceded to form their own Nee-inspired small group known here as in California as the Local Church.[48]

Barton Creek and the Local Church now stood on either side of the ideological map of Spanish Lookout signaling a seemingly never-ending debate in the community. Significantly, during this debate the concept of 'Mennonite community' was interpreted with divergent images; the ultraconservatives emphasized the idea of 'following Christ,' the progressives the admonitions to heed 'the Holy Spirit.' During the 1970s many Mennonites in Canada and the United States invigorated religious commitment by rediscovering in sixteenth-century Anabaptist accounts of 'peace, discipleship and brotherhood' a 'useable past.'[49] Spanish Lookout Mennonites, however, found reinvigoration by contrasting themselves to a modernistic Canadian community and some by tapping into the evangelicalism of a small, California-based movement. Significantly, during these tumultuous 1970s the leaders made few appeals to sixteenth-century Mennonite history,[50] or even to past practices. Members of the Kleine Gemeinde church now increasingly searched for new models to enrich the old faith.

Re-establishing Social Boundaries

If the internal meaning of being Mennonite was constantly re-evaluated, so too was the image that the community sought to project to the outside world. During the 1970s the Spanish Lookout Mennonites were separated from the wider world by the Belize River and its slow, manually propelled ferry. Still this was the decade in which pioneer tractor power gave way to trucks and cars travelling the limestone *caleche* all-weather roads.[51] Increasingly, colonists also travelled abroad, most notably by regular jet airplane service through Miami, Florida, and beyond. These ties were never simply threats to Spanish Lookout, but links that could serve the wider interests of the colony. Indeed, these new ties came to represent anything but an easy accommodation with

Spanish Lookout's host society or other societies that lay beyond Belize. Links to unknown California evangelicals, unfamiliar Swiss Mennonites in Pennsylvania, and old friends in Mexico were used to bolster religious life at Spanish Lookout. Other ties in Canada, Honduras, Guatemala, and the wider society of British Honduras were seen ambivalently, each simultaneously representing threat and opportunity.

Increasingly close links to the outside world, of course, had the potential for making the enforcement of old-order values difficult. During the 1970s disgruntled members could leave the colony and seek reintegration into the modern and more progressive Canadian Mennonite communities. Spanish Lookout ministerial reports from the 1970s identified members who had not only returned to Canada but were 'working on Sundays,' attending public schools, and 'idealizing the Canadians.' A report of a respected widow, 'our fellow sister,' who had returned to Canada put the plain-living British Honduras brethren in a special quandary for when it was reported that she owned 'a radio there' it was also noted that she 'uses it to listen to German-language sermons,'[52] a spiritual lifeline in a foreign land. Ironically, the very existence of Canada could also serve to strengthen the unity of Spanish Lookout. The reason was that several of the Spanish Lookout residents who moved to Canada during the 1970s were excommunicated members who had fallen out of grace with the community. Ministers who visited the banned members in Canada returned to British Honduras with reports of 'unhappy,' 'cold and apathetic,' 'devious,' 'insolent,' and 'empty' men and women.[53] Close ties to Canada were necessary, not to discover progressive methods to renew Spanish Lookout colony, but because the British Honduras church felt a responsibility for the moral condition of excommunicated members who lived there. As the ministers noted, 'so long as they are unrepentant, we feel we cannot leave them alone.'[54] The very presence of the excommunicated in Canada, no doubt, helped crystallize opposition to Canadian Mennonite lifestyles and served to relegitimize the migrations of 1948 and 1958. Signalling their continued mistrust of their modernistic Canadian kin, when some of the Spanish Lookout people sought economic opportunity and social security by moving to Canada in 1984, they elected to settle in the eastern province of Nova Scotia, more than 1500 miles from their former homes in Manitoba.[55]

Spanish Lookout Mennonites' activities in neighboring Central American countries and the British Honduras host society also served contradictory ends. On the one hand they represented the immoral wider world filled with temptations; on the other they presented the colony with the opportunity to reach out with material aid, thus bolstering its sense of moral purpose. True, the British Honduras society that lay across the Belize River from the colony was perceived as hostile and threatening. Already in January 1959 the Bruderschaft raised a concern that some of 'our unconverted [unbaptized] youth ... carry on rowdy lives on the other side of the river' and only a month later ministers were approached by a young woman who 'confessed to going over the river to listen to the radio,' acknowledging that this kind of behavior 'does not belong in the kingdom of God.'[56] By the 1970s the colony had established an *Auswärtige Hilfe Komitee*, literally a foreign aid committee that sought opportunities to assist Spanish Lookout's neighbors who lived on the non-Mennonite side of the river.[57] In 1974, for example, donations of beans and corn were made to the 'poor indigenous people'; 1 percent of each farmer's harvest was solicited, placed first in the colony's 'Goodwill Speicher,' the goodwill granary, and then distributed through 'Mr. McDougal, the Social Development man.'[58] In the same year the colony donated a tractor and plough for the poor in nearby Belmopan and provided aid for 'Dr Mundal's clinic.' During the following year, donations of lumber were made following the 'great fire in Belize City,' and an outright gift of money plus the services of a Mennonite teacher were offered the town of Democracia. For the Spanish Lookout residents the outside world stood both as a recipient of their goodwill and as a temporal society that must be avoided. It simultaneously drew good Christians and repelled them.

A similar ambivalence shaped relationships with communities in neighboring countries. Colonists could relate stories of respected men who had fallen into sin in Guatemala City and of brethren tempted to leave their conservative ways by progressive Mennonite missionaries in Honduras.[59] But overall, increased associations with these countries served to undergird the very existence of Spanish Lookout within this Third World setting. After Nicaragua's devastating earthquake in December 1972 the colony moved quickly to 'find out if we can be of help.'[60] A September 1974 hurricane in Honduras and a January 1975 earthquake in Guatemala created other possibilities of service.[61] Within a short time of both disasters, Spanish Lookout had sent men to the scenes of tragedy who soon sent reports outlining the need, not for manual labor, but for skilled supervision. These messages in turn were followed by reports of Spanish Lookout's part in constructing hundreds of homes and the religious satisfaction that derived from giving this aid; as one recently returned worker reported to the Bruderschaft in March 1975, 'a cheerful giver has God's love.'[62]

Given the colony's confidence that it could control social boundaries, members by the 1970s also began pressing for the introduction of English instruction in the schools. Ironically in 1958 the colonists had chosen an English-speaking country as the best location in which to safeguard their German language and senior members acknowledged that their English schooling in Canada helped them negotiate with both state and market. Now this contradiction surfaced again. In January 1974 it came to a head when an English-speaking American Holdeman Mennonite missionary approached the Spanish Lookout ministerial with the request 'to use one of our school buildings for English instruction.' The ministers responded by striking their own committee of lay members to consider English instruction.[63] By May 1974 a morning session of English language instruction had been commenced and just two months later it was also considered for 'our day schools.' Still the issue raised much ambivalence. The question 'on what can we base it when we don't want to learn the language of the country' was met with counterquestions of how can we 'realize the true objective of our migration here' if English is learned. In the spring of 1975 a bilingual school policy for the upper grades was finally accepted by the ministers, for the simple reason that 'many brothers are in favor.'[64]

Spanish Lookout's separateness was guaranteed not only by the broad, unbridged Belize River and teachings to avoid the world that lay on its opposite bank. Race, too, came to define the self-identity of this ethnoreligious community. At no other time had these Mennonites or their ancestors been surrounded by non-whites as they were at Spanish Lookout. Their neighbors were mostly Mayan Indians and Creole Blacks.[65] The 1958 settlers had been acutely aware of their own racial uniqueness, some wondering if they, Caucasian Mennonites, belonged in this environment.[66] The boundary between the Mennonites and their new neighbors was obvious. Mennonites wrote about their neighbors with a sense of respect: natives had warned Mennonites of the river's flood plain and they could 'hunt for hardwood trees all day without eating.'[67] The Mennonites even knew their names: Gordon Elias was 'a negro man ... who heroically crossed the swollen Jinny Creek' on the day of Hurricane Hattie to ensure his family's safety; Dario and Arturo Martinez spoke Creole and having 'grown up on [our] land ... [were]

right at home on it.'[68] This admiration and familiarity, however, did not translate into full openness. Rather, colonists readily declared that racial differences were natural barriers that should be respected. Even 'mission work to other cultures represented a problem,' noted a colony couple, for it 'brings people together from different upbringings' and the resulting 'intermarriages' simply 'don't work.'[69] The colony administration agreed, noting bluntly in August 1971 that 'we want Moody [a logger] to move his house as there are too many native workers who live there which is bothersome to us and leads to disorder.'[70] The Bruderschaft similarly moved in March 1974 to investigate the presence of a 'seemingly suspicious native beggar woman' and set out to discover 'from where she comes and under what circumstances she lives.'[71] When in the mid-1970s some ministers were attracted to missionary work, they went to preach at Santa Familia, seven miles distant, and there established a mission church, well removed from the colony itself.[72] During the 1970s Spanish Lookout remained an almost ethnically homogeneous Euro-Mennonite community. Race, added to geography and ideology, worked to provide a high degree of exclusivity for the community.

Relations with the British Honduras government represented the greatest challenge in the keeping of social boundaries. Geographer Jerry Hall noted in his 1970 work that because Spanish Lookout 'colony administrators ... act as the representative agents to the British Honduras government' it was unnecessary for the brethren 'to associate with any authority other than their own leaders.'[73] Yet the relationship between colony and state was a dynamic one. Especially significant was the economic power Spanish Lookout wielded in a country as small as British Honduras. Geographer Leonard Sawatzky observed in 1971 that Spanish Lookout's extraordinary productivity was well known by the government and noted that 'it is the expressed wish of the premier that the rest of his countrymen emulate it.'[74] The government's admiration was not lost on even the first Mennonite settlers. Some years after the 1957 scouting trip to British Honduras John D. Friesen recalled how he and other delegates had become 'acquainted with the Minister of Mines and Natural Resources, Honorable George Price, who soon became the Prime Minister of British Honduras for about 20 years.'[75] Friesen was struck by the irony that at 'the magnificent Fort George Hotel [in Belize City] ... we as a group of lowly Mennonite farmers dined at the same table as the Hon. George Price.'[76] This direct association with government officials and the colony's economic strength provided Spanish

Lookout Mennonites with an ironic confidence; they were accepted as citizens without any participation in the country's civic politics. This confidence was apparent in local historian Gerhard Koop's observation in 1973 that 'the government is pleased when we are successful with our agricultural pursuits,' because Mennonite success secured national self-sufficiency and 'an improvement for our foreign exchange.'[77]

This self-assured position was apparent in the colony's other dealings with government. Colonists had few problems accepting government assistance in jungle clearing, as it enabled farmers to turn five acres of jungle into arable land for only $40 an acre.[78] Similarly they felt comfortable in approaching the government for a five-year, $20,000 loan when their second payment to the land vendor, Olga Burns, came due in 1960. And they accepted government help in the construction of a ferry after two primitive ferries were swept away by flooding.[79] Yet colonists became more hesitant when government initiatives threatened to have a long-term effect. Thus in October 1960 when colonists were asked 'whether we wish to hand over our main road to the government' they were unequivocal: 'we consider it ours, that is to be understood [owned by] our church membership and our road committee.'[80] Indeed, given Spanish Lookout's status as a semi-autonomous colony, the colonists never accepted government initiatives without serious reflection. Even an October 1958 report in which the British Honduras government mandated daylight saving time of half an hour led the colonists to debate the question, 'do we want the same?'[81] Just a month later when colonists heard of British Honduras's mandatory two-week wait between the reading of marriage banns and the wedding compared with the one week to which the Mennonites were accustomed, the colonists sent a spokesman to ask whether 'we can have it like we used to.'[82]

Feelings were even more mixed on questions of colony-police relations. The terms of the December 1957 'Charter of Privileges' had committed the government to protect the colonists and the colonists to accept that protection. Yet Mennonites were a pacifist, sectarian people who were leery of police protection. In July 1959, for example, after a theft on the colony, ministers bluntly asked whether we 'should ... report wrong doings to the government' as this might 'violate God's plan and ... [lead] Him [to] withdraw his hand [of protection].' Their conclusion at this juncture was that they would 'rather suffer wrong, than do wrong.'[83] Over time this thinking led to awkward situations. Police presence was considered an intrusion on the colony. Even in

January 1961 when the colony experienced its first murder, the night-time shooting by thieves of twenty-one-year-old Jake Reimer as he ran to the assistance of the thieves' victim, brought about an uneasy situation. As the account went, 'Jake had to remain' lying on the ground, unconscious with three shotgun pellets lodged in his brain, 'until the police had investigated the incident.'[84] Then in 1972 shortly after the colony's second murder, colonists were told via a minister 'to respect our policemen more, as they have heard we don't trust them.'[85] Yet with continued thievery and occasional assaults, some colonists themselves began considering bringing in the police. Significantly, after each theft or assault the ministers' central concern seemed to be the question of how 'our brothers after such an experience [will] maintain their non-resistant feelings.'[86]

The ministers had reason to be concerned. In December 1974 the two colony mayors without consulting the ministers provided a car to the Belizean police for the purposes of patrolling the colony over the Christmas break. A sharp response from the ministers did not deter the colony mayors from seeking official support.[87] Just six months later the mayors acted again, this time inviting the police to intervene on the colony to confront rowdy Mennonite boys and summon them to a meeting where they could hear the police inspector 'on how they should improve themselves.' Not surprisingly, old ideas of complete separation caused an 'uproar to ensue,' especially from 'several fathers.'[88] So intense was the feeling that colony mayor Dietrich Friesen rose at a Bruderschaft to state 'that he had distressed some brothers with his handling of the rowdy youth.'[89] Mennonites in British Honduras could seek to be the 'quiet in the land,' but direct association with government authority and occasional acts of violence forced them to re-evaluate that traditional designation in new and changing circumstances.

Inventing the Colony System

The reinvigorated Mennonite community also relied on new approaches to the development of the colony's economy. Borrowing a term from other Mennonites in Central and South America, the Spanish Lookout farmers spoke of the 'colony system.'[90] In this arrangement the colony administration experimented with new crops under new growing conditions and on unknown and untested soils. Moreover, it guided farmers' efforts to produce commodities for the marketplace. Neither the experimentation nor the commodification of crops were new. Mennonites in Russia, Canada, and the United States long had drawn attention from outside observers for their seemingly contradictory strategy of adopting commodity production in order to create a strong, separate community. Put another way, they seemed to court modern economic forces in order to sustain an antimodern culture.[91] What was new at Spanish Lookout was the corporate, colony-centered, approach to interacting with the market and to the building and maintaining of the colony's physical infrastructure. This system affected the way in which settlers perceived the very nature of land and property. It also affected in a very basic, ontological sense, their view of community. The colony system, for example, ensured the maximum degree of exclusivity because most individual initiatives in the wider market were either forbidden or made redundant. Individuals worked through the colony administration not only to attain land, but to market product and secure credit. Colony representatives dealt with wholesalers and retailers and with government marketing boards and inspection agencies. In the process, a dualistic world developed, one that asked members to yield to one another, but encouraged unrelenting optimism in market economics through a unified voice. The *Allgemeine Versamlung*, the Colony Assembly of September 1960 contained elements of this dichotomous agenda. There were hints of a closely interwoven community, but also examples of a more aggressive relationship to the outside world. The meeting began with prayer by colony mayor Johann Barkman and the singing of *Jesu, Du Alein*. Then it heard reports on the colony's roads, the drainage system, its land distribution, where to invest the last $700 U.S. payment for land sales at Quellen Kolonie in Mexico, and how to organize the production of marketable vegetables.[92] The very operation of the colony administration brought colonists together for frequent meetings, close interrelationships, and mutual identification.

The Spanish Lookout Mennonites created a remarkably strong array of institutions, approaching what sociologists have dubbed 'institutional completeness.'[93] Not only was the colony interlaced with parochial schools, mutual aid societies, and estate transfer committees, but there were democratically elected subcommittees regulating almost every aspect of the colony's economy. In 1961 alone the colony administration oversaw the work of the Road Committee, the Land Committee, the Bush Committee, the Ferry Committee, the Abattoir Committee, the Planting Committee, the Sawmill Committee, and the Fruit Tree Committee. In addition, separate Village Meetings were headed by the mayors of each of the villages. And elected positions for Colony Secretary, Colony Auditor, and Cat Overseer, that is, the overseer of the colony's Caterpillar crawler tractor, added to the elaborate bureaucratic structure. Even more associations were promised by the 1961 decision of farmers to construct a colony-owned general store, the Farmers' Trading Centre, and in their wish to erect a colony-owned cannery.[94]

Adding to the cohesive culture in the colony administration was its internal tax system. To make the settlement work, the colony administration levied a complex series of annual taxes including a one-half of 1 percent gross income tax on commodities, a 2 percent tax on most vehicles and tractors, and a 2 percent sales tax on selected goods purchased off the colony. The administration held such moral power on the colony that during the first decade there is no record of a colonist disputing the landownership system and only one of a farmer refusing to pay his taxes. In the one instance of a stubborn tax evader, the colony administration simply mandated that enterprises or farmers purchasing his beans and corn charge him the tax and forward the same to the colony office.[95]

As ultimate landowner the colony administration also regulated residency. In the first years it distributed all the land parcels and building sites. Then over the years in consultation with the ministers, the colony administration decided who could or could not purchase land on the colony. In August 1966 the colony administration reported that 'Peter R. Banmann,' a forty-one-year-old Old Colony Mennonite with a wife and eight children, has 'asked for permission to buy land on our colony,' but noted that it 'had not yet given permission.'[96] The Banmann family eventually was allowed to move onto the colony and four years later Peter and his wife, Anna, joined the Kleine Gemeinde church. The administration, however, did not automatically approve such requests. In November 1969 it declared that temporary Old Colony Mennonite employees from Shipyard Colony had created a 'disorder' and warned Spanish Lookout employers to exercise 'careful responsibility while [workers] are in their employ.' At the very minimum it asked the temporary workers 'declare themselves to the Colony Mayors' when they intended to live on the colony.[97] In an incident in 1968 even Spanish Lookout farmers who were out of step with the church, that is, 'those who do not come to church,' were permitted to purchase the high-quality land in the colony's Barton Remy district only after consulting the 'district mayors and the ministers.'[98]

Finally, the administration also did its part in redrawing the map of an acceptable wider Mennonite community. There is no record of any association with the Canadian Mennonite communities the Kleine Gemeinde migrants left in 1948. In contrast, new ties to Mennonites in Pennsylvania and Paraguay were created soon after settlement in British Honduras in 1958. In 1961 the colony administration heard a report from farmer Bernard P. Plett about his fact-finding trip to the Menno and Bergthal Mennonite colonies in Paraguay. His mission had been to study the administrative methods of these colonies since their respective inceptions in the 1920s and 1940s.[99] Throughout the 1960s other associations were created with American-Swiss Mennonites, encouraged by the Swiss-American-run 'Mennonite Centre' in Belize City; this center, an economic development agency, quickly became the agency through which Spanish Lookout farmers marketed their commodities in the city.[100] A sense of trust was soon established. In 1960 Spanish Lookout received 'a gift of purebred Holstein heifers' from Swiss-American Wisconsin Mennonites; a year later, when the last land payment was due, Spanish Lookout sent two delegates 'to ask some [Swiss-American] Mennonites in the eastern United States for a loan'; then in about 1967 another delegation traveled to the Pennsylvania Mennonite community to purchase second-hand pasteurizing equipment for a new dairy and secure a loan for it through the Eastern Mennonite Mission Board.[101] Distance from Dutch-descendant Mennonites in Canada did not preclude a relationship with Swiss-descendant Mennonites in the United States.

If the colony administration helped define the immediate Mennonite community and redraw the map of an acceptable wider Mennonite world, it also served to set the tenor of relations with the non-Mennonite world. Indeed, in these relations the colony leaders seemed markedly more aggressive. The marketplace was not merely a site in which to sell commodities, it was a site to be manipulated. In October 1960, a scant two years after arriving in the British Honduras jungle, the colony administration recorded that it 'once again had chickens in "cold storage"' awaiting more favorable prices and in December took note of product 'shrinkage' and sales 'commissions' before deciding to sell the chickens into the market.[102] In this same spirit the colonists considered the 1963 fruit deal with Peter Butland of Ontario and in 1964 entered into dialogue with a 'Mr. Aberhard Reusse' concerning tomato exports to the United States and with 'Mr. Harris' who 'wants our "Orange Tree acreage"' for his factory.[103] Within a decade of the colony's founding it seemed at home in a wider world, certainly as a major player in the tiny British Honduras economy, but also amid multinational corporations and even international markets. By 1961 colony farmers were air lifting 'baby chicks' from the United States and slaughtering 350 birds a week for resale in Belize City, a number that rose to 6000 birds a week just twelve years later. By 1965 colony farmers had also met with government health officials to consider the possibilities of a milk-pasteurizing plant and begun laying the groundwork for their very own Western Dairies, British Honduras's only modern dairy. In 1968 the colony also began exporting commodities to the Caribbean world; in that year after British Honduras's marketing board rejected the colony's corn harvest, presumably because it was not 'dry enough,' colony leaders announced confidently that it would try 'to sell cracked corn to Jamaica.'[104] There were other forays into Costa Rica to acquire pineapple plants, into Guatemala for cattle, and into the United States for trucks and tractors. Confrontations with large corporations were also undertaken with a measure of ease; in 1964 the colony defended itself against the Central American Investment company after it accused Mennonite loggers of straying off colony land and in 1968 the colony confronted the Chevron Oil company after it damaged 'the fence' on one occasion, and the 'road north of the Rosenort school' on another.[105] United behind colony structures, the Mennonites of Spanish Lookout readily took on the wider world.

Mythologizing the Rainforest

A final set of changes that can be observed among Spanish Lookout Mennonites was their approach to the environment. In chapter 2 we observed that the symbols of dust bowl and snowdrift illustrated the environmental challenges facing the Kansas and Manitoba farmers. The symbol of rainforest spelled it for the Mennonite farmers of Spanish Lookout Colony. These conservative Mennonites had chosen British Honduras despite the requirement that they adapt a high-latitude, grain-based farm economy to a rainforest. Although Spanish Lookout was located in the high altitude of Cayo District sixty miles inland it was still a tropical environment. The environmental challenges for the Mennonites here were numerous: instead of the twenty inches of annual precipitation they were accustomed to in Canada, they faced an average annual rainfall of sixty-two inches in a high humidity milieu;[106] instead of working flat, open plains they encountered a land covered with dense jungle and then, as land was cleared, a geography of steep slopes and intersecting creeks and rivers; and instead of squeezing their labor into a six-month, intense, summertime growing season, they had two annual crop seasons, that required landwork almost year-round. Even the jungle's black chernozem soils that had seemed familiar at first proved to be shallow clays, sticky when wet and rock hard when dry.[107] Despite these challenges the Spanish Lookout Mennonites survived. Indeed, through cooperative effort, a colony system of governance, trial and error cropping methods, and a commitment to developing a commodity export economy, they managed to survive successfully.

But they did so only because they adapted old ways to an alien environment. The first glimpses of Spanish Lookout fixated on the unfamiliar tropical forest. The rectangular land block the settlers had purchased was about four miles by twelve miles in area extending in a northwesterly direction from the Belize River to the Green Hills near the Guatemala border, and it was covered by bush and jungle. On the first page of his 1973 history of Spanish Lookout, Gerhard Koop imagined the thoughts of the first settlers looking over to the 'northern bank of the river' and seeing there a 'dark and forbidding jungle with its strange noises and smells.' Koop cast the challenge as one in which the fainthearted quivered, murmuring, 'why did the Lord bring us to this land to allow us to fall by ... "tropical diseases"?'[108] For the first two years naysayers filled with 'discouragement and despondency' spread 'rumours ... that the tropical climate was intolerable for the white race.' They feared the 'heat, the insects, and climate change' and the great 'impenetrable forest.'[109] From this departure, Koop the historian outlined the remarkable success of Spanish Lookout. Within a generation the colony had established itself as a highly successful farm model, with 'crop yields ... on a par with those of the successful Green Revolution countries.'[110] Geographer Jerry Hall's 1970 study described a colony that had successfully introduced a northern 'agricultural technique' to a tropical environment and as such provided 'a basis for increased food production in British Honduras.'[111] Spanish Lookout Mennonites had cleared the jungle, created a log-exporting business, imposed a square-grid survey system on the rolling landscape, established a central trade center, and had become self-sufficient in meats and vegetables. They had even replicated Canadian-style farmyards in which frame houses were 'surrounded by hedges, lawns and flowerbeds.'[112] Most importantly, by trial and error they had learned how to raise red kidney beans the winter months, chickens fed on corn grown in the summer months, and dairy products from cattle on *milpa* (cornfield) pasture.

The road to survival was a story of triumph over an environmental challenge. Poetry written by colonists depicts the process as an inevitable triumph. A twenty-eight-stanza poem in German entitled, 'Fuer Johann J. Reimers' and written on the occasion of the Reimers' fiftieth wedding anniversary devotes five stanzas to the pioneer years:

Hacking bush was now your choice
by axe and by machete
for you and others, oftentimes
bereaved by sting of the honey bee
this work was one you revelled in
your spirit it rejuvenated
so too, your neighbor's in the bush
the jungle then was lit on fire
and on it corn was planted ...
yet, success could not be counted on
for among all ashes we find coals
that sometimes even burn our feet.

The slash-and-burn technique depicted in the Reimer poem was described more scientifically by Hall in 1970. He noted that the Mennonites had quickly learned that 'handsaw and axe were no match for the hardwood trees such as bullet wood, rosewood or even mahogany.'[113] They thus adopted a Mayan milpa technique of slash-and-burn. First, scrub bush was felled by machete or gasoline-powered chainsaw. Then log trees were cut and removed by tractors. Next the excess bush was burned, followed by corn plantings by dibble stick among the smouldering stumps. For general land-breaking the farmer elected one of two avenues: the more expensive method, employed on well-drained, fertile soils, saw the $30,000 colony bulldozer move in to remove the smouldering stumps. In the less expensive approach farmers turned the land into a milpa pasture of jaragua grass and then after four years of decay they initiated a second burning to remove the scrub brush and weeds that had grown up in the meantime.[114] In either case, bush burning was part of the process, although over time the pioneers became more discerning in the use of fire. During the first years, writes Hall, burning or 'firing was a laissez faire activity' often resulting in a 'sizeable reserve of valuable trees being burned.' But by 1961 a variety of trees – sapodilla, cedar, mahogany, Santa Maria, Billy Webb, nargusta, timbersweet, cypress, bullhoff, and prickly yellow – had become valued for hardwood lumber. Not only were such trees harvested, but cohune palms were 'saved for shade.' Even then, however, in mid-April the area to be cleared was set on fire and kept burning until mid-May.[115]

Taking possession of the land also required drawing straight lines through the jungle floor, replicating not only the square-grid survey system of the North American plain, but lines that followed cardinal directions. As Koop recalled, one of the first tasks was to 'cut a line from the south side of the settlement, beginning at the B.B. Dueck farm and then headed four miles north. The line was called the "meridian,"' testimony to the reference line on the Canadian prairies.[116] A second challenge was the creation of a road system. By 24 September 1960, the date of the first extant minutes of a colony assembly meeting, Spanish Lookout's basic road system had been established and farmers were already preoccupied with improving the primitive infrastructure: 'The culverts on the colony will have to be strengthened. A bridge is needed at P.R. Pletts' and H.H. Duecks.' Also a road is needed at B.B. Duecks' and Jo.W. Pletts' ... About a bridge or ferry; it was discussed but not decided.'[117]

Another challenge was the development of an export economy. Minutes from another early meeting on 22 October 1960 suggest that farmers were enthusiastically exploring a number of options: colony administrator 'Peter D. Reimer reported that he once again had chickens in "Cold Storage,"' and thus 'Johann W. Reimer was elected to be of assistance ... [to] get sales going again.' Meanwhile farmer 'Johann D. Friesen reported on the foreign export of vegetables,' noting that the 'prices have not yet been received.' Over the course of the next few years farmers experimented with different ways to extract yield from the jungle floor. In 1961 they seemed especially enthusiastic about the prospect of fruit and vegetable growing; they ordered grapefruit, orange, and apple trees but payed special attention to tomatoes, noting that unlike in Canada, in British Honduras 'tomatoes should be planted regularly throughout the year.'[118] Then in 1963 the colony farmers debated entering into business with Peter Butland of Ontario, Canada, who was planning to build 'a large fruit packing plant.' Butland wanted a 'wide variety' of 'first quality fruit,' promised to pay 'even keel world prices' and provide farmers with 'first class information on insecticides and fungicides.' The colonists clearly were cautious and within three years many Spanish Lookout farmers had soured on the idea of fruit growing.[119] As a later colony mayor, Abe D. Loewen, recalled, Butland's 'venture was too late at Spanish Lookout. We had already discovered that we were able to gain a livelihood through cultivation'[120]

In particular, the farmers had discovered a liking for corn and beans and within ten years of settlement had created a seasonal and gendered rhythm growing these two crops. The 1968 English-language diary of Linda Dueck Thiessen, a young woman who had married Ben P. Thiessen in 1957 and was a mother five young children – Leona age ten, Maria eight, Irvin five, David two, and Albert one – suggests the basic pattern.[121] As beginning farmers, neither Linda nor Ben spent much time on the farm fields: Linda spent endless days baking, sewing, cleaning, and painting; Ben spent much of his time keeping colony financial records and working at the sawmill. Still, both were brought outdoors into a theater built on climate and soil. It was Linda's challenge to try 'drying the wash' in a rainy milieu and her vocation to tend the garden; it was Ben's to oversee land clearing and raise farms crops. The gardening in 1968 began on 4 January when Linda planted 'beets, carrots, peas, beans and "cukes"' and Ben 'put up the tomato sticks.' The recorded field work for the year began on 17 January when Ben 'cultivated the beans' that had been planted in December. Numerous other days saw Ben 'in the bush' and on at least one day he took with him 'bush workers.' The first two weeks in March were devoted to the three-step bean harvest: family members 'pulled' the beans, then Ben 'threshed beans,' and finally 'the children and I [Linda] sorted beans,' the latter task going on throughout April. During the second half of March the beanfield was ploughed, a task repeated at the end of April. In early April Ben 'brought beans away,' presumably to market, and Linda was canning 'white beans' and turning the cabbage patch into sauerkraut.

By late May, Ben planted the second crop of the year, corn, and then two weeks later on 13 June he 'cultivated the whole day,' presumably on the cornfield. Then came the very wet summer months. In 1968 heavy rains left Ben and Linda, who had been attending to medical and shopping needs in Belize City, stranded, unable to return home as 'no one from Spanish Lookout came to Belize' that day for the 'river [was] too high' and was 'still very high' until noon the next day. On 8 October the four-step corn harvest commenced when 'Ben got two loads of corn from [the land at] Barton Remie,' corn that had earlier been 'bent' or 'broken' and then 'pulled.' The 'pulling' and 'hauling' continued as rainy weather allowed until 30 October when the custom thresher arrived at the Thiessens' 'in the afternoon [and] Clarence threshed corn at our place, 83 sacks.' By November the Thiessens had begun the three-step planting of kidney beans: on 14 November Ben 'went to plough at Barton Remy,' on 23 November he 'disced at Barton Remy,' and on 7 December he 'finished planting at Barton Remy.' Christmas Eve brought more 'rainy weather' and the annual process of farming in the tropics began again.

The 1968 German-language diary of forty-seven-year-old Anna Loewen Dueck provides another perspective. Anna lived on a more established farm with her husband Heinrich and twelve children, ages four to twenty-four (the thirteenth child, Abram, twenty-seven, was married but worked closely with the parental household; a fourteenth child had died in 1951).[122] As such, her farm household varied from Linda Thiessen's.[123] But its differences existed chiefly in that it suggested the shape of a more complex agrarian household and in the extent to which the conservative Mennonites had begun to employ machines and chemicals in their bid to transplant their northern worlds to British Honduras.[124] Although Anna's diary for January 1968 makes no mention of tending the beanfields, it does mention a field of tomatoes which on 27 February was 'fertilized and sprayed.' This process was repeated in the 'warm and dry' month of April when tomatoes were planted again and then 'watered and fertilized.' Even though these were relatively dry months, the beans that the family threshed in March could spoil and so on 8 May they were 'fumigated.' In early June just as the corn planting commenced, attention was again paid to the garden when on 4 June the boys fertilized the 'sweet corn.' A note of scientific farming was struck on 18 July when the two older boys, 'Menno and Hein [ages twenty-two and sixteen] ... sprayed the corn because of worms.'

While the corn grew in summer, the boys repaired fences and worked with lumber but also focussed on the mechanical side of farming. On 2 August, for example, 'Anton, Abram, Frank and Menno [ages twenty-seven to twenty-two] were busy building a bean thresher.' The corn harvest began on 1 October. But the pulling of the corn by the 'school-age children [Lena thirteen, Otto twelve, Tina ten, Paul eight, and Klaas six] and Papa and I,' hauling it home with the 'Cat and trailer,' and the mechanical threshing of up to 169 bags, were only the first three steps. The corn harvest was not completed until the Dueck boys had 'taken the corn to David J. T[hiessen] for drying' with a propane-powered dryer, a process that took longer than expected. After a day of drying the 167 bags of corn 'remained too wet to take back home.'[125] Even as the corn harvest continued, the older boys began turning the cornfield into bean acres. They travelled 'to Barton Remy to plow with the Cat' on 2 October, seeking the narrow window of opportunity when just the right amount of moisture allowed for plowing (it was something that eluded Anton and Menno on 2 November when they 'drove to Barton Remy with the Cat to plow, but [found it] too wet).' The second step of disking began on 11 November, but it too failed when the disc broke down as they tried cutting through the hard, black clay aggregates. The disker had to be disassembled and fitted with new bearings. A sign of the pervasive hold of technology on the Dueck farm occurred on 14 January when Franz, age twenty, 'bush-hog[ged]' the meadow with a heavy-duty mower.

Fertilizers, fungicides, and insecticides were used alongside diesel, propane, and gasoline power to replicate a North American farm culture in Central America. It may seem that the Spanish Lookout farmers took an aggressive attitude to their environment and specifically in the ways they cleared the jungle after 1958. They wove the colony together in the early 1960s with straight lines of roads and fences. They used technology and accepted at least some chemical products. They created a commodity export economy of corn-fed chickens and red kidney beans by the 1970. Then they rapidly increased their commodity output during the 1970s, building their corn production from 5.5 million pounds in 1971 to 9.3 million in 1981, their bean crop from 577,500 pounds to 805,000, the number of their laying chickens from 24,000 birds to 50,000, and the number of broiler chickens from 220,000 birds to 896,000.[126]

Despite the surface appearance of environmental destruction, the Mennonite colony showed a complex and even respectful approach to the soil. If the initial settlement seemed to speak of a culture of gaining dominion over the land, the communitarian nature of the colony created a culture of environmental reverence. If the subordination of nature was required to create an egalitarian society of humility, the indirect consequences of the latter translated into greater environmental sensitivity. In 1970 geographer Jerry Hall observed that Mennonite farmers objected to the full commercialization of farming. Spanish Lookout farmers told Hall 'that farming is the only occupation where one may be self-sufficient ... Hard work is good and a humble person is one who works close to the ground in direct contact with nature. [Only] some members stated that God is nature and that he is all around in the physical world. [But they all agreed that] one communes most closely [with God] by the reality of work.'[127] Hall also saw farmers balk at a full acceptance of mechanical and scientific farming. True, in 1970 most farmers had 'larger-than-needed-tractors,' but the fact was that most colonists still used tractors and trailers for general road travel and did not own motor vehicles.[128] Most colonists also used compacting tractor power only for planting and tillage, and not for harvest. Among the older Mennonites Hall observed considerable opposition to the 'use of chemicals.' They expressed concerns that chemicals were 'unnatural or unnecessary or both,' and certainly that there was 'no direction in the Bible for their use.'[129] Hall also noted a concerted effort among Spanish Lookout households to secure food self-sufficiency: 'daily family requirements [were] kept at a minimum as it is thought that to be wasteful or excessive in the use of one's resources is sinful.' No household in 1970 even used electricity in the home.[130] Hall concluded that 'the efficiency of resource use is not maximized because the Mennonite "way of life" does not incorporate profit maximization as a goal.'[131]

The records of the Colony Assembly support Hall's observations that Spanish Lookout farmers constantly were asked to guard against full farm commercialization or land commodification. Their intention was that humility and equality should be written into the very geography of Spanish Lookout. The practice of registering land in the name of the community, specifically in the name of the Spanish Lookout's Kleine Gemeinde church, was deliberate.[132] In May 1961, for example, when a $33,000 loan from the country's Agricultural Credit Fund was made contingent on the colony becoming a cooperative of individual farmers, colony administrators sent a delegation to the United States to seek credit from another source.[133] The church-centered practice of land registration ensured cultural homogeneity because no farmer could sell land to a non-Mennonite. More importantly, some argued that the practice placed a check on growing wealth differentiation, especially as no individual farm family could mortgage its land to raise credit and thereby increase the farm size and place upward pressure on land prices. The congregational ownership of all land also gave colony administrators means to maintain social equality. The Colony Assembly alone considered land purchases outside the colony. Through an elected Land Committee it ensured that land parcels remained limited and that young farmers had first opportunity to purchase new sources of land.[134] The Land Committee, for example, had a special role in dividing the most treasured land, the red loamy land near the Belize River.[135] It also played a special role in 1968 when the colony purchased a 1400-acre parcel of similar land near the Belize River. The parcel, known as Barton Remy, became synonymous with good soil. The committee showed leadership not only by negotiating the $137,000 purchase price, but also by regulating the division of the tract into twenty-acre parcels.[136] It further introduced measures to privilege young farmers. It ruled in

March that 'he who has no land shall pay $10 on the first 20 acres, $20 on the next 20 acres; he who already has land shall pay $20 on the first 20 acres, and $50 on the next 20 acres.'[137] In 1971 when a field at Barton Remy came up for auction, the Land Committee decided that 'only those who do not yet have any red soil will have opportunity to buy.'[138] Small parcels of land distributed fairly marked the social practice of a culture rooted in a respect for environmental resources.

The ways in which they adapted to their new environment revealed the Spanish Lookout people's communitarian cosmology. They knew that nature secured sustenance for them. It allowed them to maintain the old Mennonite practice of bilateral, partible inheritance, and the cultural practice of inter vivos partitioning of land equally among boys and girls. It allowed them to make generational succession of land a central goal for the houshold. When, for example, the young couple Anton Loewen and Nettie Penner married in 1968 at the ages of twenty-three and twenty respectively, they were able to draw on two important sources for farmland: the piece of red soil at Barton Remy that Anton had been able to purchase from the colony upon reaching the age of majority and then two fifteen-acre parcels of arable farmland Anton and Nettie received from their respective parents at the time of their wedding. The farmers also knew that land was linked to their very cosmology. As a 1981 Spanish Lookout school social studies textbook asserted, 'God has made our country very nice.' After rich descriptions of the animal and plant kingdoms of British Honduras, the textbook declared 'we should always remember that it is God who makes the plants grow.'[139] If this was true, stated the social studies instructors, farmers should also respect the soil and heed 'government [which] would like the farmers to plow their fields instead of cutting and burning' them. Clearly the aim was not to extract as much as the soil could possibly give. The land was no guarantee of luxury or status. The only guarantee was that hard physical work would be required. But this promise was its blessing: 'roll up their sleeves and go to work on the land,' stated the textbook to the Spanish Lookout children. The newly independent country of Belize, it said, could use more producers of food, besides which, God 'blesses the work we do for our fellow man.' Continued adaptation to the challenges to a tropical environment would secure the aims of the 1958 pioneers.

Mennonites came to British Honduras to resist change. A consumer culture, evangelical trends, and an intrusive state in Canada had sent the Kleine Gemeinde Mennonites to Mexico in 1948 and the reappearance of similar threats in Mexico had sent them farther south to seek even more exclusion in 1958. If the colonists assumed that they would simply maintain the authentic, time-tempered voice of being Mennonite by removing themselves from worldly influences they were wrong. Exclusivity was maintained at one level, but it was safeguarded by both geographic distance and unforeseen social forces. The very test of settling in a hostile environment, the social distance available to the colonists in the form of racial difference, and the economic clout of the colony in the small British Honduras economy provided the Mennonite community with the cultural material with which to reinforce its social boundaries. The dissatisfaction of members on the inside – from the Barton Creek antimodernists to the Local Church pietists – however, signalled that isolation bolstered by racial and class differences would not keep the colony from changing. As their Mennonite kin in Canada changed ideologically and as Spanish Lookout became aware of them, those changes became part of the cultural map of the colonists. The old binary paradigm of faithful communities in the south and modernistic evangelicalized Mennonite communities in the north remained. But conservative Swiss American Pennsylvania Mennonites now received greater respect and Kleine Gemeinde brethren in Mexico who had once been viewed as having stumbled in the cause of Mennonite isolation were once again fully accepted.

The Spanish Lookout Mennonites revered their ancestors who came to Canada in the 1870s and who had rigorously confronted the worldly society in the new land. But this Canadian Mennonite pioneer society differed significantly from that of Spanish Lookout Colony a hundred years later. During their first two generations in Manitoba between 1874 and 1919, Kleine Gemeinde Mennonites had fully accepted individually titled property, household marketing strategies, a voluntary-based mutual aid society, secular-grounded municipal government, state intervention in schools, full farm mechanization, and a geography of scattered farmsteads. The Kleine Gemeinde Mennonites who moved to Mexico and to British Honduras may have thought they were stopping time and change; they were in effect partly reversing it and partly inventing something completely new. Within the more exclusive settlements provided by the governments of Mexico and British Honduras, these Mennonites elevated certain symbols as signs of cultural authenticity. The early refusal to accept cars, telephones, and electricity, the strict shunning of excommunicated members, and the primacy given to agricultural vocation reflected an early-twentieth-century North American Mennonite agenda. But the colony system, with its centrally planned economy and the practice of placing legal title of all lands in the name of the church, reflected a strategy that the Kleine Gemeinde borrowed not from the past, but from Mennonites in other communities in Latin America. Then too, the Spanish Lookout Mennonite acceptance of Low German and an emphasis on the inner spiritual life encouraged a subjective religiosity that reflected elements of American evangelicalism.

Most obvious of all changes in Spanish Lookout was its agriculture. The farmers' daunting challenge was to tame a rainforest, to turn its fragile soils into sustainable cropland, harness its year-long fecundity, accept the jungle as a home for northerners, and direct its bounty to undergird a close-knit community. The frequency with which farmers would allude to the chaotic, mud-filled days that followed Hurricane Hatti of 31 October 1961, suggested their preoccupation with the new physical environment. The record of their farming – the host of new farming methods, the efforts to shore up poor roads, the energy put into marketing strategies – was a measure of just how new the new setting was. To meet these requirements British Honduras farmers engaged in great cooperative effort, censuring upward mobility even as they courted the agents of the global export market with deliberation. Moreover, they were almost unpacifist in their cavalier drive to tame the seemingly indominatable jungle; they slashed, burned, and bulldozed their way through the bushland. Yet all this change too was directed to the economic construction of a close-knit, solidaristic community. In British Honduras land was seen as a divine gift for a communitarian people to use in their effort to reinvigorate a life of community-centered Christian humility.

Ironically, the Spanish Lookout Mennonites engaged in a discourse of tradition without examining closely the historical record. At the very time that Canadian Mennonites were rediscovering in sixteenth-century Anabaptist accounts what Mennonite historian Paul Toews has called a 'useable history,' the British Honduras Mennonites de-emphasized centuries-old Anabaptist literature. In their search for an authentic tradition they created the strong foundation for a new one. The Spanish Lookout community may have spoken of survival and persistence, but a historical examination illuminates the extent to which it created new social mechanisms and refashioned its identity. To the outsider, Spanish Lookout may have been a place firmly set in tradition; in fact its culture was the product of vibrant, creative effort as fertile as the jungle in which it was rooted.

9 Fragmented Freedoms: Studies of Mennonites in Winnipeg and Denver

Cityward

Far-reaching social changes in mid-twentieth-century rural society sent many of the most conservative North American Mennonites into both a virtual and real diaspora. In the eastern half of the continent – especially in Ontario, Pennsylvania, and Ohio – intrusive governments and consumer cultures caused Swiss-descendant Old Order Mennonites and Amish to reassert themselves in highly visible agrarian communities, private schools, and communitarian churches.[1] In western Canada conservative Dutch-descendant Mennonite groups separated themselves physically, undertaking costly migrations southward to Paraguay and northern Mexico, with secondary migrations to British Honduras, Bolivia, and southern Mexico. But at the very time that the Great Disjuncture was propelling the conservative wing of the Mennonite community to become even more antimodern, the rural transformation was sending many others to consider a full acceptance not only of modernity, but the postmodern 'soft city.' In Jonathan Raban's classic words, cities are 'unlike villages' in that they 'are plastic by nature'; they are places of 'polymorphus correlations,' places of 'illusion, myth, aspirations, [and] nightmare.'[2] Here, as newcomers to cities elsewhere, Mennonite newcomers found their 'ethnicity, culture and identity' interrelated in a process that was 'contested, temporal and emergent.'[3] They became affiliated to different classes, religions, professions, political affiliations, places of residence, and forms of leisure. In the process they 'invented' new identities, affected by a 'cross cultural' experience, sometimes by 'multi-ethnic' intersections, always leading to 'cultural fragmentation.' In the fashion of newcomers in other cities, a younger generation rose to challenge the culture of an older one, working to 'wring their own past from generalized amnesia,' writing a 'useable history' that served more to 'reinforce group solidarity' than transplant a 'traditional identity.'[4]

By 1970 more Mennonites in North America lived in cities and towns than on farms and in villages. The main city of choice for the Rural Municipality (RM) of Hanover Mennonites was of course Winnipeg, its closest point lying only twenty miles to the northwest and said to possess the single largest concentration of urban Mennonites and urban Mennonite institutions in the world.[5] Here Mennonites found work in all economic sectors, but especially in the teaching and medical professions and in construction and manufacturing. The city of choice for Meade County Mennonites was less clear-cut, situated as they were a fair distance from any large city. Many found their way to small cities, central Kansas's Wichita and Hutchinson and California's Fresno, for example. But giant Denver, three hundred miles to the northwest of Meade County, held special appeal. As cities go, it was relatively close to Meade and it had hosted the single largest group of 1-W Mennonites, the conscientious objectors, during and after the Second World War.[6] Numerous 1-W men who had worked as orderlies in hospitals returned to the city after marriage to work in construction and other trades and as college-trained professionals.

The Mennonite presence in North American cities has generated significant interest among scholars and Mennonite scholars in particular. The appeal is to sort out a riddle: how did Mennonites who were lodged in the North American imagination as a quintessentially rural, sectarian, and quiescent people, adapt to the city to which they came lately? Between 1941 and 1971 the number of Mennonites in Canadian cities of more than 100,000 persons grew more than tenfold, from 5100 to 61,000.[7] A different set of statistics reveals less of a tendency towards urbanization among Mennonites in the United States, but a trend nevertheless: between 1940 and 1960, the percentage of members of the largest of the American Mennonite denominations, the Mennonite Church, that lived in cities of more than 10,000 almost doubled, from 6 percent to 11 percent. By 1972 the two Mennonite denominations most numerous in Kansas, the General Conference Mennonite Church (GC) and the Mennonite Brethren Church (MB) showed a particular openness to urban life; nationwide, 23 percent and 36 percent of their members respectively lived in cities of 25,000 or more.[8]

An often-quoted observation by Mennonite sociologist Winfield Fretz has become a reference point in discussion of the group's urbanization.

In 1956 Fretz remarked that 'where Mennonites have gone to the cities, the solidarity of the communities has been shattered' and Mennonites have 'lost their identity as Mennonites.'[9] Historians examining the urbanizing generation of Mennonites have concluded the very opposite. T.D. Regehr's *Mennonites in Canada, 1939–1970*, in observing the range of urban Mennonite educational, medical, financial, and media institutions, argued that 'a look at a map of any Canadian city to which they moved in large numbers quickly demonstrates that [their] identity has not been lost but in fact ... strengthened.'[10] Paul Toews's the *Mennonites in American Society, 1930–1970* reached a similar conclusion. During these years, he argued, 'being Mennonite had less and less to do with the practice of nonconformity visually defined, with speaking German, with being rural ... More and more, ideology, servant activism and voluntarism were replacing cultural markers as the central carriers of Mennonite peoplehood.'[11] These markers were often associated with the term Anabaptist, a reference to the Mennonites' sixteenth-century, socially engaged ancestors who could often be found in towns and cities.

Other evidence suggests that the picture may be even more complex than the transition from Mennonite sectarianism to a neo-Anabaptist social activism. Mennonite sociologist Leo Driedger suggests that the city created a 'Mennonite mosaic, a kaleidoscope of ferment and change.'[12] True, the city proved to be a ground on which Mennonite newcomers turned their Anabaptist past into a 'usable history,' finding in it models for inner-city service and the pursuit of social justice. But as sociological surveys suggest, the city also gave birth to evangelical fundamentalists who voted conservatively and to impatient, young, secularized Mennonite writers and teens who strayed from their parents' teachings and found 'difficulty relating to their parents.'[13] And the group quickly divided itself into distinctive economic classes; entrepreneurs, professionals, and laborers crafted distinctive work cultures, attitudes to authority, religious practices, residential patterns, and even voting patterns.[14] The urban Mennonite world was not homogeneous socially or culturally.

On the surface, the RM of Hanover Mennonites who went to Winnipeg and the Meade County Mennonites who went to Denver created a sense of ethnicity and embraced a religious faith that was antithetical to the culture of their second and third cousins in northern Mexico or in interior British Honduras. But upon closer inspection a majority urban Mennonite culture cannot be neatly defined. Indeed if the forces of the Great Disjuncture fragmented the Mennonite societies of North America physically, ethnically, and religiously, the fragment that was sent to the city seemed divided into even smaller pieces upon its arrival. The very dynamic of the postmodern urban culture presented an evolving multiplicity of networks and boundaries.

'Rural' Networks in Winnipeg

A simple contradiction was evident in southeastern Manitoba after the war. As farm folk saw it, the city-bound migrants were those people of the southeast who had not survived the postwar rural transformation. As town folk perceived it, the urban migrants were the rising stars, young people who could not tolerate the closed, parochial culture of the countryside. At midcentury, Hanover's youth in Winnipeg did include many young female domestics, but just as often they were college kids attending either the Mennonite Brethren Bible College or the Canadian Mennonite Bible College or one of the secular places, the downtown United College or giant, suburban University of Manitoba.[15] And oftentimes the graduates in Winnipeg were only at the beginning of their upward mobility. In 1960 it was reported that Dwight Reimer, in possession of a newly minted Bachelor of Commerce degree from the University of Manitoba, had been hired by Cessna Aircraft company in Toronto, that Eric Rempel had earned a Bachelor of Agriculture degree and had left for a new job in Ottawa's Department of Agriculture, and that Albert Hiebert's Bachelor of Arts certificate was taking him to Chicago's Trinity College and Seminary. The list went on. Reports also came of Hanover musicians making good in the city. In 1960 Alvina Klassen was awarded Winnipeg's 'Sacred Music Society's Cup' with highest honors, and in the same year Glenn Loewen won the prestigious 'Women's Music Society of Winnipeg Award' at a piano recital at United College in Winnipeg, an award that carried him to the Royal Conservatory in Toronto.[16] Occasionally, word was broadcast of Hanover Mennonites coming close to the center of the privileged British Canadian upper classes: the June 1960 marriage of trucking firm magnate Frank F. Reimer's son Gerald to June Faith Gowler, daughter 'of Mr and Mrs Spencer Gowler of Winnipeg' took place in the city's stately Portage Avenue Elim Chapel in the company not only of the grandparents and uncles and aunts from Steinbach, but also 'His Worship, Lieutenant Governor ... Willis and Mrs Willis.'[17] Within Hanover's media, the *Carillon News* and Radio CHSM, the city was the appropriate destination for local achievers.

Another image of the city lurked in the shadows. It was the place of hard knocks and insidious temptations. Not unrepresentative was the story of a Hanover family that moved to Winnipeg before the Second World War. Anna Toews Reimer, daughter of the kindly, local centenarian John B. Toews, was an early pioneer in Winnipeg. She had married into the Reimer merchant family in Steinbach and during the Depression, as many other Mennonites hunkered down to a life of bushland subsistence, the Reimers moved to Winnipeg. Here 'she took in roomers and boarders, she sewed clothes ... out of material and castoff clothing. She never stopped working ... while Dad was ... beating the pavement trying to sell cars that nobody had money to buy and fuel savers that nobody except Dad believed in.' Anna Reimer disliked Winnipeg. As her daughter Elizabeth later noted: 'Mother tried to keep the evils of the outside world away from us. She felt that Steinbach was the only safe place for her daughters to be.'[18] After the war the family did return to Steinbach where daughter Elizabeth married Bruno Derksen, one of the owners of the *Carillon News*. In later years Elizabeth wrote an autobiographical novel in which she noted that leaving Winnipeg was as if 'we came out of exile. But not to a strange land – coming to Millbach [the novelist's name for Steinbach] was like coming home to the village of my childhood ... The sky was clear. Lilacs bloomed in the hedge ... Strangers who had a familiar look ... greeted us in Low German ... I was at home.'[19]

For most Hanover Mennonites in Winnipeg, the city had little of either Gerald Reimer's glamor or Elizabeth Reimer's drudgery. The city offered a middle-class suburbia – in East Kildonan, Charleswood, Fort Garry, and St Vital – where Mennonite networks were indelibly rooted in a local Mennonite church. As scholars of immigration have increasingly observed, places of worship were crucial in the creation of a virtual community for dispersed urban newcomers. This importance can be seen in the story of one of the smallest of the Mennonite denominations in Winnipeg, the Evangelical Mennonite Conference (EMC), descendant body of the conservative Mennonite Kleine Gemeinde. EMC people predominantly from Hanover founded four churches in the city between 1951 and 1976. Their first church was begun when Steinbach's large EMC church helped organize a fellowship in rented quarters on Ellis Avenue in Winnipeg's inner city. Unlike other early Mennonite churches in Winnipeg, the Ellis Avenue church was not primarily a mission church; it was founded after 'a survey was conducted in order to see if there were enough EMC members to warrant establishing a

local church.'[20] By 1954 the congregation had purchased its own building on the inner-city Aberdeen Avenue and by 1957 the congregation
was accepted into the wider EMC with a membership of fifty-five. It
depicted itself as both a social and spiritual site for rural families
entering the city and for rural youth who came there to work temporarily. It reported that its membership seemed to fluctuate with the
'coming and going of people, as is often the case in an urban church,'
but insisted that it was offering 'a heavy schedule of regular services
and meetings.' Membership transfers usually recorded a rural to urban
migration: the first official membership transfers to the Aberdeen church
were said to be those of 'Miss Lena Brandt ... from the Blumenort EMC
and Mr and Mrs Albert Kroeker ... from the Steinbach EMC.'[21] This
pattern became well established at Aberdeen and in successive years
the church attracted numerous members from outlying rural EMC
churches in Hanover, in the Interlake district to the north and the
Rosenort district to the southwest. The church's 1972 notice in the
Messenger, the EMC's periodical, welcoming 'young people coming to
Winnipeg to study or work' to attend the church's new 'College and
Career group [that] has been meeting every other Thursday,' was representative of its pitch.[22]

The same pattern can be observed in the establishment of EMC
churches in Winnipeg's well-defined suburbs: the west-end Crestview
EMC begun in 1967, the east-side Braeside EMC established in 1968,
and the south-end Fort Garry founded in 1976. Each of the churches
appealed to rural newcomers and membership acceptances read like a
record of immigration from the farm districts to Winnipeg's growing
residential quarters. The year Crestview was begun it published an
invitation in the *Messenger* for 'young people from the country [who
are] working in the city to come to our Friday night Young People's
at 8 o'clock.'[23] In October 1974 when the church reported that it had
baptized Norman Solnik, a man not bearing a traditional ethnic Mennonite surname, it also announced that members with traditional rural
Mennonite surnames – Friesen, Neufeld, Dyck, and Reimer – were
welcomed into fellowship as transferred members.[24] The Braeside church
experienced a parallel growth: in a single service in 1970, sixteen new
members included predominantly rural, ethnic Mennonites: EMC members from the Hanover districts of Steinbach, Kleefeld, and Landmark;
EMC members from churches at MacGregor and Portage la Prairie to
the west of Winnipeg; and members of the rural conservative Bergthaler
and Old Colony Mennonite denominations.[25] By 1976 when the Fort

Garry EMC was begun it followed a well-established pattern: it credited its beginning to the fact that 'a few families in the area, living a
good distance from any EMC congregations had contemplated this
move' for some time, and that the church could be attractive to 'students at nearby University of Manitoba.'[26] Both groups, it said, could
benefit from a 'sense of community' that the church saw itself providing.[27] And like the other EMC churches, Fort Garry issued a special
message for newcomers from the countryside: in a September 1980 ad
in the *Messenger* it boldly declared that the 'Fort Garry Church Needs
You: If you are planning to move to Winnipeg to work or study this fall,
consider helping the Fort Garry EM Church' by providing leadership in
Sunday school, music, or children's clubs.[28] Rural migrants had their
urban niche.

Winnipeg's Ideological Ferment

The EMC churches, however, were much more than rural havens. They
charted pathways into the heart of urban culture. True, the churches
might have had rural roots, but they made evangelistic outreach the
centre of their church ethos. In 1967 when the Crestview church opened
its doors, it recalled that its genesis made 'this church ... unique' for it
had its 'beginning in a country church, Kleefeld, from where the workers went out every Sunday to [the Winnipeg suburb of] Charleswood to
conduct Sunday School' and after December 1961 when actual services
began with only twelve people a 'door to door religious census was
made and householder mail sent out to promote the work.'[29] Informal
programs in church basements also brought remnants of ethnic culture,
mostly in familiar ethnic foodways, but an evangelical agenda was
never far off. In the winter of 1973 the Crestview Young People's association ended an evening of tobogganing and Christian fellowship by
consuming *Kommst Borscht*; in the winter of 1978 the Braeside church
celebrated its tenth anniversary by sitting down to a 'delicious *Faspa*,'
the traditional Low German Sunday late-afternoon meal of cold meat,
cheese, bread, jam and coffee.[30] But during the very month in which the
Crestview youth consumed their borscht they hosted a Mr. Gawryletz
of the Overseas Missionary Fellowship and Crestview's children organized a 'Christian Olympics Club' that sang Christian songs at the
interdenominational Heritage Lodge Home.[31] At the 1978 meeting in
which Braeside folks consumed their *Faspa* pastor Cornie Plett reminded
members that 'our purpose in the Braeside Park Community is to

combat evil and to make the opportunity to know God available to the people' and he challenged them 'to take on their responsibility to get the Gospel out to the people of this community, rather than waiting for them to come and get it.'[32]

No shortage of evangelical concern existed among the Winnipeg EMCs. In fact Mel Koop, the EMC minister appointed to counsel students at the University of Manitoba, was unequivocal on the matter: in a December 1966 gathering at the university he declared that 'the vocation ... prepared for and entered in [by] the student must be considered in the light of Christ's Great Commission' and that students should seize the day at the university, 'now in the evangelicalization of their fellow man.'[33]

The mission of evangelism gave the rural migrants to Winnipeg a reason for being that took them beyond the attainment of suburban comfort and professional self-actualization. However, few Hanover migrants were primarily evangelistic in religious orientation. Even within the four EMC churches some members preferred the socially progressive Christianity expressed by the internationally focused Mennonite Central Committee (MCC). The Crestview church, for example, was home to MCC Canada's executive secretary, Dan Zehr, and occasionally offered him a public forum: in November 1970 Zehr preached a sermon on Jesus's socially engaging words, 'as you have done to the least of these, you have done to me,' and in December 1975 he reported on his controversial trip as part of a peace delegation to North and South Vietnam.[34] During the same evening that Zehr reported on Vietnam, another member, Reg Toews, originally of Steinbach and the future executive secretary of MCC headquarters in Akron, Pennsylvania, reported on his tour of poverty- and conflict-ridden areas of Africa and the Middle East.[35]

Other EMC members openly criticized the fundamentalist and moralistic bent of evangelicalism and even aired their views in the *Messenger*. In 1969 Glenn Klassen, a high school teacher from Steinbach who had returned to university for graduate work in biology declared at one of the EMC university student meetings that 'what [is] going on in our church buildings from week to week [is] a hindrance to our witness in the present generation.' He went on to say that he 'was embarrassed by the vocabulary used, the songs we sing, and by the oppressive atmosphere created by formality and lack of true openness.' In a subsequent letter Klassen stoked the fire by asserting that the debate pitting liberals against fundamentalists within the EMC and the preoccupation with 'hair, skirts, tobacco, guitars and other trivia' shamed the church.[36] Klassen was sharply rebuked by some EMC ministers. That 'there are no absolutes [in universities] is becoming more obvious,' wrote Mel Koop.[37] But Klassen was not alone in his questioning. In a September 1970 letter Agatha Fast, a Winnipeger with Blumenort roots, wrote boldly that she was attending a non-Mennonite church and had joined a 'Friday night cell group' consisting of 'Roman Catholics (including priests and nuns), Anglicans, Mennonites, Brethren, Lutherans, Presbyterians, church tramps and un-churched believers [and] seeking-unbelievers.' As she saw it, the strict ethical code of 'don'ts' was irrelevant where 'love' was at work: 'I believe that love has an evaluation system all its own in discerning the right or wrongness of matters ... and it is a great deal more accurate than the most fool-proof work of moral codes.'[38] Fast in turn was supported in 1971 by Elizabeth Friesen who called for social action, quoting one social activist preacher as saying that the 'church is an awful place for an unbeliever,' and exhorting members to consider 'the need of Children's homes in the city ... It would be good to see a Christian couple interested in these unhappy children ... Jesus loves them! Do we?'[39] In an especially pointed 1973 letter, Winnipeg schoolteacher Wally Doerksen, also originally of Blumenort, chastised church leaders for overemphasizing 'personal evangelism.' Using biblical metaphors Doerksen lauded the task of symbolically 'sprinkling salt' for as Christians 'we ARE the salt' in the world. It was a task, however, not achieved by 'visitation, tract distribution, singing, etc.,' but in 'our community involvement, business transactions, social interactions.'[40]

The Mennonite newcomers to the city who felt uncomfortable with the evangelical imperative would find a cultural home in neo-Anabaptism, celebrating the social activism of their sixteenth-century antecedents. These voices equally disparaged the Low German rural Mennonites and those who had adapted a North American fundamentalist evangelicalism. University students in particular were critical of either the ethnic or the evangelical label. In November 1974 student Ray Friesen, who had spent his childhood in the Blumenort district, wrote critically of a peace conference held at the University of Winnipeg where Mennonites had put themselves to shame by being unable to articulate a clear position on pacifism. Friesen concluded that to be a Mennonite had become 'synonymous to being called a Dutch Prussian Russian Canadian.' He granted that 'our "Mennonitism" will become a great historical heritage but [it] will not describe our beliefs.' This religious articulation was possible, he insisted, only once Mennonites saw themselves not as 'ethnic,' but as 'Anabaptists.'[41]

The term 'Anabaptist' gained new currency in city circles during the 1970s. In April 1978 student Travis Kroeker, who had spent his childhood in Steinbach, wrote to the *Messenger* to report on his attendance at the Mennonite World Conference in Wichita, Kansas. 'The conference,' he noted, 'reinforced my Mennonite identity by providing me with a conclusive definition of what it means to be a Mennonite.' It was a religious identity only, specifying 'a spiritual descendant of Menno Simons and the sixteenth century Anabaptists.' The 'appellation "Mennonite,"' wrote Kroeker, 'should be disassociated with a particular culture or ethnic heritage. At the conference this belief was confirmed as thousands of Mennonites from all parts of the world assembled to create a colorful mosaic composed of many cultural traditions and diverse lifestyles. Our commonness was not rooted in cultural homogeneity or common ancestry, but in our common commitment to Jesus Christ and the teachings of our Anabaptist forebears.'[42] Students such as Friesen, Kroeker, and others not only embraced the term Anabaptist and its social agenda, they slammed the personal moralism of evangelicalism. In 1978 Friesen critiqued the link between evangelicalism and middle-class complacency: It is when 'social action requires us to look at our affluence and threatens our life style' that 'we suddenly decide that our emphasis should be evangelism. It's much safer.'[43] In the same year Kroeker called on church members to consider a 'holistic expression of life in Christ,' that is, one which venerates 'sacrificial love ... and a prophetic lifestyle,' which in turn 'attempts to come to grips with the inequalities, injustices and ills of our world.'[44]

The two poles within the EMC, the middle-class evangelicals and the social activist neo-Anabaptists drew on a common desire to create of their Mennonite religiousness a relevant force within the city. In this respect both created a means into urban culture. At the same time, both also contributed to the emergence of greater cultural distance between the city and the countryside. Rurality became an 'other,' the force against which one defined a new urban identity. It was an antipathy that crossed ideological boundaries and lines of gender.

The advance guard of Mennonites in Winnipeg, and indeed of other Canadian cities including Vancouver and Saskatoon, were single women who worked as domestics and raised badly needed hard currency for debt-ridden rural households. Much has been written about these single women, their residences in Mennonite-run 'girls homes,' female networks, sense of importance, and the effect of their cultural assimilation upon their return to the farms.[45] But single women also figured prominently in the post–Second World War era, especially those rural women who found a sense of independence in remaining single while pursuing professional jobs in Winnipeg. Alice and Linda Doerksen, for example, were sisters who had been born in Haskell County, Kansas, and migrated to the RM of Hanover during the Great Depression. They came to Winnipeg in the 1950s where eventually they joined the Aberdeen EMC church. The move, however, was not apolitical. As Alice Doerksen recalled, rural 'people would criticize the girls who were going to the city,' but as she saw it, 'it's their own fault because they don't pay' the salaries required to keep the youth in the countryside. Linda Doerksen echoed this sentiment: 'When we left the community, there were people there who said Alice and I were going to the bad city now and this is it, you've lost your girls, they're out in the world ... [It's] pretty well going to the devil if you came to Winnipeg.' If the rural folk were suspicious of the city, Linda Doerksen had her reservations about the countryside: 'We've had a good life and a happy one and even if our start in the city was a rough one ... But I've adjusted and I like the city; I never want to move back on the farm.'[46]

Two other sisters, Doris and Esther Loewen, originally of Steinbach and later members of the Aberdeen EMC church, had a similar experience.[47] One of them recalled warnings about coming 'to the city to work because ... the city was such a worldly place. You could ... just go wrong. And the scuttlebutt we heard, the rumors we heard!' Doris and Esther would prove their critics wrong: it 'doesn't necessarily mean that when you move to the city that you stop going to church and stop being a Christian.' So secure were they in their urban church, they quite enjoyed the 'scuttlebutt.' In fact, 'we were quite happy about hearing [about it]. That's the kind of rumors you like to hear.' They too would turn the tables, becoming as sceptical of farm life as the rural folks were of urban life. The city was especially liberating for Doris and Esther as women, for 'in the fifties and sixties when a lot of people were moving off the farm ... there weren't a lot of opportunities ... especially for women.' All that women could do was 'cleaning or working in a sewing factory or getting married and having kids and living on a farm.' 'The city' was simply 'a much better place to work and a much better place to live' than the countryside. There were 'more things to do ... and there's bus service if you want to go somewhere.' Then, too, urban life provided opportunities to do good works. Esther recalled her satisfaction when, while working 'at the switchboard at City Hall,' she was told by a co-worker, 'Thank you for telling me so much about God,' not verbally, but sharing God through actions, 'without knowing that I've done that.' In addition, there was the freedom of the 'city because you have an eight-hour shift and then ... that's it,' none of the 'twenty-four hours a day, especially [in the] spring and fall ... [on the] dairy farm.' In the city one is 'off at four o'clock and you're off.' Finally, as Doris recalled, 'you get paid for your work. That was a big thing.'

The sense of liberation marked the experience for a fifth single woman in Winnipeg, schoolteacher Margaret Toews of Blumenort.[48] She too spoke of initial opposition from the elders to her education, her determination to leave, and her appreciation of the city for its freedom 'to move around and go places ... [by] bus or streetcar, in the old days.' In fact, as she saw it, there 'are more ways to express oneself spiritually in the urban rather than the rural area,' something possible even in going 'out to restaurants with a group of close friends' because they 'are all Christians ... from different churches.' As she saw it, 'how can you be a light if you don't mix into the world and hold your own?'

Significantly, these women who came to spurn the countryside were not religious radicals. Each was an evangelical Mennonite Christian, a member of the Aberdeen EMC. Indicating a convergence of thought on one level, they shared their misgivings of rurality along with the most radical of the newcomers to the city, the secularized, non-churched Mennonites.

Assimilated Mennonites in cities, wishing to distance themselves from their religious and ethnic identities, are perhaps the most difficult to trace and document. Only crude statistics can identify the number of Mennonites who joined other religious groups – Anglican, Pentecostal, Baptist, Catholic, Jewish – or who became secularized and chose not to express a religious affiliation on the national census. A study of Winnipeg's telephone directory suggests that the number of secularized Mennonites or ethnic Mennonites with no religious Mennonite affiliation is as high as 31 percent of persons who can be identified in some way as Mennonite or of Mennonite background.[49] Many families had their 'lost sons and daughters,' those who joined the military during the Second World War.[50] But many more had children who moved to the city, obtained an education, and then through marriage, upward mobility, or further migration became removed from the Mennonite community, maintaining only loose kinship ties. Some of these individuals were remembered by local history books for having become successful and prominent North Americans; others were cited in church meeting records as having 'fallen into sin' and for having become entirely 'associated with the world.'[51] The best known ex-Mennonites in Winnipeg who hailed from Hanover were the published poets and novelists, some of whom gained national, even international, stature with their stories of smalltown repression in Steinbach and city libera-tion in Winnipeg. No particular trend can be identified, but considering the stories of three Steinbach-raised writers, each with roots in the town's EMC church, and each of whom moved to Winnipeg – one leaving in the 1950s, another in the 1960s, a third in the 1970s – suggests they all saw a separation from Mennonite religiousness and small-town culture as a liberation.

Al Reimer, whose father was Peter J.B. Reimer, one of the evangelical lay ministers in the Steinbach EMC church, left Hanover and the Men-nonite faith in the early 1950s, and returned to it only at mid-life. He eventually found his way to Yale University, where he earned a PhD in English literature, and then moved to Winnipeg in the 1960s to teach at the University of Winnipeg. Later he wrote fiction in which the Menno-nite ministers of Steinbach figured prominently. He described two Second World War–era ministers who confront a young soldier who shows up for a Sunday morning worship service dressed in his khaki uniform. Reimer's depictions were not kind. They included: 'Ohm Toews, the *Eltesta*, stooped and bald with a thin fringe of white' who 'shuffled to the pulpit to sigh out his usual German words of greeting, followed by a few meagre introductory remarks and a scripture reading, before making way for the first sermon.' After the first sermon, 'Jake Plett, a prosperous farmer only recently elected to the ministry, but already an imposing figure in the pulpit with his ruddy broad face, bull-dog neck and robust middle-aged bulk,' moved in place to offer the second sermon.[52] Later, in another piece of writing, Reimer spoke of his exodus from the myopic and repressive town: 'I made my get away from Steinbach with ill-concealed haste, and congratulated myself on having made a clean escape. I couldn't believe my new freedom. I kicked up my heels like a spring-sprung colt. How exhilarating to be able to pass for "white" in the world out there, to find that I wasn't carrying my Mennonitism around on my back like a telltale lump ... I considered myself to be fully assimilated, my ethnic background fading behind me. I married a non-Mennonite wife and began raising a family in a non-Mennonite social and religious environment.'[53]

An equally cutting criticism of life in Steinbach came from another

Winnipeg resident, the acclaimed poet Patrick Friesen. In a 1980 publication, *The Shunning*, he drew a scathing portrait of the rural Mennonite church that foreshadowed Reimer's observation.[54] And in a 1988 piece, Friesen spoke of finding a kind of liberation in the world beyond Mennonitism: 'I have been ashamed of my heritage. I have been proud. I have been confused by this heritage ... Why, given their spiritual and social heritage do most North American Mennonites appear to be socially conservative ... Religiously I'm not Mennonite. In other important ways I am. Some days I feel Mennonite, other days not. It doesn't really matter. I was born into this ... I could have been born in Spain.'[55]

The tone in Friesen's poetic work was foreshadowed by a series of heated exchanges published in 1967 in the *Carillon News* when he was a university student in Winnipeg. Friesen pointedly let his rural elders know of his liberation in the city and their pathetic rural conformity. In an October letter he was baited into the exchange by a report that Steinbach businessmen wished that 'young people ... dress the way employers want their employees to dress.' Friesen saw this as evidence of continued rural repression: 'the trouble is not so much with the young people as it is with an archaic school system taught and supported ... by business-minded people [who] don't believe that many young people have grown very tired of old systems.' As the university student saw it the church elders who had once demanded conformity from Steinbachers had now been replaced with 'another version of the middle ages, with businessmen replacing the church as to who will establish standards.'[56] Friesen was sharply rebuked by Elbert Toews, the vice-principal of Steinbach Collegiate, who detected in the young scribe 'a person with considerable inner turmoil and confusion' who might be well advised to clear his 'mind of the bitterness and prejudice which appears to permeate it and start thinking and writing positively.'[57] From Winnipeg, Friesen responded a month later with a declaration that he detected in Toews a system in which 'the student is set in ... the direction which will please society in general and especially (in rural areas) his community.' John Milton's 1644 observation that if the streams of truth 'flow not in perpetual progressive, they sicken into a muddy pool of conformity and tradition,' argued Friesen, was relevant to Steinbach.[58] Patrick Friesen was supported in the 1960s by several former Steinbachers living in Winnipeg. In one letter university student Ralph Friesen, another son of a Steinbach EMC minister, sided with his friend Patrick, and suggested that as Vice-Principal Toews did not know Pat, it was clear that in Steinbach 'a person [is] full of turmoil, confused, bitter and prejudiced only when he criticizes that which we don't like to have criticized.' Ralph Friesen detected a trend in small-town high schools that socialize students to attend 'university for no other reason than to make money' and don't 'encourage original thinking.'[59]

Miriam Toews was another Steinbach resident who left town for Winnipeg (she as a teenager in about 1979) and went on to write several novels notably critical of the town. In her award-winning *A Complicated Kindness* the protagonist, a troubled 1970s-era teenager, Nomi, rebels against a stifling combination of inherited pacifism and learned evangelicalism. East Village, a thinly disguised Steinbach, is a town that provides services to its rural hinterland, and is located within striking distance of a large city. In the novel, Nomi's mother and sister leave town for the liberation of the city after confrontations with the town's leading minister, The Mouth. Nomi longs to leave as well and contemplates the irony of the name 'East Village' the name not only of her town, but 'of the area in New York City that I would most love to inhabit,' a place where 'we would all sleep till noon, then play Frisbee in Central Park, then watch [Lou Reed] play in clubs.'[60] Other cities beckon as well: there is the Prague of 'lovers and laugh and drink' and the Paris of 'baguettes and wine and fresh flowers.'[61] Time and again the city spells Nomi's only hope. What other townsfolk see as liberating, C.S. Lewis's *Narnia* books, for example, Nomi spurns: 'I dream of escaping into the *real* world ... I would love to read the diary of a girl my age – a girl from the city. Or a textbook on urban planning. Or a New York City phone book. I would kill to own a New York City phone book.'[62] On occasion, Nomi climbs Abe's Hill on the outskirts of town to watch in the distance the 'lights of the city c[o]me on, slowly at first and then faster, like they were giving in, like the people in charge of turning on the lights were thinking all right already, it's dark, let's just turn on the lights.' The same lights for the townspeople, however, signal sinfulness: For them 'the city was the dark side, the whale's stomach. It flickered off and on in the distance like pain. It was the worst thing that could happen to you. If you go for any length of time you don't come back, and if you don't come back you forfeit your place in heaven's lineup.'[63]

If moving to Winnipeg for some was a way cutting loose from the Mennonite faith, the city represented a place of rejuvenated religious commitment for others. Indeed, its numerous Mennonite churches provided instant homes for most migrants from rural districts. But the churches did not represent a network of staid tranquillity. A sharp debate took place within the churches and between newcomers to the city and their rural homeland. The rural folk who found themselves in the city seemed to agree that the move was culturally liberating, but they disagreed on how best to become fully integrated into the city. One common element among the evangelicals, social activists, and literary critics was that they each cultivated a Mennonite identity. Each accepted a symbolic Mennonite ethnicity, but also grappled with the ideological implications of Mennonite religiousness. For one group the historic teachings on pacifism and social justice were secondary to evangelicalism; for the young neo-Anabaptists, those teachings were profoundly relevant in the city; for secularists, the old teachings were repressive and myopic, but culturally informative. Ironically, each of the three representations offered a congenial pathway into urban life.

One group of newcomers to the city not represented above were the Mennonites who lost both their religious and their cultural affiliations. Their story usually produced no public expression in church periodicals, published fiction, or rural newspapers. Census records only hint at the large percentage of Mennonite farm folk entering the city who did not associate with a Mennonite church or other Mennonite institution. These city dwellers quietly amalgamated into suburban life, joined a mainstream evangelical or liturgical church or none at all, and found alternative social associations in class-appropriate local clubs, community ventures, or political parties. A hint of their story appears in the accounts that emanated from Denver.

Residual Mennonitism in Denver

Scholars have argued that a large difference exists between Canadian and American Mennonite views of the city. Using Winnipeg as an example, it is said that Mennonites in Canada readily found a comfortable niche in the medium-sized or even large city where they developed considerable 'critical mass' and an 'institutional completeness.' In contrast, relatively few Mennonites in the United States chose life in the large city; most found themselves drawn to large towns. Among the Mennonites attracted to large cities were the Meade County folk in Denver. Their story of constituting a tiny minority supported by few ethnic institutions is part of the North American Mennonite mosaic.

Not large enough to establish their own church, Meade Mennonites who came to Denver in the 1950s chose between two existing Mennonite church options, the more liturgical but also more socially engaged First Mennonite Church of the General Conference (GC) Mennonite denomination or the more evangelistic and more politically conservative Garden Park Church of the Mennonite Brethren (MB) denomination.[64] More Meade Mennonites chose the latter than the former as they found within the MB church an ideology and worship culture similar to the Emmanuel Mennonite Church and Evangelical Mennonite Brethren Church of Meade. The MB church was overtly evangelistic but residually Mennonite, giving at least some observance to historic Mennonite teaching on pacifism, service, and humility. If the MB church in Denver resonated with the theology of the Meade churches, its urban setting made it more avant-garde. It seemed more ready to debate the great moral issues of the twentieth-century city and more at ease in an alignment with a nationally anchored evangelical agenda.

From accounts in the MB magazine, the *Christian Leader*, Denver's Garden Park MB church was a confident institution in every respect, both within its chosen city of Denver and within the larger North American MB denomination. It was self-consciously an urban church set in a metropolis. In 1971 the church hosted the annual North American MB conference with promises that the Loretto Heights College conference site, while overlooking 'the busy city ... will be isolated so [that delegates] can concentrate on the conference ... yet be within minutes of the majestic mountains and the busy city.'[65] The conference itself seemed to relate well to Garden Park's large-city concerns: it directly confronted issues including anti-institutionalism, male-female roles, misdirected social activism, and the 'dangers' of charismatic groups that led to an 'erratic kind of Christian Life.'[66] But Garden Park also turned to offer the city its solution to modern anomie. Shortly after the 1971 conference, for example, the Garden Park church board voted to 'enlarge its ministry in radio and television,' signalling that an experiment of running 'a 15 minute program of Christmas music' and 'brief spots' promoting the church's programs' in the electronic media had been successful.[67] In time the church demonstrated an even more outgoing personality. In April 1973 it fully participated in the national, interdenominational 'Convocation for Evangelism' facilitated with resource persons from 'Campus Crusade, the Navigators, and the Kennedy School for Evangelism.'[68] By this time plans for a second MB church in Denver's southwest quadrant had been planned and the church planters received a boost when 'three to four carloads' of delegates from the evangelism convocation 'canvassed' the district for potential converts.[69]

Church growth continued unabated; just a month later in May, a third MB church was announced for North Denver, and in March 1974 a fourth in the suburb of Littleton.[70] The new churches were a mark of the success of evangelicalism; as Pastor Roland Reimer noted, they marked the consequence of a 'deliberate and unified result of the outreach efforts' of local church people.[71]

If the Denver MB churches made a physical impression, they also seemed culturally astute, addressing urban issues without abandoning middle-class evangelical concerns. A letter published in 1965 from 'a Negro man' in Denver, asserting that he had 'never clamored for civil rights,' in large part because 'only Jesus Christ ... will end the hatred so prevalent,' exemplified the conservative tenor of Mennonite Brethren ministries.[72] A 1966 book by Garden Park pastor Dan E. Friesen entitled *The End of the Struggle*, outlined the promise of evangelical Christianity as it would show up 'the many things we have today ... radio, televisions, cars, planes, telephones, recording machines and Dictaphones.' But first, said the pastor, the modern church would have to 'turn ... cities upside down' in the manner of 'a giant stalking through the land on the offensive,' and not as 'a beggar at the side of the road apologetically offering a bit of spiritual salve.'[73] Within the criticism, of course, was a blueprint for action that would make any group of evangelicals proud of their pastor.

In fact as their own record of church growth demonstrated, the Garden Park church was anything but a 'beggar at the side of the road.' Its members, and its women in particular, were active in the church. At the 1971 MB conference women were congratulated for attending a workshop on abortion, lending 'an in-depth, feeling ... of realism which was intensely helpful in this predominantly male audience.' At the 1973 evangelism convention Denver members heard the wife of MB evangelist Waldo Wiebe, 'Mrs Wiebe,' lead 'women in training for ... evangelistic Bible coffees.' In 1975 women from the Denver churches launched a six-week study in expressing love which 'climaxed with an overnight retreat' led by 'Mrs Leonard Vogt and Mrs Roland Reimer, pastors' wives.'[74] The Denver church even addressed racial issues. In a highly publicized 1977 baptism of nineteen individuals at Garden Park, for example, the church accepted not only two American Catholic women who 'desired believer's baptism,' but 'eight young men and women from an Venezuelan family,' unilingual Spanish speakers but conversant in evangelicalism as the mother 'had accepted Christ at a Billy Graham crusade in Venezuela.'[75]

The Denver Mennonite Brethren churches' dynamism, however, had its limits. If they earned the respect of the national MB constituency and found a niche in mainstream evangelical discourse, they, alongside Denver's First Mennonite (GC) Church, missed appealing in the long run to many Mennonite newcomers from the countryside. Interviews with three former Meade County residents – two married men and one single woman – suggest in fact that the Mennonite churches had a limited role to play in their integration into Denver. More important were the newcomers' vocations that linked the work culture of the countryside to that of the city, secured a new set of social networks, and offered a sense of pride and belonging that removed any desire to return home. Significantly, neither a reinvented Mennonite ethnicity nor a reformulated neo-Anabaptism served a purpose in their integration. These newcomers who assimilated in Denver rejected ethnic labels, abandoned Mennonite church membership, and limited their links to Meade County to visits with family members still in the countryside. They would have found little affinity with any of the Winnipeg Mennonite manifestations, be it the revivalist Evangelical Mennonites, the radicalized neo-Anabaptists, or the rascal poets and writers of fiction. Still, within their cosmologies the newcomers to Denver possessed everyday values that they insisted had been inherited from their parents and their lives on the dusty plains of Meade County. These first-generation sojourners in the city could be termed 'near-Mennonites' in their minds, possessed of a 'residual Mennonitism.' But they were out of reach of either First Mennonite or Garden Park MB.

Ben Janzen's (not his real name) entry to city life was not unusual for either a Meade County boy or any other American Mennonite farm boy drafted for military service during the 1950s.[76] Ben made his way to Denver in 1952 where he served as a conscientious objector (CO) under the 1–W program. Like many COs he worked in the medical field, as an orderly St. Luke's General Hospital, and his wife Nancy (not her real name) worked in the hospital's cafeteria and then became a ward clerk. Even though Denver was foreign for Ben, urban life soon became agreeable. Ben and Nancy lived in a multi-apartment house with several Meade County boys and felt welcomed at the First Mennonite Church. After the two-year 1-W program ended, Ben and Nancy moved to Hutchinson, Kansas, and then to Danuba, California, where they linked up with Mennonite churches. But Ben wanted to return to Meade as he 'wanted to farm awfully bad.' He even approached an elderly Anglo-

American neighbor and former employer named Drake with the assertion 'I believe it's time I rent your ground.' Unfortunately a more well-
to-do Mennonite farmer beat Ben to it. Ben's only consolation was that
in the 1950s a 'half section doesn't do anything.' Life in Meade County
held little promise and even though 'Mom would have liked us to build
a house across the road' from the home place, the fact was that 'wild
sunflowers don't taste too good.' Thus permanent city life was the only
option and in 1957 Ben and Nancy reasoned that if they would have 'to
live in the city, then it'll be Denver' and they made it their permanent
home.

Denver presented Ben with a range of familiar networks and a novel
vocational path. At first Ben hoped to work in music, especially to
pursue his love of singing, and he even had a contact – the music
director at Denver's Rockmount College. But a growing family compelled him to take jobs where they were available. He found work with
'some Mennonites' for a large poultry company, hauling eggs and
frozen meat from plants in Nebraska and Kansas to small retailers in
the Denver region. In time he moved on to similar work for a dairy
company and here he learned refrigeration. Tipped off by a fellow 1-W
alumnus, Ben and his brother Mel (not his real name), also a 1-W
alumnus, enroled in classes that eventually earned them each a certificate in refrigeration and air conditioning maintenance. When one of the
instructors informed them that the public service of Colorado was
about to hire, both Ben and Mel applied and found work. For the next
twenty-one years Ben worked in the same building. He maintained the
air conditioning and heating system, calibrated the eighty thermostats
each floor possessed, and fixed light fixtures. All the while he developed a pride in his work, asserting that 'we had the finest building in
the state.' He loved his work and aspired to a management position.
But having finally won a supervisory position he soon quit, even though
his fellow workers championed him as 'the only guy who can stand up
to the boss.' In the end, 'the fight, the political jargon, it was absolutely
not worth it ... not with the values I grew up with.' He found that he
needed to 'compromise my integrity' and he would not do so. 'I wouldn't
play the game ... it didn't matter if it was the president of the company
or the janitor,' if it was '"nuts and bolts" or high-up.' Thus Ben 'went
back to be a classified mechanic.' The only time he came close to
violating a Mennonite teaching on the job was when he joined the
union, an action considered militant by Mennonite elders. Even then

old values of thrift and peace guided this decision. As he saw it, 'why pay dues and not belong?' He reasoned that no coercive strikes would ensue because 'the utilities had a no-strike clause.'

In time, Ben and Nancy established a typical, suburban American home: Ben worked for the utility, and Nancy tended the four children. The family members cultivated their Mennonite identities, attending the Garden Park MB church for seventeen years. However, the church relationship waned over time. Ben felt that even as an evangelistic Mennonite church, Garden Park was not fully integrated into Denver. As he recalled, 'any rural Mennonite church has a hard time making it in the large city' because of the 'cultural gap between the Mennonites and the average English speaker.' He sensed that the church seemed rooted in the MB's Tabor College in the small town of Hillsboro, Kansas, and that this rural site was 'still the capital.' He was very disappointed when one of the pastors at Garden Park was compelled to leave because 'he wanted to have the service for everyone, including the Spanish, but the people were against it.' The subsequent upheaval made Ben nostalgic for the old Mennonite Kleine Gemeinde in Meade County where, as he recalled, 'like-minded' people worked together. Of course it was a romantic notion, for the people of Meade 'didn't realize how secluded they were,' being out of touch with 'what happened in the wider world,' and obsessed with 'cruel' questions of 'who would rent what ground' and who would 'get to buy the home place.' At the time he also felt drawn to the First Mennonite Church, but found it 'very liberal.' Making the 'salvation story secondary,' they emphasized 'conscientious objection and that's it.' Even when his old friend and Meade County compatriot Walt Friesen left his place as psychologist at Kansas State University at Manhattan, Kansas, to become the pastor of First Mennonite church in Denver, Ben resisted joining. He would speak to Walt in Low German, but told him that 'I wanted to keep him as a friend,' and Walt responded that Ben 'was the only deacon he had.' The shade of Mennonite ideology or the intensity of Mennonite identity would not affect his friendships. In about 1974 Ben and Nancy broke their last official tie with the Mennonites, left Garden Park church, and joined a nearby Baptist congregation, hoping for a more fully integrated life in Denver.

Ben may have felt out of step with each of the Mennonite churches he knew, but still he cultivated a Mennonite identity. For example, he maintained his time-honored pacifism: 'I have too much Mennonite blood that the M1 rifle [could never be] my best friend.' He also said that even though he believed in the death penalty, 'I wouldn't pull the switch and ... wouldn't ask anyone else to do it either.' Ben recalled with pride the story in one of 'the big American weekly magazines' reporting on a visit by President Harry Truman to Fort Simmons Army Hospital where he asked to be photographed with a 1-W orderly, dubbing the young conscientious objector 'tougher than the army.' Over time Ben maintained other ties to the Mennonites, volunteering for the Mennonite Disaster Service and insuring the family home through a Mennonite Mutual Aid agency. Throughout these years Ben and Nancy returned to Meade County with the words, 'let's go home.' They went for the holidays – Thanksgiving, Christmas, and Easter – or on occasion for a wedding or funeral. Here they would meet the parents, the uncles and aunts, and a favorite Emmanuel Mennonite Church deacon, who Ben still remembered as 'a peach of a guy, my cousin.' Thus even though Ben claimed that 'I'm glad I didn't stay in Meade' as it was 'too compressed,' and that he 'would be hard pressed to think of a Meade person [in Denver] who is still a Mennonite,' he 'wouldn't trade my first twenty years of upbringing for anything.' Ben Janzen's Mennonitism had become symbolic.

The life story of David Kliewer (not his real name) parallels Ben Janzen's story even though Kliewer experienced both greater upward and lateral mobility than did Janzen.[77] David too was born on a farm in Meade County in the mid-1930s and also relocated to Denver after having served in the 1-W program in that city, in his case between 1954 and 1956. He too lived with fellow Mennonite boys from Meade County and rendered his service at a medical supply warehouse. After 1–W he also turned to making a living in Kansas, working for his uncle in Wichita, as his youngest brother took over the home place and his oldest brother bought land from an uncle. It was not difficult in this context to leave the intense heat of the Kansas summer and return to Denver. Here he eventually found his way into the electrical trade he had learned during the REA days of rural electrification in Meade County in 1947. After five or six years he became a licensed electrical technician and spent the 1960s and 1970s in the field, all the while thinking quietly that 'sooner or later I would take a shot' at putting in his own bid on a job and venturing out on his own. As David put it, 'if you were farming, you would want your own farm.' In 1979 he obtained the chance and after a year business flourished to the point where he no longer needed a listed telephone number. He was the provider of electrical and computer services to blue-chip Denver firms.

Unlike Ben Janzen, David Kliewer charted a life in Denver outside the Mennonite community from the outset. He had attended an 'Old' Mennonite Church fellowship in Denver during his 1-W years, but found that these Swiss-American Mennonites dressed even more conservatively than the Mennonites back in Meade. Thus, shortly after returning to Denver he began attending a Baptist Church and married a young Baptist woman he had first met during his 1-W years. If David was astonished that the pastor 'preached a lot on hell,' he was impressed that the pastor was 'on fire for Christianity.' In time David rethought his pacifist position, realizing that although 'I would rather not kill, I would not stand idly by' and 'I would protect my country.' For David pacifism became a matter of personal behavior: I 'turn my other cheek' in business, 'in everyday life I have never sued anyone and if some one doesn't pay I don't collect.' This teaching is something David learned from his father for 'it didn't bother Dad if it cost him some money to tell the truth.' But again as David saw it, 'this is not Mennonite, it is a biblical principle.' Like other successful business owners, David enjoyed the good life, golfing and eventually taking annual week-long trips to Hawaii. Visits to Meade occurred annually, but they represented a 'time with the family' and a tight schedule forced the Kliewers to 'turn down invitations' from members of the community. David felt no great sympathy or antipathy for Meade County; for others 'the greatest thing was to leave Meade,' but not for him.

Unlike Janzen and Kliewer, Ruth Bartel of Meade County first came to live in Denver in the 1970s.[78] But like the men, Ruth found her way outside of membership in a Mennonite church, even though she venerated some aspects of her Mennonite culture. Before coming to Denver she had studied for three years at Grace Bible Institute, a fundamentalist college in Omaha popular with Mennonites. Here she was drawn to the teaching English as a second language program. It was a linguistic bent inherited from her mother who 'had a tremendous love for languages' and perhaps it derived from Ruth's own acquired knowledge of Low German, honed enough to speak with her grandparents. Ruth's links with Mennonites, however, waned when she graduated from Grace in 1971 and her mother drove her to Denver to look for work. Having no close Mennonite links, Ruth stayed at a YWCA hostel and visited an employment agency to find her first job. The next day her mother returned to Meade County, as she told Ruth later, crying all the way home. At first Ruth went through jobs quickly, as a telephone solicitor for a land development company, as an employee of a depart-

ment store, and then as a traveling salesperson for the land development company. Through the Baptist church she attended, a 'big wig'
division chief with the Colorado Department of Agriculture invited her
to apply with the department. She began working the next day and
three months later, in April 1972, she had become a 'certified state
employee.' This vocation became her life. She took a stint at an out-of-
town job and even became seriously involved with a fellow employee, a
divorcee.

Neither the Mennonite churches nor any Mennonite networks for
that matter had much appeal for Ruth. It wasn't that she felt especially
un-Mennonite. In fact, the ties to Meade County remained important
and at first she returned several times each year; later, she only went
for Christmas. Even though relatives back home peppered her with
questions as to when she would eventually marry, she found herself
irresistibly drawn to large family gatherings in Meade.

Perhaps Ruth's interest in the Meade Mennonites represented an
unusual bond. Certainly it was not shared by her younger sister Wilma
who had joined Ruth in Denver. Wilma saw in Mennonite culture a
prohibition against dancing, a parochialism that castigated wide travel,
and an imbedded parsimony; not only did Wilma not attend a Mennonite church, she pursued no Mennonite friendships.[79] Nonetheless Ruth's
ties with the Mennonite perspective were strengthened by a deep respect she developed for the historic Mennonite peace position. It is true
that she felt little appreciation for 'the underlying philosophy' of the
Mennonites, because 'they follow tradition rather than the Bible.' She
was even 'aware that if I had been a boy,' during the Vietnam War, 'I
would have been drafted' and would 'not have gone [only] because of
Mom and Dad's stance on [the issue of] conscientious objection.' In fact,
'when I went to Grace [Bible Institute] I would [have] killed someone if
they had hurt me or someone I loved.' Her own pacifism came slowly
and ironically after she had left Meade County. Some years after arriving in Denver, 'Dad gave me his diary [of his time at] a CO camp in
North Ridge, California, and then [at] a Wisconsin dairy farm. It was an
eye opener. I had never known his thought process before, the real
impact of what it meant for a nineteen- or twenty-year-old boy. I found
myself retelling this story.' I learned that 'the CO stance was not fear of
death, [it was] a true belief, a system that says one trusts God who is
capable of taking care of me. They would not compromise ... This life is
God's gift. Dad took this to any part of life ... There are stories of Dad's
father in World War I and he kept a diary in a [Gothic] handwriting that

no one can read; but there are stories of persecution there; Grandpa would not talk about it at that time. I can only imagine the rough times.' Thus she felt drawn to the Mennonites' historic stance, but it became an individualized attraction shared neither by her pastor nor the Evangelical Free Church she eventually joined.

Life in the city for midcentury Mennonites was uncertain and dynamic. In fact so profound was the change that awaited the Mennonites in the city that oftentimes the only perception the newcomers shared was that they comprised, in Leo Driedger's ironic rebuke, 'ethnic villagers who look back to the fleshpots of "rural utopias"' with a sense of relief.[80] The city had become less morally suspect than the countryside. Few of the newcomers harboured romantic ideas of rurality; instead it came to represent repressiveness, isolation, and cultural myopia. And it did so for groups of Mennonites who would not have recognized each other as Mennonite. The religious revivalists found in the city a subjective religiosity that called them to convert non-evangelicals in the mainstream population or in other ethnic groups. The social radicals, socially conscious, and professional found in the city the opportunity to establish organizations that critiqued society's middle-class structures. The cultural rascals turned from all formal religion and focused especially on the arts, music, literature, and philosophy. The residual Mennonites forsook old ethnic markers, joined non-Mennonite churches, but insisted nevertheless that their cultural roots informed their daily life.

Each of these groups gave up the old markers of their ethnicity – plain dress, Low German, anti-modernity. Yet through symbolic ethnicity and various degrees of ethnic inventiveness they found the cultural material with which to enter the wider society while retaining a degree of continuity and legitimacy. The rascal poets' eloquent and prophetic voices, able to identify the shibboleth of rural Mennonite society, earned them the attention from city and national media. The radical neo-Anabaptists found in their sixteenth-century antecedents a critique of middle-class opulence and narcissism and the trappings of a new identity. The revivalists accepted the language of national and international evangelical figures, but honored historic Mennonite teachings on pacifism and social service. The residual Mennonites believed that their stolid, middle-class honesty and work ethic were rooted in rural Mennonite values and they venerated the memory of their parents' deep Anabaptist beliefs. Many other Mennonites drifted from any sort of ethnic identity and any form of religious participation. As they neither contested nor attempted to refashion old identities, their story remains unrecorded in this chapter only because of the completeness of their assimilation. The members of these loose groupings were all second and third cousins. Many enjoyed Low German banter, ethnic baking, and extended clan gatherings on special weekends, but they lived in distinct worlds. It was as if the anonymity, class structure, and polyethnicity of the city atomized the newcomers. Freedom in the city had led to a further fragmentation and reformulation their lives.

Conclusion

The middle decades of the twentieth century shook the foundation of rural North America. Economic transformation, social change, and cultural reinvention seemed intertwined to make for a great disjuncture in the countryside. Several studies have identified this change in the lives of typical farm families. This book has examined its effect in the world of conservative, ethnoreligious people who inhabit the farms of Canada and the United States in large numbers. Studies have demonstrated that these were decades of transmutation for a variety of such communitarian people, including Jewish farmers from upstate New York, Dutch Calvinists of Iowa, Quebec-descendent French Catholics of Manitoba, Amish farmers in Pennsylvania, Mormon families in southern Alberta, and Japanese Buddhist farmers in California. These studies have spoken about one-way migrations from farm to city, the intrusion into agraria of large farm corporations, the rise of a highly personal evangelicalism, the arrival of proactive state agents in rural society, the separation by generation of adults from university-bound children, the effect of highly technological and chemicalized farming, and the cultural responses to consumerism and electronic communications. The list could continue, but the fact was that over the course of fifty years as farm populations dropped by 80 percent and faced unprecedented dispersion, the countryside became transformed.

This study has sought to contribute to this enquiry by focussing on the history of two Mennonite communities, one located in the Rural Municipality (RM) of Hanover in Canada and the other in Meade County in the United States. It suggests, first, that the midcentury years can be more fully understood through a study of conservative Mennonites, descendants of sixteenth-century Protestant Anabaptists who over the centuries had developed a religious commitment to the simplicity, peacefulness, and communitarian nature of rural farm life. Indeed, insofar as the Mennonites changed, the breadth of the wider transformation can be illuminated. Second, because Meade and Hanover were located in two corners of an international grassland in Canada and the United States, the promise of comparative study can be realized: certainly the transnational character of this transformation as well as such variables as physical environment, national culture, and federal farm policies can be more fully identified. Third, such a comparative study becomes especially effective when two communities of similar background with defined social boundaries can be discovered. This comparative study has identified certain lines of query and the interplay of specific variables including economics, religion, ethnicity, gender, and environmental imagination. Fourth, this study has employed the concept of diaspora in the study of local responses to midcentury transformation, and examined the effect on people of dispersion, both locally within rural districts and more broadly throughout the North American continent.

This story has suggested that Meade in the United States and Hanover in Canada shared a common mindset in the 1930s and even as late as 1937, when the Great Depression began lifting. Their mindset represented a 'culture,' a concept defined by Clifford Geertz as a 'frame ... of meaning within which people live and form their convictions, their selves and their solidarities.'[1] They were mostly agrarian people, committed to age-old ideas of communitarian cohesion, a stubborn anticonsumerism, a sectarian cosmology, and an implicit antimodernism. They were conservative members of a self-conscious ethnoreligious Christian minority. They were especially sceptical of modernity with its promises of consumer culture, government programs, and agricultural science. Certainly they had contested urbanizing forces in North America for decades. Their centuries-old commitment to a pacifist, communitarian Christianity made them especially recalcitrant to change during the social storm of the mid-twentieth century. The intensity of their cultural struggle suggested the depth of the change that the mid-century signalled, in particular as measured by changes in their cultural lives, and by the Mennonites' consequent physical dispersion.

But the Mennonites' story makes it clear that this midcentury moment of transnational social and economic upheaval did not simply result in a rural transformation. True, modernity, with its attending concepts of individualism, formalism, and rationalism, now shaped

North American society. True too, farm families became more integrated into state-sponsored social welfare programs, an urban-based
consumer culture, technologized agriculture, and a culturally homogeneous national or international culture. Certainly old ideas of community became disjoined from their moorings. And with that disconnection
came a diaspora of sorts, a cultural fragmentation and sets of physical
relocations. By 1980 specific communities of Hanover and Meade Mennonites could be found in the original rural townships founded in 1874
and 1906 respectively, especially in the southeastern townships in Meade
and in the northern townships in Hanover. By 1980 too, distinctive
Mennonite networks had been transplanted in towns, in Hanover's
Steinbach and Meade County's town of Meade. In turn, other social
conglomerates were obvious in Winnipeg and Denver. By that time as
well, a thriving community consisting to a large extent of one-time
Hanover Mennonites existed at Spanish Lookout Mennonite colony in
British Honduras. Within this physical scattering lay a cultural fragmentation. The geographic dispersion paralleled and gave expression
to an evolving and diverging mindset.

But if the virtual and physical rural diaspora involved fragmentation,
it also left in its wake a cultural reformulation. People within dispersed
and distinctive social units re-established themselves in their new settings and embraced coherent and distinct cultural expressions. Their
new cosmologies revealed a dynamic dialectic between inherited
ethnoreligious symbols and an imagined regional and even national
culture. The dialectic was made more complex by the fact that the
dispersed subjects of this study found within the wider society a diverse range of cultural artifacts that could either replace or be added to
old ideas.[2] This dialectic was itself propelled by emerging forces in the
economy, agricultural science, communication technologies, consumer
markets, and state programs. In the process a variety of new identities
and sets of understandings were employed to shape and bring order to
new social realities.

In this account, the 1930s marked a last decade of conservative cohesion. The cultural crescendo of this decade occurred in 1937 when
elders representing old-order forces in both Meade and Hanover met to
seek ways to maintain and nurture a communitarian culture. Insofar as
the Great Depression had reaffirmed mixed-farming practices and new
levels of community cooperation, the envisioned old order had a good
chance of survival. But the year 1937 also marked a wider recovery
from the Great Depression and the commencement of four decades of

profound change. Especially during and after the Second World War a re-emerging global market for wheat and suburban demands for meat and dairy products commercialized the countryside in new ways.

A comparative analysis suggests that the farm market and agricultural science worked their magic in different ways and with different results in the far corners of the North American grassland. Aided by disparate American and Canadian farm policies, two specific agricultural economies came into being: land allotment programs and laws enabling agricultural consolidation in the United States seemed to exacerbate rural depopulation by encouraging the reduction of family farm production, while the Canadian Wheat Board and marketing board programs north of the border strengthened rural communities by pooling income or guaranteeing production levels at profitable prices. In both the United States and Canada the overall farm transformation sent a large number of rural people into town. Here a much more significant fragmentation occurred. The combination of ethnic critical mass in Hanover and the multicultural policies in Canada had a specific effect on Steinbach's Mennonites, which made their experience somewhat different than that of the Meade Mennonites, situated as they were as a minority in a frontier-celebrating, Republican-dominated, western American town.

Similar differences appeared in gender relations. Certainly both the women and men of Hanover and Meade underwent significant gendered changes in the faces of economic dislocation, consumer culture, and a more integrated world. The women of Meade made changes that were especially public; indeed, given the culture and economy of western Kansas, Meade women readily joined Home Demonstration Units and then as married women readily worked in town jobs, bringing somewhat greater change to their lives than seen in those of their counterparts in Manitoba. Similarly the men of Hanover underwent especially public changes; technological innovation and political initiatives seemed to have a direct effect on the mindset of the men of Hanover's livestock and poultry operations, while the particular cultural makeup of Hanover encouraged non-farm Mennonite men to express their masculinities in specifically public ways. The gendered, public expressions of the poultrymen and car dealers of Hanover and the cheerful homemakers and office workers of Meade seemed to point to a sharp cultural break with a gendered communitarian past, but also signalled that even the nature of broad changes in gender varied by degree depending on local circumstance.

Somewhat more pronounced differences appeared in the church life of Meade and Hanover. In the churches, evangelicalism refashioned the old communitarian faith, providing its adherents with both a social path into the heart of the new, more integrated society, as well as a new set of social boundaries. As in the economic sphere, the religious transformation worked itself out differently in Canada and in the United States. The Canadian church moved toward the individualistic and progressive religiosity of evangelicalism, but at a much slower pace than its American counterpart. Throughout the 1970s the Canadian church strongly supported old Anabaptist teachings on pacifism, amillennialism, and separation from the wider world, especially from nationalism and consumerism. And it was the Canadian church that gave birth to a conservative sector that was so committed to preserving a communitarian faith that it joined a Mennonite emigration to Latin America and sided with other old order groups in North America that resisted consumerism, individualism, and cultural associations with the wider world.

Revealing the depth of the cultural fragmentation in the two communities, this study followed its most conservative and most progressive members into new locations. Hanover Mennonites who migrated to Mexico in 1948 and then on to British Honduras in 1958 exhibited a remarkably different culture than did those who went to Winnipeg in the 1950s and 1960s, or their Meade counterparts who moved to Denver. In British Honduras Mennonite farmers embarked on a cavalier assault on the rainforest, the opposite approach of their counterparts in Meade County who had accepted a government-sanctioned culture of soil conservation. Still, the attending social views contradicted the environmental approaches. The conservative Mennonites of British Honduras revealed a profound skepticism of capitalistic agriculture, especially its full acceptance of competition, economies of scale, and scientific farming. The same distinctive mindset was apparent in their religious commitment to construct a lasting old order community, separate from the world, united by a communitarian faith and a life of agrarian simplicity.

In the cities of Winnipeg and Denver newcomers expressed an impatience with the very ideals they believed the British Hondurans venerated, agrarian parochialism and communitarian conformity. The urban Mennonites, however, seemed to agree only that their cultures should relate to the needs of the complex urban environment: evangelical Mennonites accepted a new, more subjective meaning of religious sal-

vation in the city; neo-Anabaptist progressives reinvented sixteenth-
century stories in addressing urban ills; secularized poets turned stories
of rural social oppression into narratives of cultural illumination; mainstream evangelicals treasured memories of parental pacifism, frugality,
and honesty that had currency in suburban culture. The fragmentation
that began in the countryside continued and in fact took on greater
force and momentum in the city.

Always the diasporic fragments entered into phases of cultural
renewal. The lines between the fragments were not always clear.
Certainly binary opposites were envisioned and often constituted a
fundamental aspect of each fragment's cosmology. As social organisms
they demonstrated human agency in searching for, studying, and adapting ideologies from within the wider society that would at once legitimate aspects of an inherited culture and set the course for respectable
integration in the wider world. From the wider fields of evangelicalism,
communitarianism, social activism, or secularism Mennonite newcomers in the cities borrowed, tasted, and usually accepted some form of
novel culture. But each of the groups represented a change from the
overarching mindset one might have been able to identify that ordered
rural community in the 1930s. The subgroups could not easily be judged
by standards of continuity with the past, even though each would have
readily agreed that the British Honduras old order conservatives and
Winnipeg secularists were located on the far poles of some kind of
cultural paradigm. But the conservatives were less in harmony with the
past and the so-called assimilated Mennonites more in touch with their
history than either was prepared to acknowledge. Each of the groups
used historical reference points to give legitimacy to their understanding of themselves. Each group too went beyond old boundaries by
accepting transfusions of energy and new thought. Having been invigorated by these cultural borrowings, each of the various groups could be
assured that they had transcended the past, while retaining a logical
connection to it. The subgroups could then turn to the old Mennonite
community they had left and challenge it to improve itself, but they
could also turn to the wider society with the same message. The
communities broke from the parent communities, but they reattached
themselves to the memories of those communities in new ways.[3]

The dispersed fragments, however, were not merely drifting in a
murky morass of meaninglessness. The student of the descendant
midcentury groups cannot but notice what David Harvey concedes are
the positive features of postmodern analysis: 'its concern for differ-

ences, for the difficulties of communication, for the complexity and nuances of interest, culture and places' and its acknowledgement of the 'multiple forms of otherness as they emerge from differences in subjectivity, gender and sexuality, race and class, temporal ... and spatial geographies, locations and dislocations.'[4] Certainly, rural society itself was complex, divided within specific communities by disparate identities and shaped within the wider region by divergent national policies and specific physical environments. And through the course of what Shover dubbed the Great Disjuncture that society became even more complex. But as Clifford Geertz, Ulf Hannerz, and other theorists have argued, diversity is not synonymous with hopelessness and meaninglessness. Culture, writes Hannerz, is 'not in The Mind, or in just any minds. Rather it is in particular ways in particular minds, and when it is public, it is made available through social life by particular people, to particular people.'[5] These cultural expressions were always compelling in specific communities. But the specific communities themselves did not negate the existence of a wider human community or understandable broader experience. As Geertz argues, 'if the general is to be grasped at all ... it must be grasped not directly, all at once, but via instances, differences, variations, particulars – piecemeal, case by case. In a splintered world, we must address the splinters.'[6] The fragments were compelling cultural reformulations; they were also testimony to the far-reaching significance of twentieth-century economic changes and political differences.

The Great Disjuncture that visited the countryside of the North American grassland in the mid-twentieth century caused a social upheaval and a subsequent scattering of rural people. Some farm families commercialized their holdings, other joined old-order communities in distant places, while most embraced the urban milieu of towns and cities. Each of these disparate places became associated with distinctive expressions of gender, ethnicity, religion, and environmental concern. Physical relocation was accompanied by a virtual migration, a divergence in thinking, a diaspora in the countryside. Kith and kin had become separated from each other; moving in diverse directions, they had become as strangers to one another. Mennonites in two corners of North America's interior grassland, one in Canada and the other in the United States, were confronted by a common, global culture of capitalism and consumerism. The ways in which they responded to this pervasive force, using inherited ideas in various ways to interpret new worlds, resulted in remarkable diversity. Just which path was the most authentic is not the subject of this study; certainly human foibles along the way provided grist for debates within particular communities. What is indisputable is the significance of change, the range of diversity, and the ingenuity of people in new places. Clearly, in each of the scattered settings human creativity responded to new circumstances with an eternal search for meaning and order, for truth and social harmony.

Notes

Preface

1 I am indebted to Mary Ann Loewen, a student of English literature, for introducing me to these concepts. For historians who position themselves in histories they have written see Aritha Van Herk, *Mavericks: An Incorrigible History of Alberta* (Toronto: Viking, 2001); Leora Auslander, *Taste and Power: Furnishing Modern France* (Berkeley and Los Angeles: University of California Press, 1996); Brian W. Beltman, *Dutch Farmer in the Missouri Valley: The Life and Letters of Ulbe Eringa, 1866–1950* (Urbana: University of Illinois Press, 1997).

Introduction

1 This book tends to use the term 'North America' as synonymous with the countries of Canada and the United States, although it recognizes that Mexico and other parts of Central America such as Belize technically fall in the geographic category of 'North America' and hence uses the term at moments also to include those more southern countries.
2 I Peter 1:1 and 18, *The New Jerusalem Bible*. See Ecclesiasticus 36:10 for the yearning of exiled Hebrew people to be 'gather[ed] together [as] the tribes of Jacob.'
3 See Robin Cohen, *Global Diasporas: An Introduction* (Seattle: University of Washington Press, 1997). On the Telegu in South Africa see www.telegudiaspora.com; on Africans in Latin America see www.lanic.utexas.edu/ba/region/african; on Palestinians in the Gulf States see www.mondediplo.com/map/refugeesdiaspora/paldp/2000; on French Canadians in the United States see www.en.wikipedia.org/wiki/Quebec_diaspora (accessed 10 May 2005).

4 Cohen, *Global Diasporas*, x.

5 Donna R. Gabaccia, *Italy's Many Diasporas* (Seattle: University of Washington Press, 2000), 5.

6 Angelika Bammer, ed., *Displacements: Cultural Identities in Question* (Bloomington: Indiana University Press, 1994), xi, 156.

7 Dirk Hoerder, *Cultures in Contact: World Migrations in the Second Millennium* (Durham: Duke University Press, 2002).

8 John L. Shover, *First Majority – Last Minority: The Transforming of Rural Life in America* (Dekalb: Northern Illinois University Press, 1976), xiii. I am indebted to John Herd Thompson for introducing me to Shover's work.

9 Ibid., 16, 50, 57.

10 Ibid., 71, 102.

11 Ibid., 73, 80, 93.

12 Clifford Geertz, *After the Fact: Two Countries, Four Decades, One Anthropologist* (Cambridge: Harvard University Press, 1995), 43.

13 Ibid., 57.

14 Shover, *First Majority*, 4.

15 In some ways the figures are undramatic. Between 1950 and 1970, the total number of Americans who were recorded as rural inhabitants in the U.S. census, that is, farm or small town dwellers, dropped relatively slightly, from 54,478,981 to 53,585,309 and similarly in Canada from 5,191,792 to 5,157,325. But because of high postwar urban-bound migrations, with the number of Americans designated urban rising from 151 to 203 million and doubling in Canada from 8.8 to 16.4 million, the percentage of folks designated as rural dropped from 36 percent to 26 percent of the total population in the United States and from 37 percent to 24 percent of the population in Canada. The actual number is 151,325,798 in 1950 and 203,302,031 in 1970 in the United States and 8,817,637 in 1951 and 16,410,785 in 1971 in Canada. Census of Canada; www.usda.gov/agency/ nass/pubs/trends/farmpop/-labor.csv (accessed 17 April 2005).

16 The number of Canadians living on farms declined from 4,804,728 in 1931, to 3,152,449 in 1941, to 2,789,286 in 1951, to 2,072,785 in 1961, to 1,419,795 in 1971. Table 4: Population 1790–1990; Census of Canada, 1931; 1941; 1951; 1971. For a discussion on rural depopulation during these years see also John Porter, *The Vertical Mosaic: An Analysis of Social Power and Class* (Toronto: University of Toronto Press, 1965), 142, 146, 164. In the United States the number of farm inhabitants actually rose from 30,529,000 to 30,547,000 in the 1930s, but then dropped to 23,048,000 in 1950, 13,445,000 in 1960, 9,712,000 in 1970, and 6,051,000 in 1980. See www.usda.gov/ agency/nass/pubs/trends/farmpop/-labor.csv (accessed 17 April 2005).

Another set of statistics records the decline of the number of farm workers in the United States from 13.4 million in 1920, to 11.0 million in 1940, to 7.0 million in 1960, to 3.0 million in 1980. See www.ctaitc.org/pdf/popchart.pdf (accessed 17 April 2005).

17 Shover's work is an exception to this observation and so too is Gilbert C. Fite, *American Farmers: The New Minority* (Bloomington: University of Indiana Press, 1981). Studies that examine specific rural themes and regions in the middle decades include: Ronald R. Kline, *Consumers in the Country: Technology and Change in Rural America* (Baltimore: Johns Hopkins University Press, 2000); Katherine Jellison, *Entitled to Power: Farm Women and Technology, 1913–1963* (Chapel Hill: University of North Carolina Press, 1993); R. Douglas Hurt, ed., *The Rural South since World War II* (Baton Rouge: Louisianna State University Press, 1998). For local studies that examine these decades see Rhonda F. Levine, *Class, Networks, and Identity: Replanting Jewish Lives from Nazi Germany to Rural New York* (Lanham, MD: Rowman and Littlefield, 2001); Leonard N. Neufeldt, *Village of Unsettled Yearnings: Yarrow, British Columbia: Mennonite Promise* (Victoria, BC: Horsdal and Schubart, 2002); David Walbert, *Garden Spot: Lancaster County, the Old Order Amish and the Selling of America* (New York: Oxford University Press, 2002); Kenneth L. Kann, *Comrades and Chicken Ranchers: The Story of a California Jewish Community* (Ithaca, NY: Cornell University Press, 1993); Valerie J. Matsumoto, *Farming the Home Place: A Japanese American Community in California, 1919–1982* (Ithaca, NY: Cornell University Press, 1993). For a history that discusses themes linked to the Great Disjuncture see Mary Neth, *Preserving the Family Farm: Women, Community and the Foundations of Agribusiness in the Midwest, 1900–1940* (Baltimore: Johns Hopkins University Press, 1995). For histories that incorporate these decades into larger studies see David B. Danbom, *Born in the Country: A History of Rural America* (Baltimore: Johns Hopkins University Press, 1995); John Herd Thompson, *Forging the Prairie West: The Illustrated History of Canada* (Toronto: Oxford University Press, 1998); R. Douglas Hurt, *Problems of Plenty: The American Farmer in the Twentieth Century* (Chicago: Ivan R. Dee, 2002).

18 Hal S. Barron, *Mixed Harvest: The Second Great Transformation in the Rural North* (Chapel Hill: University of North Carolina Press, 1997); Marie Kathryne Dudley, *Debt and Dispossession: Farm Loss in America's Heartland* (Chicago: University of Chicago Press, 2000).

19 For studies up to 1950 see Ian MacPherson and John Herd Thompson, 'The Business of Agriculture: Prairie Farmers and the Adoption of "Business Methods," 1880–1950,' *Canadian Papers in Business History* 1 (1989):

245–69, and G.E. Britnell and V.C. Fowke, *Canadian Agriculture in War and Peace, 1935–1950* (Stanford: Stanford University Press, 1962). For chapters on the middle decades see Gerald Friesen, 'The New West since 1940,' in *The Canadian Prairies: A History* (Toronto: University of Toronto Press, 1984), 418–60; Gerald Friesen, postscript, in James Giffen, *Rural Life in Manitoba, 1946* (Winnipeg: University of Manitoba Press, 2004), and Thompson, *Forging the Prairie West*, 137–68.

20 Over the past decade a number of works have addressed the features of this emerging society: the more intrusive federal and local governments; the new suburbia where families became more private and gender more rigidly defined; radio, and increasingly television, that now introduced to the nation a common language, identity, and array of symbols; the churches that drew more people into more spacious buildings and often to a message of individualized, subjective religiosity. In Canada see Paul Rutherford, *When Television Was Young: Primetime Canada, 1952–1967* (Toronto: University of Toronto Press, 1990); Mona Gleason, *Normalizing the Ideal: Psychology, Schooling, and the Family in Postwar Canada* (Toronto: University of Toronto Press, 1996); John G. Stackhouse, *Canadian Evangelicalism in the Twentieth Century: An Introduction to Its Character* (Toronto: University of Toronto Press, 1993); Doug Owram, *Born at the Right Time: A History of the Baby-Boom Generation* (Toronto: University of Toronto Press, 1996); Alvin Finkel, *Our Lives: Canada after 1945* (Toronto: J. Lorimer, 1997); Joy Parr, *Domestic Goods: The Material, the Moral, and the Economic in the Post-War Years* (Toronto: University of Toronto Press, 1999); Gerald Friesen, *Citizens and Nation: An Essay on History, Communication, and Canada* (Toronto: University of Toronto Press, 2000). In the United States see Rusty L. Monhoon, *'This Is America?': The Sixties in Lawrence, Kansas* (New York: Palgrave, 2002); Adam Rome, *Bulldozer in the Countryside: Suburban Sprawl and the Rise of American Environmentalism* (New York: Cambridge University Press, 2001); Nicholas Dagen Bloom, *Suburban Alchemy: 1960s New Towns and the Transformation of the American Dream* (Columbus: Ohio State University Press, 2001).

21 Bruce L. Gardner, *American Agriculture in the Twentieth Century: How It Flourished and What It Cost* (Cambridge: Harvard University Press, 2002); G.S. Basran and D.A. Hay, eds., *The Political Economy of Agriculture in Western Canada* (Toronto: Garamond, 1988).

22 For histories of North American Mennonites during these decades see Paul Toews, *Mennonites in American Society, 1930-1970* (Scottdale, PA: Herald Press, 1996); T.D. Regehr, *Mennonites in Canada: A People Transformed* (Toronto: University of Toronto Press, 1996).

23 Leo Driedger and J. Howard Kauffman, 'Urbanzation of Mennonites: Canadian and American Comparisons,' *Mennonite Quarterly Review* 56 (1982): 269–90.

24 Levine, *Class, Networks, and Identity*, esp. chap. 7, 'Continuities and Discontinunities,' 133–53; Kann, *Comrades and Chicken Ranchers* esp. chap. 12, '"They Just Came in and Took Your Place": Family Farming in Crisis,' 221–42. Matsumoto, *Farming the Home Place*, esp. chap. 6, 'Reweaving the Web of Community,' 149–78; Giffen, *Rural Life*; Hurt, ed., *The Rural South*, especially the chapters on labor relations and evangelical faith; Kenneth Sylvester, *The Limits of Rural Capitalism: Family, Culture, and Markets, Montcalm, Manitoba, 1870-1940* (Toronto: University of Toronto Press, 2000), esp. chap. 7, 'Leaving Rural Life,' 168–90; Jane Marie Pederson, *Between Memory and Reality: Family and Community in Rural Wisconsin, 1870–1970* (Madison: University of Wisconsin Press, 1992), esp. pp. 115, 134–15, 151, 183–14; Rob Kroes, *The Persistence of Ethnicity: Dutch Calvinist Pioneers in Amsterdam, Montana* (Urbana: University of Illinois Press, 1992), esp. chap. 8, 'You Can't Keep the World Out: Changes Ahead,' 122–34.

25 Hans Medick, '"Missionaries in a Rowboat?" Ethnological Ways of Knowing as a Challenge to Social History,' *Comparative Studies in Society and History* 29 (1987): 82.

26 Henri Lefebvre, *Critique of Everyday Life*, 1947, trans. John Moore (London: Verso, 1991), 57.

27 Kathleen Neils Conzen, 'Making Their Own America: Assimilation Theory and the German Peasant Pioneer,' *German Historical Institute Annual Lecture Series* 3 (1990): 7.

28 Clifford Geertz, *The Interpretation of Cultures: Selected Essays* (New York: Basic Books, 1973), 5, 12. In a similar vein, Hans Medick argues that 'meaning ... is never just ... transmitted in unchanging ways. ... [It] is constantly recreated by the participation of the actors.' Medick, 'Missionaries in a Rowboat,' 97.

29 See, for example, Allan Bogue's review of Susan Sessions Rugh, *Our Common Country: Family, Farming, Culture and Community in the Nineteenth Century Midwest* (Bloomington: Indiana University Press, 2001) in *American Historical Review* 107 (2002): 874–5, and Deborah Fink's review of Melissa Walker, *All We Knew Was to Farm: Rural Women in the Upcountry South* (Baltimore: Johns Hopkins University Press, 2000) in *American Historical Review* 106 (2001): 1395–6.

30 Robert A. Nisbet, 'Community as Typology: Toennies and Weber,' in *The Sociological Tradition* (New York: Basic Books, 1966), 71–83; Robert Redfield, 'The Folk Society,' *American Journal of Sociology* 52 (1947): 293–308.

31 For histories of these two congregations see Delbert Plett, *Saints and Sinners: The Kleine Gemeinde in Imperial Russia, 1812–1875* (Steinbach, MB: Crossway Publications, 1999); Calvin Redekop, *Leaving Anabaptism: From Evangelical Mennonite Brethren to Fellowship of Evangelical Bible Churches* (Telford, PA: Pandora, 1998). For official histories of these churches see Peter J.B. Reimer and David P. Reimer, *The Sesquicentennial Jubilee: Evangelical Mennonite Conference* (Steinbach, MB: Evangelical Mennonite Conference, 1962); G.S. Rempel, ed., *A Historical Sketch of the Churches of the Evangelical Mennonite Brethren* (Rosthern, SK: D.H. Epp, 1939).

32 Donald B. Kraybill and Carl F. Bowman, *On the Backroad to Heaven: Old Order Hutterites, Mennonites, Amish and Brethren* (Baltimore: Johns Hopkins University Press, 2001), x–xi. For a more personal definition of old-order society see the insightful and sprightly work Isaac Horst, *A Separate People: An Insider's View of Old Order Mennonite Customs and Traditions* (Waterloo, ON: Herald Press, 2000).

33 See Royden Loewen, *Family, Church and Market: A Mennonite Community in the Old and New Worlds, 1850–1930* (Urbana: University of Illinois Press, 1993).

34 For histories of other conservative rural communities set in earlier periods in the American Midwest see Steven D. Reschly, *The Amish on the Iowa Prairie, 1840–1910* (Baltimore: Johns Hopkins University Press, 2000); Rod Janzen, *The Prairie People: Forgotten Anabaptists* (Hanover, NH: University Press of New England, 1999); Anne Kelly Knowles, *Calvinists Incorporated: Welsh Immigrants on Ohio's Industrial Frontier* (Chicago: University of Chicago Press, 1997); Robert P. Sutton, *Les Icariens: The Utopian Dream in Europe and America* (Urbana: University of Illinois Press, 1994); Kroes, *The Persistence of Ethnicity*. For rural histories set in western Canada that discuss antimodernity in earlier periods see R.W. Sandwell, *Peasants on the Coast? Contesting Rural Space in Nineteenth Century British Columbia* (Montreal: McGill-Queen's University Press, 2004); Kenneth Sylvester, *The Limits of Rural Capitalism: Family, Culture, and Markets, Montcalm, Manitoba, 1870-1940* (Toronto: University of Toronto Press, 2000); Carl J. Tracie, *Toil and Peaceful Life: Doukhobor Village Settlement in Saskatchewan, 1899–1918* (Regina: Canadian Plains Research Center, 1996).

35 The boundaries of the RM of Hanover during the 1950s were almost identical to the 1873 boundaries that defined the Mennonite East Reserve, a land block set aside by the Dominion government for the exclusive use of the Mennonites. The East Reserve was organized politically according to Russian practices of local government among foreign colonists; in 1881, however, a new Manitoba Municipal Act reorganized the reserve accord-

ing to municipal law. The RM of Hanover would remain almost homoge-
neously Mennonite until the 1890s when the municipality expanded to
include a small Anglo-Canadian settlement on its eastern boundary, and
when German and Ukrainian settlers began settling in the southern
sections of the municipality. While separate statistics for the ethnic composition of Hanover during the 1950s were unavailable for this study, 79.7
percent of Steinbach residents were members of the Mennonite religious
denomination according to the 1961 federal census. For standard accounts
of the RM of Hanover see John Warkentin, *The Mennonite Settlements in
Southern Manitoba: A Study in Historical Geography*, 1960 (Steinbach, MB:
Hanover Steinbach Historical Society, 2000); Lydia Penner, *Hanover: 100
Years* (Steinbach, MB: RM of Hanover, 1982); Abe Warkentin, *Reflections on
Our Heritage: A History of Steinbach and the R.M. of Hanover from 1874*
(Steinbach, MB: Derksen Printers, 1971).

36 Jürgen Kocha, 'Comparison and Beyond,' *History and Theory* 42 (2003):
39–44. I am grateful to my colleague Tamara Myers for introducing me to
this work.

37 Thomas Archdeacon, 'Problems and Possibilities in the Study of American
Immigration and Ethnic History,' *International Migration Review* 19 (spring
1985): 112–34.

38 For another study that compares two distinctive environments on different sides of the continental grassland, one located in Alberta and the
other in North Dakota, see Molly P. Rozum, 'Indelible Grasslands: Place,
Memory, and the "Life Review,"' in Robert Wardhaugh, ed., *Toward Defining the Prairies: Region, Culture and History* (Winnipeg: University of
Manitoba Press, 2001), 119–35.

39 Thomas R. Dunlap, *Nature and the English Diaspora: Environment and
History in the United States, Canada, Australia and New Zealand* (New York:
Cambridge University Press, 1999).

40 See for example, Beth LaDow, *The Medicine Line: Life and Death on a North
American Borderland* (New York: Routledge, 2001).

41 Donald Worster, 'Two Faces West: The Development Myth in Canada and
the United States,' in Paul W. Hirt, ed., *Terra Pacifica: People and Place in the
Northwest States and Western Canada* (Pullman: Washington State University Press, 1998), 74.

42 John Higham, 'The Cult of the "American Consensus": Homogenizing Our
History,' in Richard M. Abrams and Lawrence W. Levine, eds., *The Shaping
of American History* (Boston: Little Brown, 1965), 704; J.M.S. Careless,
'"Limited Identities" in Canada,' *Canadian Historical Review* 50 (1969): 4.

43 For a full account of the migration from Canada to Mexico and British

Honduras see H. Leonard Sawatsky, *They Sought a Country: Mennonite Colonization in Mexico* (Berkeley: University of California Press, 1971).

44 See Fred Kniss, *Disquiet in the Land: Cultural Conflict in American Mennonite Communities* (New Brunswick, NJ: Rutgers University Press, 1997). Kniss's model allows one to avoid simple binary opposites, conservatives versus progressives. Kniss creates a four-pointed spatial model that allows an analysis of rural conservative, town-based progressive, city-based secular and evangelical groups, or socially conscious 'liberals.'

45 David Harvey, *The Condition of Postmodernity: An Enquiry Into the Origins of Cultural Change* (New York: Blackwell, 1989), 45.

46 See Joy Parr, 'Gender History and Historical Practice,' *Canadian Historical Review* 76 (1995): 354–76.

1. The 'Great Disjuncture' and Ethnic Farmers: Life in Two Corners of a Transnational Grassland

1 See E.K. Francis, 'The Adjustment of a Peasant Group to a Capitalist Economy: The Manitoba Mennonites,' *Rural Sociology* 17 (1952): 218–28.

2 For a detailed description of Hanover before the Second World War see E.K. Francis, *In Search of Utopia: The Mennonites in Manitoba* (Altona, MB: D.W. Friesen and Sons, 1955); Warkentin, *Mennonite Settlements*.

3 The small farms also translated into less land tenancy: in 1956 when almost a third 29.7 percent of the land in Manitoba was rented, only 14.3 percent was rented in Hanover. *Census of Canada*, 1956, Vol. 2, Table 15-1.

4 Census statistics in Francis, *In Search of Utopia*, 218 and 220, indicate that wheat production declined from 7045 acres to 5313 acres during this time and that oat production increased from 14,888 acres to 20,086 acres.

5 Manitoba farmers on the whole grew slightly more wheat than oats (1.0 acre of wheat for .96 acres of oats); Hanover farmers planted five times as many acres of oats than of wheat (1.0 acre of wheat to 5.2 acres of oats). There was a similar ratio of wheat to feed grain acres, 1.0 acre of wheat to 1.7 acres of feed wheat in Manitoba compared to 1.0 acre of wheat to 8.3 acres of feed grain in Hanover. See *Census of Canada*, 1956, Vol. 2, Table 17-2. Indicative of the same trend was the fact that although during the 1950s Hanover farmers owned only half as many combines per farmer as did the average Manitoba farmer, .44 combines per Manitoba farmer compared to .19 combines per Hanover farmer, they owned as many tractors, 1.2 tractors per Manitoba farm compared to .96 tractors per Hanover farm and .58 trucks per Manitoba farm compared to .62 per Hanover farm. *Census of Canada*, 1956, Vol. 2, Table 16-1.

6 The average farm in Hanover kept 18.3 swine, 24.7 cows, 640 chickens or turkeys, while the average Manitoba farm kept 6.3 swine, 4.5 cows, 122 chickens or turkeys. *Census of Canada*, 1956, Vol. 2, Table 16-2.

7 Warkentin, *Mennonite Settlements*.

8 Penner, *Hanover*, 63.

9 Bruce Fast, 'Dairy Farming in Hanover since 1873,' term paper, University of Manitoba, n.d.; Ron Andres, ed., *Silver Jubilee Steinbach D.H.I.A.* (Steinbach, MB, 1980).

10 Francis, *In Search of Utopia*, 223.

11 Shover, *First Majority*, 144. According to Shover, between 1935 and 1960 the number of chicken broilers produced in the United States rose fifty-fold and per capita poultry consumption tripled; annual poultry consumption rose from 16 pounds per capita in 1940 to 50 pounds in the 1970s, whereas beef consumption rose from 60 pounds to 116 pounds.

12 *Prairie Agricultural Census*, 1956 and 1966.

13 Royden Loewen, *Blumenort: A Mennonite Community in Transition, 1874–1982* (Blumenort, MB: Blumenort Mennonite History Society, 1990), 501–8.

14 Warkentin, *Mennonite Settlements*, 252. In 1951 Steinbach had a population of 2155. Ibid., 244.

15 *Carillon News* (hereafter *CN*), 25 June 1957.

16 Thompson and MacPherson, 'Business of Farming'; Britnell and Fowke, *Canadian Agriculture*, 120.

17 *CN*, 27 June 1968.

18 Ibid.

19 Steinbach Credit Union, *A Look at Fifty Years of Service, 1941–1991* (Steinbach, MB, 1991), 7.

20 *CN*, 7 Feb. 1973. Later that spring the local high school announced a 'pilot computer sciences program' which was 'subsidized by the provincial government' in recognition of the 'ever-increasing number of businesses utilizing computer service for payroll, bookkeeping and general accounting' Ibid., 7 March 1973.

21 Gertie Klassen Loewen, diary, 23 Nov. 1973, writes she visited a lawyer's office where 'I signed to transfer Dave Loewen to Greenridge' Farm Inc.

22 *CN*, 6 Oct. 1962.

23 In fact, soon after the Turkey Growers Association confronted the government on the fat content issue, they cooperated with the government on issues of production and marketing. In 1963 the *Carillon* reported with a hint of local pride that district farmer Ben L. Reimer 'was among the board members of the Canadian Turkey Association summoned to Ottawa this

week by the federal minister of agriculture ... to discuss pressing problems
related to the turkey industry.' Ibid., 5 July 1963. The consumption of
chicken and turkey rose in particular. Turkey consumption in Canada rose
from 127,000 per year between 1958 and 1962 to 210,000 in 1970; in Manitoba it rose from 18,000 to 19,000. The consumption of chicken rose in
Canada from 381,000 to 750,000 and in Manitoba from 25,000 to 44,000. The
production of eggs in Canada rose only slightly from 438 million dozen
per year between 1958 and 1962 to 471 million dozen in 1969; but in
Manitoba it rose from 37 million dozen to 63 million dozen. Contrary to
these trends, the total production of milk in Canada between 1958 and
1970 rose from 17.95 billion pounds to only 18.50 billion pounds. The
Canadian Department of Agriculture, *The Canadian Agriculture Outlook*
(Ottawa: Agriculture Canada, 1970), 55, 70, 75.

24 For an overview of 'marketing boards and the Canadian food system' see
J.D. Forbes, R.D. Hughes, and T.K. Waverly, *Economic Intervention and
Regulation in Canadian Agriculture* (Ottawa: Ministry of Supply and Services, 1982), 5–18. This work defines the marketing board system 'as
statutorily sanctioned, compulsory, horizontal cartels of the producers of
agricultural products.'

25 *CN*, 21 Feb. 1973.

26 Ibid., 14 Dec. 1962.

27 Ibid., 29 Nov. 1963.

28 See Forbes, *Economic Intervention*, 5. Farmers' support for marketing
boards was much more positive than that of Jake Epp, a Mennonite
schoolteacher from Steinbach who was elected as the region's member of
Parliament in 1973 on a free market, laissez faire, and lower taxes platform. He only tacitly supported the marketing boards. In his maiden
speech in January 1973 he lauded the western farmers for having 'consoli-
dated ... and become more efficient,' thus surviving 'not because of government programs, but possibly despite them.' *CN*, 24 Jan. 1973. And just
three months later he noted that while 'marketing boards are becoming
more and more of a fixture in agriculture, one caution must be kept in
mind ... Marketing boards must ... make their number one priority [the]
develop[ment] of new markets for their products so that production can
be expanded.' Ibid., 21 March 1973.

29 *CN*, 2 May 1968.

30 Ibid., 15 Feb. 1968, 2 May 1968.

31 Ibid., 4 April 1968.

32 Ibid., 3 Jan. 1973.

33 Loewen, *Blumenort*, 507, 508, 513. Local support for the marketing boards
was significant even though Mennonites had traditionally been leery

of both government intervention and organizing across ethnoreligious boundaries. The marketing boards were seen simply as the panacea for the preservation of the family farm. Rural depopulation was on their minds and warnings from the local Ag Rep office that in 1971 'only 8.6% of the people in Canada lived on rural farms ... a decrease from 9.5% in 1966' were commonplace. *CN*, 17 Jan. 1973. Local politicians began lining up behind the marketing board system. In fact at one all-candidates' meeting during the election in 1968 it was reported that only the Social Credit candidate did not express 'the need to maintain the family farm through marketing boards,' while the other parties questioned the sincerity of one another's support for marketing boards. Conservative candidate Warner Jorgenson for one expressed skepticism of the Liberal policy: 'Mr. Trudeau is a very prize animal in the show ring,' declared Jorgenson, but 'farmers know that such an animal has to be ROP tested.' Ibid., 12 June 1968.

34 Personal letter to author from Loudel F. Snow, Michigan State University, 31 October 1994.

35 *Meade Globe Press* (hereafter *MGP*), 26 June 1947. *Meade Globe Press* became the name of the newspaper on 4 March 1954, replacing *Meade Globe News*. To avoid confusion we have used the term *Meade Globe Press* or *MGP* throughout the book.

36 Walter Friesen, 'History and Description of the Mennonite Community and Bible Academy at Meade, Kansas,' MA thesis, State Teachers College, Emporia KS, 1957. By 1970 many of the Mennonites had left for Meade or another urban centre in the western United States, but the federal census of that year still recorded that 550 of the 4912 respondents claimed German as 'mother tongue,' a relative measure of the continued existence of Low German, the Dutch Mennonite dialect. *U.S. Population Census*, Kansas 1970, Table 119.

37 Gilbert C. Fite, *American Farmers: The New Minority* (Bloomington: Indiana University Press, 1981), 26.

38 Ibid. The number of tractors more than quadrupled on the Great Plains in the 1920s, from 82,000 to 274,000, and the number of combines in Kansas alone rose to 8300 machines.

39 Kansas State Agricultural Census, 1915, 1925, Kansas State Historical Society (hereafter KSHS); Kansas Board of Agricultural Census, 1950, KSHS.

40 Interview with Martin and Helen Bartel and John and Anne Reimer, Meade, Kansas, July 1992. And family histories that indicate that 'in the dust bowl years ... [our parents] struggled to make a living ... rais[ing] chickens and ... selling eggs to buy groceries,' support the idea of a renewed emphasis of mixed farming. Larry Beard, *Centennial History of Meade, Kansas* (Meade, KS, 1985), 157.

41 Ibid., 152.
42 Anna Z. Friesen Siemens, ed., *Genealogy and History of the J.R. Friesen Family, 1782–1990* (Meade, KS: self-published, 1990). Other women like Susie Z. Friesen located temporarily to far-off places in California to earn extra money and then joined Civilian Public Service as a show of solidarity with their brothers. Ibid. For a fuller discussion of the role of Mennonite women during the Second World War see Rachel Waltner Goossen, *Women against the Good War: Conscientious Objection and Gender on the American Home Front, 1941–1947* (Chapel Hill: University of North Carolina Press, 1997).
43 Daniel J. Classen, 'The Kleine Gemeinde of Meade, Kansas,' research paper, Bethel College, Newton KS, ca1950.
44 *MGP*, 31 July 1947.
45 Kansas Board of Agriculture, 1950, 1961, 1976.
46 Ibid.
47 Ibid.
48 *MGP*, 17 Oct. 1957, 11 Feb. 1960.
49 Fite, *American Farmers*, 255.
50 Post–Second World War advertisements such as the boast by McCormick Deering of the combine's 'one man, one engine' technology, were really not necessary in Meade County. *MGP*, 3 May 1945.
51 The auction sales took place in 1948, 1954, 1956, and 1960 and were all advertised in the *MGP*.
52 Meade farmers received their rural electricity lines through the Rural Electrification Agency (REA) in the late 1940s and did so unreservedly. The Emmanuel Mennonite Church, for example, passed a resolution in June 1945 that 'we hook up to the REA line when they build the line.' And electricity knew no social boundaries; when the lines came through the last of the Mennonite townships in 1948, each of the households, from the progressive, well-to-do farmer, John N. Ediger, to the poorer household of the 'Bartel Sisters' subscribed. Emmanuel Mennonite Church Membership Meeting Minutes, 17 June 1945, Emmanuel Mennonite Church, Meade; *MGP*, 20 June 1948.
53 Theodore Saloutos, *The American Farmer and the New Deal* (Ames: Iowa State University Press, 1982), 204.
54 Interview with Cornie Z. Friesen, Meade, July 1992.
55 *MGP*, 4 June 1948.
56 Ibid., 8 April 1948.
57 Ibid., 29 July 1948.
58 It was eight years according to ibid., 17 March 1960.

59 Ibid., 16 Sept. 1969.
60 Ibid., 8 Oct. 1959, 16 July 1959.
61 Ibid., 1 April 1948.
62 Ibid., 11 March 1954.

2. Snowdrift and Dust Bowl: The Environment and Cultural Change

1 William Cronon, *Changes in the Land: Indians, Colonists and the Ecology of New England* (New York: Hill and Wang, 1983), vii, quoted in Brian Q. Cannon, 'Pushing History Beyond Human Institutions: Studying the Rural Environment.' Paper presented to the New Trends in Rural History conference, April 2004, Iowa State University, Ames IA.

2 Patricia Limerick and others have noted that in recent decades the 'environment ... is no longer a resistant barrier to be overcome, but a vital historical component that itself changes with human interaction even as it shapes western economic and social patterns, not to mention the western imagination.' Patricia Nelson Limerick, Clyde A. Milner II, and Charles E. Rankin, *Trails: Toward a New Western History* (Lawrence: University Press of Kansas, 1991), xi.

3 See J. Donald Hughes, *An Environmental History of the World: Humankind's Changing Role in the Community of Life* (New York: Routledge, 2001).

4 Richard White, 'Environmental History: Watching a Historical Field Mature,' *Pacific Historical Review* 70 (2001): 105.

5 Ibid., 110.

6 Adam Rome, 'What Really Matters in History? Environmental Perspectives on Modern America,' *Environmental History* 7 (2002): 307.

7 Simon Schama, *Landscape and Memory* (New York: Knopf, 1995), 9. In fact, Schama suggests provocatively that the creation of landscape by humans is 'a cause not for guilt ... but celebration.'

8 For a fuller discussion of this paradox see Calvin Redekop, ed., *Creation and the Environment: An Anabaptist Perspective on a Sustainable World* (Baltimore: Johns Hopkins University Press, 2000); see also Royden Loewen, 'The Quiet on the Land: Mennonites and the Environment in History,' *Journal of Mennonite Studies* 23 (2005).

9 Beard, *Centennial History*, 131.

10 *Familienfreund*, Oct. 1937.

11 *Meade Globe Press* (hereafter *MGP*), 21 April 1955.

12 Ibid., 14 March 1957.

13 Ibid., 21 March 1957.

14 Ibid., 11 April 1957.

15 Ibid., 26 April 1945; 31 May 1945; 4 Dec. 1947; 29 Feb. 1948; 19 Sept. 1957; 14 April 1960.
16 Ibid., 25 June 1959; 30 May 1957; 11 June 1959; 10 June 1954.
17 Ibid., 26 June 1958.
18 Henry A. Friesen, diary, 1952, 1968, Dr Menno Friesen, Goshen, IN.
19 Helena Doerksen Reimer, 'Tagebuch,' 1948, Helena Reimer Bartel, Meade, KS.
20 *MGP*, 3 May 1957.
21 Twenty years later semi-retired farmer Henry A. Friesen's 1968 diary shows the same cycle. Technology might change, seasons did not. The first sign of life in 1968 occurred with the brusque statement of 1 February that 'today 1st calf dropped, h[ei]f[e]r calf.' This was followed by the birth of a 'bull calf' on the sixth, three more calves, two bulls, and a heifer on the ninth, and then on the tenth when yet another two were born, Friesen appended a note that he had 'moved calves to ... wheat pasture.' By the end of March the cattle were juggled from one field to another; on the sixteenth it was time to remove the cattle from the 'Loewen land'; on the twenty-first Friesen 'turned cows on wheat pasture at home' and on 13 April he took the 'heifers off the wheat pasture of Wilson land.' June and July were the months of the harvest and a sign of the importance of the end of the harvest was the fact that Friesen had only three entries for June: the entry of Elda leaving for Haiti, a note on the fifth that 'Robert Kennedy was assassinated in Los Angeles,' and the note of the twenty-ninth that he had 'finished cutting wheat at 11.45 p.m. at home.' In the succeeding days the senior Friesen was able to 'help cut wheat at John K. Isaac ... with [son] Marvin's combine' or observe Marvin custom cut for other neighbors, although the 'used cutter' broke down and had to be hauled to Liberal for repairs on warranty. On 16 September, having taken a vacation to Oregon and British Columbia at the end of August, Henry was ready to pitch in again, this time on 17 September by 'driving truck [during] silage cutting' and by 8 October he noted that the farm had 'finished cutting at Dan Post.' On 29 October he offered a hand again, this time he 'drilled ... wheat on Nichols' section, summerfallow is all 'Scout' wheat, on stubble reseeded with 'Bison' wheat'; on the thirty-first Marvin 'redrilled wheat on Wilson on east side ... with Scout and Bison wheat.' On 29 November Henry helped grandson Stanley 'put electric fence at ... rented field at Arnold Reimer' and on 9 December Henry noted that he 'moved our calves on Nichols' section – 16 head' and the season had truly begun again. And although Friesen drove to Meade for haircuts, the shopping center, and

the restaurant as if nothing had changed, Friesen even took days off to butcher hogs, pick up alfalfa pellets and hog feed, repair the pig barn, and then also to butcher a 760 pound heifer, can three and a half bushels of peaches with in-laws, share strawberries with a neighbor, plant a cherry tree, and watch his wife 'dress 13 hens.'

22 Donald Worster, *Dust Bowl: The Southern Plains in the 1930s* (New York: Oxford University Press, 1979), 174. For similar observations about the Mennonites of Haskell County, some of whom were first cousins to the Meade Mennonites, see Katherine Jellison, *Entitled to Power: Farm Women and Technology, 1913–1963* (Chapel Hill: University of North Carolina Press, 1993), 37–8.

23 Pamela Riney-Kehrberg, *Rooted in Dust: Surviving Drought and Depression in Southwestern Kansas* (Lawrence: University Press of Kansas, 1994), 172.

24 *MGP*, 3 May 1948; 12 Aug. 1954.

25 Ibid., 1 May 1954; 4 June 1947; 4 June 1947.

26 Ibid., 6 Nov. 1947.

27 In July 1947 the Ernest Drilling Company from Dodge City made it look feasible: a turbine pump cost as little as $600, a 65-horsepower Buick engine to power the system, $810; 16-inch casing cost only $12 a foot; drilling itself 65 cents a foot; for everything included, a 180-foot well would mean spending as little as '$2000.' Ibid., July 1947.

28 Ibid., 28 Feb. 1957.

29 Michael P. Malone and Richard W. Etulain, *The American West: A Twentieth-Century History* (Lincoln: University of Nebraska Press, 1989), 95.

30 *MGP*, 8 May 1969.

31 Ibid., 1 Feb. 1948.

32 Ibid., 21 March 1948.

33 Ibid., 26 June 1947. The American farmer, noted the American Steel and Iron company ad in November 1947, is 'alone among the farmers of the major nations ... able to feed his own countrymen,' and his 'efficiency' too is the reason why Americans are 'better fed, better clothed and have more automobiles, refrigerators, telephones and radios per capita than any other country.' Ibid., 30 Nov. 1947; 27 June 1948.

34 Beard, *Centennial History*, 64.

35 Malone and Etulain, *The American West*, 96.

36 *MGP*, 29 April 1948.

37 There is only circumstantial evidence that Mennonite farmers attended these films. The *Globe Press* noted that these films drew over a hundred farmers at a time to consider soil management ways.

38 Ibid., 12 Feb. 1948; 14 Feb. 1957; 21 Feb. 1957; 26 Sept. 1957.
39 The *Globe Press* reported in 1957 that irrigation systems were purchased in 'all parts of the country except the southeast.' Ibid.
40 Interview with Abe Isaac, Meade, KS, July 1992.
41 Friesen, diary.
42 Ibid., 8 April 1954.
43 Ibid., 22 July 1959.
44 Donald Edward Green, *Land of Underground Rain* (Austin: University of Texas Press, 1973).
45 *MGP*, 16 May 1948.
46 Ibid., 14 March 1948; 18 April 1948.
47 Ibid., 3 June 1948.
48 Ibid., 25 July 1957.
49 Interview with Ben Classen, Dallas OR, July 1992.
50 Although less fertilizer was used on dry land than on irrigated land, by the 1960s fertilizer usage seems to have become general. The local Co-op elevator rented fertilizer pellet spreaders or special twelve-foot-wide cultivators and three-point hitch-mounted tanks that could apply a gaseous form, anhydrous ammonia, at $3.50 an acre less than the dry form. *MGP*, 19 March 1959. But even then few Mennonite farmers used fertilizers such as ammonium nitrate that could be purchased at C.W. Cone in 1954 and was said to be used 'everywhere in the county' to 'boost yields.' *MGP*, 4 March 1954.
51 Ibid., 15 July 1954.
52 Ibid., 26 Oct. 1947. The price for this week was quoted as $2.81 a bushel.
53 Ibid., 6 Feb. 1948 reported wheat at $2.17 per bushel; ibid., 13 Feb. 1948 quoted it as $1.95 per bushel.
54 Ibid., 18 June 1959; 11 June 1960.
55 Plank, *Twas Home on the Range*, 55.
56 *MGP*, 31 July 1947; 30 Oct. 1947.
57 Ibid., 21 Nov. 1957; 9 July 1959.
58 Beard, *Centennial History*, 8.
59 Ibid., 9.
60 *MGP*, 3 May 1945; 2 Oct. 1947; 6 Feb. 1948; 8 June 1948.
61 Ibid., 4 Sept. 1954.
62 Ibid., 4 April 1957.
63 The mean income for Meade County was $3188, for Harvey County $2545, for Marion County $1879, and for McPherson County $2347. *U.S. Census, Kansas,* 1960.
64 Beard, *Centennial History*, 9.

65 *MGP*, 24 June 1957.
66 Ibid., 25 April 1957; 31 June 1957; 15 Oct. 1959.
67 Ibid., 27 Nov. 1958.
68 Interview with Ben D. Reimer, Steinbach, MB, June 1992.
69 Minutes of the Membership Meetings, 1944–1960, Emmanuel Mennonite Church, Meade, KS.
70 *Carillon News* (hereafter *CN*), 9 May 1973.
71 Ibid., 4 Jan. 1968.
72 Ibid., 2 May 1973.
73 Ibid., 16 May 1968.
74 Ibid., 24 May 1963.
75 Ibid., 9 April 1963.
76 Ibid., n.d., 1962.
77 Ibid., 15 Nov. 1963.
78 *Canada Census, Prairie Agriculture*, 1946, 1976.
79 *CN*, 4 Oct. 1963.
80 Ibid., 27 Sept. 1963.
81 Sometimes the signs of change came in the form of cautionary advice: in June 1963 he warned 'all dairymen not to use Deldrin or DDT on any feed or bedding' and further warned poultry farmers against misusing Malathion or face the possibility, as had one farmer, of losing 'a few hundred laying hens and the litters from eight sows.' Ibid., 7 June 1963.
82 Ibid., 7 June 1963.
83 Ibid., 5 July 1963.
84 Examples of folklore passed on to me by my father, Dave P. Loewen, my neighbor Ken Reimer, and ag rep Rod Siemens.
85 *CN*, 21 June 1963.
86 For a more detailed expose of this inheritance system see Royden Loewen, '"If Joint Heirs of Grace, How Much More of Temporal Goods?": Inheritance and Community Formation,' in *Hidden Worlds: Revisiting the Mennonite Migrants of the 1870s* (Winnipeg: University of Manitoba Press, 2001), 33–150.
87 *EMC Estates Committee*, 1974, 6,10.
88 Book B10, folio 18, St Boniface Probate Court (hereafter SBPC), St Boniface, MB.
89 Book 8, folio 977, SBPC.
90 Book 10, folio 396, SBPC.
91 Book 8, folio 674. SBPC.
92 Book 13, folio 106, SBPC.
93 Book 10, folio 406, SBPC. Of the seven people who bequeathed money to

charity four were women and two were businessmen. Reflecting a new mindset was the will of Steinbach lumber merchant and small wood-products factory owener, C.T. Loewen, who died in October 1960 after a long illness. He bequeathed $10,800 to a variety of organizations, with the single largest bequest of $4000 left for his home church. Of this he designated $1000 for the 'foreign missionary department,' $1000 for the church mutual-aid society known as *Hilfwerk*, and $2000 'to be divided equally among the ministers of the said church.'

94 My father, a master farmer, once told me with reference to his bitter disappointment of having been shut out of a land deal, that his pain derived from the fact that 'next to my love for the Lord and for my family, I love land the most.'

95 See Michael Hadley, 'Education and Alienation in Dyck's *Verloren in der Steppe*,' *Canadian-German Yearbook* 3 (1976): 199–206.

96 Yi-Fu Tuan, *Space and Place: The Perspective of Experience* (Minneapolis: University of Minnesota Press, 1977), 148. Historical geographer John Warkentin asserts that Manitoba Mennonite farmers found themselves in the 'rigid, unswerving geometrical gridiron of the regular section land survey' that turned 'its rapid, uncompromising spread across the plains' into a 'controlling, enclosing, cage' for Mennonites. See John Warkentin, 'Going on Foot: Revisiting the Mennonite Settlements of Southern Manitoba, *Journal of Mennonite Studies* 18 (2000): 59–81. Where Mennonites were not caught in 'rectangularity,' they invented it, making 'straight rows amid the burnt stumps and debris' in Spanish Lookout and surveying straight terrace lines in the post-dust bowl. See Higdon, 'Farm Diversification,' 33.

3. 'Hold Your Heads High in Your Usual Unassuming Manner': Making a Mennonite Middle Class

1 For novels that depict town life in the RM of Hanover in these terms see David Bergen, *Year of Lesser* (Toronto: Harper Collins, 1996) and Miriam Toews, *A Complicated Kindness* (Toronto: Knopf, 2004). For the viewpoint that the city represented a cultural renaissance for Mennonites see Leo Driedger, *Mennonites in the Global Village* (Toronto: University of Toronto Press, 2000).

2 Warkentin, *Mennonite Settlement*, 101.

3 For contextual literature on these themes see Werner Sollers, ed., *The Invention of Ethnicity* (New York: Oxford University Press, 1989); Benedict Anderson, *Imagined Communities: Reflections on the Origin and Spread of*

Nationalism (London: Verso, 1991); Ulf Hannerz, *Cultural Complexity: Studies in the Social Organization of Meaning* (New York: Columbia University Press, 1992); Orm Overland, *Immigrant Minds, American Identities: Making the United States Home, 1870–1930* (Urbana: University of Illinois Press, 2000).

4 Maurice Halbwachs, *On Collective Memory*, 1941, trans. Lewis A. Coser (Chicago: University of Chicago Press, 1992), 188. To place Halbwachs in a wider context see Jeffrey K. Olick and Joyce Robbins, 'Social Memory Studies: From "Collective Memory" to the Historical Sociology of Mnemonic Practices,' *Annual Review of Sociology* 24 (1998): 105–40.

5 Halbwachs, *On Collective Memory*, 38.

6 Brian W. Dippie, 'American Wests: Historiographical Perspectives,' in Patricia Nelson Limerick, Clyde A. Milner II, and Charles E. Rankin, eds, *Trails: Toward a New Western History* (Lawrence: University Press of Kansas, 1991), 116; Henry Nash Smith, quoted in William G. Robbins, 'Laying Siege to Western History,' in ibid., 184. The region seemed cognizant of its place in 'the expansion to the west [that] was regarded as proof that the American nation was unique and destined to greatness.' Jon Gjerde, *The Minds of the West: Ethnocultural Evolution in the Rural Middle West, 1830–1917* (Chapel Hill: University of North Carolina Press, 1997), 26.

7 Leland Harder, *Steinbach and Its Churches* (Elkhart, IN: Mennonite Biblical Seminary, 1970), 15 and 16.

8 Quoted in Harder, *Steinbach*, 15.

9 Only 15.3 percent of Steinbach workers were listed as professional or laborers; the majority were craftsmen (31.1%), service workers (13.3%), managers (12.0%), sales personal (10.6%), and clerks (10.0%). Statistics from Harder, *Steinbach*, 28.

10 Abe Warkentin, *Our Heritage: A History of Steinbach and the RM of Hanover* (Steinbach, MB: Derksen Printers, 1971). Also see Rachel Mills, 'Gender, Ethnicity and Religion in the Context of Entrepreneurship: The Loewen Lumber Businessmen of Steinbach, Manitoba, 1877–1985' (MA thesis, University of Winnipeg, 2003).

11 *Carillon News* (hereafter *CN*), 31 Oct. 1973.

12 Ibid., 7 Nov. 1973.

13 Ibid., 3 Jan. 1973. That same year the sixty-five employees of the Winnipeg-owned Friendly Family Farms poultry killing plant located just north of town also unionized.

14 Ibid., 24 Jan. 1973.

15 Ibid., 7 Feb. 1973.

16 Ibid., 4 April 1973; 6 June 1973.

17 Ibid., 23 May 1973.
18 Ibid., 5 Jan. 1954; 19 Feb. 1960.
19 Ibid., 3 June 1960.
20 Ibid., 5 Feb. 1960.
21 Warkentin, *Mennonite Settlements*, 243.
22 Ibid.
23 *CN*, 6 Dec. 1957.
24 For another late-century history of Steinbach see Gerald Wright, *Steinbach: Is There Any Place Like It?* (Steinbach, MB, 1991).
25 T.J. Jackson Lears, Introduction in Richard Wightman Fox and T.J. Jackson Lears, eds., *The Culture of Consumption: Critical Essays in American History, 1880–1980* (New York: Pantheon, 1983), vii–xvii.
26 Francis, *In Search of Utopia*, 250.
27 In December 1947 the *CN* ran a photo of rows of tall maples, announcing that 'only ten years ago Main Street looked like this,' *CN*, 17 Dec. 1947. Only a week later it ran the related story that the grand 'H.W. Reimer resident' built in 1911 from the profits of early-century retailing had been moved 'from main street.' Ibid., 20 Dec. 1947.
28 Ibid., 1 Feb. 1949; 5 Feb. 1957; 13 Sept. 1957.
29 Warkentin, *Mennonite Settlements*, 243.
30 *CN*, 19 March 1954. In the five years between 1956 and 1960 the amount of money spent on dwellings in Steinbach rose each year, increasing from $180,000 to $536,000 during this time. In 1960 alone fifty-five houses were constructed for a total of $536,000. Harder, *Steinbach*, 16.
31 Janis Thiessen, 'Immigrant Mennonite Factory Workers: Ethnicity, Class and Integration,' paper presented to the Return of the Kanadier conference, University of Winnipeg, October 2002.
32 Census statistics as reproduced in Harder, *Steinbach*, 31, indicate that these groups comprised 31.7, 28.3, 19.1, 7.0, and 6.5 percent, respectively, of the total population base of 28,734.
33 *CN*, 24 June 1973; The newspaper, in an apparent show of support for assimilation, also lamented in 1968 that 'majority opinion should realize what dangers lie in not explaining itself ... more forcibly' and denounced 'minority groups which ... stage demonstrations, sit-downs or sit-ins.' Ibid., 22 Aug. 1968 Another voice for assimilation came in 1963 when a Mary Thiessen wrote to the *Carillon* to complain that while 'there's every imaginable [group] in the US [at least they] have laws setting one cultural group above the other.' Ibid., 16 Aug. 1963. In Ottawa, meanwhile, Jake Epp downplayed the polyethnic dimension of his constituency, proclaim-

ing that no 'person should be judged by the national background of his forefathers.' Ibid., 24 Jan. 1973.

34 In time the German language was increasingly seen as not crucial in the maintenance of the integrity of the community. As E.K. Francis noted, 'once the Kanadier Mennonites recognized that the adoption of English did not necessarily lead to a loss of group identity, they ceased to resist its use as a lingua franca.' Francis, *In Search of Utopia*, 277.

35 *CN*, 9 July 1954.

36 Ibid., 29 April 1973.

37 Ibid., 15 April 1973.

38 John C. Reimer, ed., *75 Gedenkfeier der Mennonitischen Einwanderung in Manitoba, Canada* (North Kildonan, MB, 1949), 102.

39 For a view of this sense of Mennonite history see Thielman J. van Braght, *Martyrs' Mirror: The Story of Seventeen Centuries of Christian Martyrdom, from the Time of Christ to A.D. 1600.* Joseph F. Sohm, trans. (Scottdale, PA: Herald Press, 1950).

40 The value increased from $159,017 to $1.67 million. See, *CN* 25 Jan. 1957; Mel Toews, *The First Forty Years; The Story of the Steinbach Credit Union Limited* (Steinbach, MB, 1986), 29.

41 *CN*, 23 Sept. 1960; 5 Feb., 1960; 8 April 1960; 13 Sept. 1963.

42 Halbachs, *On Collective Memory*, 38.

43 *CN*, 31 Dec. 1973.

44 Ibid., 13 Jan. 1973; 4 April 1973; 21 Feb. 1973; 21 Feb. 1973.

45 Ibid., 28 March 1946.

46 Ibid., 7 June 1954. The majority of residents who had deep reservations of this medium, no doubt, saw it as ironic that when a local supermarket gave away a free TV set to one of its patrons, the winner was the owner of the Tourist Hotel. *CN*, 16 July 1954.

47 By 1951 nine of ten Canadian homes owned a radio. Rutherford, *Prime Time*, 12.

48 *CN*, 27 March 1947; 3 Oct. 1947.

49 *Steinbach Post*, 13 Feb. 1957.

50 *CN*, 15 March 1947; Interview with Ralph Friesen, Winnipeg, MB, March 1993.

51 *CN*, 15 March 1957.

52 Ibid.

53 Ibid., 4 Jan. 1968; 11 Jan. 1968.

54 Ibid., 4 Jan. 1968.

55 Ibid.

56 Ibid., 8 Aug. 1973.
57 *CN*, 20 June 1946.
58 Ibid., 1 March 1957.
59 Ibid., 12 July 1963.
60 After the rookie member of the Legislative Assembly (MLA), Ed Schreyer of Beausejour, wrote to defend the NDP by suggesting that 'Presidents Eisenhower and Kennedy' also had been cited for being 'soft on communists,' the *CN* shot back that it was anathema to link Kennedy with the NDP as the president was 'the top man in the world today, a man doubtlessly sent by God in an hour of crisis' and should not even be 'associated with the NDP.' Ibid., 23 April 1963.
61 Ibid., 18 Jan. 1968.
62 Ibid., 10 Oct. 1973.
63 *U.S. Census*, 1950, Kansas, Table 6.
64 Rural places are defined here as places of less than 2500 people.
65 *U.S. Census*, 1970, Kansas, Table 18-13.
66 *U.S. Census*, 1950, Kansas, Table 6.
67 *MGP*,10 July 1947; 10 June 1954.
68 Friesen, 'Mennonite Community,' 38.
69 *U.S. Census*, 1960, Kansas.
70 *Meade County Telephone Directory*. According to this source, the total number of Mennonite households rose steadily from 82 in 1938 to 119 in 1951, indicating both a rise stemming from natural increase and perhaps the return of some Meade families following the Great Depression. A further rise to 155 households in 1970, however, was made possible only through significant urbanization.
71 Friesen, 'Mennonite Community,' 32.
72 *MGP*, 14 June 1947; 19 June 1947.
73 Ibid.
74 Ibid., 20 Sept. 1945; 29 Oct. 1954; 24 Nov. 1955; 10 Sept. 1959.
75 Beard, *Centennial History* (Meade, KS, 1985), 29.
76 *MGP*, 23 Aug. 1945.
77 Ibid., 26 June 1947. It was an optimism rooted in the context of general urban growth in Kansas. Cities like Kansas City and smaller centers like Emporia, Manhatten, and Wichita grew, even by 1950 when census takers increased the size of the town qualifying for urban status. *U.S. Census*, 1970, Kansas, Table 18:7.
78 *MGP*, 23 Oct. 1947.
79 Ibid., 22 April 1948.

80 Ibid., 11 Nov. 1954. Increased license plate or license tag sales also indicated a rising number of cars. In fact Meade County officials reported
that in 1947 they had sold almost 10 percent more tags than in 1946, 1534
compared to 1397. Ibid., 15 Feb. 1948.

81 Ibid., 26 Oct. 1947.

82 Classen, 'Kleine Gemeinde'; *MGP*, 11 March 1954.

83 Interview with Dave and Martha Classen, Hillsboro, August 1992.

84 True, Ben Loewen's Loewen Oil Company, operating out of a new 'ultra-
modern gas and tire station' in town and servicing the traffic of Highway
54, did seem to spell escape and not rootedness. But other businesses
embraced agriculture. *MGP*, 15 April 1954; 14 Dec. 1959.

85 Beard, *Centennial History*, 139.

86 Ibid.

87 *MGP*, 17 Nov. 1966.

88 Friesen, 'Mennonite Community,' 33.

89 *MGP*, 22 Oct. 1958.

90 Ibid., 17 Nov. 1966; 26 Sept. 1968.

91 Beard, *Centennial History*, 112; *MGP*, 23 Oct. 1947.

92 Ibid., 150.

93 Ibid., 153.

94 *MGP*, 26 Sept. 1968.

95 Ibid., 3 June 1957.

96 Beard, *Centennial History*, 136.

97 *MGP*, 27 May 1954; 26 April 1954.

98 Ibid., 28 Aug. 1969.

99 Ibid., 16 July 1959.

100 Ibid., 6 May 1954. The Kiwanis supported local Boy Scouts, 4-H Achievement Days, City-Farm relationship programs, and senior citizen programs. Beard, *Centennial History*, 58.

101 *MGP*, 2 June 1960.

102 Ibid., 4 March 1954. In 1959 locals celebrated the feat of a 'former Meade
boy' and 'son of Mr. and Mrs. C.Z. Wiebe [of the] ... southeastern part of
Meade,' developer John A. Wiebe, who had just begun developing a
$10,000,000 shopping mall in Omaha.

103 Ibid., 4 March 1948.

104 Ibid., 12 June 1947. Only occasionally were Mennonites reported as part
of mainstream community life: in May 1948 two Mennonite girls, nine-
year-old Donna Lee Cornelsen and four-year-old Connie Lou Cornelsen
were photographed and placed alongside four other children on the front

page with the designation, 'Meade Citizen of Tomorrow'; in May 1957 high school student Paul Harms, son of 'Mr and Mrs Isaac Harms,' was highlighted as a member of the football team, the glee club, and the student council, and as someone who 'likes Western music and money ... [and] dislikes ... hard work and school.' Ibid., 1 April 1948; 2 May 1957.

105 Ibid., 25 March 1954.

106 Ibid., 4 Nov. 1954; Beard, *Centennial History*, 36.

107 *MGP*, 23 Sept., 1954; 29 Oct. 1954; 24 Nov. 1955; 27 May 1957; Beard, *Centennial History*, 13.

108 *MGP*, 21 Dec. 1947.

109 Ibid., 8 March 1945; 3 May 1945; 17 May 1945; 14 June 1945; 31 May 1945; 19 July 1945.

110 Ibid., 8 April 1948.

111 Ibid., 5 June 1947.

112 Images of the militarism could be seen frequently: in mid-March 1954 alone the *Globe Press* ran stories of a 'jet bomber' crashing near Meade, of the county's Veterans of Foreign Wars reorganizing, and of the Meade Theatre screening *Mission over Korea*,' dubbed a 'Thrilling Account of American Airforce.' Ibid., 26 Oct. 1947; 11 March 1954; 6 May 1954; 21 March 1954.

113 Ibid., 12 Dec. 1957. County residents were exuberant when they came close to the nation's centre: in June 1947 it was worth a front-page story when two local men visiting Kansas City came 'within 20 feet of President Truman, General Ike Eisenhower ... and other big wigs'; in September 1964 when Bob Dole appeared at Meade Park organizers prepared enough meat for 1000 people. Ibid., 19 June 1947; 24 Sept. 1964.

114 Ibid., 19 Oct. 1947; 17 June 1954.

115 Bertha Classen, 'The Mennonite History of the Kleine Gemeinde,' term paper, University of Wichita, 1959, 25.

116 Friesen, 'Mennonite Community,' 39.

117 *MGP*, 7 Aug. 1947; 17 Oct. 1947.

118 Ibid., 2 June 1965; 12 July 1965.

119 Beard, *Centennial History*, 137.

120 Emmanuel Mennonite Church, 'Anniversary of the Emmanuel Mennonite Church, Meade County, Kansas, 1944–1974,' n.p.

121 Ibid.

122 Beard, *Centennial History*, 3.

123 Ibid., 144–5.

124 *U.S. Census*, 1950, Kansas, Table 6.

125 See Marcus Lee Hansen, 'The Third Generation Immigrant,' in Peter

Kivisto and Dag Blanck, eds., *American Immigrants and Their Generations: Studies and Commentaries on the Hansen Thesis after Fifty Years* (Urbana and Chicago: University of Illinois Press, 1990), 191–203; Herbert Gans, 'Symbolic Ethnicity: The Future of Ethnic Groups and Cultures in America,' in H. Gans, ed., *On the Making of Americans: Essays in Honor of David Riesman* (Philadelphia: University of Pennsylvania Press, 1979), 193–220; Porter, *The Vertical Mosaic*; Kathleen Neils Conzen, David A. Gerber, Ewa Morwa-ska, George E. Pozzetta, and Rudolph Vecoli, 'The Invention of Ethnicity: A Perspective from the USA,' *Journal of American Ethnic History* 29 (1992): 3–41; Overland, *Immigrant Minds*.

4. Joy and Evangelicalism: Rediscovering Faith in Kansas

1 In Canada classic studies by S.D. Clark, C.A. Dawson, and others use frameworks to analyse nineteenth- and twentieth-century settlement history that pitted 'sect versus church' or individualized communities versus 'group settlements.' In the United States a more recent examination of the 'minds of the west' by Jon Gjerde portrays an endemic conflict between intentionally segregated and 'corporatist configurations' of continental European descent and the liberal, upwardly mobile, volatile Yankee communities. See C.A. Dawson, *Group Settlement* (Toronto: Macmillan, 1936): S.D. Clark, *Church and Sect in Canada* (Toronto: University of Toronto Press, 1948); Gjerde, *Minds of the West*, 3.

2 Kroes, *The Persistence of Ethnicity*, 120. For a view from a more progressive community see Pederson, *Between Memory and Reality*. For responses from a denominational perspective see Alan Graeber, *Uncertain Saints: The Laity in the Lutheran Church–Missouri Synod, 1900–1970* (Westport, CT: Greenwood Press, 1975); Armand L. Mauss, *The Angel and the Beehive: The Mormon Struggle with Survival* (Urbana: University of Illinois Press, 1994); Kniss, *Disquiet in the Land*; Gerald Tulchinksy, *Branching Out: The Transformation of the Canadian Jewish Community* (Toronto: Stoddart, 1998).

3 For these biblical references to 'joy' see Psalm 51:12, Isaiah 35:1, James 1:2, and I Peter 1:8. For examples of this typology in Canada see David B. Marshall, *Secularizing the Faith: Canadian Protestant Clergy and the Crisis of Belief, 1850–1940* (Toronto: University of Toronto Press, 1992); see as well Stackhouse, *Canadian Evangelicalism in the Twentieth Century* and Robert K. Burkinshaw, *Pilgrims in Lotus Land: Conservative Protestantism in British Columbia, 1917–1981* (Montreal: McGill-Queen's University Press, 1995). For an overview of the history of religion in Canada see Robert Choquette, *Canada's Religions: An Introduction* (Ottawa: University of Ottawa Press, 2004).

4 Geertz, *After the Fact,* 43. See also Fredrik Barth, *Balinese Worlds* (Chicago: University of Chicago Press, 1993), 7.
5 Eviatar Zerubavel, *The Fine Line: Making Distinctions in Everyday Life* (New York: Free Press, 1991), 13.
6 For general histories of American Mennonite churches during this time see Toews, *Mennonites in American Society;* Kniss, *Disquiet in the Land;* Perry Bush, *Two Kingdoms, Two Loyalties: Mennonite Pacifism in Modern America* (Baltimore: Johns Hopkins University Press, 1998). For histories of the Emmanuel Mennonite Church see Meade County, *Pioneer Stories;* Beard, *Centennial History;* Henry L. Fast, 'The Kleine Gemeinde in the United States of America,' in Delbert F. Plett, ed., *Profile of the Kleine Gemeinde, 1874* (Steinbach, MB, 1987), 87–140; G.S. Rempel, ed., *A Historical Sketch of the Churches of the Evangelical Mennonite Brethren* (Rosthern, SK, 1939). For accounts of Kansas Mennonites see Dennis Engbrecht, *The Americanization of a Rural Immigrant Church: The General Conference Mennonites in Central Kansas, 1874–1939* (New York: Garland, 1990); David Haury, *Prairie People: A History of the Western District Conference* (Newton, KS: Faith and Life Press, 1984).
7 Interviews with Henry F. Loewen, Meade County, October 1987; Arnold and Helen Reimer, George J. and Maria Friesen Rempel, Herman and Eva Reimer Rempel, Andrew and Rosella Bartel, Pete and Deloris Loewen, Corny Z. Friesen, Dick Unruh, Abe Z. Friesen, Elias D. Friesen, John D. and Anne Reimer, George D. Reimer, Marten and Helen Reimer Bartel, Ruth Bartel, Anna Friesen Siemens, Meade, Kansas, July 1992; interview with Ben Classen, Ben Rempel, Dallas, Oregon, July 1992; Al Isaac, Hillsboro, Kansas, July 1992; Will Classen, Bertha Classen Johnson, Steinbach, Manitoba, July 1994; *Meade Globe Press* (hereafter *MGP*), 1945–8, 1954, 1957, 1960; Beard, *Centennial History;* Meade Historical Society, *Pioneer Stories.*
8 Kevin Enns-Rempel, 'The Fellowship of Evangelical Bible Churches and the Quest for Religious Identity,' *Mennonite Quarterly Review* 63 (1989): 247–64; Bertha Classen, 'Kleine Gemeinde at Meade, Kansas,' unpublished term paper, Bethel College, Newton, KS, 1949.
9 Will Herberg, *Protestant-Catholic-Jew: An Essay in American Religious Sociology* (New York: Doubleday, 1955), 4.
10 George Marsden, *Religion and American Culture* (San Diego: Harcourt Brace, 1990), 312.
11 Evangelicalism is defined by Martin E. Marty, *Religion and Republic: The American Circumstance* (Boston, Beacon Press, 1987), 275, as 'turning from the old self and world ... through an intense experience of Jesus Christ ...

[that is] reinforce[d] with a fresh resort to biblical authority ... [and followed by] a plea for ordered moral behavior and efforts to ... share the faith in the form of evangelism.'

12 The Third Great Awakening between 1890 and 1920 mixed religious revivalism with the fundamentalist concern over biblical inerrancy and was passed directly to Mennonites via Dwight L. Moody in the 1870s and 1880s and Rueben Torrey, a graduate of Moody Bible Institute and President of the Bible Institute of Los Angeles, in the 1920s. See James C. Juhnke, *Vision, Doctrine, War: Mennonite Identity and Organization in America, 1890–1930* (Scottdale, PA: Herald Press, 1989). In this sense it was 'traditionalist and backward looking,' as W.G McLoughlin argues. Billy Graham and other evangelicals of the post-war period 'demonstrate[d] that Fundamentalism was not dead but in fact held the key to the return of law, order, decency and national progress.' W.G. McLoughlin, *Revivals, Awakenings and Reform* (Chicago: University of Chicago Press, 1978).

13 It was to be distinguished from earlier fundamentalism: it was had less to do with concerns about 'the dissolution of personalistic, patriarchal notions of order and social religion and their replacement by depersonalized principles' than with other matters such as a closing world, a feeling of having lost true faith. See Martin Riesebrodt, *Pious Passion: The Emergence of Modern Fundamentalism in the United States and Iran*, trans. Don Reneau (Berkeley: University of California Press, 1993), 16. Nor was here no sense of having 'deviated so far from accepted (traditional) norms.' See George Rawlyk, 'New Lights, Baptists and Religious Awakenings,' in Mark McGowan and David Marshall, eds., *Prophets, Priests and Prodigals* (Toronto: McGraw-Hill, 1992), 53.

14 McLoughlin, *Revivals*, 18.

15 Marty, *Religion and Republic*, 274.

16 Ibid., 276.

17 Ibid.

18 Marsden, *Religion and American*, 217.

19 Worster, *Dust Bowl*, 4; interview with Ben Classen, Dallas, OR, July 1992.

20 Bartel, *Emmanuel Church*, 19–21.

21 Ibid., 24.

22 Ibid.

23 Ibid.

24 Interview with Rev. Sam Epp, Steinbach, MB, June 1992.

25 *Christlicher Familienfreund* (hereafter *Familienfreund*), October 1937. This was the received wisdom too; Klaas H. Reimer, a local farmer and carpenter, would later pen the words, 'live peaceably with all men,' in his

264 Notes to pages 86–7

daughter's autograph book. Interview with Helena Reimer Bartel, Meade, July 1992.

26 Classen, 'Kleine Gemeinde,' 20.

27 In a typical 1937 report the Canadians learned that 'Nick Reimers' baby is improving,' that 'Frau Heinrich F. Isaac suffers from hayfever,' that the house of A.E. Reimers has suffered a fire, that Isaac T. Brandts have returned from a 'roundtrip' of California, Oregon, British Columbia, and Manitoba, that Rev Gerhard Klaassen can because of health no longer carry out the duties of his office. *Familienfreund*, July 1937.

28 *Familienfreund*, Oct. 1937.

29 Fast, 'Kleine Gemeinde.' Meade families recall other links, especially times when favorite Manitoba ministers came to preach and during those visits officiated at Kansas weddings. Rev Henry R. Dueck of Kleefeld, Manitoba, for example, is remembered as a popular minister who also happened to marry the Kansas couples Ben Classen and Anne Rempel, and Ben Rempel and Elisabeth Classen in 1934. Interview with Ben Classen and Ben Rempel. In fact, preacher exchanges between the two communities was common and other social links were made in the process. Bishop Jacob F. Isaac, for example, strengthened such a link in 1936 when after his first wife died he married the Manitoba woman Maria Dueck, fourteen years his junior, but a daughter of an influential Manitoba Kleine Gemeinde preacher. John Dueck, Willie Dueck, and Nettie Peters, eds., *Descendants of Jacob and Maria L. Dueck, 1839–1986* (Steinbach, MB, 1986), 84. See also interview with Abram R. Reimer, July 1981: Evangelical Mennonite Conference Archives (hereafter EMCA).

30 Fast, 'Kleine Gemeinde,' 137–8.

31 Ibid.

32 Others attended revival meetings in outlying areas; Helen Reimer Bartel notes that she and several others 'accepted Christ as a non-Mennonite revival meeting, at the Church of God in Satanta, Kansas.' Interview with Helen Reimer Bartel.

33 Friesen, 'Mennonite Community,' 25; *MGP*, 11 March 1948; 21 March 1948; 29 July 1954.

34 For a history of the EMB see Redekop, *Leaving Anabaptism*.

35 Friesen, 'Mennonite Community,' 15.

36 Ibid., 16.

37 O.J. Wall, ed. and trans., *A Concise Record of Our Evangelical Mennonite Brethren Annual Conference Reports, 1889–1979* (Frazer, MT, 1979), 34–5. George Schultz, 'Autobiography, 1880–1950,' Beatrice Schultz, Monterey, CA, 2. Friesen, 'Mennonite Community,' 23, notes that the Meade EMB had annual revival meetings during the 1940s.

38 Its roots lay in the Oklahoma Bible Institute of Meno, several hours from Meade.

39 Rempel, 'Evangelical Mennonite Brethren,' 61, notes that in 1947 the EMB conference 'recommended that the Grace Bible Institute in Omaha, Nebraska be recognized an approved school.'

40 In 1947 after a productive farm year, the Meade EMB donated over $9000 to mission work. Walter Friesen notes that in 1948 the EMB collected $8000 for relief. Wall, *Concise Record*, 37; Friesen, 'Mennonite Community,' 23.

41 Four sermons were preached: 'The Rapture of the Church' by George P. Schultz, 'The Tribulation Period' by John R. Dick, the 'Eternal State of the Wicked' by George S. Rempel, and 'The Eternal State of the Saved' by Henry P. Fast. Wall, *Concise Record*, 31.

42 Rempel, 'Evangelical Mennonite Brethren,' 117.

43 Friesen, 'Mennonite Community,' 41.

44 Classen, 'Kleine Gemeinde,' 27.

45 Fast, 'Kleine Gemeinde,' 133; interview with Ben Rempel, Dallas, OR, July 1992.

46 Classen, 'Kleine Gemeinde,' 28.

47 Bishop Isaac had allowed or invited preaching from John Enns and Isaac Penner from a more progressive church in Inman, Kansas, and even reported on their message of 'come to me all you who are heavy burdened and I will give you rest.' *Familienfreund*, Sept. 1937; Classen, 'Kleine Gemeinde,' 29; Helen Reimer Bartel. He is also reported to have preached extemporaneously in the fashion of more evangelistic preachers, and not in 'two hour' written sermons as some residents later noted. Interview with Ben Classen.

48 *Familienfreund*, Oct. 1937.

49 Classen, 'Kleine Gemeinde,' 29.

50 Ibid., 30. For a much more thoroughly researched account of these events see Merle Loewen, 'Aeltester Jacob F. Isaac, 1883–1970,' *Preservings* 25 (2006).

51 Margaret J. Loewen, diary, 31 January 1943 (note provided by Merle Loewen, Goshen, IN, personal correspondence to author, May 2004).

52 Classen, 'Kleine Gemeinde'; ibid.

53 'Reasons for and Organizing of the Emmanuel Mennonite Church,' unpublished document, 20 March 1944, Emmanuel Mennonite Church Office, Meade, KS.

54 'Minutes of the Membership Meetings,' Feb. 1944, Emmanuel Mennonite Church, Meade, KS.

55 The speakers brought in were no strangers, they were from other EMB churches and included A.T. Doerksen from Steinbach, Manitoba, and H.P. Fast from Orients, Oklahoma.

56 Emmanuel Mennonite Church, 'Anniversary of the Emmanuel Mennonite Church, Meade County, Kansas, 1944–1974,' n.p.

57 Indicating the depth of the feelings for reform is the fact that one of the five was H.F. Isaac, a brother to the bishop, I.W. Loewen, a respected community leader and a major land owner, P.L. Classen, a preacher in the Kleine Gemeinde, and Geo. J. Rempel, a deacon in the Kleine Gemeinde. The other member was Henry L. Classen.

58 Minutes of the Membership Meetings, 15 May 1944.

59 Henceforth religion had less to say about consumerism, marriage patterns, lifestyle, and political power within the community: it would become personalized. For another example of this transition see William Westfall, *Two Worlds: The Protestant Culture of Nineteenth-Century Ontario* (Montreal: McGill-Queen's University Press, 1989), 16.

60 Minutes of the Membership Meetings, 8 April 1945; 31 December 1946; Friesen, 'Mennonite Community,' 35. Friesen notes in 1957 that the 'practice' of anyone visiting 'a neighbor or fellow church member ... without invitation ... has become less common in recent years,' although 'it is still acceptable.'

61 Minutes of the Membership Meetings, 25 August 1944; Emanuel Mennonite, 'Anniversary,' n.p.

62 Minutes of the Membership Meetings, 29 July 1947; 3 Sept. 1947; 4 Nov. 1947.

63 Friesen, 'Mennonite Community,' 27. The Emmanuel church purchased a piano in 1950, but only after a vote in which only half of the members (thirty-seven for, thirty against, three undecided, four abstentions) indicated support for it. Church Minutes, 15 November 1949. The German language died out slowly: by 1951 one service a month still included a German sermon. Interview with Sam Epp; Classen, 'Kleine Gemeinde,' 30.

64 *MGP*, 7 June 1947; 19 June 1947.

65 Ibid., 22 February 1948.

66 Ibid., 23 May 1948.

67 Ibid., 11 April 1948.

68 For examples of these traditions see Peter and Elfrieda Dyck, *Up from the Rubble* (Scottdale, PA: Herald, 1991); Wesley Berg, *From Russia with Music: A Study of the Mennonite Choral Singing Tradition in Canada* (Winnipeg: Hyperion Press, 1985).

69 Minutes of the Membership Meetings, 22 Oct. 1944. In 1946 the church moved to 'support Rev and Mrs Klaas Kroeker, that is the monthly support, on their mission field in Africa.' Ibid., 3 March 1946.

70 Interview with Corny Z. Friesen; *MGP*, 9 Dec. 1954. The fact that he had

sold 5000 mills did not discourage him; he invested thousands of dollars and was said to have 'led' 1000 Americans to the Lord.

71 The knowledge of German was still a measure of distinctiveness for the Mennonites: one observation from 1957 was that '"Low" German ... is still quite universally spoken by the Meade people, including many of the young people.' Friesen, 'Mennonite Community,' 21.

72 *Familienfreund*, Nov. 1945.

73 Minutes of the Membership Meetings, 24 July 1956.

74 Ibid., 11 Nov. 1958. Ministers who visited the Emmanuel church during the first ten years of its existence recalled that although the church was evangelistic, 'mission-mindedness was slow in coming.' Interview with Rev Ben D. Reimer, Steinbach, MB, 22 May 1992; others recalled that the older people, although they 'loved the Lord ... found it difficult to use [evangelistic] terms.' Interview with Rev Sam Epp, June 1992.

75 Rempel, 'Evangelical Mennonite Brethren,' 68.

76 *MGP*, Sept. 1947.

77 For the policies of Cliff Hope see James L. Forsythe, 'Cliff Hope of Kansas: Practical Congressman and Agrarian Idealist,' *Agricultural History* 2 (1977): 406–20.

78 Friesen, 'Mennonite Community,' 37. Electoral analysis of Logan and Sandcreek Townships, the only townships in which Mennonites held a majority, indicates that their leanings followed county-wide leanings except that they were more predictably Republican than were other county residents; on the combined vote for senator, congressman, and governor, the Republican vote in Logan and Sandcreek townships was 70.67 percent of the 300 votes cast, compared to 60.49 percent of the 3745 votes cast for the three offices in the wider county. *MGP*, 4 Nov. 1954.

79 Interview with Pete and Delores Loewen, and Arnold and Helen Reimer, Meade, July 1992.

80 Quoted in Friesen, 'Mennonite Community,' 30.

81 Ibid., 31.

82 Ibid., 29.

83 Ibid., 31.

84 Ibid., 43.

85 In 1954 only one of twenty-eight Meade Public High School graduates, Jimmie Friesen, had a traditional Mennonite family name; only one of the forty-one-person Meade High football team, Marvin Cornelsen, held a Mennonite family name. *MGP*, 13 May 1954; 21 Oct. 1954.

86 Emmanuel Mennonite, 'Anniversary,' n.p.; interview with Pete Loewen, et al.

87 Friesen, 'Mennonite Community,' 57, 59, 134. There was also a clear 'prefer[ence for] instructors with a Mennonite background.'
88 Ibid., 45.
89 Ibid., 46, 69, 86, 87.
90 Ibid., 88.
91 Ibid., 54.
92 Ibid., 78.
93 Ibid., 67.
94 *MBA Progress*, Feb. 1959.
95 *MGP*, 13 May 1954.
96 Friesen, 'Mennonite Community,' 36.
97 Friesen, 'Mennonite Community,' 36, 60, 61, 65, 83. The only exception to interacting in the public sphere was made for music competitions, where MBA student performances were said to have been 'very commendable.' Ibid., 60.
98 Ibid., 111, 46.
99 Ibid., 64.
100 Ibid., 100.
101 Ibid., 98. In 1965 there were thirteen members of the Emmanuel Church at Tabor College and Grace College, five at trade and nursing schools, none at a university. Indicating the strength too of Mennonite networks was the fact that although 89 percent of the MBA youth indicated in 1957 that they would 'date or marry a non-Mennonite Christian' it is revealing that according to county histories that relatively few had. Ibid., 66.
102 Emmanuel Mennonite, 'Anniversary'; Minutes of the Membership Meetings, 6 May 1963. The decision was taken after a vote of thirty-three to twenty to build the needed church building in the 'city.' 'When they built they saw the future with people living in town.' Herman Rempel, interview.
103 Meade County, *Pioneer Stories*, 37ff.
104 *Emmanuel Mennonite Church Yearbook*, 1965, 8: $4447 to foreign missions, $1973 to Meade Bible Academy, $1271 to Mennonite Central Committee.
105 *Emmanuel Mennonite Church Yearbook*, 1965, 24–5.
106 Emmanuel Mennonite, 'Anniversary,' n.p.
107 'Constitution and Handbook,' Emmanuel Mennonite Church, Meade, KS, ca 1950; 'Constitution and Manual,' Emmanuel Mennonite Church, Meade, KS, ca 1975.
108 *U.S. Census*, 1970, Kansas, Table 119. A total of 533 of 1674 adult men were veterans; this compares to 2737 of 8612 in McPherson County and 1168 of

4877 in Marion County, two counties in Central Kansas with sizeable Mennonite populations.

109 Rempel, 'Evangelical Mennonite Brethren,' 93–4.

110 *MGP*, 19 April 1954.

111 'Constitution and Manual,' 1975. In 1966 the Emmanuel church moved for the last time to excommunicate a member for joining the military (the navy) and chastise the parents for their son's action. In 1976 a member joined the marines without recrimination. Interview with Marten and Helen Bartel, July 1992; interview with Ruth Bartel, July 1997.

112 In 1975 both churches had Mennonite Disaster Service committees and despite the fact that the EMB officially severed its ties to the Mennonite Central Committee (MCC) in 1969 it, as did the Emmanuel church, supported MCC's meat canning projects, in which a mobile meat canning unit visited the county and took donations of meat for distribution among the urban poor.

113 'Constitution and Manual,' ca 1975.

114 *Emmanuel Mennonite Church Yearbook*, 1966, 1967, 1968. The others attended a Missionary Church, a Gospel of Grace Church, a Friends Church, a Bible Church.

115 *Our Church* (Yearbook), Evangelical Mennonite Brethren, Meade County, 1976, 14–15.

5. Beyond Shunning: Reconfiguring the Old Manitoba Bruderschaft

1 Most Mennonite churches of Dutch/North German-descent practiced Bruderschaft in some fashion, although some denominations called it a *Gemeindestunde*, a congregational hour, and others employed the innocuous English term membership meeting. In some churches the meeting was held at least monthly, in others when the bishop called it, and in some instances only annually. In some churches financial and spiritual concerns were delegated to separate meetings, a *Wirtschaftlicher* and an *Innerliche* Bruderschaft; most churches saw little difference in these designations. In some progressive churches it was a meeting to debate ecclesiastical policy and approve annual church budgets. In some churches both men and women attended, in most it was a meeting only for male members. The Bruderschaft was linked to two other types of church meetings. It was usually preceded by a *Dieneramt*, a meeting of the elders, ministers, and deacons, who often created the agenda for the upcoming Bruderschaft. An assembly of all members, men and women,

occurred only twice a year in preparation for the semi-annual communion service; this was the *Geschwesterversamlung* and it was called to make sure that all members had the opportunity to make amends for any wrongdoing prior to the communion and to ensure that the congregation was in a state of general harmony.

2 A history of Mennonite Brethren women notes that it was at the Bruderschaft that women officially were silenced. See Gloria Neufeld Redekop, *The Work of Their Hands: Mennonite Women's Societies in Canada* (Waterloo, ON: Wilfrid Laurier University Press, 1996). See also Regehr, *Mennonites in Canada*, where Bruderschaft is the site of raucous wars pitting progressive urban Mennonites against a conservative rural folk.

3 But the very closed nature of these records also meant that they were records of intense and personal debate, heartfelt anguish, communitarian forthrightness. Certainly they were records of churches that were out of step with the general trend that saw urbanized Mennonite churches develop public programs that were evangelistic or socially progressive. Ironically, as the churches became more evangelistic their records took on a more formal format, often obscuring the nature of the debates. Over time the churches became open to the study of their records by historians. The Bruderschaft minutes of the Manitoba churches for the period from 1930 to about 1970 are housed in the Evangelical Mennonite Conference Archives in Steinbach, Manitoba.

4 Patrick Friesen, *The Shunning* (Winnipeg: Turnstone, 1980), 22 and 68; for a similarly negative view of the Bruderschaft see Rudy Wiebe, *Peace Shall Destroy Many* (Toronto: McClelland and Stewart, 1962).

5 Barth, *Balinese Worlds*, 5.

6 *Kleine Gemeinde Allgemeine Bruderschaft Protokullbuch* (hereafter *Bruderschaft*), 4 July 1934, Evangelical Mennonite Conference Archives (hereafter EMCA), Steinbach, MB.

7 *Bruderschaft*, 3 Feb. 1935; 10 Feb. 1934; *Kleine Gemeinde Dienersitzung Protokullbuch* (hereafter *Dienersitzung*), EMCA, 1 Aug. 1938; 3 June 1936; 5 Oct. 1941.

8 *Bruderschaft*, 29 Aug. 1934.

9 *Dienersitzung*, 6 March 1936.

10 *Bruderschaft*, 15 Dec. 1936.

11 Ibid., 17 Oct. 1935.

12 *Familienfreund*, Dec. 1937.

13 *Dienersitzung*, 19 Feb. 1935.

14 Peter J.B. Reimer and David P. Reimer, *The Sesquicentennial Jubilee: Evangelical Mennonite Conference* (Steinbach, MB: Evangelical Mennonite

Conference, 1962), 32; *Bruderschaft*, 30 Aug. 1934. The reason for this was simple: the ingrained religious meaning of this service for Mennonites was found in its German name, *Einigkeit*, that is, 'unity,' and attendance at such services for Mennonites was an act of conformity to church practice.

15 *Bruderschaft*, 28 May 1935; 21 July 1935.

16 Ibid., 27 April 1941; 2 June 1941; 17 Jan. 1941.

17 *Dienersitzung*, 1 Oct. 1941; 23 Feb. 1942.

18 *Bruderschaft*, 28 Sept. 1945

19 Ibid., 7 Sept. 1936; 7 Dec. 1936; 7 Oct. 1940; 23 Oct. 1941; 23 Feb. 1942. Early in the war the idea arose that given the different social contexts of the church split into separate church districts. The proposal was first made on 3 February 1941, and then raised again in October 1945 with the added urgency that 'we see it as timely to begin organizing our church here in districts and that we do the same at a minister election in Prairie Rose.'

20 John K. Reimer, *Cornelius R. Reimer, 1902–1959* (Belize, CA: n.p., n.d.).

21 *Steinbach Bruderschaft Protokullbuch* (hereafter *Steinbach Bruderschaft*).

22 Ibid., 28 Dec. 1945.

23 Ibid.

24 *Mennonite Encyclopedia*, 1955, vol. 3, 'Mexico.' By 1950 there were a total of 16,000 Canadian-descendent Mennonites in Mexico, 12,000 in Chihuahua, 3000 in Durango, and 1000 elsewhere.

25 *Familienfreund*, 17 Dec. 1948. Early in 1948 the deal was closed and mapping of the Hacienda had commenced, laying out six villages and superimposing the square grid system that Mennonites had learned to love in Canada. By the end of 1948 half of the eighty-five families had migrated and there were optimistic reports of good oat crops and garden yields of tomatoes, plums, and apples. During 1949 two schoolhouses and a church were constructed and the church leadership and traditional doctrinal statements were reaffirmed. *Familienfreund*, 25 March 1949. For a thorough pictorial history see Arden M. Dueck, Myron P. Loewen, Leslie L. Plett, and Eddy K. Plett, *Quellen Kolonie* (Torreon, Coahuila, Mexico: Impresora Colorama, 1998).

26 *Familienfreund*, 3 Dec. 1948.

27 Ibid., 11 Feb. 1949; 25 Feb. 1949.

28 Ibid., Feb. 1949.

29 Ibid., 6 May 1949.

30 Ibid., 25 March 1959. Soon reports followed that upon reorganizing in Mexico the church had 'reaffirmed,' along with elected ministers and the

concept of a unified Gemeinde, the old 'Twenty Articles' document that
the Canadian church had begun changing. To underscore the value of
unity the elderly bishop, Peter P. Reimer, noted that 'unity' would occur
by 'brothers giving their united answer quite simply with writing a "yes"'
to the question. To underscore a refounding of old ways, however, members were asked to reaffirm old teachings on lifestyle, the 'right order'that
the church of God had practised 'from the time of Christ.' Raising this
affirmation to a serious level it was also decided that 'to establish who is a
member of the church and freely wants to be, it was ... always, "do you
wish to hold to these guidelines?"'

31 Ibid., 7 Oct. 1949.
32 Ibid., 1 July 1949.
33 Ibid., 24 Sept. 1948.
34 Interview with Dietrich P. Loewen, Blumenort, MB, June 1996.
35 C.B. Loewen, *I Remember: Riverside and the Regions Beyond* (Morris, MB,
    1995), 138.
36 Sue Barkman, *Ever-Widening Circles: EMC Missions Silver Jubilee, 1953–1978*
    (Steinbach, MB, 1978), 58.
37 Reimer, *Sesquicentennial*, 109.
38 *Blumenort Bruderschaft Protokoll Buch* (hereafter *Blumenort Bruderschaft*),
    10 August 1950, EMCA; Reimer, *Sesquicentennial*, 109.
39 Ibid.
40 *Blumenort Bruderschaft*, 14 July 1955; *Familienfreund*, 21 Jan. 1955; 'Eine
    Darlegung der Kleingemeinde, Quellenkolonie, Mexico, June 3, 1955,'
    EMCA, Box 96.
41 Reimer, *Sesquicentennial*, 100.
42 For a first-hand experience at the Tabernacle see Al Reimer, 'Coming in
    from the Cold,' in Harry Loewen, ed., *Why I Am a Mennonite* (Scottdale,
    PA: Herald Press, 1988): 254–7.
43 Ralph Friesen, 'The Diary of Peter D. Friesen,' unpublished document,
    courtesy the author.
44 *Steinbach Bruderschaft*, 7 Sept. 1947. Still, during the same year the
    Steinbach leader, Peter D. Friesen, 'spoke about the seriousness of disci-
    pline and shunning and the need for us to do it.' *Steinbach Bruderschaft*, 8
    June 1946.
45 Peter P. Reimer, 'Eine Erafung, February 1946,' EMCA.
46 *Steinbach Bruderschaft*, 10 Sept. 1946.
47 Ibid., 30 April 1948.
48 Ibid., 4 Dec. 1948.
49 Ibid., 16 April 1949.

50 The assembly insisted on a 'dress of old fashion' but was willing to compromise on other wedding practices.
51 The Steinbach EMC was the main church behind the Steinbach Bible
Institute, which in April 1960 drew a total of 1800 people to its school's
graduation in two ceremonies. *CN*, 15 April 1960.
52 Sometimes the ministers were turned away: in September 1958 Archie
Penner visited a couple in Winnipeg, had an 'earnest conversation,' but
found that 'they were no longer oriented to Christianity.' Steinbach Ministerial, 26 Sept. 1958; 5 Feb. 1952; 10 Feb. 1947.
53 It announced as early as 1946 that English worship services would be held
from time to time, and decided by 1965 to restricting German to a special
'service during Sunday School.' *Carillon*, 17 Oct. 1946; Steinbach Ministerial, 20 Dec. 1965. In 1952 when the church purchased the piano, it raised
such opposition from rural churches that the town church wondered
'how can we work in the conference with blessing.' Steinbach Ministerial,
23 June 1953. In 1964 when local businessman Ben L. Reimer asked for
permission to place an organ in the church for his daughter's wedding,
the ministers voiced no objection and sent the matter on to the 'brethren.'
Steinbach Ministerial, 18 March 1964. Just a year later the church began
seriously discussing the purchase of an organ for between $4300 and
$7300. Steinbach Ministerial, 18 May 1965.
54 The Steinbach church also continued violating the wishes of the conservative sections of the Kleine Gemeinde. In March 1945 the church deliber-
ately joined a town-based program to encourage ministers from other
Mennonite denominations to preach, noting in the brotherhood minutes
that 'Sunday morning, the 18th of March was the first time that in our
church here in Steinbach, preachers from among the other Mennonite
churches, held morning worship services.' *Steinbach Bruderschaft*, 3 Feb.
1945. It was a particularly significant move as one of the ministers, Rev.
Isaac P. Friesen, was a progressive General Conference Mennonite based
in Winnipeg; it was significant, too, because just three days later when two
Ruednerweider Mennonite ministers from the West Reserve 100 miles to
the west visited Steinbach, the leader, Peter D. Friesen, invited the men
to preach for two nights beginning that night and 'hurriedly telephoned
to make it known.' *Steinbach Bruderschaft*, 18 March 1945. The Mexican
Mennonites strenuously objected to this interchurch practice. Yet their
migration opened the door in Manitoba to a decade-long association with
any travelling ministers, so long as they were 'evangelistic.' Some examples are Rev Schmidt from the Leper's Mission in May 1956, the 'Janz
Team' in May 1955, and the Mennonite [Radio] Hour Quartet with pastor

in June 1958. By 1958 when the church planned its revival meeting for the next year, Pastor Archie Penner warned that 'if we want an evangelist for next spring ... it is time we should look after this now,' and suggested three names, one each from Colorado, Ontario, and Minnesota. Steinbach Ministerial, 20 June 1958. In 1965 when a group of Pentecostal revivalists came to town to hold their emotional healing meetings in a tent on the edge of town, the ministers raised a concern about the 'many fakes in their healing,' but agreed 'as long as Christ is preached' they could pray for the meetings. Steinbach Ministerial, 19 July 1969.

55 Correspondence from Ralph Friesen, January 2004; Al Reimer, 'Revival,' *Journal of Mennonite Studies* 16 (1998): 203–13.

56 Among visits from Mennonite ministers were the March 1953 visits from Harold S. Bender from Goshen, Indiana, and a Rev Graber.

57 Harder, *Steinbach*, 41–2. Conversely, the Steinbach EMC's competitors, the Emmanuel Free Church and the Mennonite Brethren, grew by only 26 percent and 6 percent respectively during these years. A constant barrage of new programs was discussed: summer vacation Bible school in 1955, 'dedication services' for infants in 1955, a 'Coffee House' in 1970. Its leadership in Sunday school conventions, Bible schools, summer camps for children, and senior citizens' homes was second to none. In 1960 the new 'Invalid Home,' the Sunset Home, was built across the street from the EMC, a $160,000 building that the local newspaper described as possessing 'almost unbelievable, long, spotless corridors stretch[ing] out in either wing.' *CN*, 27 May 1960. And it was the church that in 1965 created a scientific division of powers by which it graphed lines of authority and responsibility and specific job descriptions for the ministerial, the Pulpit Committee, the Spiritual Concerns Committee, the Trustee Committee, and the Church board. The EMC presented itself competitively as a visible, community-based church, in 1956 with a special 'letterhead,' and in 1965 with 'visitor cards.' Steinbach Ministerial, 20 Jan. 1956; 28 April 1965.

58 Steinbach Ministerial, 19 June 1957; 12 Jan. 1957; 20 June 1958.

59 Ibid., 16 June 1958; 20 Dec. 1965.

60 Ibid., 24 Jan. 1958.

61 Ibid., 26 May 1964. The church insisted that the exchange of rings not be part of the ceremony, but by 1965 it relented here as well; those practising such ceremonies should receive 'wise counseling towards God's will, rather than [the] strict letter of the law.'

62 Ibid., 4 March 1957; 26 Oct. 1954.

63 Ibid., 18 March 1964.

64 Archie Penner, *The Christian, the State and the New Testament* (Altona, MB: D.W. Friesen and Sons, 1959), 122.

65 Steinbach Ministerial, 14 Nov. 1963.

66 Ibid., 6 Jan. 1965. In 1958, the year after radio CFAM went on air, the church announced that 'a radio broadcast from our church is to be brought again.' Steinbach Ministerial, 20 Sept. 1958.

6. The Rise and Fall of the Cheerful Homemaker: Womanhood in Kansas

1 A version of this chapter has appeared earlier as Royden Loewen, 'Household, Coffee Klatsch and Office: The Evolving Worlds of Mid-Twentieth Century Mennonite Women,' in Kimberly D. Schmidt, Dianne Zimmerman Umble, and Steven D. Reschly, eds., *Strangers at Home: Amish and Mennonite Women in History* (Baltimore: Johns Hopkins University Press, 2002), 259–83. A number of chapters in that volume are relevant to this chapter: Beth E. Grabyill, '"To Remind Us of Who We Are": Multiple Meanings of Conservative Women's Dress,' 53–77; Katherine Jellison, 'The Chosen Women: The Amish and the New Deal,' 102–20; Marlene Epp, 'Weak Families in the Green Hell of Paraguay,' 136–59; Steven D. Reschly, '"The Parents Shall Not Go Unpunished": Preservationist Patriarchy and Community,' 160–81; Kimberly D. Schmidt, 'Schism: Where Women's Outside Work and Insider Dress Collided,' 208–36; Jane Marie Pederson, '"She May Be Amish Now, but She Won't Be Amish Long": Anabaptist Women and Antimodernism,' 339–63.

2 Helena Doerksen Reimer, 'Tagebuch, 1949,' George D. Reimer, Meade, KS.

3 Beard, *Centennial History*; Meade County, *Pioneer Stories*.

4 For works that examine Mennonite women using textual analysis see Pamela Klassen, *Going to the Moon and the Stars: Stories of Two Russian Mennonite Women* (Waterloo, ON: Wilfrid Laurier University Press, 1994); Marlene Epp, *Women without Men: Mennonite Refugees of the Second World War* (Toronto: University of Toronto Press, 2000).

5 Martine Segalen, *Love and Power in the Peasant Family: Rural France in the Nineteenth Century*, trans. Sarah Matthews (Chicago: University of Chicago Press, 1983), 9.

6 Louise Tilly and Joan Scott, *Women, Work and Family* (New York: Rinehart and Winston, 1978), 54; Pederson, *Between Memory and Reality* 159; Deborah Fink, *Agrarian Women: Wives and Mothers in Rural Nebraska, 1880–1940* (Chapel Hill: University of North Carolina Press, 1992); Sally McMurry, *Transforming Rural Life: Dairying Families and Agricultural Change, 1820–1885* (Baltimore: Johns Hopkins University Press, 1995); Jane H.

Adams, 'The Decoupling of Farm and Household: Differential Consequences of Capitalist Development on Southern Illinois and Third World Family Farms,' *Comparative Studies of Society and History* 30 (1988): 453–82; Neth, *Preserving the Family Farm*. See Royden Loewen, 'Potato Patch in the Cornfield: The Worlds of Mennonite Immigrant Women, 1881–1906,' in *Hidden Worlds*, 51–68; 'Farm Women and Town Ladies,' in Loewen, *Family, Church and Market*, 218–36; '"The Children, the Cows, and My Dear Man," The Transplanted Lives of Mennonite Farm Women, 1874–1900,' *Canadian Historical Review* 73 (1992): 344–73.

7 Veronica Strong-Boag, '"Pulling in Double Harness or Hauling a Double Load": Women, Work and Feminism,' *Journal of Canadian Studies* 21 (1986): 32–52; Fink, *Agrarian Women*, 10.

8 See Jellison, *Entitled to Power*.

9 Personal correspondence from Pamela Riney Kehrburg, Iowa State University, 13 January 2004. See also Pamela Riney-Kehrberg, ed., *Waiting on the Bounty: The Dust Bowl Diary of Mary Knackstedt Dyck* (Iowa City: University of Iowa Press, 1999).

10 For other studies of western Kansas Mennonite farm women of this time see Riney-Kehrberg, *Waiting on the Bounty*, and Jellison, *Entitled to Power*. Jellison (37) writes that 'Mennonite women in Haskell County, Kansas, were excluded from mainstream rural society by their unique religious customs, their German language, and their families' reliance on traditional, labor-intensive farming methods.' In the latter respect, as indicated in chapter 2, above, Meade County Mennonites seem to have differed from the Haskell County Mennonites.

11 Reimer, Tagebuch; interview with Martin and Helena Bartel, Meade, KS, July 1992.

12 Klaas Reimer, Account book, 1950, Helena Reimer Bartel, Meade, KS.

13 Reimer, Tagebuch, 19 May 1949; 29 March; 24 April.

14 See Royden Loewen, 'If Joints Heir of Grace, How Much More in Temporal Goods? Inheritance and Community Formation,' in Loewen, *Hidden Worlds*; 'The Mennonites of Waterloo, Ontario and Hanover, Manitoba, 1890s: A Study in Household and Community,' *Canadian Papers in Rural History* 9 (1993): 187–209.

15 Interview with Dr. Menno Friesen, Goshen, IN, May 1995.

16 Interview with Helena Reimer Bartel. The Reimer diary indicates that the children also received equal gifts of livestock, such as on 30 November 1949 when the two married children, twenty-six-year-old Heinrich and twenty-five-year-old Helena, joined by their spouses, visited their parents to 'each get themselves a fresh heifer.' A third source indicates that 'father

financed his children's efforts to farm and each child got an equal share of land at one point in the early fifties; father kept back 240 acres and bought back machinery from the estate sale.' Interview with Al Isaac, Hillsboro, KS, July 1992.

17 *Meade Globe Press* (hereafter *MGP*), 13 April 1959.

18 Meade County Tax Rolls, Meade County Court House, Meade, KS.

19 Tagebuch; *CN*, 11 June 1948. Board of Agriculture Population Schedule for 1950 indicates another spinster household, that of Helena H. Reimer, age sixty-five, who owned 70 acres of land in 1950, five cows, two head of cattle, one hundred and fifty chickens and ten peach trees.

20 Beard, *Centennial History*, 112; Meade County, *Pioneer Stories*, 108.

21 Interview with Corny Z. Friesen, Meade, KS, July 1992. The official family history offers a different sequence, one that suggests that one of the brothers moved to the farm owned by his wife's parents and that 'one year later [he] bought the farm from her parents.' Siemens, *J.R. Friesen*, n.p.

22 Sonya Salamon, 'Land Ownership and Women's Power in a Midwestern Farming Community,' *Journal of Marriage and the Family* 41 (1979): 109–79; Ernestine Friedl, 'The Position of Women: Appearance and Reality,' *Anthropological Quarterly* 40 (1967): 97–108.

23 Beard, *Centennial History*, 152.

24 Kansas Board of Agriculture, Population Schedule, 1937, 1950, 1961, 1976, Kansas State Historical Society, Topeka, KS.

25 *MGP*, 17 October 1963.

26 For statistics indicating this trend see Board of Agriculture, 1950; 1961; 1976. For a fuller description of mid-century farm women adopting 'urban' consumption patterns see Jellison, *Entitled to Power*, 149–80.

27 Meade County, *Pioneer Stories*, 188.

28 Beard, *Centennial History*, 83.

29 Elda Plank, 'Twas Home on the Range: A Story of the Henry A. Friesen Family (Lancaster, PA: self-published, 1981), 40, 44.

30 Ibid., 44.

31 Menno M. Friesen, 'How He Works and What Happens if He Doesn't: A Look at Mid-Life Crisis,' in Calvin Redekop and Urie Bender, eds., *Who Am I? What Am I?: Searching for Meaning in Your Work* (Grand Rapids, MI: Academie Books, 1988), 202–13.

32 Plank, 'Twas Home on the Range.

33 *MGP*, 17 July 1947.

34 Ibid., 12 May 1960.

35 Ibid., 4 March 1954.

36 Demographic surveys between 1935 and 1950 were not available for this

study, but a genealogical study of two extended Meade families – Abraham H. Friesen (1878–1927) and Cornelius J. Classen (1863–1931) – suggests falling birth rates in the 1930s and 1940s. Records of ten families married between 1912 and 1928 reveals an average of 9.1 children; however, twenty-seven of these children who married between 1935 and 1945 had only an average of 3.6 children themselves, while thirty-one of these children who married between 1946 and 1956 had an average of 3.1 children. Plank, 'Twas Home; Siemens, J.R. Friesen.

37 Board of Agriculture.
38 Donald H. Parkerson and Jo Ann Parkerson, '"Fewer Children of Greater Spiritual Quality": Religion and the Decline of Fertility in Nineteenth-Century America,' Social Science History 12 (1988): 49–70.
39 Emmanuel Mennonite Church Membership Minutes, 1944, Emmanuel Mennonite Church, Meade, KS.
40 Ibid., 8 March 1955; 'Constitution and Manual,' ca 1975, Emmanuel Mennonite Church.
41 MGP, 3 June 1948.
42 Ibid., 10 June 1954. There were new definitions of the ideal mother. Obituaries in the 1930s had described a woman's relationship to children as a natural duty over which little agency was exercised: when Katherina Ratzlaff Friesen died in December 1938 it was noted that 'of [her first] marriage 10 children were born' and after her second marriage she 'took on motherly duties of [an additional] six daughters and two sons.' Familienfreund, June 1939, 8. However, when Marie Classen Reimer died in 1959 there was a somewhat different tone to the obituary: she was described 'as mother of the home who gave herself unreservedly to seeing after the welfare of the home, physically and also spiritually, having the salvation of her children at heart.' CN, 6 August 1959.
43 Familienfreund, June 1939; 8; MGP, 6 Aug. 1959.
44 Thomas Laqueur, Making Sex: Body and Gender from the Greeks to Freud (Cambridge, MA: Harvard University Press, 1990).
45 MGP, 11 July 1957.
46 Neth, Preserving the Family Farm; Jellison, Entitled to Power.
47 Beard, Centennial History, 57 and 58.
48 MGP, 14 February 1957.
49 For a study that identifies a similar process among rural women in Iowa see Jennifer Ellen Barker, 'Working for Farm and Home: The Iowa Farm Bureau Federation Women's Committee, 1921–1974,' MA thesis, Iowa State University, 2003.
50 Beard, Centennial History, 57.

51 *MGP*, 14 February 1957.

52 'Constitution and Handbook,' ca 1950, 11.

53 Siemens, *J.R. Friesen.*, n.p.

54 Emmanuel Mennonite Church, *Yearbook*, 1965; 1966.

55 Letter to author from Bertha Classen Johnson, August 1994.

56 Interview with Helen Loewen Reimer, Meade, KS, July 1992. Other accounts trace this development: Margaret Isaac Friesen went to nurses training against her mother's wish and but later her mother was said to have been proud of her; Helen Reimer Bartel wanted to attend nurses' training but father said 'no,' for which he later was sorry. Interviews, July 1992.

57 Friesen, 'Mennonite Community,' 51.

58 In April 1954 Agnes Classen was hired as fifth grade teacher; Mr Richard Enns was hired as sixth grade teacher. *MGP*, 12 April 1954.

59 See: Friesen, 'Mennonite Community,' 68.

60 Beard, *Centennial History*, 136.

61 The Centennial History of Meade notes that while eighteen women founded the Cheerful Homemakers Club in 1952, the club had only nine members in 1985; the Live 'n Learn club had similarly declined in membership from twenty-one to fourteen in 1984. Beard, *Centennial History*, 57–8.

62 Tilly and Scott, *Women, Work and Family*, 229.

63 Shover, *Last Majority*, 158.

64 These figures may not reflect the rise in actual numbers of women working, as the actual number of male employees dropped from 2012 in 1940 to 1272 in 1970, reflecting a general trend of rural depopulation throughout the United States. These figures are almost identical to the central Kansas county of MacPherson where 13.4 percent of the work force was female in 1940 and 29.1 percent in 1960. *U.S. Census*, 1960, 'Characteristics of the Population,' Kansas, Table 83, 18-244; 1970, table 121, 18-381.

65 Ibid., 1960, Table 36, 18-167; 1970, Table 121, 18-381.

66 Beard, *Centennial History*, 137.

67 Board of Agriculture statistics reveal that the average Mennonite farm in 1975 operated 249.5 acres.

68 Interview with Marten and Helen Bartel, July 1992.

69 See Beard, *Centennial History*, 83, 97, 137, 143, and Siemens, *J.R. Friesen*, n.p., for experiences of other women of small farms. At least one exception to this pattern is Dan Loewen, who raised 700 acres of wheat in 1975 and whose wife Vesta began teaching in about 1958. Beard, *Centennial History*, 123.

70 Ibid., 112, 137.
71 Ibid., 108, 139.
72 Ibid., 153, 108.
73 Ibid., 118.
74 This figure is derived from comparing the number of Mennonite families in the Board of Agriculture, Population Schedule, 1961, with the number of Mennonite households listed as living in Meade according to the *Southwestern Bell Telephone Directory*.
75 Interview with Helena Reimer Bartel.
76 Beard, *Centennial History*, 56, 58, 62.
77 Ibid., 136 and 138.
78 For a similar observation for farm women finding paid labor in towns see Jellison, *Entitled to Power*, 170.
79 Tilly and Scott, *Women, Work and Family*.
80 *MGP*, 25 February 1960.
81 *MBA Progress Report*, February 1959, 2.
82 *MGP*, 28 March 1948.
83 Friesen, 'How He Works.'
84 For similar conclusions see Veronica Strong-Boag, 'Home Dreams: Women and the Suburban Experiment in Canada, 1945–60,' *Canadian Historical Review* 72 (1991): 471–504; Caitlin Flanagan, 'Housewife Confidential: A Tribute to the Old-Fashioned Housewife, and to Erma Bombeck, Her Champion and Guide,' *Atlantic Monthly*, September 2003, 141–50.

7. Poultrymen, Car Dealers, and Football Stars: Masculinities in Manitoba

1 Joan Wallach Scott, *Gender and Politics in History* (New York: Columbia University Press, 1988), 29.
2 See Kathryn McPherson, Cecilia Morgan, and Nancy M. Forestell, eds., *Gendered Pasts: Historical Essays in Femininity and Masculinity in Canada* (Toronto: Oxford University Press, 1999).
3 Daniel Coleman, *Masculine Migrations: Reading the Postcolonial Male in New Canadian Narratives* (Toronto: University of Toronto Press, 1998); E. Anthony Rotundo, *American Manhood: Transformation in Masculinity from the Revolution to the Modern Era* (New York: Basic Books, 1993); Robert A. Nye, *Masculinity and Male Codes of Honor in Modern France* (New York: Oxford University Press, 1993); Michael Roper and John Tosh, eds., *Manful Assertions: Masculinities in Britain Since 1800* (New York: Routledge, 1991).
4 Joy Parr, *Gender of Breadwinners: Women, Men and Change in Two Industrial*

Towns, 1880–1950 (Toronto: University of Toronto Press, 1999), 141, 155.

5 *Carillon News* (hereafter *CN*), 31 May 1957.
6 See for example Helmut Harder, *David Toews Was Here, 1870–1947* (Winnipeg: CMBC Publications, 2002); Ester Epp Thiessen, *J.J. Thiessen: A Leader for His Time* (Winnipeg: CMBC Publications, 2001); Albert N. Keim, *Harold S. Bender, 1897–1962* (Scottdale, PA: Herald Press, 1998).
7 Marlene Epp, 'Heroes or Yellow Bellies? Masculinity and the Conscientious Objector,' *Journal of Mennonite Studies* 17 (1999): 108.
8 John C. Reimer, *Familienregister der Nachkommen von Klaas und Helena Reimer* (Winnipeg: n.p., 1958), 55, 115, 217, 258.
9 *CN*, 30 Sept. 1949; 30 April 1954; 7 June 1954; 3 Feb. 1957; 8 Jan. 1960.
10 Ibid., 14 March 1946.
11 Ibid., 3 April 1960: 95 men, but only 10 women worked for C.T. Loewen and Sons; 53 men but only 3 women worked at Barkman Hardware.
12 Ibid., 21 May 1954.
13 Ibid., 19 Aug. 1960.
14 First published in 1954, by 1960 Dyck had become a celebrity with reports of a 'tremendous run on sales of his latest book, *Koop en Bua en Dietschland.*' *CN*, 8 April 1960. Al Reimer, 'Innocents Abroad: The Comic Odyssey of *Koop enn Bua opp Reise,*' *Journal of Mennonite Studies* 4 (1986): 33.
15 For a discussion of this phenomenon in the United States see Jellison, *Entitled to Power*, 157.
16 Jeffrey Taylor, *Fashioning Farmers: Ideological Agricultural Knowledge and the Manitoba Farm Movement, 1890–1925* (Regina: Canadian Plains Research Center, 1994), 68.
17 *CN*, 21 Nov. 1946.
18 Ibid., 19 Dec. 1946.
19 Ibid., 7 Jan. 1949; 2 Dec. 1949.
20 Ibid., 16 Jan. 1947; 19 Aug. 1960; 13 March 1947; 7 Oct. 1955; 23 Oct. 1959.
21 Francis, *In Search of Utopia*, 225.
22 *CN*, 12 Sept. 1954.
23 Ibid., 29 July 1955; 2 Dec. 1949; 18 Feb. 1949; 25 Sept. 1959.
24 Ibid., 5 Dec. 1946; 9 Sept. 1955.
25 Ibid., 26 July 1957. 'The turkey grower in this province is a very discouraged person,' reported the *CN* in 1960, as 'he ... chose to grow too many turkeys basing his production decisions on the relatively high prices he received in 1959.' Ibid., 5 Feb. 1960.
26 Warkentin, *Mennonite Settlement*, 248.
27 *CN*, 1 Feb. 1957.
28 See: Rachel Mills, 'Masculinity, Entrepreneurship and Religion: Lumber-

man C.T. Loewen of Steinbach, Manitoba,' *Journal of Mennonite Studies* 23 (2005): 213–29.

29 *CN*, 4 Nov. 1955; 21 Oct. 1955; 9 Sept. 1955.

30 Warkentin, *Our Heritage*, 108.

31 *CN*, 20 Dec. 1947; 24 Dec. 1954.

32 Ibid., 25 March 1960.

33 Ibid., 20 May 1960.

34 Ibid., 8 Nov. 1957.

35 Ibid., 14 Oct. 1960.

36 Ibid., 9 July 1954.

37 Warkentin, *Our Heritage*, 80.

38 Ibid., 82.

39 *CN*, 19 Dec. 1947.

40 Francis, *In Search of Utopia*, 229.

41 *CN*, 12 Feb. 1960.

42 Miriam Toews, *Swing Low: A Life* (Toronto: Stoddart, 2000), 91.

43 As told to the author by Abe G. Penner, Blumenort, MB.

44 *CN*, 15 Jan. 1957.

45 Ibid., 15 Jan. 1957.

46 Ibid., 8 Jan., 1960.

47 Ibid., 15 Jan. 1957; 5 Feb. 1960; 21 Nov. 1946; 10 Apr. 1970.

48 Wright, *Steinbach*, 113.

49 *CN*, 17 Sept. 1954.

50 Ibid., 27 Sept. 1957.

51 Ibid., 26 Dec. 1957.

52 In time these hunting and fishing stories became popular. In September 1955 a front page story told of 'Mr. C.F. Friesen, also known as CCF, one of Southeastern Manitoba's most ardent anglers (at age 78)' who snagged such a large Jackfish in the local Seine River that he 'fell into the river.' Ibid., 16 Sept. 1955.

53 *Steinbach Post*, 19 Nov. 1924.

54 Reimer, *Sesquicentennial Jubilee*, 33.

55 *CN*, 5 Dec. 1946.

56 Ibid., 16 Jan. 1947; 23 Jan. 1947.

57 Ibid., 6 Feb. 1947.

58 Michael Oriard, *Reading Football: How the Popular Press Created an American Spectacle* (Chapel Hill: University of North Carolina Press, 1993), 191.

59 Rotundo, *American Manhood*, 241.

60 *CN*, 27 Feb. 1947.

61 Ibid., 12 Dec. 46 Youth pastor Lando Hiebert speaking at the eighth annual

Youth Conference in June 1947 began each of his talks with a pitch to 'energy.' He spoke of 'Spirit-Filled Lives,' called the youth to 'Win the Fight,' and in counselling them on personal relations reminded them to 'Fly in Formation.' Ibid., 20 June 1947.

62 Ibid., 20 Nov. 1959.

63 Ibid., 27 Nov. 1959.

64 Ibid., 8 Nov. 1957.

65 Interview with Wilmer Penner, October 1995.

66 *CN*, 8 Nov. 1957.

67 Evangelical Mennonite Church (EMC) Ministerial Meeting Minutes (hereafter EMC Ministerial), 3 April 1958; 6 Feb. 1958, EMCA.

68 *CN*, 1 Nov. 1957.

69 Interview with Wilmer Penner, October 1995.

70 EMC Ministerial, 10 Oct. 1960.

71 Warkentin, *Mennonite Settlement*, 231 and 235.

72 Among scores of loud ads in the 1954 issues of the *CN*, Marvel Ladies Apparel of Steinbach promised that with its 'full bloom revolutionary new flexes bra' it had the answer to 'how skinny girls get curves.' *CN*, 11 June 1954.

73 Ibid., 12 Sept. 1946; Reimer, *Sesquicentennial*, 144–5.

74 *Census of Canada*, 1956, Population, Table 12, 9. In a November 1946 poll at Steinbach Collegiate only one of the twenty-two students planning to attend university was a girl; one-third of the forty-nine girls were planning to become nurses, one-fifth secretaries, another one-fifth were undecided. *CN*, 21 November 1946.

75 Ibid., 9 Dec. 1949; 21 May 1954; 27 May 1960.

76 *Messenger*, 12 June 1964.

77 Ibid., 5 June 1970.

8. Reinventing Mennonite Tradition: Old Ways in the Jungles of British Honduras

1 Kathleen Neils Conzen, David A. Gerber, Ewa Morawska, George E. Pozzetta, and Rudolph J. Vecoli, 'The Invention of Ethnicity: A Perspective from the USA,' *Altreitalie* (1990), 43.

2 Anderson, *Imagined Communities*, 38.

3 See Royden Loewen, *The Making of Ethnic Farm Culture in Western Canada*, Canada's Ethnic Group Series (Ottawa: Canadian Historical Association, 2003).

4 Kelly Hedges, '"Plautdietsch" and "Huuchdietsch" in Chihuahua: Lan-

guage, Literacy, and Identity among the Old Colony Mennonites in Northern Mexico' (PhD diss., Yale University, 1996), 323.

5 Steven D. Reschly, 'Alternative Dreams and Visions: The Amish Repertoire of Community on the Iowa Prairie, 1840–1910' (PhD diss., University of Iowa, 1994). The work was later published as *The Amish on the Iowa Prairie, 1840–1910* (Baltimore: Johns Hopkins University Press, 2000).

6 Conzen, 'Invention of Ethnicity,' 38.

7 Werner Sollors, *The Invention of Ethnicity* (Oxford: Oxford University Press, 1989), xiv.

8 See the *Vorsteher Komitee and Allgemeine Versamlung Protokollbuch* (the minutes of the colony mayor committee and general colony meeting) (hereafter *Versamlung*), Spanish Lookout Colony Administration Office. In particular see, *Versamlung*, 17 Oct. 1966. See also H. Leonard Sawatsky, *They Sought a Country: Mennonite Colonization in Mexico* (Berkeley: University of California Press, 1971); John C. Everitt, 'The Recent Migrations of Belize, Central America,' *International Migration Review* 18, no. 2 (1984): 319–25; 'Mennonites in Belize,' *Journal of Cultural Geography* 3 (1983): 82–93; Paul Martin, 'The Mennonites of Belize,' *National Studies* 1 (1973): 12–13; Thomas A. Minkel, 'Mennonite Colonization in British Honduras,' *Pennsylvania Geographer* 5 (1967): 2–7; Joseph M. Perry, 'Mennonite Agricultural Enclaves and Economic Growth in Belize,' Paper Presented to the Association of American Geographers 88th Annual Meeting, San Diego, CA, 20 April 1992; G.A. St. John Robinson, 'German Migration to Belize: The Beginnings,' *Belizean Studies* 13 (1985): 17–40; Higdon, 'Farm Diversification and Specialization.'

9 Jerry Alan Hall, 'Mennonite Agriculture in a Tropical Environment: An Analysis of the Development and Productivity of a Mid-Latitude Agricultural System in British Honduras' (PhD diss., Clark University, 1970), 80ff, 344.

10 The British Honduras Mennonites, like the 10,000 other Canadian Mennonites who migrated to Mexico and Paraguay, were 'traditional' only in a sense. Over the centuries Mennonites had developed a cultural repertoire of negotiated group migration. Ancestors in Canada, Russia, and Poland engaged in migration as a form religious resistance; when pacifist and sectarian ways seemed threatened, the community attained promises of military exemptions, parochial schools, and block settlement from foreign states whose central demands were that upon immigration, the Mennonites develop a rural economy. This pattern began in Poland after 1550, continued in Russia after 1789, and in Canada after 1874. For a standard history of Mennonites that describes these various migrations see C.J.

Dyck, *An Introduction to Mennonite History* (Scottdale, PA: Herald Press, 1993).

11 Jacob U. Kornelsen, *25 Jahre in Mexico: Beschreibung Von der Quellenkolonie, 1948–1973* (Cuauhtémoc, Mexico: self-published, 1973); interview with Menno Dueck and George Kornelsen, Los Jagueyes, Mexico, July 1997.

12 Regehr, *Mennonites in Canada*, 13–14. Several influential teachers at Steinbach Bible Institute in Steinbach, Manitoba, had attended Goshen College, Goshen, Indiana, where Harold S. Bender was leading a generation of scholars seeking to revitalize sixteenth-century Anabaptist history by asserting its relevance to the issues of the midcentury. One such graduate of Goshen College was Harvey Plett, author of *Seeking to Be Faithful: The Story of the Evangelical Mennonite Conference* (Steinbach, MB: Evangelical Mennonite Conference, 1996); another was Archie Penner, author of *The Christian, the State and the New Testament*.

13 See Royden Loewen, 'Mennonite "Repertoires of Contention": Church Life in Steinbach, Manitoba and Los Jagueyes, Chihuahua, 1945–1970,' *Mennonite Quarterly Review* 72 (1998): 301–19

14 Klaas C. Penner, 'Denkschrift,' 1972, 31, Abram C. Penner, Landmark, MB. See also K.C. Penner, 'Emigration Trip,' in Gerhard S. Koop, *Pioneer Years in Belize* (Belize City: privately printed, 1991), 43.

15 Peter F. Kornelsen, 'Moving to British Honduras,' in Koop, *Pioneer Years*, 28.

16 Sawatzky, *They Sought a Country*, 334–5.

17 John D. Friesen, 'Looking at a New Country,' in Koop, *Pioneer Years*, 21.

18 Ibid., 26.

19 Kornelsen, 'Moving to British Honduras,' 35.

20 Ibid., 36; Letter from Albert and Liesbeth Dueck, Spanish Lookout, to Linda, Ben, and Leona Dueck, Quellen Kolonie, 30 March 1958.

21 Koop, *Pioneer Years*, 38 and 44.

22 Ibid., 37.

23 Ibid., 64.

24 Spanish Lookout Kleine Gemeinde *Bruderschaft Protokullbuch* (hereafter *Bruderschaft*) and Spanish Lookout Kleine Gemeinde *Dienersitzung Protokollbuch* (hereafter *Dienersitzung*), June 1958–July 1959, as read to the author by Bishop Abram K. Reimer, Spanish Lookout, December 1991.

25 *Bruderschaft*, 8 June 1958; *Dienersitzung*, 1 August 1958. Even the song leaders were elected on an interim basis only and were asked to resist sitting on the leaders' platform at the front of the church. This changed in February when hope of all the Mexican song leaders coming to British Honduras ended. *Dienersitzung*, 27 Feb. 1959. On 5 October 1958 Reimer

initiated the baptism of the youth by 'reading' the old, 1632 'articles of faith' and five days later by initiating the old rite of baptizing those youth who had applied for full adulthood and been accepted by the Bruderschaft as morally fit for baptism.

26 *Bruderschaft*, 4 August, 8 Sept., 31 October 1958. The brethren also agreed to re-establish their fire insurance agency with the only caveat being that they should 'keep in mind ... [that] our [wooden] houses are worth more here' than the brick houses back in Mexico.

27 Koop, *Pioneer Years*.

28 See ibid., 125. *Bruderschaft*, 30 Jan. 1959 notes that Gerhard Koop was appointed 'colony secretary' by the Bruderschaft. All Vorsteher Komitee meetings and Allgemeine Versamlungen meetings began with prayer and scripture reading.

29 *Bruderschaft*, 8 Sept. 1958. See also Koop, *Pioneer Years*, 40. By mid-September Johann L. Barkman had been elected to assist Friesen. *Bruderschaft*, 28 Nov. 1958. One of the depositors wrote about the crisis with a sense of understanding: 'Many of us had deposited money into the colony treasury in Mexico and here sought to withdraw it to pay for farm investments and ... daily living expenses.' But then the writer who was also appointed auditor noted that 'no dishonesty had occurred' and listed the reasons for the empty treasury: the construction of five immigration houses; slow internal land payments; the costly initial survey; a bulldozer and sawmill purchase; land payments to Olga Burns.

30 *Bruderschaft*, 8 June 1958. The palm roof was an inexpensive method of church building, but the porous material absorbed so much sound it was difficult to hear and the church body considered the merits of a built-in wooden ceiling. The climate was so hot that the time for meeting was changed to an early 8:30 a.m. Ibid., July 1958. After only nine months the initial covering of palm leaves was in need of replacement. Ibid., 2 Feb. 1959.

31 Ibid., 8 June, 6 October 1958; 6 April 1959.

32 Ibid., 26 May, 1 June 1959.

33 Ibid., 29 Sept. 1958. This is the only item of business revealed to the author by Abram Reimer. It became apparent too that even some of the preachers were leery about the British Honduras option. One reportedly did so 'against his own conviction' and two others 'rolled along with the general feeling.' Klaas C. Penner, a respected colony farmer, is said to have led the charge, saying that if 'everyone moves here, an election there is not necessary.' Interview with Menno Loewen, Dec. 1991.

34 Ibid.
35 *Bruderschaft*, 3 Oct. 1958.
36 Ibid., 3 Nov. 1958; *Dienersitzung*, 30 Jan., 27 Feb. 1959; *Bruderschaft*, 6 July 1959.
37 *Bruderschaft*, 2 Aug. 1959; *Dienersitzung*, 23 Aug. 1959; Koop, *Pioneer Years*, 63.
38 Interviews with Gerhard Koop and Menno Loewen. Loewen singled out his uncle, Abram P. Loewen, as one of the most energetic conservatives. It was said that the permission that colonists received to own large trucks was a capitulation by Bishop Dueck. Others blamed an aggressive colony administration for the acceptance of telephones in 1963. For a fuller account of Peter R. Dueck's life see Royden Loewen, 'Cars, Commerce, Church: Religious Conflict in the Urbanizing World of Steinbach, Manitoba, 1900–1930,' *Journal of Mennonite Studies* 11 (1993): 111–34.
39 Interview with Menno Loewen. One conservative member at Spanish Lookout was quoted as having said that it 'was unfortunate that they [the Old Colonists] had left their moorings.' Meanwhile there was 'continual agitation for a complete break from Mexico.'
40 Koop, *Pioneer Years*, 135.
41 Sawatzky, *They Sought a Country*, 362. An Amish community had been established along upper Barton Creek under the leadership of Albert Stahl and along the same creek the Spanish Lookout conservatives established their community. At this moment of discontent at least two other conservative, American-based Swiss Mennonite groups solicited support from a few families: in 1968 Titus Hoover, a former Holdeman Mennonite minister, arrived at the colony to declare himself the leader of the true Church of God. When his credibility suffered, Corny L. Friesen from Mexico, a Kleine Gemeinder turned Holdeman Mennonite, arrived to steer the Hooverites into the fold of the North American Holdeman Mennonite church. At the same time, in 1967 a few other Spanish Lookout members joined the Beachy Amish church of the United States, arguing that the Holdemans were too exclusive. Interview with Menno Loewen.
42 *Bruderschaft* 1966, 1972–6 and *Dienersitzung*, 1966, 1972–6, Bishop John B. Loewen, Spanish Lookout, Belize. To protect the privacy of these persons the exact dates of discussion are not provided.
43 Ibid. To protect the privacy of these persons the exact dates of discussion are not provided.
44 *Bruderschaft*, 16 March, 2 July, 9 July, 30 Aug. 1975.
45 *Dienersitzung*, 30 Jan., Sept. 1975.

46 *Dienersitzung*, 13 June 1975; 12 March 1976.
47 Interview with Harvey Plett, Steinbach, MB, Sept. 1997; *Dienersitzung*, 11 March 1976.
48 Interview with Menno Loewen.
49 See Toews, *Mennonites in American Society*.
50 By my count they did so once when they considered Menno Simons's refusal to allow the excommunicated to attend church. *Dienersitzung*, 2 March 1976.
51 I first visited Spanish Lookout in December 1980 by flying from Winnipeg through Minneapolis and Miami to the international airport at Belize City. I then traveled by car along the paved Western Highway past the capital of Balmopan, and then by ferry and along all-weather unpaved roads to the colony.
52 *Dienersitzung*, 31 July 1974; 6 Feb. 1974; 31 July 1974. *Bruderschaft*, 9 April 1975.
53 Ibid.
54 *Dienersitzung*, 11 March 1976.
55 See Karen Pauls, 'Northfield Settlement, Nova Scotia: A New Direction for Immigrants from Belize,' *Journal of Mennonite Studies* 22 (2004): 167–84.
56 *Dienersitzung*, 6 Jan. 1959; 2 Feb. 1959.
57 *Bruderschaft*, 5 Feb. 1976.
58 *Dienersitzung* 1 March 1974; *Bruderschaft* 8 Dec. 1974; 7 Feb. 1975.
59 Ministers were 'concerned that our brothers who are working there [in Honduras] might accept strange [teachings] under the influence of various Mennonites in the world.' *Dienersitzung*, 17 Feb. 1975.
60 *Dienersitzung*, 30 Dec. 1972.
61 Ibid., 15 Oct. 1974; 9 Feb. 1975; 21 Feb. 1976.
62 *Bruderschaft*, 16 March 1975.
63 *Dienersitzung*, 14 Jan. 1974.
64 It was agreed to only after the ministers raised the concern that 'our younger members [should] know our reasons for holding onto the German language.' Ibid., 4 April 1975.
65 The School Board, *Our Country of Belize* (Spanish Lookout, Belize, 1981), 22.
66 Interview with Abe D. Loewen, Spanish Lookout, December 1991.
67 *Koop, Pioneer Years*, 59, 65, 144.
68 Koop adds that Elias 'was very glad when he was across the creek. It was obvious that he loved his family just as much as we loved our families.' Ibid., 58.
69 Interview with Nettie Penner and Tony Loewen, Spanish Lookout, Dec. 1991.

70 *Versamlung*, August 1971.
71 *Bruderschaft*, 10 March 1974.
72 Interview with Menno Loewen. He notes that only one non-Mennonite, Robert Pabb, a worker for one of the colonists, was baptized at one of the Spanish Lookout churches, but noted that 'he was too much alone and never joined.'
73 Hall, 'Mennonite Agriculture,' 92.
74 Sawatzky, *They Sought a Country*, 361.
75 Koop, *Pioneer Years*, 19.
76 Ibid., 20
77 Ibid., 112.
78 Ibid., 53. Gerhard Koop also notes that in 1960 when the second payment was due to Olga Burns 'our leaders asked the British Honduras government, if they had any type of assistance in our dilemma. They had the Agriculture Credit Fund [which was] ... intended for the native Belizeans. But enough of the board members were in favor of granting us a loan of $20,000 at 6% interest for a five year period.' Ibid., 127.
79 Ibid., 117. In a reversal of trends in Canada and the United States, the colony provided grants to the government; in 1971 a fifth ferry was constructed after 'our colony offered the government $7000 in order for them to build a steel ferry.' See ibid., 120.
80 *Versamlung*, 22 Oct. 1960.
81 *Bruderschaft*, 31 Oct. 1958; on 3 Nov. 1958 they accepted the new time.
82 *Bruderschaft*, 3 Nov. 1958. The Bruderschaft's argument was that the traditional week-long courtship would be undermined by accepting the government directive. The Bruderschaft protested internally that 'eight days is a better length of time for introductions, than 15.' Even the government directive for mandatary smallpox vaccinations were discussed and a colony couple elected to accompany the nurses around the colony. *Dienersitzung*, 2 Jan., 6 Jan. 1959. The colony also sent along an observer or assistant during the taking of the 1960 national census. In his diary for March 1960 Klaas C. Penner noted that 'I assisted a policeman to take a census on our colony, traveling with him from household to household.' Koop, *Pioneer Years*, 63.
83 *Bruderschaft*, 20 July 1959.
84 Koop, *Pioneer Years*, 129.
85 *Dienersitzung*, 24 June 1972.
86 *Bruderschaft*, 15 Feb. 1974; *Dienersitzung*, 14 June, 27 Sept. 1974.
87 *Dienersitzung*, 27 Sept. 1974; 3 Jan. 1975; *Bruderschaft*, 6 Jan. 1975.
88 *Dienersitzung*, 13 June 1975.

89 *Bruderschaft*, 9 July 1975.

90 Interview with Abe D. Loewen.

91 See for example E.K. Francis, 'The Adjustment of a Peasant Group to a Capitalist Economy: The Manitoba Mennonites,' *Rural Sociology* 17 (1952): 218–28.

92 *Versamlung*, 24 Sept. 1960.

93 Raymond Breton, 'Institutional Completeness of Ethnic Communities and the Personal Relations of Immigrants,' *American Journal of Sociology* 70 (1964): 193–205.

94 *Versamlung*, 30 Jan. 1971. In addition, all male members belonged to road work crews that served at least three days a year.

95 To ensure payment the administration mixed church-based community consensus with other incentives: a congratulatory note was sent to the village of Rosenhof in 1964 for having been 'the first to have paid both [the cattle and the corn] taxes.' Ibid., 28 March 1964. In 1969 when a farmer refused to pay his taxes the administration sent out a directive that noted that whereas a colony member 'will not pay the 2% tax when he sells his beans, he shall see his taxes paid by the purchasers of the beans.' Ibid., 22 Feb. 1969.

96 Ibid., 27 August 1966.

97 Even in 1972 when the government asked that Spanish Lookout host 'several 16 year old boys ... to teach them to work on the farm' the colony moved tentatively: 'if it is only for a short time then perhaps there would be little concern.' Ibid., 29 Jan. 1972; see also 29 April 1972.

98 Ibid., 27 March 1968. Jerry Hall notes that 'members of the congregation may hold land by payment, but it may be recalled for any major transgression against the group or the church.' See Hall, 'Mennonite Agriculture,' 61.

99 *Versamlung*, 24 Sept. 1960.

100 Sawatzky, *They Sought a Country*, 345.

101 Koop, *Pioneer Years*, 55, 128, 137.

102 The very next year the Komitee recorded that because egg prices were low as a result of 'overproduction' in the country, the colony was holding some fifty cases in Belize City and only a short time later recorded that Belize City buyers would 'willingly take all our eggs.' *Versamlung*, 27 May, 30 Sept. 1961

103 Ibid., 17 October 1966; see also Sawatzky, *They Sought a Country*, 347; *Versamlung*, 30 May, 8 July 1964.

104 Ibid., 17 July 1961; Koop, *Pioneer Years*, 100; *Versamlung*, 27 Nov. 1965; 29 Jan. 1966; 25 May, 26 Oct., 28 Dec. 1968.

105 Ibid., 25 May, 28 Dec. 1968.
106 Rain record, 1968–89, David J. Thiessen, Spanish Lookout Colony, Belize. The lowest rainfall occurred in 1974 when 47.24 inches fell, the highest in 1979 when 84.58 inches fell. Usually the months of June, July, and August alone produced 24 inches.
107 Hall, 'Mennonite Agriculture.'
108 Koop, *Pioneer Years*, 4. This statement is a paraphrase of Numbers 14:3.
109 Ibid., 122. Gerhard Koop recalls that unfortunately for Vorsteher Peter Friesen, his wife hailed from a particularly strong-willed clan, and 'she said, no way, she wasn't moving back.' Interview with Gerhard Koop, December 1991. See also Koop, *Pioneer Years*, 122, 125.
110 Hall, 'Mennonite Agriculture,' 29, 42.
111 Ibid., 201.
112 Ibid., 63.
113 Ibid., 187.
114 Ibid., 194.
115 These are the trees mentioned in the colony administration minutes for 25 November 1961 with the words 'decision taken to cut the following kinds of wood.'
116 Koop, *Pioneer Years*, 124.
117 *Versamlung*, 24 Sept. 1960.
118 Ibid., 16 Sept. 1961.
119 See also Sawatsky, *They Sought a Country*, 347. See also *Versamlung*, 17 Oct. 1966.
120 Koop, *Pioneer Years*, 95.
121 Linda Dueck Thiessen, diary, 1968, Linda Thiessen, Spanish Lookout, Belize; Spanish Lookout Birth Registry. Leona was born on 10 March 1958; Maria on 22 Feb. 1960; Irvin 15 April 1963; David on 15 April 1965; Albert on 12 March 1967. Other children were born in later years: Johann was born 15 June 1969; Elma 27 June 1972; Lydia 18 July 1975.
122 C.W. Friesen and Peter J. Penner, eds., *The Peter Penner Genealogy, 1816* (Roblin, MB, 1973).
123 Anna Loewen Dueck, Tagebuch, 1968, Dietrich Dueck, Spanish Lookout, Belize.
124 Ironically, as Koop notes, the 'hot and humid climate' would not allow vegetables they had known before to grow and the settlers could not develop a taste for sweet potatoes or plantains, and so employed insecticides, fungicides, and fertilizers to allow them to grow the vegetables they 'had raised in Mexico and Canada.' Koop, *Pioneer Years*, 94.
125 An openness to chemical usage was again demonstrated on 15 October

when daughter Anna, cleaning the 'ice cellar' and discovering rats and cockroaches in it, relied on the cats to drive out the former and 'poison' to kill the latter.

126 Francis Xavier Higdon, 'Farm Diversification and Specialization: The Adaptation of Mennonite Households in Spanish Lookout, Belize' (PhD diss., University of Pittsburgh, 1997), 46, 48. The output continued to grow rapidly during the 1980s: corn production increased to 24,866,800 pounds, laying hens to 132,310 birds, and broiler chickens to 2,146,991 birds. The number of cattle also increased, from 3144 head in 1971 to 5882 in 1991.

127 Hall, 'Mennonite Agriculture,' 87.

128 The Land Committee also dictated that 'the land is to be paid off with [annual payments of] one half of [the gross value of the annual] crop or in three years, whichever comes first.' *Versamlung*, 27 March 1968.

129 Hall, 'Mennonite Agriculture,' 192

130 Ibid., 76, 317.

131 Ibid., 334.

132 Sawatzky writes of the British Honduras Mennonite colonies that 'property deeds to all colony land are held in the name of the respective church groups, plus, usually, two named individuals who act as custodians. Individual ownership rests on colony registry only.' Sawatzky, *They Sought a Country*, 350. According to the colony assembly minutes in November 1971 the colony decided to 'make land titles, for each one a title, as they have it at Quellen Kolonie' in Mexico, but the decision seems not to have been acted upon. *Versamlung*, 27 Nov. 1971. A consensus that the colony system required a general title seemed to hold. Gerhard Koop observed that 'if everyone had his own title, it would soon be quite mixed up.' It would lead to a situation in which 'mortgages were taken in the banks' and in the event of debt default 'someone else would move in. Soon the colony would be hybrid. Who knows how many years one would lose? A girl who marries a non-Christian does not succeed.' Interview with Gerhard Koop, Spanish Lookout Colony, Dec. 1991.

133 *Versamlung*, 27 May 1961.

134 Ibid., 29 Oct. 1966; 25 July 1970.

135 Ibid., Nov. 1960.

136 The Land Committee negotiated all details of the deal with landowner Charlie Nord; the price was $137,000, $13,000 less than he had asked for. The committee made a loan for $100,000 at 9.75 percent interest. *Versamlung*, 13 Jan. 1968; 27 March 1968.

137 Ibid., 3 March 1968.

138 Ibid., 13 Jan. 1968; 24 Feb. 1968; 18 March 1968; 27 March 1968; 23 Jan. 1971. In order for the colony to qualify for a three-year mortgage from Barclay Bank it decided that 'there shall be five names on the title.' The names included the following: Abram D. Reimer, Ben L. Friesen, D.R. Friesen, Peter L. Dueck, and Dietrich L. Dueck. *Versamlung*, 18 March 1968.
139 School Board, *Our Country of Belize*.

9. Fragmented Freedoms: Studies of Mennonites in Winnipeg and Denver

1 Kraybill and Bowman, *On the Backroad to Heaven*.
2 From Jonathan Raban's *Soft City* (1974) quoted in Harvey, *The Condition of Postmodernity*.
3 George J. Sánchez, *Becoming Mexican American: Ethnicity, Culture and Identity in Chicano Los Angeles, 1900–1945* (New York: Oxford University Press, 1993), 8.
4 Mario Maffi, *Gateway to the Promised Land: Ethnic Cultures in New York's Lower East Side* (New York: New York University Press, 1995), 24, 43.
5 Driedger, *Mennonites in the Global Village*.
6 Toews, *Mennonites in American Society*, 245–7. For a first-hand account of the CO experience in a camp near Denver see Robert S. Kreider, *Looking Back into the Future* (North Newton, KS: Bethel College, 1998). For full histories of the U.S. Mennonite experience during the Second World War see Perry Bush, *Two Kingdoms, Two Loyalties: Mennonite Pacifism in Modern America* (Baltimore: Johns Hopkins University Press, 1998); Rachel Waldner Goossen, *Women against the Good War: Conscientious Objection and Gender on the American Home Front, 1941–1947* (Chapel Hill: University of North Carolina Press, 1997).
7 Leo Driedger, 'Post-War Canadian Mennonites: From Rural to Urban Dominance,' *Journal of Mennonite Studies* 6 (1988): 70–88.
8 Toews, *Mennonites in American Society*, 188.
9 Quoted in Regher, *Mennonites in Canada*, 169.
10 Ibid., 192.
11 Toews, *Mennonites in American Society*, 213.
12 Driedger, *Mennonites in the Global Village*, 20.
13 Ibid., 162.
14 See for example Roy Vogt, 'Entrepreneurs, Labourers, Professionals and Farmers: A Response to Mennonites in Canada,' *Journal of Mennonite Studies* 15 (1997): 134–41; Janis Thiessen, 'Mennonite Business in Town and City: Friesens Corporation of Altona and Palliser Furniture of

Winnipeg,' *Mennonite Quarterly Review* 73 (1999): 585–600; Johann Funk
and Ruth Kampen, 'Urban by Default: Mennonites in Lower Mainland
of British Columbia,' *Journal of Mennonite Studies* 20 (2002): 199–224; Di
Brandt, 'The Poet and the Wild City,' *Journal of Mennonite Studies* 20 (2002):
89–104; Bruno Dyck, 'Exploring Congregational Clans: Playing the "Mennonite Game" in Winnipeg,' *Journal of Mennonite Studies* 21 (2003): 137–54;
Sam Steiner, 'The City and the Formation of "Mennonite Church Eastern
Canada,"' *Journal of Mennonite Studies* 21 (2003): 155–74; Joe Friesen, '"It's
not that the Tories are closer to God, they're furthest from the Devil":
Politics and Mennonites in Winnipeg, 1945–1999,' *Journal of Mennonite
Studies* 21 (2003): 175–90.
15 *Carillon News* (hereafter *CN*), 26 June 1953; 8 June 1967; 8 June 1967.
16 Ibid., 10 June 1960.
17 Ibid., 17 June 1960.
18 Ibid., 8 May 1981.
19 Elizabeth Bartel, *Even Such Is Time* (Victoria, BC: Trafford, 2002), 77.
20 Reimer and Reimer, *The Sesquicentennial Jubilee*, 68.
21 *Messenger*, 25 June 1965. In another typical early membership acceptance
meeting the church accepted members Allan and Laura Friesen from the
Interlake district north of Winnipeg, Sarah Reimer from Blumenort to the
southeast of Winnipeg, and Myrna Friesen from Rosenort to the southwest
of Winnipeg. Ibid., 25 Sept. 1970.
22 Ibid., 11 Feb. 1972.
23 Ibid., 27 Oct. 1967.
24 Ibid., 4 Oct. 1974.
25 Ibid., 25 Sept. 1970. The newcomers came to study and returned to the
rural districts as teachers or as employees to earn enough money to put a
down payment on a farm. In June 1975, for example, the Braeside Church
bade farewell to seven couples returning to Kleefeld, Rosenort, and
Steinbach and three persons transferring in from Steinbach and Morris.
Ibid., 29 June 1975.
26 Ibid., 29 Oct. 1976.
27 The search for a location was crucial: 'we wanted it near the University
and we wanted it near a good bus route,' wrote the founders. They found
that place in 1977 in a vacant 7–11 convenience store within walking
distance of the university. Ibid., 30 Jan. 1981.
28 Ibid., 12 Sept. 1980.
29 Ibid., 3 Feb. 1967.
30 Ibid., 23 March 1973; 17 March 1978.
31 Ibid., 23 March 1973.

32 Ibid., 14 March 1969. The assumption was that the vast majority of people in the neighborhood of the church were not church attenders. The anniversary report noted with some pride that four thousand homes had received literature explaining 'what the EMC church is.' It was an ambitious plan, for the literature was to be 'followed up by a visitation program called "Salvation by Appointment"' that entailed a Bible study 'with those who are interested and thus lead them to Christ.' Ibid., 14 March 1969. When the Braeside church began in 1968 it invited revivalist Marvin Eck of Fayetteville, Arkansas, to preach an eleven-day 'deeper life' sermon series, it saw to it that 'every home in the neighborhood has received a bulletin urging them to attend these meetings,' it trained spiritual counsellors, and it hosted prayer meetings in the hope that Christians and non-Christians alike would 'place Christ at the centre of their lives.' Ibid., 24 May 1968.

33 Ibid., 3 Feb. 1967. In September 1965 Harvey Plett was appointed 'EMC representative to our College and University students studying in Winnipeg.' Ibid., 15 Oct. 1965. In 1966 he was replaced by Melvin Koop with the note that all 'those in our Conference who are pursuing their studies in institutes of higher learning' should take note that Koop 'would appreciate hearing from you.' Ibid., 28 Oct. 1966.

34 Dan Zehr was executive director of Mennonite Central Committee Canada from 1970 to 1976; ibid., 4 Dec. 1970; 23 Jan. 1976.

35 Ibid., 23 Jan. 1976. Moreover the EMC students were invited to participate in the 'Inter Mennonite Campus Ministries' that supported the promotion of Mennonite Central Committee and Mennonite Disaster Service at the university campuses. Ibid., 11 June 1974.

36 Ibid., 19 Dec. 1969.

37 Ibid., 30 Jan. 1970.

38 Ibid., 25 Sept. 1970.

39 Ibid., 17 Dec. 1971.

40 Ibid., 29 Dec. 1973.

41 Ibid., 15 Nov. 1974.

42 The impact of the Wichita Mennonite World Conference was widespread. Arden Thiessen, a minister from the rural district of Blumenort, wrote the following: 'For a few hundred years we have been dividing ... Now we came together – European theologians, American charismatics, dancing drum-pounding Kenyans, social radicals from Columbia, plus a hundred other types to praise our God and to rejoice in the work of our Lord Jesus Christ. It was a Babel in reverse ... I never felt as good about being a Mennonite as I did when we left Wichita.' Ibid., 15 Nov. 1974.

43 Ibid., 31 March 1978.
44 Ibid., 18 Aug. 1978. Other voices of criticism included that of John
   Schlamp, a Winnipeger from rural Saskatchewan, who wrote a stinging
   criticism of the EMC's embrace of a happy, middle-class evangelicalism: 'if
   social action militates against a concept of evangelism perhaps there is
   something wrong with our concept,' he wrote in one letter; in a subsequent letter he took up another evangelical concern, personal happiness,
   arguing that within Christianity depression cannot be deemed sinful and
   that he agreed 'wholeheartedly that to keep on smiling ... is often to live a
   lie.' Ibid., 3 March 1978; 27 Oct. 1978. In March 1978 university student
   Jake Friesen from Manitoba's Interlake district criticized the EMC for its
   belief that 'all social action must be done with the expressed purpose of
   leading a person to a personal experience with Jesus Christ.' Ibid.,
   17 March 1978.
45 See Ruth Derksen-Siemens, 'Quilt as Text and Text as Quilt: The Influence
   of Genre in the Mennonite Girls' Home in Vancouver, 1930–1960,' *Journal
   of Mennonite Studies* 17 (1999): 118–29; Frieda Esau-Klippenstein, 'Doing
   What We Could: Mennonite Domestic Servants in Winnipeg, 1920s–1950s,'
   Journal of Mennonite Studies 7 (1989): 145–66; Marlene Epp, 'The Mennonite
   Girls' Homes of Winnipeg: A Home Away from Home,' *Journal of Mennonite Studies* 6 (1988): 100–14.
46 Interview by Tina Fehr Kehler, Winkler, MB, with Linda Doerksen and
   Alice Doerksen, Winnipeg, August 1999.
47 Interview by Tina Fehr Kehler, Winkler, MB, with Doris Loewen and
   Esther Loewen, Winnipeg, August 1999.
48 Interview with Margaret Toews, June 1999, Winnipeg, EMCA.
49 A survey by the author of the 2003 Winnipeg telephone directory indicates
   a total of about 222,000 residential names. Winnipeg in that year had
   approximately 680,000 citizens, meaning that the average telephone listing
   was associated with 3.0 persons. A survey of 110 names identified by the
   author as Mennonite surnames in the same telephone directory produces
   approximately 13,000 telephone listings (that is 1194 inches of Mennonite
   names with 11 households per inch). The ten most common names included in order of number: Friesen with approximately 690 names,
   Wiebe 580, Penner 465, Klassen 445, Dyck 415, Peters 360, Doerksen (also
   Derksen and Duerksen) 353, Reimer 355, Neufeld 290, Loewen 283,
   Thiessen (also Tiessen and Thiesen) 293, Giesbrecht 280, Rempel 250,
   Hiebert 245, Enns (also Ens and Entz) 245, Schmidt 230, Dueck 205,
   Hildbrandt 200, Sawatzky (also Sawatsky) 285, Martens 185, Toews 175,

Schulz 170, Janzen 163, Kehler 160, Harder 160, Bergen 140. It is assumed that although some names such as Schultz, Schmidt, Abrams, Isaac, Peters, and Wall are shared with other ethnic groups, the author will have overlooked certain names associated with ethnic Mennonites, and therefore the figures may not be inflated. If the figure of 13,000 is multiplied by 3.0 (assuming that the average household bearing a Mennonite surname has the same number of persons as that of a household bearing a non-Mennonite name) the total number of Winnipeg residents living in households bearing ethnic Mennonite names rises to 39,000. Sociologist Leo Driedger's estimate of the total number of religiously affiliated Mennonites for the same year stood at 27,000 (telephone interview, 6 May 2005). This means that 30.8 percent of Winnipeg residents who were identified in some way as Mennonite were not religiously affiliated Mennonites. Religious affiliation in this instance, of course, is not equal to church participation, merely religious identity.

50 Regehr, *Mennonites in Canada*, 56.

51 Warkentin, *Reflections on Our Heritage*, 99–100; *Kleine Gemeinde Bruderschaft Protokullbuch*, 1934–1948; Steinbach EMC Ministerial Meeting Minutes, 1947–ca. 1965.

52 Al Reimer, 'When the War Came to Kleindarp,' *Journal of Mennonite Studies* 15 (1997): 181–6.

53 Al Reimer, 'Coming out of the Cold,' in Loewen, *Why I Am a Mennonite*, 254–67. Later, at mid-life, Reimer was baptized and joined a Mennonite congregation in Winnipeg. Ibid.

54 Patrick Friesen, *The Shunning* (Winnipeg: Turnstone, 1980).

55 Patrick Friesen, 'I Could Have Been Born in Spain,' in Loewen, *Why I Am a Mennonite*, 105.

56 *CN*, 5 Oct. 1967.

57 Ibid., 12 Oct. 1967.

58 Ibid., 23 Nov. 1967.

59 Ibid., 19 Oct. 1967. Another response came from a John Klassen who wrote to offer 'more courage to young boys like Patrick Friesen who has the intelligence ... to break the rules of conformity ... and strike out at the general hypocrisy ... hidden under the cloak of religion in the community of Steinbach.' Ibid., 7 Dec. 1967.

60 Toews, *A Complicated Kindness*, 5, 91.

61 Ibid., 87, 123.

62 Ibid., 6.

63 Ibid., 74, 58.

64 Although the GC and the MB churches were different, Garden Park pastor Dan Friesen noted in 1965 that the GCs were 'one with us in seeking the mind of Christ.' *Christian Leader*, 3 Aug. 1965.
65 Ibid., 23 March 1971.
66 Ibid., 27 July 1971. One participant at the conference argued that the 'twentieth century which knows so much of personal loneliness, disrupted relationships, violence, injustice, and war, needs to hear the full-orbed gospel of Jesus Christ.' Ibid., 7 Sept 1971.
67 Ibid., 28 Dec. 1971.
68 Ibid., 6 March 1973. The conference itself drew some seventy-seven delegates who were so moved by the messages that 'long before organized personal witnessing efforts were scheduled, participants were sharing their faith with waitresses, busboys and passersby.' Ibid., 3 April 1973.
69 Ibid., 3 April 1973.
70 Ibid., 1 May 1973; 27 May 1975.
71 Ibid., 1 May 1973.
72 Ibid., 8 June 1965.
73 Ibid., 26 Sept. 1967.
74 Ibid., 7 Sept. 1971; 3 April 1973; 10 June 1975.
75 Ibid., 29 March 1977.
76 Interview with anonymous source 1, Denver, July 1997.
77 Interview with anonymous source 2, Denver, July 1997.
78 Interview with Ruth Bartel, Denver, July 1997.
79 Ruth's brother Don was also estranged from the Mennonite community; in his youth he had charted a carefree life and his CB handle was 'Kansas Wild Man.' Ironically, he would find a culture of discipline in the Marines he joined in about 1969, even though the church warned him about a possible excommunication. Interview with Ruth Bartel, Denver, July 1997.
80 Leo Driedger, *Mennonite Identity in Conflict* (Queenston, ON: Edwin Mellen Press, 1988).

Conclusion

1 Clifford Geertz, *Available Light: Anthropological Reflections on Philosophical Topics* (Princeton: Princeton University Press, 2000), 246.
2 Hannerz, *Cultural Complexity*, 9.
3 Harvey, *The Condition of Postmodernity*, 49; Halbwachs, *On Collective Memory*.
4 Harvey, *The Condition of Postmodernity*, 113.
5 Hannerz, *Cultural Complexity*, 7.
6 Geertz, *Available Light*, 221.

Bibliography

Manuscripts: Public, Regional, and Church Archives

Emmanuel Mennonite Church, Meade, KS
  'Constitution and Handbook,' Emmanuel Mennonite Church, ca. 1950.
  'Constitution and Manual,' Emmanuel Mennonite Church, ca. 1975.
  Emmanuel Mennonite Church Yearbook, 1965.
  Minutes of the Membership Meetings, 1944–ca. 1960.
  'Reasons for and Organizing of the Emmanuel Mennonite Church,'
    20 March 1944.
  Yearbook, 1965, 1966, 1967, 1968.
Evangelical Mennonite Brethren Church, Meade, KS
  Our Church (Yearbook), 1976.
Evangelical Mennonite Conference Archives, Steinbach, MB
  'Eine Darlegung der Kleingemeinde, Quellenkolonie, Mexico. June 3, 1955.'
  EMC Estates Committee Handbook, 1961, 1974.
  Kleine Gemeinde Bruderschaft Protokullbuch, 1934–48.
  Reimer, Peter P. 'Eine Erafung. February 1946.'
  Steinbach EMC Ministerial Meeting Minutes, 1947–ca. 1965.
Kansas State Historical Society, Topeka, KS
  Kansas State Agricultural Census, 1915, 1925.
  Kansas Board of Agricultural Census, 1937, 1953, 1961, 1975.
  U.S. Census, 1950, 1960, 1970, 1980.
Legislative Library, Winnipeg
  Census of Canada, 1951, 1956, 1961, 1971, 1981.
  Prairie Agricultural Census, 1946, 1956, 1966, 1976.
Meade County Court House, Meade, KS
  Meade County Tax Rolls.
  Probated Wills.

Meade County Historical Society, Meade, KS
  Farm Directory, Meade County, Kansas, 1948.
  Meade-Fowler, Kansas, Telephone Directory, 1951.
  Southwestern Bell Telephone Directory for Dodge City, Fowler, Meade,
    Minneola, 1970.
  Telephone Directory, May Edition, Plains, Kansas, 1938.
St Boniface Probate Court, St Boniface, MB
  Probated Wills, 1900–60.

Manuscripts: Private Collections

Bartel, Helena (Reimer), Meade, KS, Klaas Reimer, account book, 1950.
Dueck, Dietrich, Spanish Lookout, Belize, Anna (Loewen) Dueck, 'Tagebuch,'
  1968.
Friesen, Dr Menno, Goshen, IN, Henry A. Friesen, diary, 1952, 1968.
Friesen, Ralph, 'The Diary of Peter D. Friesen.'
Loewen, Rev Johan B., Spanish Lookout, Belize, *Dienersitzung Protokullbuch*,
  ca. 1970–85.
Loewen, Gertie (Klassen), Blumenort, MB, notes on personal diary, 1963, 1973.
Penner, Abram C., Landmark, MB, Klaas C. Penner, 'Denkschrift,' 1972.
Reimer, George D., Meade, KS, Helena (Doerksen) Reimer, 'Tagebuch,' 1949.
Schultz, Beatrice, Monterey, CA, George Schultz, 'Autobiography, 1880–1950.'
Thiessen, Linda, Spanish Lookout, Belize, personal diary, 1968.

Interviews

By Author
  Anonymous, 1, Denver, August 1997.
  Anonymous, 2, Denver, August 1997.
  Bartel, Andrew and Rosella, Meade, KS, July 1992.
  Bartel, Marten and Helen (Bartel), Meade, KS, July 1992.
  Bartel, Ruth, Denver, August 1997.
  Classen, Ben, Dallas, OR, July 1992.
  Classen, Dave and Martha, Hillsboro, KS, July 1992.
  Classen, Will and Bertha (Johnson), Denver (in Steinbach, MB), July 1994.
  Dueck, Dietrich, Spanish Lookout, Belize, December 1991.
  Dueck, Menno, Los Jagueyes, Mexico, July 1997.
  Epp, Rev Sam, Steinbach, MB, June 1992.
  Friesen, Abe Z., Meade, KS, July 1992.
  Friesen, Cornie Z. Meade, KS, July 1992.

Friesen, Elias D., Meade, KS, July 1992.
Friesen, George J. and Maria (Rempel), Meade, KS, July 1992.
Friesen, Dr Menno, Goshen, IN (in Chicago), ca. February 1995.
Isaac, Al, Hillsboro, KS, July 1992.
Koop, Gerhard, Spanish Lookout, Belize, December 1991.
Kornelsen, George, Los Jagueyes, Mexico. July 1997.
Loewen, Abe D., Spanish Lookout, Belize, December 1991.
Loewen, Dietrich P., Blumenort, MB, June 1996.
Loewen, Henry F., Meade, KS, October 1987.
Loewen, Menno, Spanish Lookout, Belize, December 1991.
Loewen, Pete and Delores, Meade, KS, July 1992.
Loewen, Tony and Nettie (Penner), December 1991.
Penner, Wilmer, Steinbach, MB, October 1995.
Plett, Harvey, Steinbach, MB, September 1997.
Reimer, Abram R., Blumenort, MB, July 1981.
Reimer, Arnold and Helen, Meade, KS, July 1992.
Reimer, Ben D., Steinbach, MB, June 1992.
Reimer, George D., Meade, KS, July 1992.
Reimer, Helen Loewen, Meade, KS, July 1992.
Reimer, John and Anne, Meade, KS, July 1992.
Rempel, Ben, Dallas, OR, July 1992.
Rempel, Herman and Eva (Reimer), Meade, KS, July 1992.
Siemens, Anna (Friesen), Meade, KS, July 1992.
Unruh, Dick, Meade, KS, July 1992.

By Tina Fehr Kehler, Winkler, MB
   Doerksen, Linda and Alice, Winnipeg, August 1999.
   Loewen, Doris and Esther, Winnipeg, August 1999.
   Toews, Margaret, June 1999, Winnipeg, August 1999.

Newspapers

Carillon News, Steinbach, MB
Christian Leader, Hillsboro, KS
Christlicher Familienfreund, Giroux, MB
Meade Globe News, Meade, KS
Meade Globe Press, Meade, KS
The Messenger, Steinbach, MB
Steinbach Post, Steinbach, MB

Books and Articles

Adams, Jane H. 'The Decoupling of Farm and Household: Differential Consequences of Capitalist Development on Southern Illinois and Third World Family Farms.' *Comparative Studies of Society and History* 30 (1988): 453–82.

Amato, Joseph A. *Rethinking Home: A Case for Writing Local History.* Berkeley: University of California Press, 2002.

Anderson, Benedict. *Imagined Communities: Reflections on the Origin and Spread of Nationalism.* London: Verso, 1991.

Andres, Ron, ed. *Silver Jubilee Steinbach D.H.I.A.* Steinbach, MB: N.P., 1980.

Archdeacon, Thomas. 'Problems and Possibilities in the Study of American Immigration and Ethnic History,' *International Migration Review* 19 (Spring 1985): 112–34.

Auslander, Leora. *Taste and Power: Furnishing Modern France.* Berkeley: University of California Press, 1996.

Barkman, Sue. *Ever-Widening Circles: EMC Missions Silver Jubilee, 1953–1978.* Steinbach, MB: Evangelical Mennonite Conference, 1978.

Barron, Hal S. *Mixed Harvest: The Second Great Transformation in the Rural North.* Chapel Hill: University of North Carolina Press, 1997.

Bartel, Elizabeth. *Even Such is Time.* Victoria, BC: Trafford 2002.

Barth, Fredrik. *Balinese Worlds.* Chicago: University of Chicago Press, 1993.

Basran, G.S., and D.A. Hay, eds. *The Political Economy of Agriculture in Western Canada.* Toronto: Garamond, 1988.

Beard, Larry, ed. *Centennial History of Meade, Kansas.* Meade, KS: Kes-Print, 1985.

Beltman, Brian W. *Dutch Farmer in the Missouri Valley: The Life and Letters of Ulbe Eringa, 1866–1950.* Urbana: University of Illinois Press, 1996.

Berg, Wesley. *From Russia with Music: A Study of the Mennonite Choral Singing Tradition in Canada.* Winnipeg: Hyperion, 1985.

Bergen, David. *Year of Lesser.* Toronto: Harper Collins, 1996.

Braght, Thieleman J. van. *Martyrs' Mirror: The Story of Seventeen Centuries of Christian Martyrdom, from the Time of Christ to A.D. 1600.* trans. Joseph F. Sohm. Scottdale, PA: Herald Press, 1950.

Brandt, Di. 'The Poet and the Wild City.' *Journal of Mennonite Studies* 20 (2002): 89–104.

Breton, Raymond. 'Institutional Completeness of Ethnic Communities and the Personal Relations of Immigrants.' *American Journal of Sociology* 70 (1964): 193–205.

Britnell, G.E., and V.C. Fowke. *Canadian Agriculture in War and Peace, 1935–1950.* Stanford: Stanford University Press, 1962.

Burkinshaw, Robert K. *Pilgrims in Lotus Land: Conservative Protestantism in British Columbia, 1917–1981*. Montreal: McGill-Queen's University Press, 1995.

Bush, Perry. *Two Kingdoms, Two Loyalties: Mennonite Pacifism in Modern America*. Baltimore: Johns Hopkins University Press, 1998.

Careless, J.M.S. '"Limited Identities" in Canada.' *Canadian Historical Review* 50 (1969): 1–10.

Choquette, Robert. *Canada's Religions: An Introduction*. Ottawa: Ottawa University Press, 2004.

Clark, S.D. *Church and Sect in Canada*. Toronto: University of Toronto Press, 1948.

Cohen, Robin. *Global Diasporas: An Introduction*. Seattle: University of Washington Press, 1997.

Coleman, Daniel. *Masculine Migrations: Reading the Postcolonial Male in New Canadian Narratives*. Toronto: University of Toronto Press, 1998.

Conzen, Kathleen Neils, 'Making Their Own America: Assimilation Theory and the German Peasant Pioneer.' *German Historical Institute Annual Lecture Series* 3 (1990): 1–33.

Conzen, Kathleen Neils, David A. Gerber, Ewa Morwaska, George E. Pozzetta, and Rudolph Vecoli. 'The Invention of Ethnicity: A Perspective from the USA.' *Journal of American Ethnic History* 29 (1992): 3–41.

Cronon, William. *Changes in the Land: Indians, Colonists and the Ecology of New England*. New York: Hill and Wang, 1983.

– *Nature's Metropolis: Chicago and the Great West*. New York: W.W. Norton, 1991.

Dawson, C.A. *Group Settlement*. Toronto: Macmillan, 1936.

Derksen-Siemens, Ruth. 'Quilt as Text and Text as Quilt: The Influence of Genre in the Mennonite Girls' Home in Vancouver, 1930–1960.' *Journal of Mennonite Studies* 17 (1999): 118–29.

Driedger, Leo. *Mennonite Identity in Conflict*. Queenston, ON: Edwin Mellen Press, 1988.

– *Mennonites in the Global Village*. Toronto: University of Toronto Press, 2000.

– 'Post-War Canadian Mennonites: From Rural to Urban Dominance.' *Journal of Mennonite Studies* 6 (1988): 70–88.

Driedger, Leo, and J. Howard Kauffman. 'Urbanzation of Mennonites: Canadian and American Comparisons.' *Mennonite Quarterly Review* 56 (1982): 269–90.

Dudley, Kathryne Marie. *Debt and Dispossession: Farm Loss in America's Heartland*. Chicago: University of Chicago Press, 2000.

Dueck, Arden M., Myron P. Loewen, Leslie L. Plett, and Eddy K. Plett. *Quellen Kolonie*. Los Jaqueyes, Mexico: Colorama, 1998.

Dueck, John, Willie Dueck, and Nettie Peters, eds. *Descendants of Jacob and Maria L. Dueck, 1839–1986*. Steinbach, MB: Dueck Family Book Committee, 1986.

Dunlap, Thomas R. *Nature and the English Diaspora: Environment and History in the United States, Canada, Australia and New Zealand*. New York: Cambridge University Press, 1999.

Dyck, Bruno. 'Exploring Congregational Clans: Playing the "Mennonite Game" in Winnipeg.' *Journal of Mennonite Studies* 21 (2003): 137–54.

Dyck, C.J. *An Introduction to Mennonite History*. Scottdale, PA: Herald Press, 1993.

Dyck, Peter, and Elfrieda Dyck. *Up From the Rubble*. Scottdale, PA: Herald Press, 1991.

Emmanuel Mennonite Church, *Anniversary of the Emmanuel Mennonite Church, Meade County, Kansas, 1944–1974*. Meade, KS: EMC, 1974.

Engbrecht, Dennis D. *The Americanization of a Rural Immigrant Church: The General Conference Mennonites in Central Kansas, 1874–1939*. New York: Garland, 1990.

Enns-Rempel, Kevin. 'The Fellowship of Evangelical Bible Churches and the Quest for Religious Identity.' *Mennonite Quarterly Review* 63 (1989): 247–64.

Ens, Adolf. *Becoming a National Church: A History of the Conference of Mennonites in Canada*. Winnipeg: CMU Press, 2004.

Epp, Marlene. 'Heroes or Yellow Bellies? Masculinity and the Conscientious Objector.' *Journal of Mennonite Studies* 17 (1999): 107–17.

– 'The Mennonite Girls' Homes of Winnipeg: A Home Away from Home.' *Journal of Mennonite Studies* 6 (1988): 100–14.

– *Women without Men: Mennonite Refugees of the Second World War*. Toronto: University of Toronto Press, 2000.

Epp, Marlene, Franca Iacovetta, and Frances Swyripa, eds. *Sisters or Strangers? Immigrant, Ethnic and Racialized Women in Canadian History*. Toronto: University of Toronto Press, 2004.

Epp-Tiessen, Esther. *Altona: The Story of a Prairie Town*. Altona, MB: D.W. Friesen and Sons, 1982.

Esau-Klippenstein, Frieda. 'Doing What We Could: Mennonite Domestic Servants in Winnipeg, 1920s–1950s.' *Journal of Mennonite Studies* 7 (1989): 145–66.

Everitt, John C. 'The Recent Migrations of Belize, Central America.' *International Migration Review* 18 (1984): 319–25.

– 'Mennonites in Belize.' *Journal of Cultural Geography* 3 (1983): 82–93.

Fast, Henry L. 'The Kleine Gemeinde in the United States of America,' in *Profile of the Kleine Gemeinde, 1874*, ed. Delbert F. Plett, 87–140. Steinbach, MB: DFP Publications, 1987.

Fink, Deborah. *Agrarian Women: Wives and Mothers in Rural Nebraska, 1880–1940*. Chapel Hill: University of North Carolina Press, 1992.

Finkel, Alvin. *Our Lives: Canada after 1945*. Toronto: J. Lorimer, 1997.

Fite, Gilbert C. *American Farmers: The New Minority*. Bloomington: Indiana University Press, 1981.

Flanagan, Caitlan. 'Housewife Confidential: A Tribute to the Old-Fashioned Housewife, and to Erma Bombeck, Her Champion and Guide.' *Atlantic Monthly*, September 2003, 141–50.

Forbes, J.D., R.D. Hughes, and T.K. Waverly. *Economic Intervention and Regulation in Canadian Agriculture*. Ottawa: Ministry of Supply and Services, 1982.

Forsythe, James L. 'Cliff Hope of Kansas: Practical Congressman and Agrarian Idealist.' *Agricultural History* 2 (1977): 406–20.

Francis, E.K. *In Search of Utopia: The Mennonites in Manitoba*. Altona, MB: D.W. Friesen and Sons, 1955.

– 'The Adjustment of a Peasant Group to a Capitalist Economy: The Manitoba Mennonites.' *Rural Sociology* 17 (1952): 218–28.

Friedl, Ernestine, The Position of Women: Appearance and Reality,' *Anthropological Quarterly* 40 (1967): 97–108.

Friesen, C.W., and Peter J. Penner. eds. *The Peter Penner Genealogy, 1816*. Roblin, MB: privately published, 1973.

Friesen, Gerald. *Citizens and Nation: An Essay on History, Communication, and Canada*. Toronto: University of Toronto Press, 2000.

– *The Canadian Prairies: A History*. Toronto: University of Toronto Press, 1984.

– postscript, in James Giffen, *Rural Life: Portraits of the Prairie Town, 1946*. Winnipeg: University of Manitoba Press, 2004.

Friesen Gerald, and Royden Loewen. 'Romantics, Pluralists and Post-Modernists.' In *River Road: Essays in Manitoba and Prairie History*, ed. Gerald Friesen, 183–96. Winnipeg: University of Manitoba Press, 1996.

Friesen, Joe. '"It's not that the Tories are closer to God, they're furthest from the Devil": Politics and Mennonites in Winnipeg, 1945–1999. *Journal of Mennonite Studies* 21 (2003): 175–90.

Friesen, Menno M. 'How He Works and What Happens If He Doesn't: A Look at Mid-Life Crisis,' in *Who Am I? What Am I? Searching for Meaning in Your Work*, ed. Calvin Redekop and Urie Bender, 202–13. Grand Rapids, MI: Academic Books, 1988.

Friesen, Patrick. *The Shunning*. Winnipeg: Turnstone, 1980.

– 'I Could Have Been Born in Spain.' In *Why I Am a Mennonite*, ed. Harry Loewen. Scottdale, PA: Herald Press, 1988.

Funk, Johann, and Ruth Kampen. 'Urban by Default: Mennonites in Lower Mainland of British Columbia.' *Journal of Mennonite Studies* 20 (2002): 199–224.

Gans, Herbert. 'Symbolic Ethnicity: The Future of Ethnic Groups and Cultures in America.' In *On the Making of Americans: Essays in Honor of David Riesman*, ed. Herbert Gans, 193–220. Philadelphia: University of Pennsylvania Press, 1979.

Gardner, Bruce L. *American Agriculture in the Twentieth Century: How It Flourished and What It Cost*. Cambridge: Harvard University Press, 2002.

Geertz, Clifford. *After the Fact: Two Countries, Four Decades, One Anthropologist*. Cambridge: Harvard University Press, 1995.

– *Available Light: Anthropological Reflections on Philosophical Topics*. Princeton: Princeton University Press, 2000.

Gjerde, Jon. *The Minds of the West: Ethnocultural Evolution in the Rural Middle West, 1830–1917*. Chapel Hill: University of North Carolina Press, 1997.

Gleason, Mona. *Normalizing the Ideal: Psychology, Schooling and the Family in Postwar Canada*. Toronto: University of Toronto Press, 1996.

Goossen, Rachel Waltner. *Women against the Good War: Conscientious Objection and Gender on the American Home Front, 1941–1947*. Chapel Hill: University of North Carolina Press, 1997.

Government of Canada, *The Canadian Agriculture Outlook*. Ottawa: Agriculture Canada, 1970.

Green, Donald Edward. *Land of the Underground Rain*. Austin. University of Texas Press, 1973.

Hadley, Michael. 'Education and Alienation in Dyck's Verloren in der Steppe.' *Canadian-German Yearbook* 3 (1976): 199–206.

Halbwachs, Maurice. *On Collective Memory*. 1941. Trans. Lewis A. Coser. Chicago: University of Chicago Press, 1992.

Hannerz, Ulf. *Cultural Complexity: Studies in the Social Organization of Meaning*. New York: Columbia University Press, 1992.

Hansen, Marcus Lee. 'The Third Generation Immigrant.' In *American Immigrants and Their Generations: Studies and Commentaries on the Hansen Thesis after Fifty Years*, ed. Peter Kivisto and Dag Blanck, 191–203. Urbana: University of Illinois Press, 1990.

Harder, Helmut. *David Toews Was Here, 1870–1947*. Winnipeg: CMBC Publications, 2002.

Harder, Leland. *Steinbach and Its Churches*. Elkart, IN: Mennonite Biblical Seminary, 1970.

Harris, Richard. *Creeping Conformity: How Canada Became Suburban, 1900–1960*. Toronto: University of Toronto Press, 2004.

Harvey, David. *The Condition of Postmodernity: An Enquiry into the Origins of Cultural Change*. New York: Blackwell, 1989.

– *Spaces of Hope*. Berkeley: University of California Press, 2000.

Haury, David. *Prairie People: A History of the Western District Conference.* Newton, KS: Faith and Life Press, 1984.

Heisey, M.J. 'Mennonite Religion Was a Family Religion.' *Journal of Mennonite Studies* 23 (2005): 9–22.

Herberg, Will. *Protestant – Catholic – Jew: An Essay in American Religious Sociology.* Garden City, NY: Doubleday, 1955.

Hoerder, Dirk. *Cultures in Contact: World Migrations in the Second Millennium.* Durham, NC: Duke University Press, 2002.

Horst, Isaac. *A Separate People: An Insider's View of Old Order Mennonite Customs and Traditions.* Waterloo, ON: Herald Press, 2000.

Hughes, J. Donald. *An Environmental History of the World: Humankind's Changing Role in the Community of Life.* New York: Routledge, 2001.

Hurt, R. Douglas. *Problems of Plenty: The American Farmer in the Twentieth Century.* Chicago: Ivan R. Dee, 2002.

– ed. *The Rural South since World War II.* Baton Rouge: Louisiana State University Press, 1998.

Janzen, Rod. *The Prairie People: Forgotten Anabaptists.* Hanover, NH: University of New England Press, 1999.

Jellison, Katherine. *Entitled to Power: Farm Women and Technology, 1913–1963.* Chapel Hill: University of North Carolina Press, 1993.

Juhnke, James C. *Vision, Doctrine, War: Mennonite Identity and Organization in America, 1890–1930.* Scottdale, PA: Herald Press, 1989.

Kann, Kenneth L. *Comrades and Chicken Ranchers: The Story of a California Jewish Community.* Ithaca: Cornell University Press, 1993.

Kasdorf, Julia. *Fixing Tradition: Joseph W. Yoder, Amish American.* Telford, PA: Pandora Press, 2002.

Keim, Albert N. *Harold S. Bender, 1897–1962.* Scottdale, PA: Herald Press, 1998.

Klassen, Pamela. *Going by the Moon and the Stars: Stories of Two Russian Mennonite Women.* Waterloo, ON: Wilfrid Laurier University Press, 1994.

Kline, Ronald R. *Consumers in the Country: Technology and Social Change in Rural America.* Baltimore: Johns Hopkins University Press, 2000.

Kniss, Fred. *Disquiet in the Land: Cultural Conflict in American Mennonite Communities.* New Brunswick, NJ: Rutgers University Press, 1997.

Knowles Anne Kelly. *Calvinists Incorporated: Welsh Immigrants on Ohio's Industrial Frontier.* Chicago: University of Chicago Press, 1997.

Kocha, Jürgen. 'Comparison and Beyond.' *History and Theory* 42 (2003): 39–44.

Koop, Gerhard S. *Pioneer Years in Belize.* Belize City: Colorama, 1991.

Kornelsen, Jacob U. *25 Jahre in Mexiko: Beschreibung Von der Quellenkolonie, 1948–1973.* Cuauhtémoc, Mexico: Self-published, 1973.

Kraybill, Donald B. and Carl F. Bowman. *On the Backroad to Heaven: Old Order*

Hutterites, Mennonites, Amish and Brethren. Baltimore: Johns Hopkins University Press, 2001.

Kreider, Robert S. *Looking Back into the Future*. North Newton, KS: Bethel College, 1998.

Kroes, Rob. *The Persistence of Ethnicity: Dutch Calvinist Pioneers in Amsterdam, Montana*. Urbana: University of Illinois Press, 1992.

LaDow, Beth. *The Medicine Line: Life and Death on a North American Borderland*. New York: Routledge, 2001.

Laqueur, Thomas. *Making Sex: Body and Gender from the Greeks to Freud*. Cambridge: Harvard University Press, 1990.

Lears, T.J. Jackson. Introduction to *The Culture of Consumption: Critical Essays in American History, 1880–1980*, eds. Richard Wightman Fox and T.J. Jackson Lears, vii–xvii. New York: Pantheon, 1983.

Lefebvre, Henri. *Critique of Everyday Life*. 1947. Trans. John Moore. London: Verso, 1991.

Levine, Rhonda F. *Class, Networks, and Identity: Replanting Jewish Lives from Nazi Germany to Rural New York*. Lanham, MD: Rowman and Littlefield, 2001.

Limerick, Patricia Nelson, Clyde A. Milner II, and Charles E. Rankin, eds. *Trails: Toward a New Western History*. Lawrence: University Press of Kansas, 1991.

Loewen, C.B. *I Remember: Riverside and the Regions Beyond*. Morris, MB: N.P., 1995.

Loewen, Merle. 'Aeltester Jacob F. Isaac (1883–1970),' *Preservings* 26 (2006).

Loewen, Royden. *Blumenort: A Mennonite Community in Transition, 1874–1982*. Blumenort, MB: Blumenort Mennonite Historical Society, 1983.

– 'Bright Lights, Hard Truth, Soft Facts: The Evolving Literature of Ethnic Farm Life in Canada.' *Canadian Ethnic Studies* 28 (1997): 25–39.

– *Ethnic Farm Culture in Western Canada*. Canada's Ethnic Group Series. Ottawa: Canadian Historical Association, 2002.

– *Family, Church and Market: A Mennonite Community in the Old and the New Worlds, 1850–1930*. Urbana: University of Illinois Press, 1993.

– , ed. *From the Inside Out: The Rural World of Mennonite Diarists, 1863–1929*. Winnipeg: University of Manitoba Press, 1999.

– *Hidden Worlds: Revisiting the Mennonites Migrants of the 1870s*. Winnipeg: University of Manitoba Press, 2001.

– 'Mennonite "Repertoires of Contention": Church Life in Steinbach, Manitoba and Los Jagueyes, Chihuahua, 1945–1970.' *Mennonite Quarterly Review* 72 (1998): 301–19.

– 'The Quiet on the Land: Mennonites and the Environment in History.' *Journal of Mennonite Studies* 23 (2005): 151–64.

MacPherson, Ian, and John Herd Thompson. 'The Business of Agriculture: Prairie Farmers and the Adoption of "Business Methods," 1880–1950.' *Canadian Papers in Business History* 1 (1989): 245–69.

Maffi, Mario. *Gateway to the Promised Land: Ethnic Cultures on New York's Lower East Side.* New York: New York University Press, 1995.

Malone, Michael P., and Richard W. Etulain. *The American West: A Twentieth-Century History.* Lincoln: University of Nebraska Press, 1989.

Marsden, George. *Religion and American Culture.* Fort Worth: Wadsworth, 2001.

Marshall, David B. *Secularizing the Faith: Canadian Protestant Clergy and the Crisis of Belief, 1850–1940.* Toronto: University of Toronto Press, 1992.

Martin, Paul. 'The Mennonites of Belize.' *National Studies* 1 (1973): 12–13.

Marty, Martin E. *Religion and Republic: The American Circumstance.* Boston: Beacon Press, 1987.

Matsumoto, Valerie J. *Farming the Home Place: A Japanese American Community in California, 1919–1982.* Ithaca: Cornell University Press, 1993.

Mauss, Armand L. *The Angel and the Beehive: The Mormon Struggle with Assimilation.* Urbana: University of Illinois Press, 1994.

McLoughlin, W.G. *Revivals, Awakenings and Reform.* Chicago: University of Chicaco Press, 1978.

McMurry, Sally. *Transforming Rural Life: Dairying Families and Agricultural Change, 1820–1885.* Baltimore: Johns Hopkins University Press, 1995.

McPherson, Kathryn, Cecilia Morgan, and Nancy M. Forestell, eds. *Gendered Pasts: Historial Essays in Femininity and Masculinity in Canada.* Toronto: Oxford University Press, 1999.

Meade County Historical Society, *Pioneer Stories of Meade County.* Meade, KS: Meade County Historical Society, 1985.

Medick, Hans. '"Missionaries in a Rowboat?" Ethnological Ways of Knowing as a Challenge to Social History.' *Comparative Studies in Society and History* 29 (1987): 76–98.

Mills, Rachel. 'Masculinity, Entrepreneurship and Religion: Lumberman C.T. Loewen of Steinbach, Manitoba.' *Journal of Mennonite Studies* 23 (2005): 213–29.

Minkel, Thomas A. 'Mennonite Colonization in British Honduras.' *Pennsylvania Geographer* 5 (1967): 2–7.

Neth, Mary. *Preserving the Family Farm: Women, Community and the Foundations of Agribusiness in the Midwest, 1900–1940.* Baltimore: Johns Hopkins University Press, 1995.

Neufeld, Gloria. *The Work of Their Hands: Mennonite Women's Societies in Canada.* Waterloo, ON: Wilfrid Laurier University Press, 1996.

Neufeldt, Leonard N. *Village of Unsettled Yearnings: Yarrow, British Columbia: Mennonite Promise.* Victoria, BC: Horsdal and Schubart, 2002.

Nisbet, Robert A. 'Community as Typology: Toennies and Weber,' *The Socio-logical Tradition*, 71–83. New York: Basic Books, 1966.

Nolt, Steve. *Amish Enterprise: From Plows to Profits*. Baltimore: Johns Hopkins University Press, 1995.

Nye, Robert A. *Masculinity and Male Codes of Honor in Modern France*. New York: Oxford University Press, 1993.

Olick, Jeffrey K., and Joyce Robbins. 'Social Memory Studies: From "Collective Memory" to the Historical Sociology of Mnemonic Practices.' *Annual Review of Sociology* 24 (1998): 105–40.

Oriard, Michael. *Reading Football: How the Popular Press Created an American Spectacle*. Chapel Hill: University of North Carolina Press, 1993.

Overland, Orm. *Immigrant Minds, American Identities: Making the United States Home, 1870–1930*. Urbana: University of Illinois Press, 2000.

Owram, Doug. *Born at the Right Time: A History of the Baby-Boom Generation*. Toronto: University of Toronto Press, 1996.

Parkerson, Donald H., and Jo Ann Parkerson. '"Fewer Children of Greater Spiritual Quality": Religion and the Decline of Fertility in Nineteenth-Century America.' *Social Science History* 12 (1988): 49–70.

Parr, Joy. *Gender of Breadwinners: Women, Men and Change in Two Industrial Towns, 1880–1950*. Toronto: University of Toronto Press, 1999.

– *Domestic Goods: The Material, the Moral and the Economic in the Post-War Years*. Toronto: University of Toronto Press, 1999.

– 'Gender History and Historical Practice.' *Canadian Historical Review* 76 (1995): 354–76.

Pauls, Karen. 'Northfield Settlement, Nova Scotia: A New Direction for Immigrants from Belize.' *Journal of Mennonite Studies* 22 (2004): 167–84.

Pederson, Jane Marie. *Between Memory and Reality: Family and Community in Rural Wisconsin, 1870–1970*. Madison: University of Wisconsin Press, 1992.

Penner, Archie. *The Christian, the State and the New Testament*. Altona, MB: D.W. Friesen and Sons, 1959.

Penner, Lydia. *Hanover: 100 Years*. Steinbach, MB: RM of Hanover, 1982.

Penner, Mil. *Section 27: A Century on a Farm*, Lawrence: University Press of Kansas, 2002.

Peters, Doreen Reimer. *One Who Dared: Life Story of Ben D. Reimer, 1909–1994*. Steinbach, MB: self-published, 2005.

Plank, Elda Friesen. *'Twas Home on the Range: A Story of the Henry A. Friesen Family*. Lancaster, PA: self-published, 1981.

Plett, Delbert. *Saints and Sinners: The Kleine Gemeinde in Imperial Russia, 1812–1875*. Steinbach, MB: Crossways Publications, 1999.

Plett, Harvey. *Seeking to be Faithful: The Story of the Evangelical Mennonite Conference*. Steinbach, MB, Evangelical Mennonite Conference, 1996.

Porter, John. *The Vertical Mosaic: An Analysis of Social Class and Power in Canada*. Toronto: University of Toronto Press, 1965.

Rawlyk, George. 'New Lights, Baptists and Religious Awakenings.' In *Prophets, Priests and Prodigals*, ed. Mark McGowan and David Marshall, 37–59. Toronto: McGraw-Hill, 1992.

Redekop, Calvin, ed. *Creation and the Environment: An Anabaptist Perspective on a Sustainable World*. Baltimore: John Hopkins University Press, 2000.

– *Leaving Anabaptism: From Evangelical Mennonite Brethren to Fellowship of Evangelical Bible Churches*. Telford, PA: Pandora, 1998.

Redekop, Gloria L. Neufeld. *The Work of Their Hands: Mennonite Women's Societies in Canada*. Waterloo, ON: Wilfrid Laurier University Press, 1996.

Redfield, Robert. 'The Folk Society.' *American Journal of Sociology* 52 (1947): 293–308.

Regehr, T.D. *Mennonites in Canada: A People Transformed*. Toronto: University of Toronto Press, 1996.

– *Faith, Life and Witness in the Northwest, 1903–2003: Centennial History of the Northwest Mennonite Conference*. Kitchener, ON: Pandora Press, 2003.

Reimer, Al. 'Coming in from the Cold.' In *Why I Am a Mennonite*, ed. Harry Loewen, 254–7. Scottdale, PA: Herald Press, 1988.

– 'Innocents Abroad: The Comic Odyssey of *Koop enn Bua opp Reise*,' *Journal of Mennonite Studies* 4 (1986): 31–45.

– 'When the War Came to Kleindarp.' *Journal of Mennonite Studies* 15 (1997): 181–6.

Reimer, John C., ed., *75 Gedenkfeier der Mennonitischen Einwanderung in Manitoba, Canada*. North Kildonan, MB: Festkomitee, 1949.

– *Familienregister der Nachkommen von Klaas und Helena Reimer*. Winnipeg: Regehr Printing, 1958.

Reimer, John K. *Cornelius R. Reimer, 1902–1959*. Spanish Lookout, Belize: n.p., n.d.

Reimer, Peter J.B., and David P. Reimer. *The Sesquicentennial Jubilee: Evangelical Mennonite Conference*. Steinbach, MB: Evangelical Mennonite Conference, 1962.

Rempel, G.S., ed. *A Historical Sketch of the Churches of the Evangelical Mennonite Brethren*. Rosthern, SK: D.H. Epp, 1939.

Reschly, Steven D. *The Amish on the Iowa Prairie, 1840–1910*. Baltimore: Johns Hopkins University Press, 2000.

Riesebrodt, Martin. *Pious Passion: The Emergence of Modern Fundamentalism in the United States and Iran*. Trans. Don Reneau. Berkeley: University of California Press, 1993.

Riney-Kehrberg, Pamela. *Rooted in Dust: Surviving Drought and Depression in Southwestern Kansas*. Lawrence: University Press of Kansas, 1994.

– ed. *Waiting on the Bounty: The Dust Bowl Diary of Mary Knackstedt Dyck*. Iowa City: University of Iowa Press, 1999.

Robinson, John. 'German Migration to Belize: The Beginnings.' *Belizean Studies* 13 (1985): 17–40.

Roessingh, Carel, and Tanja Plasil, 'From Collective Body to Individual Mind: Changes in Leadership and Attitudes in an Old Colony Mennonite Community in Northern Belize.' *Journal of Mennonite Studies* 24 (2006): 55–72.

Rome, Adam. *Bulldozer in the Countryside: Suburban Sprawl and the Rise of American Environmentalism*. New York: Cambridge University Press, 2001.

– 'What Really Matters in History? Environmental Perspectives on Modern America.' *Environmental History* 7 (2002): 303–17.

Roper, Michael, and John Tosh, eds. *Manful Assertions: Masculinities in Britain since 1800*. New York: Routledge, 1991.

Rose, Marilyn Preheim. *On the Move: A Study of Migration and Ethnic Persistence among Mennonites from East Freeman, South Dakota*. New York: AMS, 1989.

Rosenberg, Norman L., and Emily S. Rosenberg. *In Our Times: America since World War II*. 1976. Upper Saddle River, NJ: Prentice Hall, 1999.

Rotundo, E. Anthony. *American Manhood: Transformation in Masculinity from the Revolution to the Modern Era*. New York: Basic Books, 1993.

Rozum, Molly P. 'Indelible Grasslands: Place, Memory, and the "Life Review."' In *Toward Defining the Prairies: Region, Culture and History*, ed. Robert Wardhaugh, 119–35. Winnipeg: University of Manitoba Press, 2001.

Rugh, Susan Sessions. *Our Common Country: Family Farming, Culture and Community in the Nineteenth Century Midwest*. Bloomington: Indiana University Press, 2001.

Rutherford, Paul. *When Television was Young: Primetime Canada, 1952–1967*. Toronto: University of Toronto Press, 1990.

Salamon, Sonya. 'Land Ownership and Women's Power in a Midwestern Farming Community.' *Journal of Marriage and the Family* 41 (1979): 109–79.

Saloutos, Theodore. *The American Farmer and the New Deal*. Ames: Iowa State University Press, 1982.

Sánchez, George J. *Becoming Mexican American: Ethnicity, Culture and Identity in Chicano Los Angeles, 1900–1945*. New York: Oxford University Press, 1993.

Sandwell, R.W. *Peasants on the Coast? Contesting Rural Space in Nineteenth Century British Columbia*. Montreal: McGill-Queen's University Press, 2004.

Sawatsky, H. Leonard. *They Sought a Country: Mennonite Colonization in Mexico.* Berkeley: University of California Press, 1971.

Schama, Simon. *Landscape and Memory.* New York: Knopf, 1995.

Schmidt, Kimberly D., Dianne Zimmerman Umble, and Steven D. Reschly, eds. *Strangers at Home: Amish and Mennonite Women in History.* Baltimore: Johns Hopkins University Press, 2002.

Scott, Joan Wallach. *Gender and the Politics of History.* New York: Columbia University Press, 1988.

Segalen, Martine. *Love and Power in the Peasant Family: Rural France in the Nineteenth Century.* Trans. Sarah Matthews. Chicago: University of Chicago Press, 1983.

Shover, John L. *First Majority, Last Minority: The Transforming of Rural Life in America.* Dekalb: Northern Illinois University Press, 1976.

Siemens, Anna Z. Friesen, ed. *Genealogy and History of the J.R. Friesen Family, 1782–1990.* Meade, KS: self-published, 1990.

Sollors, Werner. Introduction to *The Invention of Ethnicity,* ix–xx. Oxford University Press, New York, 1989.

Stackhouse, John G. *Canadian Evangelicalism in the Twentieth Century: An Introduction to Its Character.* Toronto: University of Toronto Press, 1993.

Steinbach Credit Union. *Steinbach Credit Union: A Look at Fifty Years of Service, 1941–1991.* Steinbach, MB: N.P., 1991.

Steiner, Samuel. 'The City and the Formation of "Mennonite Church Eastern Canada." *Journal of Mennonite Studies* 21 (2003): 155–74.

Strong-Boag, Veronica. '"Pulling in Double Harness or Hauling a Double Load": Women, Work and Feminism.' *Journal of Canadian Studies* 21 (1986): 32–52.

Sutton, Robert P. *Les Icariens: The Utopian Dream in Europe and America.* Urbana: University of Illinois Press, 1994.

Sylvester, Kenneth. *The Limits of Rural Capitalism: Family, Culture, and Markets, Montcalm, Manitoba, 1870-1940.* Toronto: University of Toronto Press, 2000.

Taylor, Jeffery. *Fashioning Farmers: Ideological Agricultural Knowledge and the Manitoba Farm Movement, 1890–1925.* Regina: Canadian Plains Research Center, 1994.

Thiessen, Janis. 'Mennonite Business in Town and City: Friesens Corporation of Altona and Palliser Furniture of Winnipeg. *Mennonite Quarterly Review* 73 (1999): 585–600.

Tiessen, Esther Epp. *J.J. Thiessen: A Leader for His Time.* Winnipeg: CMBC Publications, 2001.

Thompson, John Herd. *Forging the Prairie West: The Illustrated History of Canada.* Toronto: Oxford University Press, 1998.

Thor, Jonas. *Icelanders in North America: The First Settlers*. Winnipeg: University of Manitoba Press, 2002.

Tilly, Louise, and Joan Scott. *Women, Work and Family*. New York: Rinehart and Winston, 1978.

Toews, Mel. *The First Forty Years: The Story of the Steinbach Credit Union Limited*. Steinbach, MB: Steinbach Credit Union, 1986.

Toews, Miriam. *A Complicated Kindness*. Toronto: Knopf, 2004.

– *Swing Low: A Life*. Toronto: Stoddart, 2000.

Toews, Paul. *Mennonites in American Society, 1930–1970: Modernity and the Persistence of Religious Community*. Scottdale, PA: Herald Press, 1996.

Tracie, Carl J. *Toil and Peaceful Life: Doukhobor Village Settlement in Saskatchewan, 1899–1918*. Regina: Canadian Plains Research Center, 1996.

Tuan, Yi-Fu. *Space and Place: The Perspective of Experience*. Minneapolis: University of Minnesota Press, 1977.

Van Herk, Aritha. *Mavericks: An Incorrigible History of Alberta*. Toronto: Viking, 2001.

Vogt, Roy. 'Entrepreneurs, Labourers, Professionals and Farmers: A Response to Mennonites in Canada.' *Journal of Mennonite Studies* 15 (1997): 134–41.

Walbert, David. *Garden Spot: Lancaster County, the Old Order Amish and the Selling of America*. New York: Oxford University Press, 2002.

Wall, O.J., ed. and trans. *A Concise Record of Our Evangelical Mennonite Brethren Annual Conference Reports, 1889–1979*. Frazer, MT: N.P., 1979.

Warkentin, Abe. *Reflections on Our Heritage: A History of Steinbach and the R.M. of Hanover From 1874*. Steinbach, MB: Derksen Printers, 1971.

Warkentin, John. 'Going on Foot: Revisiting the Mennonite Settlements of Southern Manitoba.' *Journal of Mennonite Studies* 18 (2000): 59–81.

– *The Mennonite Settlements of Southern Manitoba*. 1960. Steinbach, MB: Hanover Steinbach Historical Society, 2000.

Westfall, William. *Two Worlds: The Protestant Culture of Nineteenth-Century Ontario*. Montreal: McGill-Queen's University Press, 1989.

White, Richard. 'Environmental History: Watching a Historical Field Mature.' *Pacific Historical Review* 70 (2001): 103–11.

Wiebe, Rudy. *Peace Shall Destroy Many*. Toronto: McClelland and Stewart, 1962.

Williams, Raymond. *The Country and the City*. New York: Oxford University Press, 1973.

Worster, Donald. *Dust Bowl: The Southern Plains in the 1930s*. New York: Oxford University Press, 1979.

– 'Two Faces West: The Development Myth in Canada and the United States.' In *Terra Pacifica: People and Place in the Northwest States and Western Canada*, ed. Paul W. Hirt, 71–92. Pullman: Washington State University Press, 1998.

Wright, Gerald. *Steinbach: Is There Any Place Like It?* Steinbach, MB: Derksen Printers, 1991.

Zerubavel, Eviatar. *The Fine Line: Making Distinctions in Everyday Life.* New York: Free Press, 1991.

Unpublished Theses and Papers

Barker, Jennifer Ellen. 'Working for Farm and Home: The Iowa Farm Bureau Federation Women's Committee, 1921–1974.' MA thesis, Iowa State University, 2003.

Blanke, David. 'New Directions in the History of Consumerism in the Countryside.' Paper presented to the New Trends in Rural History conference, Iowa State University, April 2004.

Canon, Brian Q. 'Pushing History beyond Human Institutions: Studying the Rural Environment.' Paper presented to the New Trends in Rural History conference, Iowa State University, April 2004.

Classen, Bertha. 'The Mennonite History of the Kleine Gemeinde.' Unpublished term paper, University of Wichita, 1959.

Classen, Daniel. J. 'Kleine Gemeinde Church at Meade, Kansas.' Research paper, Bethel College, Newton KS, 1949.

Fast, Bruce, 'Dairy Farming in Hanover since 1873.' Term paper, University of Manitoba, ca. 1980.

Friesen, Walter. 'History and Description of the Mennonite Community and Bible Academy at Meade, Kansas.' MA thesis, State Teachers College, Emporia, KS, 1957.

Gjerde, Jon. 'Do Three Peculiarities Make a Whole? The State of the Field of Immigration and Ethnicity in Rural History.' Paper presented at the New Directions in Rural History conference, Iowa State University, April 2004.

Hall, Jerry Alan. 'Mennonite Agriculture in a Tropical Environment: An Analysis of the Development and Productivity of a Mid-Latitude Agricultural System in British Honduras.' PhD diss., Clark University, 1970.

Haniewicz, Joasia. 'A Mennonite Story.' Unpublished essay, Menno Loewen, Spanish Lookout, Belize.

Hedges, Kelly. '"Plautdiestch" and "Huuchdietsch" in Chihuahua: Language, Literacy, and Identity Among the Old Colony Mennonites in Northern Mexico.' PhD diss., Yale University, 1996.

Higdon, Francis Xavier. 'Farm Diversification and Specialization: The Adaptation of Mennonite Households in Spanish Lookout, Belize.' PhD diss., University of Pittsburgh, 1997.

Perry, Joseph M. 'Mennonite Agricultural Enclaves and Economic Growth in

Belize.' Paper presented to the Association of American Geographers 88th annual meeting. San Diego, CA, 20 April 1992.

Plett, Edwin. 'The Dispersion of the Evangelical Mennonite Church (Kleine Gemeinde), 1920–1980.' Paper presented to the 150th Anniversary of the Kleine Gemeinde conference, Steinbach, MB, 1987.

Reschly, Steven D. 'Alternative Dreams and Visions: The Amish Repertoire of Community on the Iowa Prairie, 1840–1910.' PhD diss., University of Iowa, 1994.

Thiessen, Janis. 'Immigrant Mennonite Factory Workers: Ethnicity, Class and Integration.' Paper presented to the Return of the Kanadier conference, University of Winnipeg, October 2002.

Werner, Hans Peter. 'Integration in Two Cities: A Comparative History of Protestant Ethnic German Immigrants in Winnipeg, Canada and Bielefeld, Germany 1947–1989.' PhD diss., University of Manitoba, 2002.

Index

Aberdeen EM Church (Winnipeg), xiii, 119, 207, 212–13

acculturation. *See* assimilation

advertising, 39, 45, 65, 72, 121, 155, 156, 158, 251n33, 283n72

Aeltesten. See clergy

African North Americans, 8, 26, 184, 288n68

agricultural representative (ag rep), xi, 19, 23, 52, 58, 247n33

agriculture: 5ff; in British Honduras, 170, 191–9; in Canada, 20–6, 33–6, 47–57, 152–5; in Mexico, 113; in the United States, 26–47, 124–38, 142. *See also* fungicides; harvest; herbicides; insecticide; irrigation; land acquisition; mixed farming; planting; soils; tillage; and specific agricultural products

agriculture and business mentality, 22–4

agriculture and government, 13, 19, 21, 23, 24, 25, 29–32, 35, 40–1, 47, 52, 56–7, 106, 134, 152, 199, 232, 245n23, 289n78

air conditioning, 74, 76, 133, 221

airplanes, 37, 40, 62, 69, 157, 181, 259n112, 288n51

Alberta, 22, 228, 243n38

alcohol, 55, 67, 105, 112, 121, 150, 161

alfalfa, 38, 48, 53, 251n21

Amish, 170, 171, 178, 202, 228, 287n41

Anabaptists, xiii, 7, 8, 65–6, 102–3, 121–2, 169–70, 172, 181, 201, 204, 226, 228, 232–3, 285n12. *See also* neo-Anabaptists

Anderson, Benedict, 170

animals. *See* beef production; chicken production; dairy farming; dogs; hogs; horses

anniversaries, 65–7, 74, 76, 79, 81, 107, 159, 193, 208. *See also* commemorations

anomie. *See* individualism

appliances (household), 63, 132–3, 137

Arabic, 137

architecture, xii, 20, 45, 63, 66, 98, 113, 148, 153, 157, 174, 176, 192, 256n27, 268n102, 286n26, 286n30

assaults. *See* pacifism

assimilation, 64, 84, 101, 116, 170, 212, 220, 225, 227, 256n33, 259–60n104

atheism, 120

Eck, Marvin (missionary), 92, 295n32
Ediger, John N. (oil leasee), 45
education. *See* schools
egalitarianism. *See* class; status
egg production, 20, 24–5, 32, 39, 127, 174, 246n23, 290n102
Eisenhower, Dwight (general), 260n113
electricity, 21–2, 29, 63, 73, 114, 133, 137, 198, 200, 223–4, 248n52
Elias, Gordon (laborer), 184, 288n68
Emmanuel Mennonite Church (Kansas), 11, 90–101, 129, 133, 136, 218
endogamy. *See* marriage
English (language), xii, 20, 64, 78, 90–1, 107, 119, 141, 178, 184, 222, 224, 257n34, 273n53
Enns, A.J. (oil leasee), 46
Ens, Gerhard (history teacher), 66
entrepreneurship. *See* business
environment, 12, 18, 19, 34–57, 176, 191–9, 232, 249n2. *See also* climate
Epp, H.H. (revivalist), 37
Epp, Jake (Member of Parliament), 61, 67, 161, 246n28
Epp, Marlene (historian), 147
ethnicity, 26, 64, 80, 93, 95–6, 100, 165, 172, 207, 210–11, 220, 226, 267n85, 296n49
evangelicalism, 14, 82–101, 210, 218–19, 232, 262n11, 263n13, 294n32, 298n68
Evangelical Mennonite Brethren Church (Kansas/Manitoba), 10, 87–8, 89–90, 92–3, 99–100, 218
Evangelical Mennonite Conference (Manitoba), 11, 54, 115–22, 165–6, 168, 173, 206–17

Evangelical Mennonite Mission Conference. *See* Rudnerweide Mennonite Church
excommunication, 91, 106–10, 117–18, 120, 122, 166, 178, 182, 298n79
exhibitions, 66, 154, 156
export economy, 25, 28, 30, 155, 190–2, 194, 197, 201

family. *See* birthrates, kinship, men, old age, women, youth
family farms, 23, 26, 74, 125, 231
farms. *See* agriculture
farm support programs. *See* agriculture and government
fashion. *See* clothing
Fast, Agatha (city resident), 210
Fast, Jacob (judge), 106
fathering. *See* men
feedgrains. *See* barley production; corn production; oat production; sorghum
femininity. *See* women
fertility. *See* birth rates
fertilizers, xi, 21, 43, 47, 51–4, 73, 196–7, 252n50, 291n124
film, 40, 67, 69, 97, 98, 119, 121, 251n37, 260n112
Fink, Deborah (historian), 125
fires, 183, 193, 194
First Mennonite Church (Denver), 222
fishing, 51, 282n52
Fite, Gerald (historian), 27, 28
folklore, 53–4
foodways, 65, 96, 132, 174, 208, 291n124
footwashing, 99, 105
forgiveness, 46, 179

Fort Garry EM Church (Winnipeg), 206–8

Francis, E.K. (sociologist), 21, 154

French Canadians, 8, 64, 67, 165, 228

Fretz, Winfield (sociologist), 203–4

Friesen, Ben Z. (farmer), 46

Friesen, C.F. (sport fisher), 282n52

Friesen, Corny Z. (well driller), 73, 75

Friesen, Dan E. (pastor), 219, 298n64

Friesen, Dietrich (colony major), 187

Friesen, Elda (missionary), 38, 132, 250n21

Friesen, Elizabeth (city resident), 210

Friesen, Gerald (historian), 7

Friesen, Gilbert (Rhodes scholar), 150

Friesen, Henry A. (farmer), 37–9, 41, 44, 128, 250n21

Friesen, Henry L. (entrepreneur), 73, 94

Friesen, Henry Z. (farmer), 73

Friesen, J.R. (car dealer), 55

Friesen, Jacob R. (windmill agent), 47, 93

Friesen, Jake K. (migrant), 114

Friesen, John D. (migrant), 173, 185, 194

Friesen, John L. (visionary), 93

Friesen, Katherina Ratzlaff (mother), 278n42

Friesen, Katherine and Pete (farm householders), 131

Friesen, Margaret Isaac (nurse), 279n56

Friesen, Maria (homemaker), 174

Friesen, Menno (professor), 132

Friesen, Patrick (writer), xii, 103, 215, 297n59

Friesen, Peter D. (minister), 111, 117, 272n44, 273n54

Friesen, Peter F. (colony mayor), 174–6, 291n109

Friesen, Ralph (student), 215

Friesen, Ray (student), 210

Friesen, Suzie (CPS member), 248n42

Friesen, Walter (principal), 71, 96, 222

fruit growing, 28, 48, 188, 190–1, 194

frontier, 34, 59, 66, 77, 79, 81, 98, 125, 153, 159, 231, 255n6

fundamentalism, 84, 86, 88, 96, 97, 204, 209–10, 224, 263n12. *See also* dispensationalism

funeral. *See* death

fungicides, 194, 197, 291n124

Garden Park MB Church (Denver), 218, 222

gardens, 48, 56, 76, 113, 157, 195–6

Geertz, Clifford (anthropologist), 5, 9, 229, 234

Gemeinde. See church

gender relations. *See* women, men

genealogy, xiv, 64–5, 278n36

General Conference Mennonites (Kansas/Manitoba), 203, 218, 220, 273n54

German North Americans, 64, 82, 146, 243n35

Gilbert, Don (revivalist), 92

Gillet, Bob (town resident), 93

God, 35, 40–1, 56, 86, 89, 90, 93–4, 105, 108–10, 112, 114–15, 119–20, 163, 184, 186, 197, 199, 209, 213, 225, 258n60, 275n61, 296n42

Goossen, George (senior), 150

Goshen College (Indiana), 285n12

sexual behavior, 68, 109, 180

Shama, Simon (historian), 35

shopping. *See* consumerism

Shover, John L. (historian), ix, 6, 21, 23, 26, 138

shunning, 102, 108–10, 118–19, 122, 272n44

Siemens, Anna and John (health worker/well driller), 139

Siemens, Cornelius and Margaret (farm householders), 36

Siemens, Mary (wife of Frenchman), 106

Siemens, Rod (ag rep), 23, 52, 253n84

Simons, Menno, 105, 211, 288n50

singing, 89, 91, 111–12, 136, 174, 188, 208, 221, 285n25

singleness. *See* marriage

Smith, T.G. (banker), 163

Sobering, Ben (constable), 69

social activism, 204, 209–11, 217–18, 233, 296n44

social boundaries. *See* boundaries (social)

social gospel. *See* social activism

social stratification. *See* status; class

soil conservation, 30, 35, 40–1, 43, 47, 57, 232

soils, 27, 34–5, 36, 38, 40–1, 45, 47–9, 52–3, 71, 73, 173, 187, 192–3, 195, 197–9, 201

Sommerfelder Mennonite Church, 10, 103, 169

sorghum, 28, 38, 43, 127, 139

Spanish Lookout, British Honduras, xii, 169–201, 230

spirituality, 89, 92, 110, 112, 120, 133–4, 172, 179, 180–1, 201, 207, 213, 215, 219, 283n61

sports, 48, 87, 96–7, 120, 131, 143, 149, 151, 162–6, 224

status, 56–8, 79, 125, 129–30, 146, 148, 153, 160–1, 172, 199. *See also* class; middle class

Ste Anne, Manitoba, 50, 51, 67, 153

Steinbach Bible Institute (Manitoba), 67, 111, 117, 162, 168, 273n51, 185n12

Steinbach EM Church (Manitoba), 116, 119–21, 207, 214–15, 273n51, 274n57

Steinbach, Manitoba, 14, 59ff, 102ff, 116–22, 205–6, 214

Strong-Boag, Veronica (historian), 125

supply management, 13, 24–5, 57

survey (land), 42, 76, 174, 192, 194, 254n96, 271n25

Swedes, 8, 82

swine production. *See* hogs

Swiss-American Mennonites, 104, 172, 182, 190, 200, 202

Tabor College (Kansas), 88, 92, 97, 137, 222, 268n101

Tanchak, J.P. (turkey rancher), 153

Taylor, Jeffrey (historian), 152

teaching, xiii, 66, 87, 95, 105–7, 112–13, 137, 141, 160–1, 166–8, 175, 179, 183, 209–10, 213

technology (farm), barn, 21, 22, 154; hydraulics, 21, 29; power takeoff, 21, 29, 52

technology (leisure), 48, 73

telephones, 22, 63, 78, 125, 156, 178, 200, 219, 287n38

television, xii, xv, 15, 67, 76, 150, 162, 218–19, 240n20

theology. *See* religion